More Praise for *The Six Loves of James I*

"Russell is an inspired guide through the twists and turns of James' conflicted maneuverings. . . . A multidimensional, often revelatory portrait of a singular king."

—*Bookpage* (starred review)

"A sly, precise, and persuasive biography, fit for both gleeful gossips and students of Jacobean history."

—*Publishers Weekly* (starred review)

"Vivid and exciting. . . . A highly entertaining, gossipy, but polished biography."

—*Library Journal* (starred review)

"A nuanced and compassionate portrait of a complex personality."

—*Kirkus*

"Superb . . . [Russell] stands apart in its mixture of acute psychological insight and intricate research, as he brings the backbiting and power struggles of the Jacobean court to life with wit and vigor."

—*The Observer*

"Gareth Russell cannot write an uninteresting book . . . James is that most interesting of men—one whose best acts contribute to his own destruction. It is a warts-and-all story told with compassion."

—Philippa Gregory

"Brilliant. Superb scholarship, thrilling insight and gripping investigations that will keep you riveted until the end. . . . A political thriller combined with scrupulous research and analysis; an unforgettable and revolutionary insight into this often overlooked monarch."

—Kate Williams, *New York Times* bestselling author of *Becoming Queen Victoria: The Unexpected Rise of Britain's Greatest Monarch*

"Books like this don't come along very often. Told with Gareth Russell's characteristic verve and exquisite eye for detail, it is a story so compelling and surprising that it feels as if it has been hiding in plain sight for 400 years."

—Tracy Borman

"Thoroughly researched and bursting with delicious details, *The Six Loves of James I* is an important book that is both masterful and utterly captivating. This is Russell at his absolute best."

—Nicola Tallis, historian and author of *Young Elizabeth*

"A pacy, accessible book, it celebrates a force of nature who lived life on his own terms, despite the strife it caused him."

—*The Herald* (Edinburgh)

"Written with enviable clarity and full of fascinating asides."

—*The Scotsman*

"A highly-readable, highly-relevant tale of passion, politics and, above all, people."

—Steven Veerapen, author of *Witches: A King's Obsession*

"A substantial and remarkable contribution to the study of the history of Stuart Britain. . . . Russell is one of the great living historians and is setting the (very high) standard for the rest of us, and we are very lucky to have him and his work."

—Andrea Zuvich, author of *Ravenous: A Life of Barbara Villiers, Charles II's Most Infamous Mistress*

"More than just a biography, it is a reclamation. . . . This book is a vital contribution to our understanding of James, his kingship, and the complex tapestry of love and power."

—*History Today*

ALSO BY GARETH RUSSELL

FICTION

Popular

The Immaculate Deception

NONFICTION

The Emperors: How Europe's Rulers Were Destroyed by the First World War

A History of the English Monarchy: From Boadicea to Elizabeth I

Young and Damned and Fair: The Life and Tragedy of Catherine Howard, Fifth Wife of King Henry VIII

The Ship of Dreams: The Sinking of the Titanic and the End of the Edwardian Era

Do Let's Have Another Drink: The Dry Wit and Fizzy Life of Queen Elizabeth the Queen Mother

The Palace: From the Tudors to the Windsors, 500 Years of British History at Hampton Court

THE SIX LOVES OF JAMES I

GARETH RUSSELL

ATRIA PAPERBACK
New York Amsterdam/Antwerp London
Toronto Sydney/Melbourne New Delhi

ATRIA PAPERBACK
An Imprint of Simon & Schuster, LLC
1230 Avenue of the Americas
New York, NY 10020

Originally published in Great Britain in 2025 by
William Collins, an imprint of HarperCollins Publishers

First Atria paperback edition June 2026

Manufactured in the United States of America

1 3 5 7 9 10 8 6 4 2

The Library of Congress Cataloging-in-Publication Data has been applied for.

ISBN 978-1-6680-4968-6
ISBN 978-1-6680-4969-3 (pbk)
ISBN 978-1-6680-4970-9 (ebook)

For Brettne,
In friendship

Elizabeth was king,
Now James is queen.

–Anonymous English author
(c. 1623)

The mightiest kings have had their minions;
Great Alexander loved Hephaestion,
The conquering Hercules for Hylas wept;
And for Patroclus, stern Achilles drooped.

–Christopher Marlowe,
Edward II (1594)

CONTENTS

FAMILY TREES

James, the House of Stewart and the Scottish Crown

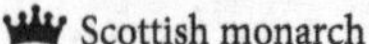 Scottish monarch

* Died violently

Names in capitals indicate one of James's regents or mentors

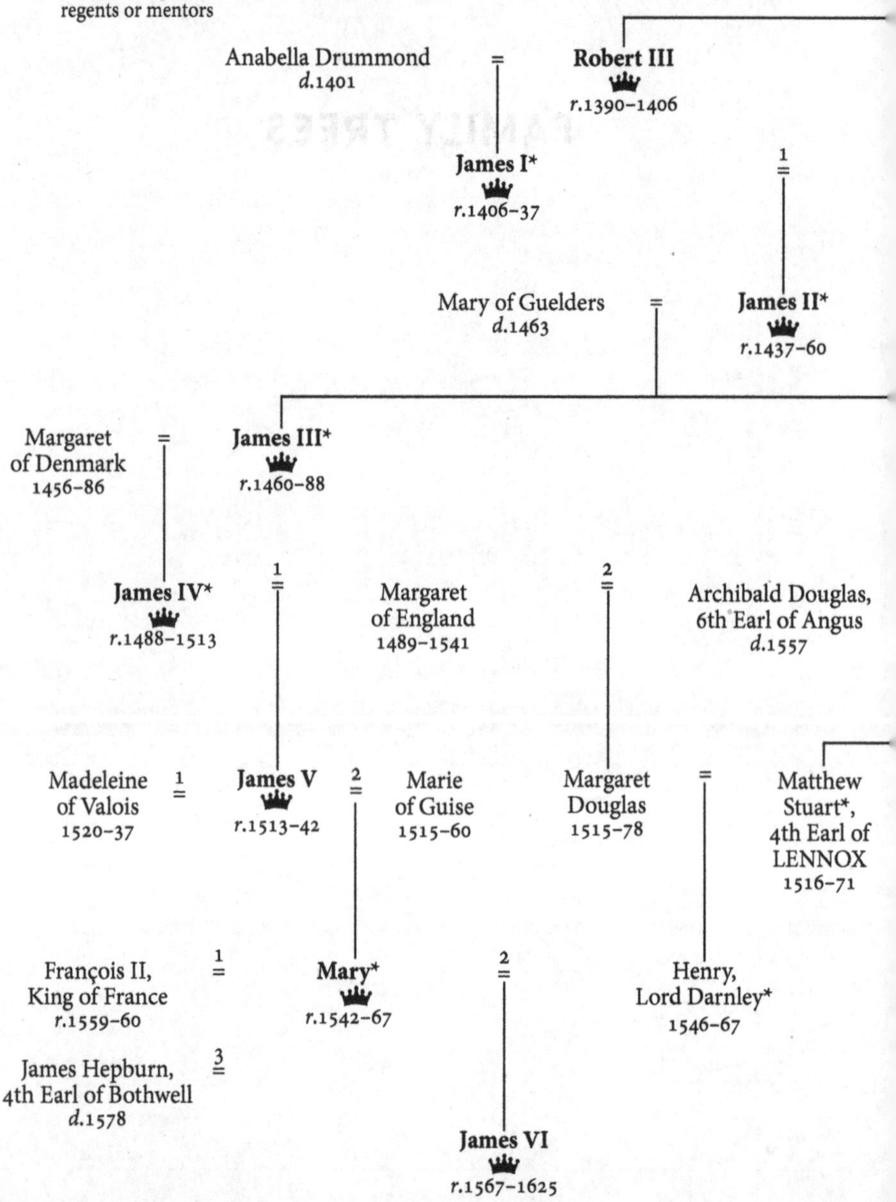

Anabella Drummond *d.*1401 = **Robert III** *r.*1390–1406

James I* *r.*1406–37

Mary of Guelders *d.*1463 = **James II*** *r.*1437–60

Margaret of Denmark 1456–86 = **James III*** *r.*1460–88

James IV* *r.*1488–1513 =[1] Margaret of England 1489–1541 =[2] Archibald Douglas, 6th Earl of Angus *d.*1557

Madeleine of Valois 1520–37 =[1] **James V** *r.*1513–42 =[2] Marie of Guise 1515–60

Margaret Douglas 1515–78 = Matthew Stuart*, 4th Earl of LENNOX 1516–71

François II, King of France *r.*1559–60 =[1] **Mary*** *r.*1542–67 =[2] Henry, Lord Darnley* 1546–67

James Hepburn, 4th Earl of Bothwell *d.*1578 =[3]

James VI *r.*1567–1625

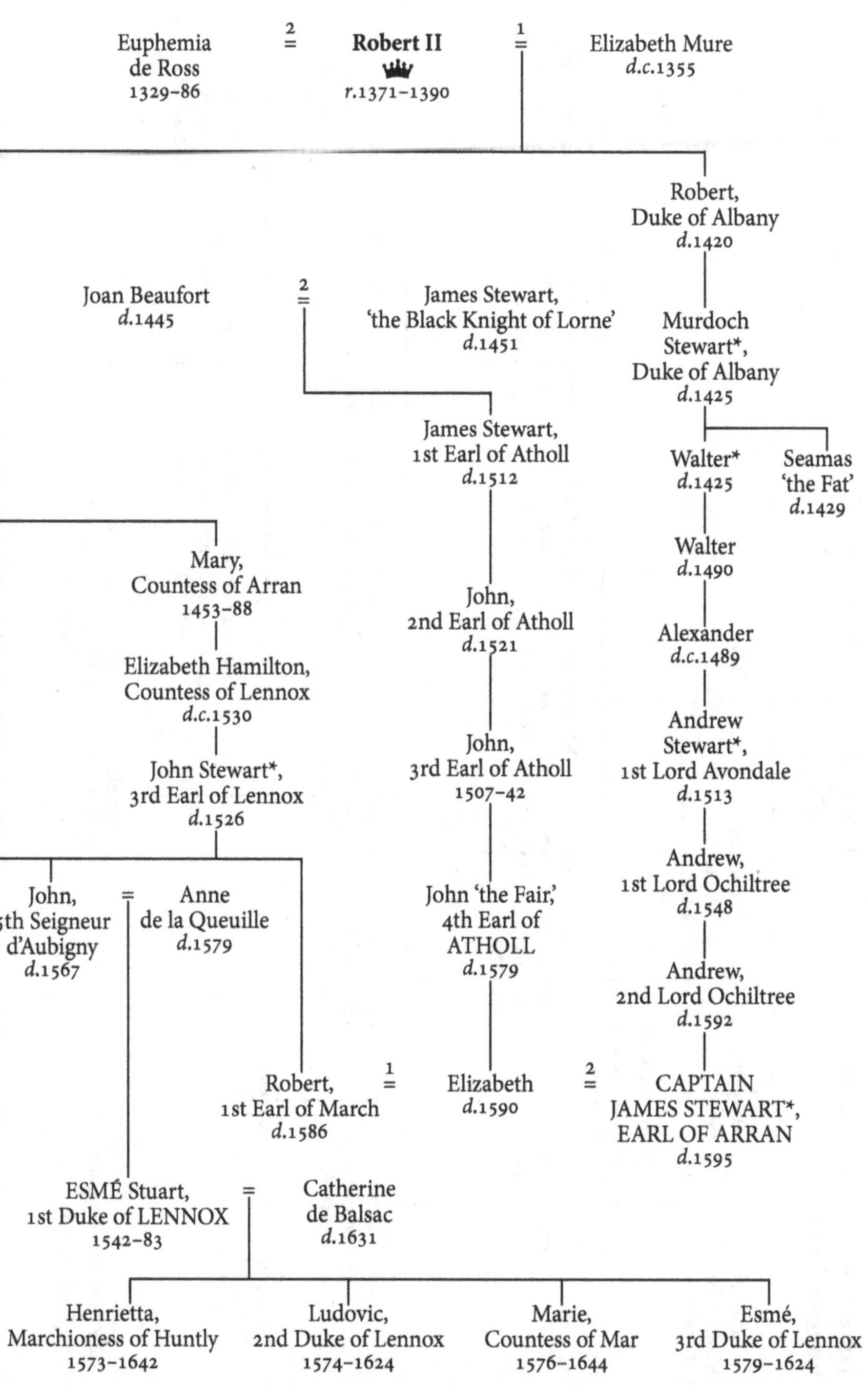

Euphemia de Ross 1329–86
2 =
Robert II
r.1371–1390
1 =
Elizabeth Mure d.c.1355
Robert, Duke of Albany d.1420
Joan Beaufort d.1445
2 =
James Stewart, 'the Black Knight of Lorne' d.1451
Murdoch Stewart*, Duke of Albany d.1425
James Stewart, 1st Earl of Atholl d.1512
Walter* d.1425
Seamas 'the Fat' d.1429
Mary, Countess of Arran 1453–88
Walter d.1490
John, 2nd Earl of Atholl d.1521
Alexander d.c.1489
Elizabeth Hamilton, Countess of Lennox d.c.1530
John Stewart*, 3rd Earl of Lennox d.1526
John, 3rd Earl of Atholl 1507–42
Andrew Stewart*, 1st Lord Avondale d.1513
Andrew, 1st Lord Ochiltree d.1548
John, 5th Seigneur d'Aubigny d.1567
=
Anne de la Queuille d.1579
John 'the Fair,' 4th Earl of ATHOLL d.1579
Andrew, 2nd Lord Ochiltree d.1592
Robert, 1st Earl of March d.1586
1 =
Elizabeth d.1590
2 =
CAPTAIN JAMES STEWART*, EARL OF ARRAN d.1595
ESMÉ Stuart, 1st Duke of LENNOX 1542–83
=
Catherine de Balsac d.1631
Henrietta, Marchioness of Huntly 1573–1642
Ludovic, 2nd Duke of Lennox 1574–1624
Marie, Countess of Mar 1576–1644
Esmé, 3rd Duke of Lennox 1579–1624

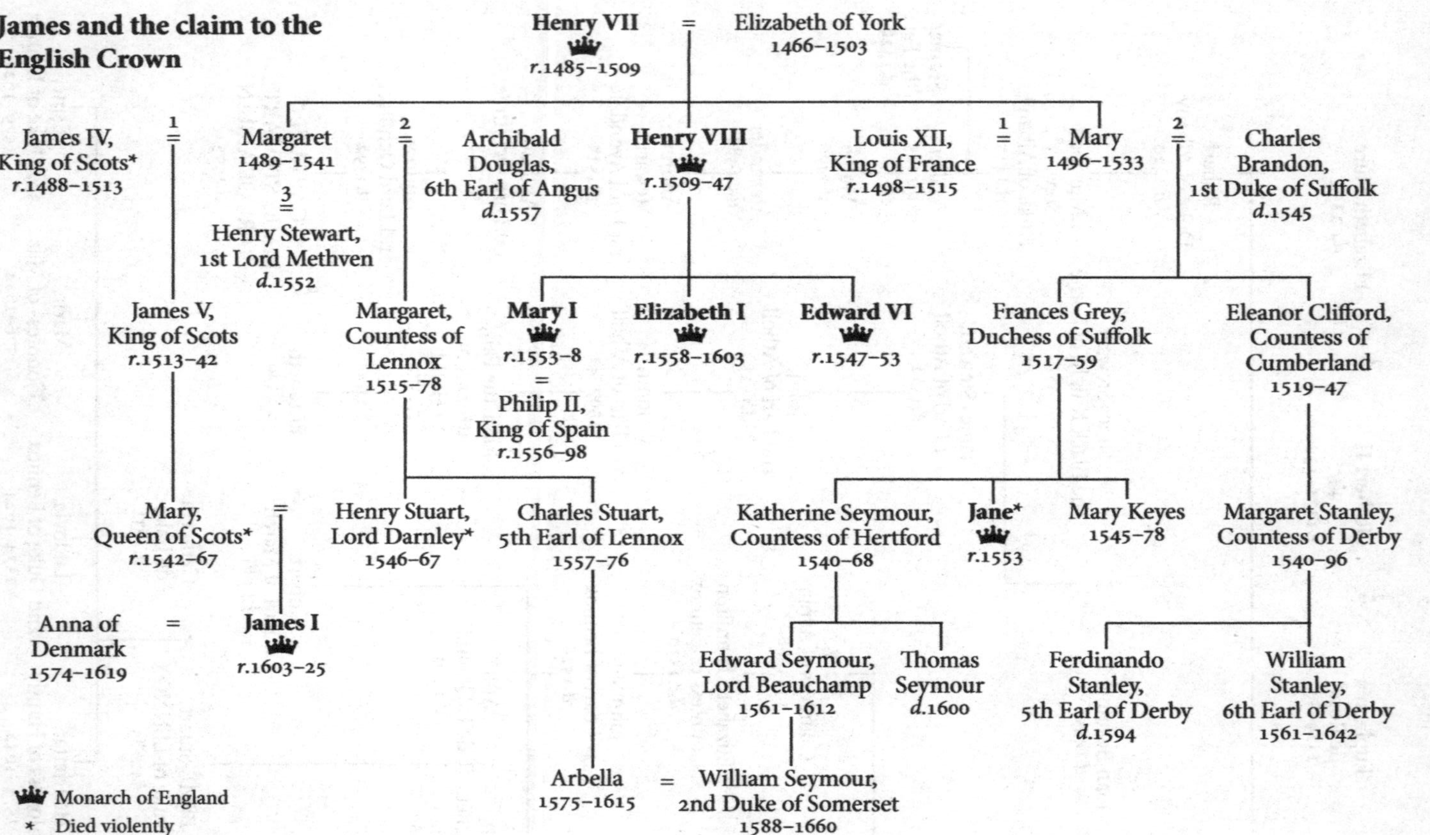
James and the claim to the English Crown
Henry VII r.1485–1509
=
Elizabeth of York 1466–1503
James IV, King of Scots* r.1488–1513
1 =
Margaret 1489–1541
2 =
Archibald Douglas, 6th Earl of Angus d.1557
3 =
Henry Stewart, 1st Lord Methven d.1552
Henry VIII r.1509–47
Louis XII, King of France r.1498–1515
1 =
Mary 1496–1533
2 =
Charles Brandon, 1st Duke of Suffolk d.1545
James V, King of Scots r.1513–42
Margaret, Countess of Lennox 1515–78
Mary I r.1553–8
=
Philip II, King of Spain r.1556–98
Elizabeth I r.1558–1603
Edward VI r.1547–53
Frances Grey, Duchess of Suffolk 1517–59
Eleanor Clifford, Countess of Cumberland 1519–47
Mary, Queen of Scots* r.1542–67
=
Henry Stuart, Lord Darnley* 1546–67
Charles Stuart, 5th Earl of Lennox 1557–76
Katherine Seymour, Countess of Hertford 1540–68
Jane* r.1553
Mary Keyes 1545–78
Margaret Stanley, Countess of Derby 1540–96
Anna of Denmark 1574–1619
=
James I r.1603–25
Edward Seymour, Lord Beauchamp 1561–1612
Thomas Seymour d.1600
Ferdinando Stanley, 5th Earl of Derby d.1594
William Stanley, 6th Earl of Derby 1561–1642
Arbella 1575–1615
=
William Seymour, 2nd Duke of Somerset 1588–1660
Monarch of England
* Died violently

MAPS

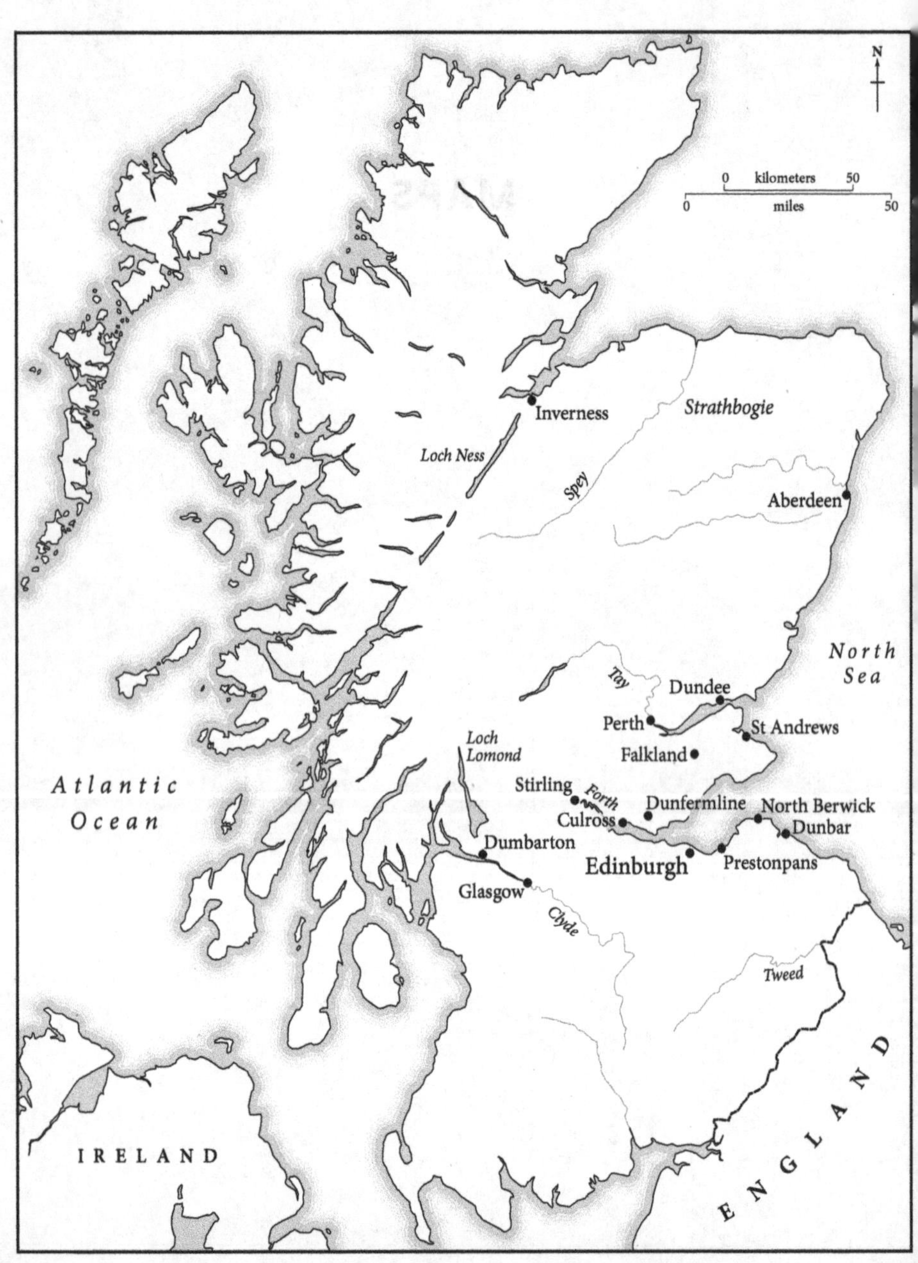
N
0 kilometers 50
0 miles 50
Inverness
Strathbogie
Loch Ness
Spey
Aberdeen
North Sea
Tay
Dundee
Perth
St Andrews
Falkland
Loch Lomond
Atlantic Ocean
Stirling
Forth
Dunfermline
North Berwick
Culross
Dunbar
Dumbarton
Edinburgh
Prestonpans
Glasgow
Clyde
Tweed
IRELAND
ENGLAND

SCOTLAND
Berwick
0
kilometers
100
0
miles
100
N
Tweed
Newcastle upon Tyne
Durham
ENGLAND
North Sea
Isle of Man
York
Irish Sea
Doncaster
Lincoln
WALES
Trent
Apethorpe
Althorp
Severn
Royston
Oxford
Theobalds
Pembroke
London
Bath
Windsor
Thames
Farnham
Portsmouth
English Channel

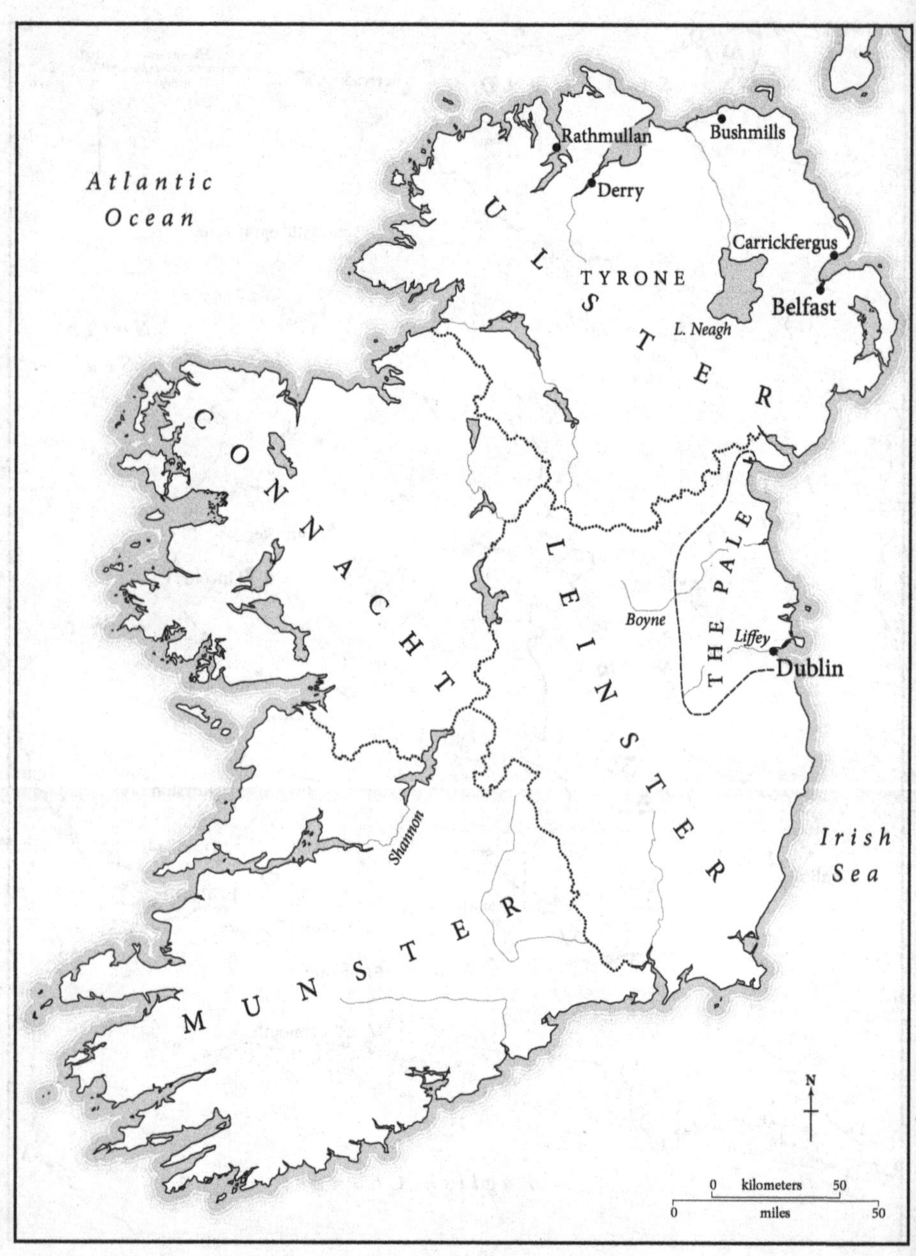
Atlantic Ocean
Rathmullan
Bushmills
Derry
ULSTER
Carrickfergus
TYRONE
Belfast
L. Neagh
CONNACHT
LEINSTER
THE PALE
Boyne
Liffey
Dublin
Shannon
Irish Sea
MUNSTER
N
0 kilometers 50
0 miles 50

THE SIX LOVES OF JAMES I

AUTHOR'S NOTE

This is a private life of James VI, King of Scots, who in 1603 became James I of England. After three chapters focusing on episodes from his early years—respectively, his mother's downfall, his education, and the end of his regencies—it aims to tell his life through the prism of the men and women James loved and those with whom he was intimate. It would, however, be impossible to write a biography of a modern constitutional monarch that made no mention of politics, much less a biography of an absolutist king or, in James's case, of an aspiring absolutist. While this is not intended as a political life of King James, politics, foreign policy, religion, economics, and social affairs are discussed where they shaped his life. James described himself as two people existing in one body, the "particular man" and "a general Christian king," and here the narrative is weighted to the former.[1]

The nomenclature of studying historical sexuality is a rich—some might say a dense—field. Reflecting on James's love affairs with men, his former courtier Francis Osborne suggested that future generations would have a better vocabulary to describe "his love, or what else posterity will please to call it (who must be the judges of all that history shall inform)."[2] I have included an appendix, explaining which terms I have used in this book and why. The appendix addresses too my approach to the lexicons of British, Scottish, English, Irish, and Welsh, as well as the vocabulary chosen in the book's discussions of folklore, religion, and witchcraft.

James VI was fond of bestowing nicknames, some of which I have used in this book. Alexander Lindsay, 1st Lord Spynie, for instance, is most frequently referred to here by James's nickname for him, "Sandy." The use of private names to describe public personalities is not to every reader's taste and, truth be told, not entirely to mine. However, this is a history with a pool of first names so small that it might better be referred to as a puddle—in the book's principals, we have two Georges, three Alexanders, two Patricks, two Annes, a smattering of Roberts, and a seemingly inexhaustible litany of Jameses—and thus I have gratefully utilized any form of demarcation available to me and for the reader.

For a similar reason and where it has not seemed jarring to do so, I have sometimes used a royal consort's original name: hence, James's maternal grandmother is named as Marie of Guise rather than the anglicized Mary. With James's wife, I have called her Anna, rather than Anne, of Denmark. She was referred to as Anne after she became queen of England and Ireland in 1603, but she was Anna as queen of Scots, as princess of Denmark and Norway, and it was as Anna that she signed herself in her correspondence.

The Jacobean aristocracies were ones with frequently changing titles; I have tried, where I could, to refer to an individual by one name throughout.[3] A list of prominent figures with the name or title by which they are most frequently referred to in the text is included at the book's end.

As will be clear to the reader, I do not believe that James VI was heterosexual. This conclusion is shared by many historians, and the belief that the King had male lovers was widespread in his lifetime.[4] In the nineteenth and twentieth centuries, there were arguments that presented James as either heterosexual or asexual.[5] I believe the argument that James was heterosexual or asexual is shaken by pieces of individual evidence from his lifetime and unsustainable when looking at that evidence in the cumulative. While the historiography of James's sexuality is relevant, rather than attempt a general discussion of why I believe he was involved with his own gender, I have discussed with each relevant relationship why the individual can—or cannot—credibly be regarded as James's lover.

I have not provided modern equivalents to sixteenth- or seventeenth-century monetary sums. This is in part because the modern figures will soon be out of date in our own economy and because of the vast differences between our century and James VI's in regard to labor costs, as well as the cost of materials and their transport, which renders misleading any attempt to provide an equivalency.

Most citations from the Bible are from the King James Version (KJV), also known as the Authorized Version, and the names used in it for different sections and books of the Bible are used here, too. In the few instances where citation has been taken from the Geneva Bible translation, this has been specified in the endnotes.

Unless specified otherwise, translations from early modern Scots into modern English are my own, as is the responsibility for any errors. All dates are given in the Old Style, except for the year, which I have counted as beginning on January 1, as is the case in Britain today and was in most of Europe during James's lifetime. Prior to 1752, the new legal year started in the British Isles on March 25—the Feast of the Annunciation—so, from January 1 to March 24, the British states were one calendar year behind most of the rest of western Europe.

PROLOGUE

Summer 1617

King James was led through a tunnel that ran beneath the waters of the Firth of Forth. He was forty-nine years old, of average height, with heavy-lidded eyes, a ginger beard, strong shoulders, thin legs, pale skin, and an old riding wound on his ankle that sometimes made walking painful.

He had been escorted from the mainland into a tower and, from it, down into the earth by his host, Sir George Bruce. This sixty-seven-year-old Scottish gentleman had been granted the lands nearly three decades earlier by a relative who had petitioned King James to approve the transfer of the estate. James had done so because Bruce was an engineering genius and there was coal lurking beneath the ground at Culross. The monks who had held the land in generations gone by, when Scotland had still been a Catholic country, had extracted some, but since their banishment, Culross had sat untapped.

James's faith in Bruce's talents was justified. He led the King into the subterranean gloom to show him a mechanism he called his "Egyptian wheel," with thirty-six buckets that drained the shaft—eighteen ascending, eighteen descending. Bruce's achievement had been so remarkable that engineers and miners came to Culross from across the British Isles to see how he had managed it.

Like many of his courtiers, Bruce knew King James to be a man of deep learning and sharp edges. For his part, James liked Bruce—he had previously served as a member of the Scottish parliament and as one of James's advisers—but it was hard to know how much to trust him. James had been betrayed by his confidants before.

James emerged from the mine to find himself surrounded by water. Realizing too late that he had wandered, again, into a trap in which he could be kidnapped or killed, he decided his best—perhaps, only—chance was to shout for help.

"Treason!" the King's screams rang across the Forth. Over and over, he repeated, "Treason!"

Such fears had followed him since the cradle. His governess had kept talismans in his childhood home to protect him from dark magic. He had seen relatives, guardians, and schoolmates bleeding in front of him. Men pushing him into his rooms when he tried to leave without permission. The arms of someone he trusted dragging him back into a tower as he screamed for help. Poison. Swords. Gunpowder. Now, drowning.

James kept shouting, heedless of the voices trying to calm him, until Bruce's broke through. He explained that this was not an attempt to drown James in the mine but an exit and entrance to another new feature designed by Bruce—a man-made island with a small dock to facilitate the swifter extraction and transport of coal.

A boat was brought, which proved Bruce's point, and fear released James as he was rowed back across the river to the splendid mansion Bruce had built on the shore with the money from his mines. Inside Bruce's Great Lodging,* with its large fireplaces, fine furniture, and marks carved into the chimney to protect its residents from witches, James drank and tried to relax.

At his side was a man in his twenties, who, when they were in private together, called the King "my dear husband."[1] Tall, athletic, with blue eyes and black hair, Lord Villiers was unusually handsome.[2] "From the nails of his fingers, nay, from the sole of his foot to the top of his head, there is no blemish in him," wrote a courtier, who did not like him very much but had to concede the fineness of his appearance.[3] "One of the handsomest bodied men in England," in the words of another.[4] He had straight white teeth. Once, when he had a toothache, he had considered having one removed, until the King begged him not to ruin his beautiful smile. James called him "sweetheart" in his letters, and when they were apart, Villiers liked to tease James by asking if he remembered when they first shared a bed—what Villiers called a night "I shall never forget."[5]

Villiers—born George Villiers into a down-on-their-luck family of the English gentry with nothing but his looks and his mother's

* Now called Culross Palace and operated by the National Trust.

determination to advance them—was the latest in a line of male favorites for King James. Long before him, there had been another who was "pre-eminently beautiful," when plots, invasions, and espionage had loomed alongside first love or infatuation.[6]

Outside the Great Lodging at Culross, the grim weather that had dominated the spring and summer of 1617 continued. Villiers had been on hand before to calm James when a dark mood swept over him. It often shocked those close to the King to see just how quickly his mind leaped to the worst possible conclusion, but it should not have been a surprise, in light of everything that had happened to him. When he was eighteen, James had been described by a visitor to his court as a young man who had been "nurtured in fear."[7]

Many times, James had tried to explain this to those around him. It was what he had meant when he told politicians that he felt as if his life had been "baptised in blood."[8]

1

A BONNY SON

For they that have not skill and craft
Are soonest caught in snare
–Anonymous Scottish ballad
(1567)

The first of the many attempts to kill James Stewart* came when he was in utero, and the plot involved his father. James's pregnant mother Mary, Queen of Scots was hosting a supper party at Edinburgh's Palace of Holyroodhouse on March 9, 1566, when she and her guests were interrupted by the perennially unwelcome company of her husband Henry, Lord Darnley, who sat next to her at the table and put his arm around her waist.

Darnley was the English son of Scottish parents. His father, the Earl of Lennox, was head of one of the great Scottish noble houses, and it was political disagreements with other aristocrats that had forced him to flee to England as a young man. There he married King Henry VIII's niece, whose Scottish father had taken her to England in her infancy after he too had fallen afoul of rival factions in his homeland's aristocracy. Years later, when Mary, Queen of Scots was looking for a husband, Darnley's parents had sent him to Scotland in the successful hope that the Queen would be attracted to him politically and physically. Mary described Darnley as one of the best-looking gentlemen she had ever seen, and their wedding took place on July 29, 1565. Their union, which was to provide Mary with a noble-born, royally connected father for her future heirs, rapidly disintegrated under the strain of political and emotional resentments.

* The Scottish spelling of the royal family's surname. *Stuart* was used by their French and English cousins; it became the more popular spelling after 1603.

Tall, athletic, handsome, and spoiled out of the vaguest possibility of usefulness by his adoring parents, Darnley proved that his infidelity to his wife had extended from personal to political as he was followed into the small dining chamber by a group of men armed with "steel bonnets, guns, pistols, swords . . . and other weapons."[1] Mary, by then six or seven months pregnant with James, demanded to know why they had disturbed her. An armor-wearing Lord Ruthven,* a forty-five-year-old Protestant and former rebel, replied that it was one guest in particular who had provoked them, "yonder man Davie," Mary's Italian secretary and confidant, David Riccio.† The conspirators ordered Riccio to come with them. Mary, described even by her enemies as having an appearance of "excellent beauty," turned to her husband and asked, "What do you know about this?"[2] Many other courtiers had liked the well-dressed Riccio, describing him as "a merry fellow and a good musician," with a beautiful bass singing voice, through which he had first come to Mary's notice, only afterward rising in her credit thanks to his fluency in French and knowledge of European diplomacy.[3] Mary's husband and his allies were less enthusiastic. According to another of Mary's advisers, as Riccio the foreigner rose in the Queen's favor, he became "much envied and hated," and "some of the nobility would shoulder and scoot him by when they entered the queen's chamber."[4]

Their intrusion upon the Queen's dinner party was more menacing than the contemptuous shoves that had come before, as were Darnley's unjust accusations that Mary and her secretary were lovers and that "David had more company of her body than he for the space of two months."[5] Riccio had feared an attack against him for some time, and it had prompted him to seek the advice of a colleague in Mary's service, Sir James Melville, as to how he could make himself more popular.[6] According to Melville, "I told him that strangers‡ were commonly envied when they meddled too

---

* Pronounced *Riven.*

† Sometimes spelled *Rizzio.*

‡ Foreigners.

much in the affairs of other countries. He said he, being secretary to Her Majesty in the French tongue, had occasion thereby to occupy Her Majesty's ear, as her former secretary used to do. I answered again that it was thought that the greatest part of the affairs of the country passed through his hands, and advised him, when the nobility was present, to give them [their] place."[7]

Even if he had heeded Melville's advice, which he did not, Riccio may have been damned as collateral damage to the cabal of noblemen who hoped to undermine Mary's regime by attacking her unpopular confidant. The palace gates had been barred at sunset to prevent the escape of a victim or the arrival of help for the Queen; Darnley had then let the conspirators enter through his apartments, from where he led them up the narrow private staircase toward his wife's.

As Riccio cowered behind his employer, grabbing hold of her skirts and begging the men to show him mercy, the plotters moved forward "so rudely and irreverently that the table, candles, meat and dishes were overthrown."[8] This was according to Sir James Melville, who was in the palace that night but not at the supper and heard about it later from one of the eyewitnesses. He was almost right in his account, except for the detail about the candles. As the table flipped over, one of the Queen's guests—her half sister the Countess of Argyll*—had enough presence of mind to catch a candelabrum and hold on to it as the others fell to the floor. From its light, they saw another of the plotters reach into Darnley's scabbard, extract his dagger, and slice past the Queen; it came so close to her face that "she felt the coldness of the iron."[9] It then stabbed into Riccio, who began "making great shrieks and cries."[10] Using Darnley's dagger showed chilling forethought, as it would make it harder for Darnley to weasel his way out of complicity in the assassination later.

Mary continued to shield Riccio from the attackers, until Lord Ruthven's nephew Andrew Kerr of Fawdonside manhandled her

* Jean Stewart (c. 1533–88), illegitimate daughter of King James V and his mistress Elizabeth Beaton. She married Archibald Campbell, 5th Earl of Argyll (c. 1532–73).

to one side and pointed a pistol at her belly. From that point onward, she had to watch as, in her own words, the men "most cruelly took him forth."[11] They dragged Riccio from the room. Mary and her guests could hear his sobs and screams, punctuated by stab after stab, until both sets of noise fell silent. Kerr let Mary go and left with most of his fellow conspirators. Ruthven could not resist returning to offer Mary a short lecture on how her actions had forced them to kill her adviser, since she had favored a lowly born foreigner who was "enemy to the nobility" and whom she had preferred to her husband.[12] In a moment of dark comedy given what he had just done, Ruthven respected etiquette by asking if he had Her Majesty's permission to drink in her presence. Sweating in his armor, he finished a goblet of wine in a gulp. Before he and Darnley slunk off into the palace, Mary told Ruthven, "If I or my child die, you will have the blame thereof."[13] When Mary could bring herself to leave the chamber, she found Riccio's corpse with fifty-six stab wounds lying in her Outer Chamber, the audience hall next to her bedchamber.

As Sunday morning dawned a few hours later, Mary spotted her adviser Sir James Melville crossing the palace courtyard. She flung open a window and called him over to her. "Go to the provost of Edinburgh," she ordered, "and bid him in my name convene the town with speed and come and relieve me out of these traitors' hands. But run fast."[14] Detained by a suspicious conspirator who initially refused to open the gates for him, Melville used their shared Protestant faith to persuade him by "saying that I was only going to a sermon at St Giles's church."[15] Once he was safely beyond the palace walls, Melville delivered Queen Mary's message to the city's authorities, only to discover that Darnley had sent an order the night before, urging them to remain calm, no matter what they heard from the palace. With no help coming from the city, Mary had to rely on her own wits to escape.

She never believed that Riccio had been the only target of the night's violence. She was certain that the plotters had meant to traumatize her into miscarrying her child, robbing her of an heir and quite possibly her life by shocking her into an early labor. With Mary incapacitated or dead, Darnley might be installed as regent or king in name—and his allies' puppet in reality. Only one source records Mary wiping her face with a handkerchief to famously say, "No more tears! I will now think upon revenge."[16] Whether she said it or not, it captured the spirit of her response to the plot.

The next day—Monday—when Darnley came to see her, Mary made sure to sow discord between him and the other conspirators. Given that her palace was surrounded by his allies, Darnley's support was the only way she could hope to escape. She had no choice but to convince her husband that she had forgiven him and that she regretted their previous estrangement. She also needed him at her side when she gave birth. For Darnley to have accused Mary of adultery when she was pregnant would, as Darnley must have known, leave that child battling accusations of illegitimacy for the rest of his or her life. Only by his being with Mary when the child was born could she hope to silence, or at the very least quiet, those rumors.

She succeeded in fooling Darnley into believing that she still loved him and begged him to protect her. He promised to do so and heeded his wife's warnings that he would soon be betrayed by his fellow assassins. She duped her illegitimate half brother, the political heavyweight the Earl of Moray, with a guarantee that she would pardon all those involved in Riccio's death. Trusting in Darnley's loyalty and in Mary's promises of absolution for all involved, the plotters left the Queen in her husband's care. That night, she and Darnley slipped out of Holyroodhouse by a side door, passing through the palace's cemetery, which unfortunately meant they had to walk past Riccio's freshly dug grave. Darnley struggled to hold back tears and launched into an impromptu graveside monologue of contrition for his role in the assassination. When he had finished his soliloquy, servants were waiting with horses for them in the grounds, and they escaped the city under cover of darkness, though not as speedily as Darnley might have liked. Knowing what the men he was abandoning were capable of, he kept chivvying his pregnant wife to ride faster: "Come on! In God's Name, come on! By God's Blood, they will murder both you and me if they can catch us. Come on! If this baby dies, we can have more."[17] Mary replied that, if he was so worried about being caught, he should ride on at speed, alone. Mistaking sarcasm for support, Darnley urged his horse on and left Mary, with her attendants, on the road.

After five hours in the saddle, Mary joined her husband at Dunbar Castle. Helped off her horse by waiting servants, she asked for eggs for her breakfast and then greeted supporters who had ridden there to aid her, thanks to the surreptitious resourcefulness of one of her ladies-in-waiting, who had also helped organize the royals' escape from Edinburgh.

Having robbed the plotters of their useful idiot in Darnley, Mary then brilliantly divided them among themselves by offering pardons to those who had supported the plot but refusing to extend that mercy to those involved in the killing itself. The conspiracy fell apart as more and more of its supporters abandoned the assassins and made their way to Dunbar to accept the Queen's conditional offer of clemency. Suddenly bereft of allies, the plot's leaders fled to England.

By the time a triumphant Mary reentered Edinburgh at the head of eight thousand loyalist soldiers on March 18, nine days after Riccio's murder, Darnley was battling with a new jealousy—this time for one of his wife's most stalwart supporters, the handsome and aggressive James Hepburn, 4th Earl of Bothwell.* When it came time for their child's birth, Mary and Darnley set up residence at Edinburgh Castle, the magnificent twelfth-century hilltop fortress overlooking the capital. Mary sent for a holy relic—the silver-gilt skull of her ancestor Saint Margaret of Wessex, Queen of Scots—and kept it with her until, after a long and difficult labor, Mary gave birth to "a bonny son" at about eleven o'clock in the morning of June 19.[18] The child was named James in honor of Mary's father, King James V, and his four immediate predecessors on the Scottish throne. Still anxious over Darnley's insinuations about her relationship with Riccio, when he came to see his child Mary made a point of swearing, on damnation of her soul, with James in her

---

* Each time a noble title is created, the incumbents are numbered. If the title falls into disuse and is subsequently revived or passes to another family, the numbering starts anew. The only exceptions are when the titles are held by immediate members of the royal family, in which case numbers are not attached.

arms, that "this is your son, and no other man's son!"[19] Darnley had the grace to blush and kissed James on the forehead, a gesture that acknowledged James as his own in front of the gathered courtiers and servants. Passed over to the care of Helena Little, his wet nurse, the baby Duke of Rothesay—the traditional title for the heirs to the throne in Scotland—was also created Earl of Carrick, Cunningham, and Kyle, Lord of the Isles, and Baron of Renfrew by his mother. With a household staff, he was sent to the "sweeter and pleasanter air" of Stirling Castle, about thirty-five miles from Edinburgh.[20]

With their baby born and acknowledged, Mary could abandon the charade of reconciliation. Sometimes, she would ask Darnley to think about what would have happened if the conspirator's pistol had gone off on the night it had been pointing at her pregnant womb. Darnley was initially perplexed by Mary's change of heart and, during one such argument, asked, "Sweet Madam, is this your promise that you made to forgive and forget all?" Mary replied that she had forgiven him, which was a lie, but that she could not forget what he had done to her, which was true.[21] Darnley soon swung back to recriminations of his own, by encouraging gossip that his wife had started an affair with Lord Bothwell.[22] Exhausted by her husband's behavior and perhaps able to take stock of what had happened to her that night at Holyroodhouse only once she had finished dealing with its political consequences, Mary suffered a physical and then a nervous breakdown. She vomited blood, was bedridden with a fever, and intermittently lost consciousness.

When she returned to her duties, she and her supporters knew that something had to be done about Darnley. Divorce or, more accurately, annulment was considered at a secret conference at Craigmillar Castle, a property just outside Edinburgh that was owned by a family loyal to Mary. The Queen and her husband were first cousins, as grandchildren of the English princess Margaret Tudor. They were also both Catholics and, before their wedding, Pope Pius IV had provided the necessary dispensation for the cousins to become spouses. As James's birth proved, the marriage had been consummated, so there were no credible grounds on which Mary could apply to Rome for its liquidation. Furthermore, the dissolution of the royal marriage might put James's legitimacy up for debate, something Mary was loath to risk. Even if she was prepared to do so, the Vatican might take years to reach a decision, and Darnley needed to be disposed of as soon as possible. Lord Bothwell joined Mary and her inner circle of advisers at the Craigmillar discussions, during which the Queen allegedly told them that she would leave the matter in their hands and would ensure that Parliament retrospectively sanctioned their actions against Darnley. The plan seemed to be that in the new year Darnley would be arrested to stand trial and, if he resisted or seemed to resist arrest, he would be killed in an alleged scuffle.

The meeting at Craigmillar Castle took place in November 1566. Keeping Darnley close in the weeks following was a sensible if unpleasant precaution. The next month, the couple traveled together to Stirling Castle for their son's baptism, where Darnley did nothing for his cause by throwing a last-minute temper tantrum that ended with him sulking in his rooms rather than attending the christening. At the Catholic ceremony in the castle's chapel, Mary delivered a stunning performance in pretending that nothing was wrong. As a Catholic queen in a predominantly Protestant country, her choice of godparents for James was pragmatically ecumenical. Three godparents were customary, two of whom were traditionally the same gender as the child. The Catholic King Charles IX of France and Emmanuel Philibert, Duke of Savoy* were invited to stand as the child's godfathers, which they accepted, as did his Protestant godmother, Queen Elizabeth I of England. In a gesture of solidarity with her Scottish cousin and disgust at the Riccio killing, Queen Elizabeth had ordered her ambassador to ignore Darnley, a diplomatic insult that may have prompted Darnley's pique. As a nod to the King of France as the senior godfather, the baby was baptized with the names Charles James, although it was the second by which he was universally known. All three godparents sent proxies to the christening, along with lavish gifts—the Duke of Savoy sent a jewel-encrusted peacock feather fan for Queen Mary,

* An independent duchy covering part of what is now southeastern France and northwestern Italy.

and the English queen gave a golden font for the baptism itself, during which the baby prince was held in the arms of his Protestant aunt, the Countess of Argyll.

James's christening was followed by three days of celebrations at Stirling, which included firework displays, balls, bonfires, and banquets by torchlight in the castle's Great Hall. Their splendor did not ameliorate Protestant distress at the Prince's baptism into the Catholic faith. As punishment for participating in the Catholic ceremony at Stirling, the Countess of Argyll was required by the Presbyterian Church to perform public penance; the process involved sitting in a special chair in front of the congregation on Sundays, often wearing a sign detailing your sin.[23] The number of Sundays was left to the discretion of the clergyman. Nor did the christening's festivities distract any of the guests from gossiping about Darnley's absence or speculating on the state of the royal marriage.

By February, Darnley was suffering from ill-health. His enemies later claimed, almost certainly inaccurately, that he had syphilis. With a small staff, he was moved into a mansion on the outskirts of Edinburgh called the House at Kirk o' Field. Still determined to keep an eye on him, Mary visited her husband often and even on one occasion spent the night, albeit in a separate bedroom. During her visits, Mary seemed sympathetic to her husband. She may have been acting, she may have been sincere, she may have oscillated between the two. Darnley, once again, was apparently convinced and in letters to his father described Mary as "my love the Queen" and "[my] natural and loving wife."[24] Another of Mary's illegitimate half siblings, Lord Robert Stewart—their father, James V, was not known for his love of sleeping alone—had been present as a guest at the fatal dinner party at which David Riccio was murdered. Despite this, he too suddenly felt sorry for Darnley and warned him that he would lose his life if he did not leave Kirk o' Field at the first opportunity. An agitated Darnley repeated this to the Queen, who asked Robert what he had meant. Frightened by whoever he knew to be plotting against Darnley, Robert answered that he had been speaking nonsense.

On February 9, 1567, the Queen called to see her husband in the afternoon. It was the last Sunday before Lent, so Mary and the Catholics in her household hoped to enjoy themselves before the more somber forty days preceding Easter. She told Darnley of a busy day that had begun with her attendance at the wedding at Holyroodhouse of courtier Bastien Pages, one of those who had helped organize the celebrations at Stirling for James's christening. Pages's wedding Mass had been followed for the Queen by a farewell lunch for the outgoing ambassador from Savoy, at which her new favorite, Lord Bothwell, had also been a guest. Mary had announced her intention to spend the night at Kirk o' Field when a retainer reminded her that Bastien Pages's wedding dance was being held at Holyroodhouse that night and she had promised to attend. Darnley was extremely upset at Mary's change of plan, unmollified by her gift of a ring as she left, and ordered his valet to bring him a bottle of wine to drink alone. As she prepared to mount her horse in the house's courtyard, Mary was surprised to spot one of Lord Bothwell's servants, a man called Paris. He was covered in dirt or soot.

"Jesu, Paris!" she exclaimed. "How begrimed* you are!"

A few hours later, a half-naked Darnley ran through the mansion's gardens. The sky lit up behind him as the House at Kirk o' Field became the first building in British history to be blown apart by gunpowder. As the light and sound of its destruction roused a sleeping Edinburgh, Darnley kept running. Somehow, his valet had found out just in time to rouse his master, and the two men scaled the mansion's walls moments before the fuse was lit.

Their luck stopped running before they did. We do not know who was waiting for them in the gardens. Whoever it was, they had left nothing to chance. Just in case Darnley escaped immolation, his killers hid by the hedges, where they caught the twenty-one-year-old and strangled him. They did the same to his valet, William Taylor, then dumped the two bodies in the garden, where they were found the next morning. The explosion that destroyed Kirk o' Field had been strong enough to shake the windows of Holyroodhouse, where Mary was asleep in her bedchamber. She allegedly awoke screaming, mistaking it in the seconds after sleep for the sound of another coup.

* Dirty.

Who killed Lord Darnley remains one of Scottish history's most famous unsolved mysteries. Thanks to his personality and actions, there were plenty of suspects. He had managed to offend nearly everybody in his short time as Mary's consort. The most popular conclusion was that he had been killed by those loyal to his wife—and the question of how much Mary knew remains controversial—but some wondered if Darnley himself had ordered the house stocked with gunpowder with the intention of luring his wife to spend one more night there, killing her in an explosion, and then assuming the regency for baby James. He allegedly had horses saddled and ready to leave at five o'clock in the morning on the night he had expected Mary to sleep at Kirk o' Field, only for her plans to change at the last moment because of Bastien Pages's wedding ball. Had somebody, perhaps Lord Bothwell, discovered this plan, maybe thanks to the sooty investigations of his servant Paris, and then decided to give Darnley a taste of his own medicine?[25] Others accused Darnley's former allies of murdering him in revenge for his betrayal of them and reconciliation with Queen Mary.

Almost as soon as the citizens had finished rummaging through the rubble for survivors, public opinion demanded justice for Kirk o' Field. Being killed in a fight was one thing; to be strangled, unarmed, defenseless, and in his night clothes, was dishonorable. The English government added their voice to the cry, as did Darnley's grieving and enraged parents, the Earl and Countess of Lennox, who believed Mary had been fully complicit in their son's murder. This was in contrast to Queen Elizabeth, who told the Spanish ambassador to London, "[I] cannot believe the Queen of Scotland can be to blame for so dreadful a thing, notwithstanding the murmurs of the people."[26] The Scottish Parliament defied international and public opinion by formally acquitting the chief suspect, Lord Bothwell, who had a town crier parade through the streets of the capital proclaiming the verdict. It made no difference. Among the citizens of Edinburgh, the consensus was that Darnley had been murdered by Bothwell, the Queen's lover who hoped to become her husband. Suspicions were heightened by rumors, which proved correct, that Bothwell had gathered potential supporters at a local tavern, where he had convinced them to sign a bond in which they pledged to support him in divorcing his wife and marrying the Queen. Mocking pamphlets circulated, pinned not just to the walls of ordinary buildings but to the palace gates, in which the Queen was depicted as a mermaid, a popular symbol for a prostitute.

In contrast, Darnley's sins were wiped away by death. Pictures were printed showing the night of the murder, with Darnley's and Taylor's bodies lying in the garden. Across the left-hand side of the image, a speech bubble curled like smoke from a cradle containing Prince James, robbed of his noble father by ignoble assassins, and pleading, "Judge and avenge my cause, O Lord." It was the first time that words were put into James's mouth by others.

As the situation around her spiraled, Mary suffered another collapse. This one proved even more severe than her first. Still wearing black for Darnley—she insisted on full mourning for forty days, with daily Requiem Masses—she granted an audience to the English ambassador, who was shown into "a dark chamber, so as I could not see her face"; some suspected that the woman he spoke with in that room was not Mary, but one of her heavy-veiled ladies-in-waiting impersonating her on her orders, because Mary was still too unwell to receive visitors.[27] Six weeks later, on April 21, the Queen was strong enough to go to Stirling to visit her son. James was ten months old, in good health, and his mother spent several days with him.

Mary was distressed and perplexed by how her life had come to this. By the time she had reached her son's age, she was already a monarch. Her father's death had made her queen when she was six days old. According to legend, James V died of a broken heart at news of his army's defeat by England's; more likely, he succumbed to cholera.[28] The consequences of the continuing war against England fell to his widow, Mary's mother, the French noblewoman Marie of Guise; to prevent Mary being captured by the English army or Scottish rebels, Marie subsequently sent her infant daughter to live with her relatives in France. Marie remained in Scotland, eventually becoming regent in her daughter's name. The House of Guise was one of the great families of the French aristocracy; they were one step from the throne in their ambition and soon, thanks to Mary's betrothal to King Henri II's eldest son, in blood.

Educated in France, Mary had never expected to spend much of her life in Scotland, despite being its reigning queen. At the time of her marriage to the future King François II, she had signed a secret promise whereby Scottish independence would be forfeited to France if she predeceased her husband.[29] The consequences of that never came to fruition—meningitis ended François's life, aged sixteen, and left seventeen-year-old Mary as a widow.[30] Mary's own mother had recently died, having succeeded in holding the Scottish throne for Mary but failing utterly to prevent the spread of Protestantism in the country. With her husband's death and then her mother's, Mary's future was in Scotland, where her illegitimate half brother the Earl of Moray had assumed power as regent after Queen Marie's death.

On Mary's return in August 1561, Moray relinquished the regency and remained at his half sister's side as her most prominent, and arguably most competent, adviser. She faced formidable challenges. In the months between her mother's death and Mary's return, Parliament abolished papal authority in Scotland. The founder of the new Scottish Protestant denomination of Presbyterianism, John Knox, wielded immense influence, and while he was left distressed when he reduced Mary to tears during their first meeting, it did not stop him calling on his followers to protest at the palace against the Queen's continued attendance at Catholic religious services. The power of the Presbyterian Kirk—from the Scottish word for "church"—extended into the aristocracy, where it had attracted the support of a faction called the Lords of the Congregation. They could be counted upon to promote the Kirk's agenda at the expense of the Crown's, as they had shown when they enthusiastically supported the anti-papal legislation of 1560. Nor was Mary initially helped much in Scotland by her education, which had focused on preparing her to be a French queen consort rather than a Scottish queen regnant.* It is not true, however, as is often assumed, that

---

* A female monarch who inherited the crown in her own right, rather than acquiring it through marriage, in contrast to queens consort. Queens regnant exercised the political power and authority of a monarch, in further contrast to queens consort who had no official power over legislation unless they served as regent.

she spoke with a French accent. She did so when speaking French; otherwise, as an Irish lawyer who met her in 1569 recorded, she spoke with a Scottish accent.[31]

Given all the obstacles in her way, perhaps what was most remarkable was the success Mary made of her personal rule in Scotland for the first four or five years. Then came the marriage to Darnley. This alienated Mary's brother Moray, who felt that his place as her adviser had been taken by the incompetent Darnley and then by the detested Riccio. Darnley had wanted the Crown Matrimonial, which would make him Mary's co-ruler and heir, rather than simply her consort. Mary made him Duke of Albany and Earl of Ross, and he was even ceremonially referred to as King Henry, but, belatedly realizing the defects in his character, she resisted giving him political authority.[32] The rot accelerated in their marriage as the denial of the Crown Matrimonial left Darnley in a mood of aggrieved and porous stupidity that led directly to his role as a pawn for disaffected nobles, who promised to give him that crown if he helped them kill Riccio and bully the pregnant Queen. In the aftermath of Riccio's murder and then Darnley's, this was the inheritance Mary might leave for James if the situation did not improve—sectarian divisions, a Presbyterian Kirk strong enough to challenge the government, a powerful nobility with constantly shifting loyalties, and the widespread suspicion that his father had been murdered on his mother's orders.

As she grappled with the enormity of the task facing her, Mary spent three days with James.[33] The Earl of Mar, head of James's household at Stirling, refused her request that he hand James over so that she could bring him back to Edinburgh with her. Mar justified his defiance with the explanation that "he had in his keeping the treasure of the kingdom and would not risk losing it."[34] To expose the ten-month-old Duke of Rothesay to the politically fraught environment in Edinburgh was a great risk, yet Mar's resolute refusal also showed how denuded Mary's authority had become, even in her own court. On Wednesday, April 23, she kissed James goodbye, left with her retinue, and never saw her son again.

Six miles from Edinburgh, at the main bridge crossing the Almond River, Mary and her entourage of about forty found their way blocked by four hundred armed horsemen, whose leader, her favorite Lord Bothwell, informed her that the capital city had risen against her. Mary went with him to Dunbar Castle, the same place to which she had fled after David Riccio's murder. Bothwell, who had made no secret of his desire to marry Mary, had fabricated the uprising in Edinburgh to trick Mary into coming with him. Once she was behind the walls of Dunbar Castle, he raped her, after which Mary—desperate to conform to contemporary standards that would have cast aspersions on her honor if she had sex outside marriage, even if that intercourse was not consensual—agreed to marry him. Some insight into her devastated mental state can be gained by the fact that, despite being a Catholic queen who was conscious of her dignity, she agreed to marry Bothwell in a Protestant ceremony at four o'clock in the morning with almost no guests. Bothwell's family—the Hepburns—were suspected of witchcraft, and there were whispers that Bothwell had picked four o'clock as the time of the wedding after consulting with necromancers, who helped him control the Queen by casting spells that befuddled her further.[35]

Some, however, were not convinced that Mary was in any way confused. Her detractors claimed that Mary was to show at several stages in her life that she had no qualms about lying, especially when it came to politics. Out of necessity, she often adopted two or three mutually contradictory policies while she waited to see which one would bear fruit. The alternative account of the 1567 abduction is that it was staged and that Mary and Bothwell had been lovers long before her captivity at Dunbar Castle. Just like everybody else in Edinburgh, Mary knew of Bothwell's hopes of marrying her, especially after his recent divorce from his wife, Lady Jean Gordon; Lady Jean had been persuaded to cooperate by her family, who were promised royal favor once Bothwell was Mary's consort. Bothwell and his father had been among the most loyal supporters of her mother's regency, Mary had trusted Bothwell since her time as Queen of France, and the Papal Nuncio to Scotland had described him as "the Queen's most trusty and obedient adherent."[36] Mary's critics suspected that she had wanted to marry Bothwell, who had been her right-hand man since the Riccio killing; she knew that Bothwell was a strong and capable warrior, who would be of great help to her in securing her regime after the scandal of Darnley's murder. Given some contemporary attitudes towards sexual coercion, allegations that he was a rapist would not have severely damaged Bothwell's reputation, especially since the thirty-three-year-old seemed indifferent to what anybody thought of him. In his early twenties, he had had an affair with Janet Beaton, a five-times-married mother of seven who was so ageless in her beauty that she was nicknamed "the Wizard Lady of Branxholm." There were mutual allegations of sorcery from the couple after their relationship broke down. During his subsequent travels in Europe, he had seduced, exploited, pretended to marry, then abandoned a Norwegian heiress. At their castle at Haddington, Bothwell had sex in the church steeple with the local blacksmith's twenty-year-old daughter, Bessie, who was employed as a seamstress by Bothwell's wife.[37]

To protect the Queen's reputation, Mary and Bothwell allegedly agreed in advance for him to "abduct" her to make it appear to the public that she had no choice but to marry him. Her critics claimed that this also explained her unusual request to take her infant son from the safety of Stirling, because she wanted to have James with her when she eloped with Bothwell. This would prevent James being seized by his mother and stepfather's enemies, who might attempt to proclaim him king in his mother's stead.

The confusion over what happened at Dunbar extended even to those close to the Queen. Mary's adviser Sir James Melville, who, crucially, was at Dunbar on the night of the abduction, was under no illusions about what had transpired, writing later in his memoirs, "The Queen could not but marry him, seeing he had ravished her and lain with her against her will."[38] This was contradicted by Sir William Kircaldy, who would later lose his life defending Mary's cause. He claimed that the Queen had told him that she loved Lord Bothwell so much that she would follow him to the ends of the earth, even if it meant losing everything.[39] Captain Blackater, a soldier in Bothwell's service, told a disbelieving Melville, while they were traveling to Dunbar, that the abduction was staged "with the Queen's own consent."[40] Mary confided in her confessor Father Mameret that she had married the Protestant Lord Bothwell to heal the sectarian divisions in Scotland, which might indicate that she entered the marriage willingly, but may conversely have been what Mary told herself and Father Mameret in the trauma following her abduction and assault.[41] In terms of firsthand testimony from Mary herself, there is a letter that she sent to the Bishop of Dunblane shortly after the wedding, in which she wrote of Bothwell, "Albeit we found his doings rude,* yet were his words and answers gentle."[42]

Given that Mary was physically and mentally unwell for months, it is possible that Bothwell took advantage of this by manipulating and, later, sexually abusing her. Mary's recollections to the Bishop of Dunblane—in which she contrasts Bothwell's aggressive actions with his gentle words—suggest that she may have been left discombobulated by Bothwell's oscillation between outright aggression and tactical adoration.[43] Equally credible is the scenario whereby Mary and Bothwell's relationship began consensually, then subsequently degenerated into one of control and abuse. With the evidence remaining incomplete and likely to stay that way after so many years, the circumstances of the Bothwell marriage will continue to provoke debate.[44]

Its consequences are far less ambiguous. The rebellions that Bothwell had fabricated to justify his marriage were turned into a reality by it. The Queen's wedding sparked public outrage, speculation, and uprisings that wove together to sweep Mary off her throne. When her army was defeated by the rebels and she was captured, she was led back into Edinburgh through crowds screaming, "Burn the whore!"[45] By then pregnant with twins she had conceived with Bothwell, Mary was imprisoned and moved to the island fortress at Lochleven, where she suffered the miscarriage of her twins and a third breakdown, during which her enemies pressured her into abdicating. Bothwell, with a price on his head, fled north with Mary's permission. He escaped to the Orkney Islands, from where he sailed to Norway and then to Denmark; the Danish king negotiated with the Scottish rebels, who encouraged him to detain Bothwell in Denmark.

---

* Aggressive.

The new Scottish government decided to keep Mary, who turned twenty-five that December, under house arrest. Her estranged half brother Lord Moray resumed his duties as regent—this time for James, who, carried in the arms of his governess, was taken from his nursery at Stirling Castle for his coronation in the local parish church of the Holy Rude.* The ceremony was a calculated repudiation of his mother's Catholicism. The sermon was preached by John Knox, one of his mother and grandmother's harshest critics, who took as his subject the life of the biblical monarch Athaliah, Queen of Judah. Athaliah was Jezebel's daughter and, like her mother, overturned the worship of God in favor of reintroducing idolatry. Knox's sermon also touched on Athaliah's grandson King Joash, whose father was murdered when he was an infant; afterward Joash was saved by godly loyalists, who hid him in the Temple in Jerusalem until a rebellion overthrew sinful Athaliah in favor of Joash.[46] It did not take a theologian to decipher Knox's point.

Following the sermon, the Protestant Bishop of Orkney anointed with holy oil the baby's forehead, shoulder blades, and the palms of his hands. The crown was then touched to James's head; the sword, representing the monarch's military duties in protecting his kingdom, and the scepter, denoting his promise to uphold the law, were brought to touch the child's hands. At each of these moments, more prayers were said.[47] The oath was sworn on James's behalf by the Earl of Morton, who had been a member of his mother's government until he betrayed her by helping lock down Holyroodhouse for the plotters on the night of Riccio's assassination. After the coronation, fireworks erupted over Stirling as they had at James's christening, while the sounds of "shooting of cannon and feasting" rang out to celebrate the coronation of His Grace James VI, By The Grace of God King of Scots.[48] He was thirteen months old.

---

* The cross upon which Christ was crucified was sometimes referred to as "the Rood" or "the Holy Rood" by medieval Scottish, English, and Welsh Christians. This spelling—*Rude*—was less common than Rood and later fell out of use.

2

CAIN BAIRN

I was alone, without father or mother,
brother or sister.
James VI, King of Scots
(1589)

Still in his cradle, James had become his mother's replacement, rival, and rebuke. Within weeks of his coronation, his mother insisted that James was a false king, through no fault of his own but due to the treachery of those who had crowned him. Once she had recovered her health on her island prison at Lochleven, the former queen revoked her abdication on the grounds that it had been elicited under duress. In correspondence with her half brother the Regent Moray, she tried to negotiate a compromise concerning her return to power. Moray rebuffed this, while Mary rejected the advice of supporters who urged her to initiate divorce proceedings against Bothwell, a move that they hoped would draw many people back to her cause.[1]

With talks at an impasse, Mary walked out of Lochleven under the cover of darkness on May 2, 1568, disguised as a servant. The guards who were supposed to be watching her were passed out in a stupor. Two teenagers who had been living in the castle—George Douglas and his kinsman William, quite possibly George's illegitimate nephew and nicknamed "Wee Willie" in the household—had been so impressed by Mary that they agreed to help her escape, despite George's brother (and possibly Willie's father) serving as Mary's chief jailer. George returned to the mainland, where he passed messages to Mary's adherents. On the pre-agreed night, Willie, who had remained on the island, got his colleagues drooling drunk. When they were halfway between a good time and unconsciousness, Willie stole the keys from them and opened the castle gates. Once the escape party was on the other side, Willie threw the keys into the mouth of a cannon and knocked holes in all the boats, bar one. Mary and two of her ladies, also disguised, boarded the undamaged boat, which took them to the opposite shore. When they arrived, George Douglas was waiting with horses for them.

By the time the guards at Lochleven had come to, realized what had happened, raised the alarm, and talked George's hungover and hysterical brother out of killing himself, Mary was well on her way to the fortress at Dumbarton, where her supporters—known as the Queen's Party or the Marians—flocked to join her. The King's Party—those who fought for Moray's regime but in baby James's name—rallied at Moray's base at the city of Glasgow. The two armies met at the Battle of Langside, which the Queen's Party lost. To the surprise of her adviser Sir James Melville, Mary's courage deserted her. Years earlier, Mary's uncle the Duke of Guise had told her, "you are as brave as my bravest men-at-arms. If women went into battle now, as they did in ancient times, I think you would know how to die well."[2] Melville, who also considered Mary one of the most courageous people he had ever met, wrote that, after Langside, his queen "took so great a fear that she rested never" as she sought to evade recapture by her enemies.[3]

Politically and militarily, all was not lost for the Queen's Party even after defeat at Langside but, in the post-battle panic, Mary could be forgiven for believing that it was. She fled south, riding through the night without stopping for food or water, until she reached the Catholic abbey of Dundrennan, where she was granted sanctuary. The next morning—May 16, 1568—she stepped onto a fishing boat that carried her across the Solway Firth to England, where she begged for and received asylum from her cousin Queen Elizabeth.* Mary's opponents were worried about a mooted meeting between the two queens and by rumors of Elizabeth's sympathy for Mary. Elizabeth's monarchist instincts recoiled at the overthrow of a fellow sovereign, and there were concerns that, if the cousins met for the first

* Technically, Elizabeth and Mary were cousins once removed but, like most of their contemporaries, they used the word "cousin" to cover a spectrum of kinship.

time, Mary might persuade Elizabeth to transform that sympathy into support. To prevent this, Lord Moray went south to England with documents that seemed to prove Mary's complicity in Darnley's murder and her adultery with Bothwell. Known as the Casket Letters, it is highly unlikely that they are authentic in their entirety; nonetheless, they achieved their purpose of decimating Mary's credibility in England.[4] They certainly helped the faction in the English government who did not want to see Catholic Mary restored to a foreign throne with their money. The new Scottish government refused to take Mary back, and since Elizabeth could not leave Mary at liberty in case she became a rallying point to disaffected English Catholics, the deposed Queen of Scots was kept in the limbo of luxurious detention in the English countryside.

Even as an exile, Mary continued to enjoy substantial support from the Scottish aristocracy and not, as some of her critics claimed, solely from her fellow Catholics. Of the kingdom's nineteen earls,* only five had attended James's coronation at Stirling, whereas twelve, including several Protestants, supported Mary.[5] This split within the aristocracy ensured that the question of Mary's and James's competing status dominated Scottish politics for half a decade after Mary's escape to England.

The resulting political chaos claimed the lives of James's first two regents, who consecutively ruled Scotland during his youth. In 1570, James's uncle Lord Moray acquired the unfortunate distinction of becoming the first head of government to be killed by a firearm when he was shot while riding through the streets of Linlithgow, a town twenty miles to the west of Edinburgh. Although he had been nicknamed "the Good Regent" by many in Scotland, Moray was detested by Mary's supporters, including the House of Hamilton, one of the great families of the aristocracy, who hired his assassin.[6] In retaliation, the Roman Catholic Archbishop of St. Andrews—a Hamilton who had helped plot Moray's murder—was kidnapped and hanged by the King's Party.[7]

---

* Then the highest title in use in the Scottish peerage. The two higher-ranking titles—marquess and duke—were at that time typically reserved for members of the immediate or extended royal family, such as Queen Mary's husbands.

Five months later, in September 1571, the new regent—James's grandfather Matthew Stewart, 4th Earl of Lennox—was shot in the back in a skirmish at Stirling with the Queen's Party. Lennox managed to ride back behind the castle walls before he collapsed off his horse. In the chaos, nobody was watching James, who wandered out of his rooms and saw his grandfather—wounded and bleeding—carried past him by frightened retainers.[8] Lennox interrupted their panicked chatter to ask about his grandson's well-being, saying, "If the bairn* be well, all is well."[9] From his deathbed, Lennox asked for a clergyman to soothe his soul and a doctor to soothe his wound, for his servants to tell his wife that he loved her, and for them all to keep James safe. Devastated by the murder of his son Lord Darnley, Lennox had stayed in Scotland to protect his grandson, secure his family's estates, and sustain the coup against his daughter-in-law. As his concern in extremis for "the bairn" showed, he had been a loving grandfather to James, and his death robbed the child of the last close relative in Scotland with whom he was in regular contact.

Lord Mar was appointed as Lennox's successor in government. He lasted thirteen months before stress sent him into the grave.[10] He was replaced by James's fourth regent and distant cousin, the grim but competent Earl of Morton. By then, most of the Marian earls had, with varying degrees of reluctance, prostrated themselves to pragmatism and accepted the new regime. Morton turned his attentions on the last serious bastion of Marian loyalism, Edinburgh Castle, which surrendered to siege in the summer of 1573.[11] After the castle's fall, many in the defeated garrison were allowed to leave as free men. Aristocrats on the losing side tended to be punished more severely, as those with greater wealth to their name made for more attractive candidates for confiscation. A few of those who lost their fortunes saved their lives by escaping to France. Some of their former comrades were less lucky. William Maitland of Lethington, Queen Mary's former Secretary of State and husband to one of her closest friends, took his own life by drinking poison.[12] The castle's

* "Child"—used most frequently in Scotland, the north of England, and northeastern Northern Ireland.

commander, Sir William Kircaldy, his brother, and two colleagues were taken by the victors to Edinburgh's Mercat Cross,* where they were hanged.

With the capitulation of Edinburgh Castle and Lord Morton establishing an iron grip on government, the chances of Mary being restored to power seemed dead, if not quite buried. As one of James's attendants put it, "When the King was set up, and the Power of the Regent almost settled, there was Quietness from Force and Arms, but the Peace was but Ticklish, Men's minds were yet in fermentation . . ."[13]

Scotland's first full census was not conducted until 1755, which makes it difficult to estimate how many people benefited from the ticklish peace that followed the events of 1573. Like many European nations, Scotland's population had endured a substantial dip in the fourteenth and early fifteenth centuries due to regular outbreaks of the bubonic plague, from which it took centuries to fully recover. A reasonable estimate would be that the Scottish population was about 750,000 by the time James became king, just over 5 percent of whom lived in towns or cities. The largest of these was the capital, Edinburgh, with approximately fifteen thousand residents. Prior to 1600, the country's other legally recognized city was Glasgow. Scattered mostly throughout the southern and eastern parts of Scotland, there were about one hundred burghs, which were towns that had received royal charters granting them the right to hold a market, fortify themselves, and elect town officials while remaining under the suzerainty of the Crown and, in many cases, their principal local aristocratic family.

Scotland had once consisted of four kingdoms, with similar but distinct cultures, the echoes of which reverberated long after the centuries-spanning process toward unification ended in the

* Historically, a structure erected in the squares of Scottish towns or cities that were permitted to hold markets. They emerged as venues to express or proclaim decisions made by the town's secular authorities. At the time of writing, Edinburgh's Mercat Cross dates from the nineteenth century and stands close to the site of the original, where Kircaldy and the others were executed. That Mercat Cross was erected about forty-five feet from the eastern end of St. Giles's in the reign of King David II (r. 1329–71); it was subsequently moved in 1617 and demolished in 1756.

late ninth century. The southeastern kingdom of Bernicia was an Anglo-Saxon monarchy, covering land in what is today southeast Scotland and northeast England, and English remained a common language in the region long after most of Bernicia had become part of Scotland. The dominant language in central and southern Scotland by James's lifetime was Scots, which had emerged alongside Old English and shared influences with Gaelic and French. By the late fourteenth century, Scots had evolved into a separate language, which, in the fifteenth century, became the preferred language of the Scottish court and southern nobility. Scots's similarities with English saw James and some of his contemporaries insist that English and Scots were dialects of the same language. This was contested both at the time and since, principally on the grounds that mutual intelligibility does not mean they are the same language; a better, although admittedly imperfect, comparison might be the ways in which many speakers of Italian can follow Spanish, or vice versa.

The Scots language had originated in the kingdom of Strathclyde, the former territories of which—along with Bernicia's—were known as the Lowlands. Most of northern Scotland was the Highlands, which consisted of the former kingdom of the Picts and the bicoastal Ulster-Scots kingdom of Dalriada that had once ruled over the western Scottish ports, along with much of what is now northeast Northern Ireland. Unlike England and Wales, the Romans had never conquered the Scottish kingdoms, and their name for the inhabitants of Dalriada, the "Scoti," eventually became the name used for the entire nation by Scots and English speakers. It was called Alba in Gaelic, the language of the majority in the Highlands.

The differences between the Highlands and the Lowlands extended beyond their languages. The Scottish aristocracy of the sixteenth century could justifiably claim to be one of the most locally powerful European elites. The influence they wielded in their ancestral lands was such that Scottish government was effectively an aristocratic federalism, under which the great houses were not just the locus of government but the focus of loyalty. The Earl of Cassilis, for instance, was nicknamed, with only mild exaggeration, "the

King of Carrick," after the area in the east from which his family ruled. In the Lowlands, the aristocracy could, on occasion, rival their monarch's power. In the Highlands, they frequently eclipsed it. Debate continues over how influential the Scottish system of clans was in certain parts of Scotland, but they were undeniably central to the Highlands. Each clan had its own head or chief, who commanded his territories and the loyalty of those who lived in them. Many tenants or farmers took the name of their local clan, further intensifying the symbiosis between lord and tenants. Feuds were not just prosecuted by the lords and clan chiefs, but by those who swore fealty to them. Conflicts arose over wealth, land, and politics. Above all, honor played a central role in perpetuating the feuds. They could last for years and, in some cases, for generations.

From the Crown's perspective, clan feuds were a menace. However, the aristocracy also enforced laws, collected taxes, and maintained tradition in the countryside. In adulthood, James was not wrong when he described the nobility as the bedrock of Scottish society.

Like most medieval kingdoms, Scotland had both a fraught and a friendly relationship with its neighbors at different points over the centuries. Relations with England had gone through high points of cooperation—in the eleventh century, Scotland's King Malcolm III had spent his youth in England and married an English princess. Their son David I was a respected voice in English politics in the twelfth century. They had reached a nadir in the thirteenth century, when England's Edward I exploited the death of Scotland's Alexander III to install an English puppet on the throne; when that was objected to, he embarked on a failed but generation-long attempt to conquer Scotland. There were cycles of rapprochement and retribution for the next three centuries. James I married an English noblewoman, and James IV married an English princess. In the 1510s, Scotland was defeated when they sent the largest army ever to invade England; in the 1540s, England was defeated when they launched a brutal invasion of Scotland. Within the Scottish elite, there were those who favored friendly ties with England and those who regarded England as Scotland's natural enemy.

England was not the sole concern of medieval Scotland's foreign policy. She had complicated relationships with her Scandinavian neighbors in Denmark and Norway. In the century before James's birth, tensions with Scandinavia had seen the most recent expansion of Scottish territory, when she annexed the Orkney Islands off the northeastern Scottish coast and, farther north and east, the Shetland Islands. When the islands became part of Scotland, their main language was Norn, which had emerged from the Vikings' Old Norse; it was being gradually superseded by Gaelic in the late sixteenth century. Also in the fifteenth century, the Scottish Crown had assumed control over the Inner and Outer Hebrides, an archipelago off the western coast. Following a rebellion by Clan MacDonald, the chief noble house in the Hebrides, the monarchy subsumed the Hebrides fully to Crown jurisdiction, and the defeated MacDonalds' former title—Lord of the Isles—was henceforth held by Scotland's monarch and their heir.

By the time he turned ten in the summer of 1576, James VI had seen little of his kingdom. He still lived safely behind the walls of Stirling Castle, while the government was led by Lord Morton. Almost equidistant between Edinburgh and Glasgow, Stirling Castle, which shared its name with the surrounding region of Stirlingshire, loomed on a crag over the burgh of Stirling that nestled at the bottom of the cliff on the castle's eastern side. The wind that blew in off the nearby River Forth, flowing east toward the North Sea, could be bitter in autumn and winter. The views were magnificent and, on days when the mists had cleared, the castle's residents looking north could see the mountains of Ben Ledi, Ben Lomond, Ben Vorlich, and Stùc a' Chroin, beyond which lay the Highlands. Three of Stirling Castle's four sides gave way to sharp drops, which made the castle difficult to besiege and explained its historical importance as a fortress.[14] Cold as it could be in autumn and winter, Stirling Castle was luxurious thanks to the money spent on it by James's ancestors, and above all it was safe, with the latest in a long series of defensive features having been installed on the orders of his grandmother Marie of Guise.

James's private quarters were in one of the castle towers, "the Prince's Tower." He slept in a bedchamber watched over by a portrait of his grandfather James V, whom he resembled with his pale complexion. James VI was tall for his age, like both of his parents, and he had the fair hair of his father, Lord Darnley. He had survived a childhood brush with smallpox unscarred; another, with rickets, caused a minor bowing of his femurs that was subsequently exaggerated into the inaccurate claim that he could not walk until he was seven years old.

His mornings began in his bedroom in the tower, where he was helped to dress by his Gentlemen of the Chamber, most of them from landed families loyal to the King's Party. The apartments contained several tributes to James's status—most obviously with his chair of estate, which was a throne canopied with his coat of arms—but they were also dotted with gifts that testified to his love of the outdoors, such as his black leather-covered quiver, bow, and arrows, or the golf clubs that had been given to him by a local laird.* He owned a hawking glove, seeded with pearls, that had been delivered to him from his grandmother in England, the Dowager Countess of Lennox. Although she was kept away by politics—neither the Scottish nor English governments trusted her, and both denied her permission to travel—the Countess frequently sent James wonderful gifts.[15]

Every morning, there were prayers. Following his mother's exile, the new regime had ensured that James's spiritual instruction was firmly Protestant. After prayers and before breakfast, ten-year-old James had his first lesson of the day, which was usually Greek, conducted through study either of the New Testament in that language or the works of philosophers like Plutarch or Isocrates.[16] Those lessons took place in a schoolroom in the same tower, and they seem to have been conducted by Peter Young, the junior of James's two academic tutors. A gently mannered scholar in his early thirties, Young had previously studied in Geneva under the famous Protestant theologian Theodore Beza; Young was well-liked by most

* The titles of lord and laird are both used in reference to the Scottish elite. "Laird," however, is not a title in the nobility; rather it designated the owner of a sizeable tract of land. This contrasts with "lord," a title that can be used by barons, viscounts, earls, and marquesses as a prefix to their territorial designation. For example, the Earl of Morton could also be Lord Morton.

people, including his royal pupil, whom he found to be an enthusiastic student.

Nature and nurture had combined to turn James into a remarkably intelligent young man. A Presbyterian clergyman who stayed at Stirling for two days when James was seven was impressed by the boy's "judgement, memory, and language" and was touched to see the King walking with his governess, eagerly discussing with her what he was studying in his schoolroom.[17] Languages were a passion. The English ambassador visited Stirling when James was eight and was amazed by how "he speaketh the French tongue marvellous well and was able extempore to read a chapter of the Bible into French and out of French into English."[18] James was fluent in Scots, English, French, Greek, and Latin; he had a strong grasp of Italian, which he wanted to improve, and he had good, if weaker, Spanish.[19]

Of these, his first language, according to James's recollections, was Latin. He typically studied Latin after breakfast. The class was conducted by his senior tutor, who argued that Latin would eventually be agreed upon as the best common language for European diplomacy and scholarship.[20] Given his proficiency in the language, James's Latin lessons placed their emphasis on philosophy or rhetoric, including the works of Roman writers such as Livy, Cicero, or the Christian philosopher Justin Martyr. Incredibly, given the thoroughness of his curriculum, James was never taught Gaelic, although it was the language spoken by most of his subjects in the Highlands. Some at court worried that this was an oversight fueled by geographical snobbery on the part of the King's Lowlander tutors, which would further cement the monarchy's trend of relocating to, and ruling from, the Lowlands.[21]

After Latin, there was a class in history, often conducted in Latin, where James studied many things useful to his inheritance. The rise and fall of the diplomatic pact between Scotland and France, nicknamed "the Auld Alliance" for its longevity in lasting from 1295 until 1560, was explained to him, along with the reasons why the government that ruled in James's name had jettisoned it in favor of closer ties with Protestant England. He was taught that, long ago, his family had been courtiers—they had served the previous royal family as stewards, from which they had derived their surname of Stewart—until they rose high enough to marry one of the princesses. Then, in 1371, the first Stewart to become a monarch succeeded his childless royal uncle. James learned too how regencies like his had been a recurring feature of Scottish political life since 1406, when the seven-year-old James I succeeded his father, Robert III. Since then, only one Stewart monarch—James V—had died of natural causes. James I was stabbed to death while hiding in a sewer from an aristocratic coup; his wounded widow managed to get their son, six-year-old James II, to safety. As an adult, James II was killed when one of his own cannons malfunctioned during a siege and exploded next to him, leaving the crown to eight-year-old James III, who in adulthood would be killed in battle; his son and heir, James IV, seemed positively wizened compared to most of the other Stewart kings, being fifteen when the crown landed on his head. His reign too ended with death in battle and the succession of a minor, eighteen-month-old James V.

James's Latin and history classes were usually taught by George Buchanan, who was in his early seventies, with a gray beard, stooped shoulders, and an iron will, which he used to maintain order in the classroom. He was such a forbidding figure that, as an adult, James started trembling when he was approached by a guest with a strong physical resemblance to Buchanan.[22]

Stirling Castle was close to home for Buchanan. He had passed a quiet Stirlingshire childhood in the care of his widowed mother, whom he adored—his farmer father died when Buchanan was seven, leaving the family close to destitute until help arrived from a moderately wealthy uncle. As a teenager, Buchanan enlisted as a soldier and, aged about sixteen, served in the unsuccessful Scottish siege of the English castle of Wark on Tweed; later, he studied at St. Andrews University, founded a century earlier on the east coast of Scotland, and then at the Collège Sainte-Barbe in Paris. His interest in Protestantism had not prevented Buchanan from working as a tutor to Catholic families in the French and Scottish aristocracies, including yet another of James's bastard uncles.* Other students

* James Stewart (1529–57), Commendator of Kelso and Melrose—an illegitimate son of King James V and his mistress Elizabeth Shaw.

of Buchanan's included the French future philosopher Michel de Montaigne and the diplomat-aristocrat Gilbert Kennedy, 3rd Earl of Cassilis. However, Buchanan's faith had earned him two serious brushes with the law. As a young man, he had been imprisoned for heresy in a Scottish jail, from which he escaped and went back to France to teach at the University of Bordeaux and then at the Portuguese university of Coimbra. There he attracted the attention of the Holy Office of the Inquisition, who sent Buchanan to a local monastery to repent. Apologizing his way to freedom, Buchanan had eventually returned to Scotland, where he taught at his alma mater of St. Andrews and was admired as a poet, playwright, polyglot, philosopher, and for his work on astronomy. Buchanan had been invited to court by James's mother, who enjoyed discussing philosophy and reading in Latin with him. He called her the "star of our age."[23] Following Queen Mary's deposition, Buchanan turned on her with the vitriol that was a recurrent and unsavory part of his character.

Previous students of his remembered Buchanan as kind, funny, and engaging. As he aged, those qualities had dimmed and then vanished. Nowhere was this more apparent than in the way he frequently cited Mary, in her son's classroom, as the exemplar of everything that could go wrong in womanhood and in monarchy. Shortly after the uprising against her, Buchanan had helped author a book attacking Mary, *Detectio Mariæ Reginæ Scotorum* ("A Detection of the Doings of Mary, Queen of Scots"), and his history lessons at Stirling spent a disproportionate amount of time focused on the sins of James's mother. Buchanan did not hesitate to supplement his lessons on Mary's political downfall with diatribes informing James of her moral failures as a wife and mother.*

Buchanan presented as fact the claims he had previously made in his book about Mary: that, as a queen, she was a manipulative tyrant and a pathological liar. In her private household, she had been even worse—an "Example of Cruelty, and such as was never heard of before," Buchanan claimed, informing his readers and

* Another attack on Mary—*Actio contra Mariam Scotorum reginam*—has also traditionally been attributed to Buchanan, but it is almost certainly not his work.

pupils that Mary had forced her ladies-in-waiting to satisfy Darnley's sexual urges on her behalf, distracting him so that she could commit adultery with Lord Bothwell, even while she was pregnant with Darnley's son, James.[24] She allegedly amused herself by picking her enemies' wives for Darnley's lovers.

Darnley, in contrast, was presented by Buchanan as a victim—"young and inexperienced . . . contemptuously and unkindly used" by his wife, who had betrayed him with Bothwell, with whom she plotted his murder. Buchanan claimed that after Darnley had been killed on her orders, Mary was physically—almost erotically—thrilled when she had his corpse brought to her so that she could "feast her eyes with the sight of his body slain. For she long beheld, and not only without grief, but also with greedy eyes, his dead corpse, the goodliest corpse of any Gentleman that ever lived in this age."[25] "In a woman, it is monstrous," Buchanan concluded, "in a wife not only excessively loved [by her husband], but also most zealously honoured, it is incredible."[26]

Outside his teaching duties, Buchanan's principal project was researching his historical account of the Scottish monarchy, which would be published in 1582 as *Rerum Scoticarum Historia.*[27] Buchanan felt that the Crown's history had hitherto been misrepresented through a combination of English derision and Scottish patriotism. "I am busy with our story of Scotland to purge it of some English lies and Scottish vanity," he wrote to a friend and—seeming to relish the coming controversy—he told another, "I am occupied in the writing of our history, being assured to content few, and to displease many."[28] A central thesis in Buchanan's book was that the House of Stewart had produced more than its fair share of monarchs who violated Scotland's political traditions in their quest to aggrandize the monarchy. Buchanan argued that the nature of Scotland's system of clans meant that the royal family was never intended to rule far above the nobility.[29] The Scottish royals were closer to being first among equals until, according to Buchanan, the Stewarts' ambition had led them to overturn that.

His relatives' lives were regularly used to ridicule James or, as Buchanan saw it, to discourage him from following in their footsteps. One day, when James was crying after accidentally killing a pet sparrow, Buchanan slapped him and taunted him with his ancestry, telling him that James was evidently "a true bird of the bloody nest of which he has come."[30] To Buchanan, James was descended from tyrants twice over. When James was six years old, he had been joined in Stirling's schoolroom by a French orphan called Jérôme Groslot, whose aristocratic relatives had brought him to Scotland after his father was one of thousands of French Protestants butchered in a series of events subsequently referred to as the Saint Bartholomew's Day Massacre, after the Catholic feast day of the apostle on which the mass slaughter commenced.* Beginning in Paris where many Protestants, including Jérôme's father, had gathered to attend the wedding of a Protestant prince to a Catholic princess, the massacre spread to the provinces, and while the exact number of victims remains unclear, the combined impact of violence and the flight of survivors saw the number of French Protestants collapse by about 87 percent.[31] International Protestant revulsion was compounded by Pope Gregory XIII's orders for services of thanksgiving in Rome, as well as his commissioning of a medal and three frescoes celebrating the massacre.[32] Given that some of them had been publicly calling for the extermination of Protestants for over a decade, James's French relatives on his mother's side, the House of Guise, were unsurprisingly judged complicit in the massacre by many; several of the family's most prominent members participated in the killings.[33] Buchanan's attitude to the bereaved Jérôme was gentle and paternal, in direct contrast to how he treated the King. Buchanan subsequently used his influence to arrange for Jérôme to continue his education in England and then in Switzerland.

Like every western European Christian in his generation, the rest of James VI's life was to some degree spent in the shadow of Saint Bartholomew's Day. The understandable, if almost certainly incorrect, belief among Protestants that the massacre was premeditated down to its last horrible detail—with even the royal wedding

---

* Sometimes called the Massacre of Saint Bartholomew's Eve. The apostle's feast is on August 24. The first of the massacres was perpetrated on the feast day in 1572. However, the initial act of violence—the attempted assassination of the Protestant leader Admiral Gaspard de Coligny—took place the evening before.

used as bait to lure the intended victims to Paris—gained widespread currency. The fear of another Saint Bartholomew's Day intensified—one might even say radicalized—anti-Catholic sentiment, especially in England, where one of Queen Elizabeth's chief advisers, Sir Francis Walsingham, had been in Paris as ambassador when the massacre occurred. Walsingham returned to England as a hard-line Protestant, with a fear-fueled hatred of James's half-Guise mother that would ultimately prove fatal to Mary.

The sins and dangers from James's Catholic family gave austere Buchanan rich material for his lessons, but he was also keen to expound political theories. He was determined to turn James into a godly Protestant king. In his correspondence with Sir Thomas Randolph, an English diplomat and fellow Protestant, Buchanan reflected on his ideal monarch:

> In chief, I would have him a lover of true piety, deeming himself the veritable image of highest God. He must love peace, yet be ever ready for war. To the vanquished, he must be merciful; and when he lays down arms, he must lay aside his hate. I should wish him to be neither a niggard* or a spendthrift, for each, I must think, works equal harm to the people. He must believe that as King he exists for his subjects and not for himself, and that he is, in truth, the common father of the State. When expediency demands that he shall punish with a stern hand, let it appear that he has no pleasure in his own severity. He will ever be lenient if it is consistent with the welfare of his people. His life must be the pattern for every citizen, his countenance the terror of evil doers, the delight of those who do well. His mind he must cultivate with sedulous care, his body as reason demands. Good sense and good taste must keep in check luxurious excess.[34]

Buchanan warned James that flattery was the nurse of tyranny and bad company was the "foster-mother of all vices," which rings as

* Deriving from the Norse *hnǫggr*, via the Middle English *nigon*, and meaning excessively parsimonious or obsessed with saving money.

good advice were it not for Buchanan's tendency to categorize any form of compliment to James as pernicious flattery. He also explained at length his theory of "lawful resistance," which had been used by the Presbyterian Kirk to justify their rebellions against James's mother. Its defenders saw lawful resistance as the right of a people to overthrow a monarch who misruled them or did not reflect their values; its skeptics saw it as post hoc justification for chaos and treason. James, eventually, fell hard into the latter camp, and it seems as if the relentlessness of his childhood lessons, at least in part, caused his ideological rebellion against Buchanan's views. Many of Buchanan's ideas, especially his belief in limited monarchy and the right of a people to oppose their leaders, were celebrated by later generations. The difficulty when looking at them in the context of his service at Stirling in the 1570s lies in how his ideology caused Buchanan to forget his humanity—and the pleasure, which at times seemed to border on the sadistic, that he took in humiliating the young king.

One such incident caused James to snap back at his tutor, during a lesson on the reign of James's great-great-grandfather James III, who had been born at Stirling Castle and had ruled Scotland from 1460 until he was killed in combat in 1488. The battle that ended James III's life had been fought against rebel nobles, who were presented by Buchanan as heroes. To his history of the Scottish monarchy, Buchanan would add the uncorroborated detail that James III had not died in the battle itself as nearly every other source stated but was instead killed while running away.[35] As Buchanan warmed to his theme of James III's myriad failings, James VI interrupted him to suggest that, maybe, James III had simply grown tired of being continually lectured by a subject. Never reluctant to administer corporal punishment and immediately picking up on James's historically cloaked insult, Buchanan dragged the King toward him and began beating him on his rear. The whipping was interrupted when the door was opened by James's governess, the Dowager Countess of Mar, who had been alerted by the sound of James's screams. As she remonstrated with Buchanan for his having dared to assault God's Anointed, an unrepentant Buchanan mockingly replied, "Madam, I have whipt his arse: you may kiss it if you please."[36]

After his history lessons, James was served his midday meal by servants wearing their livery in the Stewart dynasty's colors of yellow and scarlet. Following that, his afternoon classes could be arithmetic, which was his weakest subject, cosmography (geography), logic, or rhetoric. If the weather was good, the lessons might instead be outside in his "Manly Sports," which meant archery, golf, hawking, horse-riding, or hunting. He loved the latter two and looked forward to time spent with his instructors, Adam and David Erskine, respectively the Commendator* of Cambuskenneth and Dryburgh. Occasionally, there were games of football in the courtyard. In the evenings, there might be music, played by the four Hudson brothers, the castle's musicians, and sometimes there was dancing, which James did not overly enjoy. He was not a terrible dancer, but he was to dancing what paint by numbers is to art. The brothers later received the equivalent of a bonus for the "extraordinary pains" they had taken in teaching James to dance.[37]

Whether in his bed or in his study, James could choose his nightly reading from one of the six hundred books in Stirling Castle's library. This had become one of the largest private collections in northern Europe thanks to the diligence of his tutor Peter Young, who had bought some of the books with household funds and persuaded people to send others as gifts. Young's colleague Adam Erskine had contributed a textbook on hunting; one of the Gentlemen of the Chamber had gifted an archery textbook in French; the chaplain donated a copy of the Psalms and a manual on Protestant theology that had been translated into Italian for James, as he sought to acquire fluency in the language. The library held works by the philosophers Antonio de Guevara and Sebastianus Foxius Morzillus, which James could use to improve his Spanish; there were also some French poetry collections that had belonged to James's mother, religious treatises by the French Protestant scholar Guillaume Budé, or tracts by the English political theorist Sir

* Temporary holders of an ecclesiastical benefice, usually an abbey awaiting the appointment of a new abbot. The commendators, who were by royal appointment, could live off the abbey's income and administer its affairs until a new abbot was appointed. After the Scottish Reformation, they were often appointed until such time as the abbey could come under completely secular control.

Thomas Elyot. There were newer editions of older works, including those of the Byzantine philosopher Agapetus, as well as books on modern history, which had been presents sent to James by his grandmother Lady Lennox. She was a talented poet, an interest that James was beginning to share.

When he was ready for sleep in his bed, hung with red velvet curtains, Gentlemen of the Chamber were on hand to remove that day's clothes, including his wool-lined Moroccan leather shoes, doublets decorated with bejeweled buttons and shirts made by James's seamstress, Grissel Gray, daughter of his former wet nurse, Helena Little.[38] Ties of kinship shaped the royal household as fundamentally as they did wider Scottish society. Among the childhood trinkets in his rooms was a precursor to the snow globe—a glass ball with a castle made of wax inside it—which had been given to him by Lady Mar's sister-in-law.

Lady Mar, who turned forty in 1576, had been James's governess since he was a baby, and she slept in his bedroom until he was ten.[39] She had married into the House of Erskine when she was twenty-one but, since Scottish women at the time, especially in the aristocracy, did not typically take their husband's name, she remained Annabella Murray, Dowager Countess of Mar. As shown by her quarrel with George Buchanan, Lady Mar—described as "wise and sharp" by a fellow courtier—had done her best to protect James from his tutor's rages.[40] Buchanan and many of his fellow Presbyterian intellectuals distrusted her. She had served as a lady-in-waiting to James's grandmother and mother and her friendship with the Stewart royals, along with her love of jewelry and refusal to heed the Kirk's orders, had caused a Presbyterian clergyman to call her "a sweet titbit for the Devil's Mouth."[41]

She was devoted to James, and he to her—he privately addressed her by the nickname "Lady Minny"*—but she did not let herself, or him, forget that he was her king.[42] Her attitude to James—one of affection tempered by awe—extended to her family who, thanks to her, formed the majority of Stirling's "above stairs" residents. In part, her success in stuffing and staffing Stirling with her relatives

* A contemporary equivalent of the modern "mommy"/"mom."

could be explained by the fact that the Erskines had a long history of caring for Scotland's young royals and in keeping them safe through political upheavals, to thc extent that their office as governor and governess was almost regarded as hereditary by the sixteenth century. During Queen Mary's reign, she had confirmed it as such. Lady Mar's late husband, the 17th Earl of Mar, had been reluctantly persuaded into trading his post as James's household governor to become his third regent after Lennox's murder. He had been replaced at Stirling by his younger brother Sir Alexander Erskine, who was described by a fellow courtier as a "nobleman of a true, gentle nature, well loved and liked by all men"—no small achievement amidst the feuds of the 1570s.[43] James adored him and, in the same way that he called Lady Mar "Lady Minny" ("Mommy"), he nicknamed Sir Alexander "Lord Deddy" ("Daddy").[44]

James's physical educators, Adam and David Erskine, were also Lady Mar's kin; her brother Sir William Murray of Tullibardine was Comptroller of the Household, and his immediate superior as Master of the Household was Lady Mar's cousin John Cunningham, Laird of Drumquhassle. Contemporary estimations of the family vary. Courtier Sir James Melville, who knew them, judged Adam and David "wise and modest," but he considered Drumquhassle "ambitious and greedy, his greatest care was to advance himself."[45]

The power of kinship was compounded by Lady Mar's choice of James's schoolmates, most of whom were also her relatives. They were friendly with James—he joined in their good-natured teasing about a classmate's dreadful handwriting—but for various reasons, it took time for close friendships to develop. Some, like Lady Mar's son John (of the terrible handwriting) and her nephew Archibald, were several years older than James or, like John's cousins George and Thomas, were initially too young for a close bond to emerge. A few, such as Jérôme Groslot, did not stay for very long and went to complete their education abroad or, like the Provost of Glasgow's son, Walter, who was good with numbers but better with horses, could not keep pace with James intellectually.

After James endured the trauma of witnessing his grandfather's death in 1571, there had followed seven years in which Lady Mar was broadly successful in keeping politics a distant presence in

James's life. It was to the credit of all four of James VI's regents that none of them added to the chaos of the King's life by instituting clean sweeps of his household staff with each regime change. Lady Mar and her cousin Drumquhassle had been appointed by Queen Mary; Buchanan was a Moray appointee, as was the comptroller, Tullibardine; the governor had been appointed by Mar, and the chaplain was picked by Lord Morton. While James was a child, it was therefore in everybody's best interests at Stirling to avoid politics and leave government affairs to Morton in Edinburgh.

Only a few other matters, as far as Lady Mar was concerned, were too important to be ignored. Chiefly, the news that the Devil was active in the west of Scotland, where a local earl ordered an investigation into necromancy in the areas under his family's jurisdiction, resulting in the arrests of about one hundred and fifty local men and women.[46] Lady Mar collected amulets to protect James from sorcery. The area around Stirling was rich in folklore about black magic, including legends of the "cain bairn," children who had been kidnapped by others to offer them up as a tax to the Devil to achieve their own ends. The term *cain*—or *kain*—*bairn* can be translated to mean the child who pays the price for others, or the child who is offered as tribute.

By and large however, between the ages of four and ten, the safe limits of James VI's universe were marked by Stirling, from where he saw only the shadows of what was happening in the world beyond its walls.

3

COUSINS

The trees with Nature's tapestries
Are hung in buds and leaves;
The spider for to catch the flies
Her web and nets now weaves.

–Anonymous Scottish poem
(late sixteenth century)

James's childhood at Stirling began to change when he was eleven—his birthday was on June 19, 1577—and it ended in the autumn of 1579, a few months after he turned thirteen. In those two years, death and politics returned to dominate his life. There were happier developments for James at this time. Old age reduced George Buchanan's presence in his life. Increasingly unwell, Buchanan spent more time in Edinburgh completing his history of the monarchy.

As he left childhood, James looked for mentors in the generation above him, and family seems to have become his major preoccupation. In another set of circumstances, this might have resulted in a closer bond with his regent.[1] However, despite their kinship, Lord Morton was too often absent from Stirling to become close with James. This may have been in the best interests of others since, on the few occasions when the King and Morton established a rapport, it typically came at the expense of somebody else. James was proud of his education and, at times, a know-it-all, a trait that was magnified by the judgmental Morton. A young soldier, Captain Ninian Cockburn,* came to Stirling for an audience after several years serving abroad; before he was shown in to see them, Morton made fun of Cockburn to James, mocking his pronunciation of French,

* Pronounced "Co-burn."

as well as his general intelligence. After he had finished telling the King and the regent of his time abroad, in French "with many gestures and earnestness," James mortified Cockburn by answering, "I have not understood a single word you have spoken, and it seems to me to be true what my lord Regent says: that your French is worth nothing and your Scots scarcely more."[2] The moment he had said it, James seemed to regret it—perhaps Cockburn's face registered the embarrassment he felt—and James tried to soften the blow by complimenting Cockburn on his appearance and gracefulness.

In the absence of any sustained friendship with his regent, the mentors James gravitated toward in adolescence instead drove a permanent wedge between him and Morton. One was another distant relative, also named James Stewart. The second of the four sons of a Lowland nobleman, in 1579 Stewart became the new captain of James's personal guard, after returning from fighting for the Protestant Dutch rebels in their uprising against Spain. Described by acquaintances as outgoing, brave, eloquent, and handsome, a recurring criticism of Stewart was of an arrogance and temper that turned many people against him.[3]

An even closer emotional bond emerged between James and a nobleman brought to Stirling by its governor, Sir Alexander Erskine, who, now that James was older, no longer saw any need to disguise his dislike of the regent.[4] Among the nobles who allied with Erskine and were often hosted by him at Stirling was the Earl of Atholl. In his younger days, Atholl had been nicknamed "John the Fair" for his good looks, and he had been involved in Scottish politics for decades, beginning with his devotion to James's grandmother Marie of Guise. His Catholicism and his activity for the Queen's Party had kept him away from Stirling during James's youth—he was one of the last Marian noblemen to submit to the regency—and it was only in 1577–78 that they began to see more of one another.[5] Atholl was avuncular and intelligent. He too was distantly related to the King and was old enough to be his grandfather, which seems to be the closest comparison for how James saw him.[6]

The last of James's biological grandparents died when he was eleven. There would be no more gifts from his grandmother, the

Dowager Countess of Lennox, who passed away aged sixty-two in London. Despite their often frosty relationship, her cousin Queen Elizabeth ordered and paid for her magnificent funeral at Westminster Abbey. Lady Lennox had the horrible misfortune of outliving all her immediate family—along with the assassinations of her eldest son and her husband in Scotland, in England she had also buried six children in their infancy and then her last surviving son, James's uncle Charles, when he died of tuberculosis aged nineteen in 1576.

Five weeks after Lady Lennox, James's forty-four-year-old stepfather, Lord Bothwell, died in custody in Denmark. One day, in the aftermath of Bothwell's death, James spotted his comptroller, Tullibardine, engrossed in reading a pamphlet, which James asked that he hand over. It turned out to be an alleged confession that Bothwell had made to his captors, shortly before he died. In the "Bothwell Testament," copies of which circulated throughout northern Europe, Bothwell accepted full responsibility for the murder of James's father and specifically stated that Queen Mary had no knowledge of it. The Bothwell Testament also identified the future regent Morton as one of the men who had supported the plot to kill Darnley. Bothwell admitted that he had used witchcraft to manipulate Queen Mary and had considered using it to harm James, and he confessed to a pathological amount of sexual impropriety, including seducing numerous women in Scotland and Scandinavia with promises of marriage, then abandoning them after they slept with him.

Apart from the inherent unreliability of alleged deathbed confessions—and the possibility that the whole document was a forgery is strong*—there were many problems with its veracity. Even if he did contribute to it, Bothwell had spent years incarcerated at Dragsholm Castle, where he had allegedly been chained to a pillar by his neck and exhibited to curious visitors who paid to stare at him in his cell. If true, the rumors that Bothwell had suffered a complete and permanent psychological breakdown are hard to dismiss. Flamboyant legends about the sufferings of the histori-

* The original has never been found, leading to the suspicion that it never existed.

cally significant are legion, and it is unlikely that every gory detail told about Bothwell's final years is correct, but it is certain that he was kept in increasingly severe conditions, including being chained to the pillar, and that he was considered insane by the time he supposedly made this confession.[7]

James was delighted by what he read in the Bothwell Testament and seemed to believe it in its entirety. At supper that evening, his staff saw how happy he was when James told them that he now knew that "the very grievous accusations and calumnies" he had grown up hearing about his mother had been proved false.[8]

Politically, a consequence of the Bothwell Testament was its identification of Lord Morton as one of those who had helped kill James's father and then allowed Queen Mary to suffer for their crime. It also coincided with a period between 1577 and 1579 when James had forged attachments to Captain Stewart and Lord Atholl, both of whom were hostile to Morton. Atholl belonged to a faction in the nobility who, in the spring of 1578, put successful pressure on Morton to abolish the regency in preparation for James's twelfth birthday that June. Since the age of twelve loomed in sixteenth-century legal thought as a halfway house to adulthood, Lord Morton acquiesced and government was entrusted to a council.[9] Morton professed joy at relinquishing politics and announced his intention to retire to his country estate, where he would henceforth be occupied with nothing more onerous than straightening out the pathways in his beautiful gardens. Cynics joked that only a fool could believe that Morton cared about any path, save whichever crooked ones would lead him back to power.[10]

In the aftermath of Morton's retirement, tensions mounted within the aristocracy, which, like the council, was divided over what a post-Morton regime should look like. The Scottish public were similarly split, for although few loved Morton, many respected him as a man who had, in the words of an Edinburgh burgess, "kept the country in great justice and peace."[11]

Five events—two banquets, a parliament, a brawl, and a reception, all of which took place in Stirling's spectacular Great Hall—framed James's personal experience of this period. The first—a banquet in 1578—was overshadowed by the news that one of his household,

John Lyon, 8th Lord Glamis,* had been shot and killed in the town during an altercation with the Earl of Crawford, also on his way to the feast. Glamis was noted for his height, strength, reckless spending, and ability to hold his drink. His death left his three-year-old son in the care of an uncle and Lord Crawford imprisoned for manslaughter. It was the first time since his grandfather's death that violence had broken into James's household, and it loomed as a chilling harbinger of the dangers he would face as he grew older.

More bloodletting followed as the formerly close Erskine family at Stirling quarreled over politics. Morton made overtures of friendship to Lady Mar's son John, who had succeeded his father as earl of Mar. The new Lord Mar was about seventeen in 1578 and, although an adult by contemporary standards, he proved easily manipulated by Morton, who knew that, if he hoped to return to power, he must first divide his enemies among themselves.[12] He struck at Mar as the weak link and, through a series of insinuating letters, turned him against his uncle Sir Alexander. Hostilities grew at Stirling, where, one evening, eleven-year-old James was alerted by sounds of combat and rushed into the Great Hall to see the men of the Erskine family, and their retainers, fighting; Sir Alexander was lying wounded on the floor.[13] A few men answered the King's screams for somebody to help Alexander, who was carried from the room, injured but living. James was so distressed by the violence that he began sobbing and ripping out clumps of his own hair. Sir Alexander's fifteen-year-old son Archibald was then injured, either by an overturned piece of furniture or in the crush of fighting.[14] He too was carried from the hall but, unlike his father, he died the next day. Archibald's death seems to have chastened the extremism of the surviving perpetrators, who reconciled in its aftermath.[15] Once he had recovered, Sir Alexander relinquished the office of governor to his nephew Lord Mar.[16] James suffered from terrible nightmares that left him afraid to sleep.[17]

Exploiting this scandal, Lord Morton reemerged along the crooked paths to power in the latter half of 1578. He was appointed head of the council that conducted day-to-day government

---

* A direct ancestor of Queen Elizabeth the Queen Mother (1900–2002).

in the King's name.[18] In doing so, Morton had recaptured his former power, intact under a different title. While he insisted that "as soon as ever his Majesty shall think himself ready and able for his own government, none shall more willingly agree and advance the same [than] I," he had made similar protestations when he stepped down the previous spring.[19] A triumphant Morton summoned a parliament to meet in Stirling's Great Hall, where those attending noticed how Morton would whisper instructions in James's ear. Blushing and tripping over his words, James would then try to repeat Morton's instructions as his own orders.[20] James suspected, correctly, that Morton had recruited one of his own Gentlemen of the Chamber, Nicholas Elphinstone, to act as his spy at Stirling and that Elphinstone was tipping Morton off about which other members of James's entourage had their loyalty for sale.[21]

In April 1579, Morton returned to Stirling for a banquet in the Great Hall. It was ostensibly to celebrate the reconciliation between the former regent and his critics, including James's mentor Lord Atholl, who fell sick after the feast. Despite James ordering his personal physician, Gilbert Moncreiff, to care for him, Atholl died a few days later. James was devastated, and Atholl's widow was convinced that her husband had been poisoned—she, too, was sick, as was another guest, Lord Montrose. The Countess of Atholl's claims gained widespread support, in contrast to the government's insistence that it had been an accident. At Atholl's autopsy, a doctor who queried the suggestion of foul play was forced to lick the lining of the dead earl's stomach, after which he "almost died and was after, so long as he lived, sickly."[22] This was cited as proof that Atholl had been murdered. However, it seems somewhat possible that the doctor's illness may have been a consequence of his enforced licking of a cadaver's decomposing organ, rather than evidence of residual poison.

Allegations of poisoning in the sixteenth century were perennial. If a high-ranking person had anything more vigorous than a sneeze or a death less public than a beheading, there would be at least one claim that they had been poisoned. Poisoning at a banquet, where food was served on communal plates and wine poured from ewers when guests requested it, carried a very small chance of success, as it would be impossible for an assassin to know what their target would eat or how high a dose would need to be to kill them, as opposed to a fellow diner. Atholl's health had been deteriorating even before the banquet; he had asked the King's permission to go abroad for a time to recuperate in warmer climates. Whether it had been intentional or, as seems more probable, severe but accidental food poisoning, the belief that Atholl had been murdered because of his opposition to Morton endured.[23] Suspicions were not allayed when Morton ordered the execution of two authors who had written pamphlets attributing Atholl's death to poison.

By the time he turned thirteen, James regarded the man who headed his government as someone who had helped murder both his father and a man he regarded as a substitute grandfather, framed his mother, corrupted his household, and treated him like a puppet in front of his own parliament. He was careful to hide these feelings during Morton's visits to Stirling, which showcased the ways in which James was becoming an increasingly skilled liar.[24] He flattered the former regent by saying he wished Morton had the youth of one of his younger relatives so that he could continue to serve him as head of the council for decades to come.[25]

Morton announced that the next parliament would meet in Edinburgh in October 1579 and that he wanted James to attend, before returning with his entourage to Stirling. To maintain the fiction that James was exercising more of his powers with Morton simply serving as his chief adviser, Morton planned a series of festivities to welcome James to Edinburgh for the first time since childhood.

Thirteen days before they were due to depart, the household at Stirling hosted a reception in the Great Hall for one of James's relatives, an individual he had not previously met. The future of his grandfather's earldom of Lennox had prompted James to issue an invitation to his father's cousin Esmé Stuart. After his grandfather's murder, the earldom of Lennox had passed to James's English uncle Charles, who had married and had a daughter by the time of his death in 1576. The earldom of Lennox then went to James's great-uncle Robert, a younger brother of his assassinated grandfather. Unfortunately for the future of the earldom, Robert was an elderly former Roman Catholic bishop who, new and much younger wife notwithstanding, was unlikely to have any legitimate offspring. James agreed to his household's suggestion that they prepare the next in line, Esmé, for his future as earl of Lennox by inviting him to Scotland. Cultivating a friendship with Esmé would also further James's chances of rebuilding a powerful Stewart family network in Scotland, one whose primary loyalty would be to him rather than to Morton or any other Scottish lord, once he assumed rule as an adult king.

Esmé's late father, John, had been the youngest brother of James's grandfather. As a young man, John had inherited a French château and title from a distant relative; with his eldest brother as the heir to the Lennox earldom and the middle brother joining the Church, the youngest went to France. Esmé was born there in the same year as James's mother, whom he befriended during their shared childhood at the French court. Succeeding his father as Seigneur d'Aubigny in 1567, Esmé had served at the court of James's godfather, King Charles IX, and, after his death in 1574, joined the household of his younger brother and successor, Henri III. He had married and had five children with fellow aristocrat Catherine de Balsac. At the French court, Esmé was friendly with several Scottish émigrés who had fled there after Queen Mary's downfall, including those who had fought at the siege of Edinburgh Castle and blamed Lord Morton for the subsequent loss of their fortunes.

Well-spoken and well-mannered, elegantly dressed, and thirty-six years old, Esmé entered the Great Hall at Stirling with twenty servants following him as he walked from the entrance, past the hall's four large fireplaces, toward the dais where the King sat. James's household saw a man who looked very much like his Scottish relatives, with a trim red beard and auburn hair, but the dark brown eyes of his Bourbon and Milanese cousins on his mother's side. Knowing of his close ties to anti-Morton exiles, those at Stirling who still secretly resented Morton were delighted at Esmé's arrival. Under house arrest in England, James's mother was also thrilled. After twelve years, she and the remaining rump of the Queen's Party in Scotland finally had someone—intelligent, cosmopolitan, charming, Catholic, pro-French, and pro-Mary—at James's side.

James and Esmé conversed in French at their first meeting as they did during the rest of Esmé's visit, which James prolonged after Esmé announced that, as the next earl of Lennox, he had come only to formally pledge loyalty to his future king and congratulate him on the end of his regency. Esmé's stated intention was to return home to France, until James asked if he would like to accompany him on his ceremonial entry into Edinburgh. Esmé may have always hoped for such an invitation, although the suspicion that he did so is perhaps an example of hindsight unduly influencing history. Either way, he accepted and was a member of James's retinue when they left Stirling during tempestuous weather in the last weekend of September 1579.

The "great wind" described by a contemporary followed James to Linlithgow Palace, the lochside residence where his mother had been born.[26] At the time of writing, Linlithgow is roofless and part ruined, but it remains one of the most beautiful castles in the British Isles. In James's lifetime, the palace was admired for its architecture, its location, and the comfort of its private apartments. James broke his journey at Linlithgow for a night. The following morning, he was joined by Morton, who, with other nobles in a cavalcade of two thousand horses, accompanied James to Holyroodhouse.

Adjacent to a former Catholic abbey, from which it acquired its name, Holyroodhouse was the largest of the Scottish royal properties; despite its proximity to Edinburgh, it was at that time considered to lie outside the city proper. James's bedchamber was in the palace tower named after his grandfather.[27] Admired by foreign visitors, it was the most prestigious of James's homes, as well as his primary residence when visiting Edinburgh. Over the next few days various events were organized for James, including a visit to Morton's estate at Dalkeith, the size and splendor of which fueled rumors that Morton had a laissez-faire attitude toward where his money ended and the monarchy's began.

On October 19, dressed in white satin with cloth of silver details, James left Holyroodhouse to formally enter Edinburgh for the first time as king. At every stage of the journey, there were events or tableaux that welcomed James while simultaneously conveying a message to him from the civic authorities about what kind of monarch they expected him to be—Protestant, respectful of the city's liberties, brave, and an upholder of law. Magistrates greeted him beneath a purple canopy, burgesses in armor welcomed him, and cannon were fired from the castle in celebration. There were sermons along the way from the clergy, large painted displays celebrating the Stewart dynasty's genealogy, addresses delivered to him in Latin; "trumpets sounded melodiously," a pageant celebrating the virtues ended with a Catherine wheel of fireworks, and during another a young boy emerged from a mechanical globe to offer James the silver keys to Edinburgh. Fountains pumped wine for the revelers. Tapestries hung outside the town houses of the aristocracy, as people cheered from the windows. In the flower-strewn streets, the enthusiasm to see James was so great that several people were crushed in the crowd—fortunately, there were no fatalities.

James spent the rest of the winter at Holyroodhouse, where he kept his first Christmas outside Stirling. The Kirk discouraged Christmas celebrations, as they did with all religious holidays except observance of the Sabbath on Sundays, on the grounds that many Christmas traditions were Catholic, pagan, or both. The Kirk drew little distinction between the two. In the years since his mother's departure, Holyroodhouse had been neglected. Esmé was present to advise on its refurbishment, which included restoration of the palace's tiltyard and ballroom, or "dancing house" in contemporary parlance. He also advised James on etiquette. The King's education had barely touched upon it, thanks largely to Buchanan, who had even unsuccessfully suggested that the household at Stirling do away with royal forms of address such as "Your Majesty," "Your Highness," or "Your Grace"—all of which were later assigned to specific ranks but, at this point, were used interchangeably to refer to the Scottish monarch. The intricacies of etiquette, so central to how early modern monarchs conducted themselves, were pointedly excluded from Buchanan's curriculum, with the consequence that James emerged from his education with the mind of a scholar, but not the behavior of a king. Esmé, with his years of experience in the French royal household, set out to rectify the situation, not entirely successfully. His main achievement was to reform the royal household by instituting a strict rota and membership system for James's Gentlemen of the Chamber, whose number he capped at twenty-four, working in shifts of eight at a time, and all of whom had to be lords themselves or the sons of lords. When it came to introducing a more rigid code of manners throughout the rest of the court, Esmé did not find a willing audience. James was uninterested in decorum, especially not the elaborate interpretation of it as practiced at Henri III's court.

Unlike Buchanan, Esmé did not press the point. During their conversations, he treated James with a respect that he had not hitherto experienced by taking seriously his opinions rather than simply his rank, listening to James's thoughts on history, religion, and politics. Esmé encouraged James to attend more council meetings now that the regency was over, rather than leave them to be dominated by Morton. In the surviving sources, we see James VI take a tentative interest in government, in letters to and from ambassadors, or discussing pirates' raids on the Scottish coast.[28] Under Esmé's influence, James wrote to his mother in England more often, a development that may also have had something to do with the exoneration of her that James believed had been provided by the Bothwell Testament. Their letters to one another, in French, did however end with both signing themselves as Scotland's monarch.

The business of monarchy in the late sixteenth century had public-facing duties and private responsibilities. Diplomacy was conducted through lengthy correspondence with foreign heads of state, as well as audiences with ambassadors and high-ranking visitors from other countries. Similar audiences would often be granted to prominent nobles and clergy, especially if the topic was considered too delicate for writing. Major decisions on foreign and domestic policy were taken by the monarch or, until he reached his majority, his council. In adulthood, he would meet often, sometimes daily, with the council, whose number and membership were decided by him. Regular attendance at council was considered the mark of a diligent sovereign, although matters could be overseen by a senior councillor, usually either the President of the Council or the Lord Chancellor. Due to the speed of travel, communication could be slow, especially in winter, and the enforcement of law beyond the areas around Edinburgh and Stirling would have been expensive, futile, or both. The administration of justice in the countryside was delegated to the nobility, who, in their turn, devolved certain tasks to the gentry families under their feudal jurisdiction. This system required frequent, careful interaction between the center and the localities, which in its turn produced more paperwork and more hours at council. Fortunately for James, his favorite activity—hunting—was regarded as a cross between a royal pastime and necessity. It was something the elite could enjoy together, thereby solidifying alliances or friendships; it was also considered useful for keeping kings physically fit and in preparation for war during times of peace. The Stewart court often ate what it killed, which made regal hunting equally useful to the council chamber and the palace kitchens.

These were important lessons for any monarch, especially for one who might reign over more than one country. It was at the age of thirteen that James could anticipate one day wearing England's crown, as well as Scotland's. His mother had expressed such a hope for him at the time of his birth. However, it was dependent on his godmother, Queen Elizabeth, having no children of her own to succeed her. Elizabeth had always vacillated on the question of marriage, and her private remarks seem to indicate that she regarded it with trepidation.[29] She had nonetheless brilliantly used it as a tool of English foreign policy since becoming queen in 1558. In 1579, she discussed marriage with the Duke of Anjou,* the King of France's younger brother. To quiet the speculation that the only reason a woman would not want to get married was because there was something biologically atypical about her, Elizabeth underwent a semipublic gynecological examination, attended by members of her own household and staff sent as witnesses by the French embassy. Satisfied with Elizabeth's ability to produce children, negotiations pressed ahead, until they were scuppered for a variety of reasons, not the least of which was strident opposition from the English public to a French match, only seven years after the Saint Bartholomew's Day Massacre. Elizabeth was forty-six, and there

---

* François-Hercule, Duke of Anjou (1555–84), also known as the Duke of Alençon, the title he held from childhood.

was a sense that the Anjou match had been the last chance for her to marry and produce an heir. With its failure, the game of guessing who would succeed Elizabeth intensified. Many expected that the prize would eventually be won by James. There were, however, several claimants who remained ahead of him in the English line of succession, including his imprisoned mother.

At the end of his first winter in Edinburgh, Esmé had obtained "great favour and credit" with James, so much so that other courtiers had taken note.[30] Captain Stewart, despite having once occupied the position of idolized mentor that had apparently been usurped by Esmé, made friends with the new favorite. Anti-Morton families in the aristocracy attached themselves to Esmé, a development that a hubristic Morton did not initially consider worthy of concern. Esmé was less popular with the Presbyterian clergy, who, in their own words, "like faithful watchmen" stood in vigil against Esmé's Catholic faith and his sympathy for Queen Mary.[31]

In February, James returned to Stirling from Edinburgh, with Esmé among his retinue. A month later, he gave Esmé his father's former title of Lord Darnley and negotiated with his great-uncle Robert to relinquish the Lennox earldom in return for the earldom of March, which the elderly Robert would hold for the rest of his life. Three months after Esmé was invested with the titles associated with his and James's family, he announced his conversion to Protestantism, which he attributed to the many discussions he had about religion with James.[32] The news was greeted with skepticism in Scotland and shock in France, particularly by Esmé's wife, Catherine. On receiving a letter from Esmé proclaiming his gratitude for "how it hath pleased God, of His infinite goodness, to call me by His grace and mercy to the knowledge of my salvation," the Presbyterian General Assembly approved Esmé's admission to their faith, after which sermons criticizing him dwindled in volume and vigor.[33]

Over summer and autumn, Esmé's star continued to rise.[34] He was given control of the royal household as its Lord Chamberlain, which also made him First Gentleman of James's chamber, he was appointed Master of his Wardrobe, and he was admitted to government as a member of the council. He helped organize James's first extended tour, known as a Progress, through the central and eastern counties of the kingdom. Plays were staged for them when they visited St. Andrews.[35] They traveled west to visit the Mars at their estate in Alloway.[36] James jousted at Dundee and went to Glasgow, where, for the first time, there were rumors about a marriage for the fourteen-year-old King.[37] Diplomats speculated that it might be to Catherine of Bourbon, Princess of Navarre,* a Protestant eight years James's senior, while Catholic noblemen hoped that James would instead wed one of the Habsburg princesses.

During the progress, there was a horse-riding accident when James was pinned under his horse after a fall. His servants were in such a panic that they considered killing the horse, but calmer heads prevailed and "the King and horse at length were saved without hurt."[38] In July, it appeared as if James had contracted the plague that was spreading out from Edinburgh; his illness seems to have passed quickly, whereas adult members of his court who fell ill, including Esmé, suffered for longer.[39]

Esmé's ascent as the new Earl of Lennox, Lord Darnley, Royal Chamberlain, and First Gentleman of the Chamber had made him one of the most important men in Scotland and provided the King with an adult kinsman with substantial political power. He continued to acquire allies in the nobility throughout the summer, as speculation mounted of a coming showdown with Morton.[40] Esmé had arrived in Scotland with his sympathies firmly on the side of Morton's enemies, and he had seen nothing since to alter his prejudices.

James kept Christmas 1580 back in Edinburgh. Esmé's coup began on December 31 during a meeting of the council at Holyroodhouse, at which Morton was in attendance.[41] Captain Stewart, in what was undoubtedly a choreographed moment of outrage, "suddenly" accused Morton of complicity in Darnley's murder fourteen years earlier and fell to his knees before the King, begging for justice. Almost certainly forewarned, James agreed to the supporting suggestion by another councillor allied with Esmé that

* A kingdom in the Pyrenees, comprising territory that is now part of northwest Spain and southwest France.

Morton should be arrested. Morton, protesting his innocence, was kept under guard until he was moved to the more secure location of Edinburgh Castle. He was then taken to the fortress at Dumbarton, which James had placed under Esmé's jurisdiction and which was sixty-five miles from the capital.[42] This was to prevent Morton being rescued by his supporters, whose collective strength Esmé diligently weakened over the next few months.[43] He found pretexts to arrest some of Morton's relatives and exile others, including several of his illegitimate adult sons; he dismissed Morton's men from positions of government, and he undermined others.

Morton was brought back to Edinburgh for trial on May 23, 1581, just under five months after his arrest. Captain Stewart warned his allies that, having come so far, they must not hesitate. Morton's annihilation must be complete. If he escaped alive, he would return to power as he had before and, this time, inflict revenge on his enemies.[44] In preparation for the trial, a variety of charges were considered, including financial corruption, plotting to kidnap James, poisoning the Earl of Atholl at the Stirling banquet, and accepting a pension from the English government. It was distilled to one simple and capital offense—the "foreknowledge and concealing of the treasonable and unnatural murder" of James's father.[45]

Morton admitted that he had known of a plot by Bothwell to kill Darnley but insisted that he had not participated in the murder itself.[46] Less comfortably for James, the imprisoned Morton also insisted that Queen Mary had been involved in the plot to kill her husband and that the reason Morton had not tried to warn Darnley was because he knew, from past experience with the Riccio murder, that Darnley would likely change his mind and tell everything to the Queen. "Whom to should I have revealed it?" Morton asked rhetorically. "To the Queen? She was the doer thereof. I was minded, indeed, to the King's father, but I durst not for my life; for I knew him to be such a bairn, that there was nothing told to him but he would reveal it to her."[47]

Esmé had recruited for the jury noblemen who were enemies of Morton, and they delivered the guilty verdict on June 1. Esmé may have been needlessly thorough in his efforts to secure Morton's downfall. Sir James Melville observed of the ex-regent's allies that, when he needed them most, they were "found to be but friends to his fortune. For he was loved by none, and envied and hated by many; so that they all looked through their fingers to see his fall."[48] Morton was sentenced to be hanged, drawn, and quartered. It was the first death warrant that James was personally responsible for implementing, and he commuted the sentence to beheading.

During his last night alive, sixty-five-year-old Morton repented the sexual promiscuity of his younger days and vigorously denied that he had poisoned Lord Atholl, a charge against his character that seemed to bother him more than the others.[49] The next morning at Holyroodhouse, James was so agitated that he paced back and forth in his apartments, unwilling or unable to sit or stand still, clicking his fingers and refusing to read the letter Morton had sent him from prison.[50] Morton was taken to the Mercat Cross, where, in front of a large crowd, he was beheaded by the Maiden, a precursor to the guillotine.

4

HATE AND WAIT

Be careful, ay, for to invent
The way to get thine own intent.
. . . With patience then see thou attend
And hope to vanquish in the end.
—James VI, King of Scots
(c. 1582)

Morton's execution strained diplomatic relations with England, where he was regarded as an ally and French Esmé as a threat. An angry Elizabeth sent a letter to James, warning him that he might one day learn the consequences of "what it is to prefer an Earl of Lennox before a Queen of England."[1] Tensions abated when it became clear that James's bond with Esmé posed no immediate threat to Scotland's uneasy peace with England through any resurrection of the "Auld Alliance" with France.

The rest of 1581 passed happily for James. At court, he had more opportunity to interact with young men his own age; several of them became friends and often accompanied the King on his hunting trips, during which he typically spent several days away from court. James was a superb horseman, and his times at the hunt were his happiest. He had a new horse, presented to him by the Earl of Rothes, and with it came a blue velvet saddle. Later, another nobleman sent him a pet otter, which James loved and for which he ordered special leashes so that he could take it for walks.[2] Pipers entertained him and his friends after banquets, he participated in a joust at Easter, and he sat for two official portraits. His interest in poetry grew, and he hosted a literary salon, where he both experimented with his own compositions and heard the works of other poets invited to join him. These included the Hudson brothers—his former music and dancing tutors at Stirling—the visiting Irish poet Fearghal Óg Mac an Bhaird, Alexander Montgomerie, a Catholic writer from the Highlands, and Christian Lindsay, whose husband served in James's household as his Master of the Carriage. James seemed relaxed in this environment. He good-naturedly teased Montgomerie after his horse, whose prowess Montgomerie had boasted about in their last gathering, finished dead last in a race. Later in his life, James would be the first monarch in the British Isles to become a published poet.[3]

In government, Esmé became de facto chief minister. Among other prizes, he was given Morton's seized estate at Dalkeith, while James elevated his title from Earl to Duke of Lennox, making Esmé the only duke in the Scottish nobility at the time. Esmé avoided Morton's mistakes by continuing to encourage James to learn about, and participate in, government. Until such time as James married and produced children, there was discussion of naming Esmé heir to the throne. Under normal circumstances, this would have been a genealogical stretch. In terms of royal blood, Esmé was a descendant only in the senior female line from King James II, who had died over a century earlier. However, thanks to a dearth of Stewarts by 1581, he had a better claim than most.[4] James VI was the unmarried only child of a queen whose legitimate brothers had died in infancy, as had her father's full siblings. Her grandfather James IV had two brothers—one a priest and the other an unwed teenager when he died—and the other male-line descendants of James III had stumbled into extinction with bishops, bastards, and tragic early deaths.

According to a mutual colleague in the King's household, Captain Stewart, who had been made Earl of Arran for his role in Morton's downfall, secretly came to resent Esmé.[5] Their friendship had frayed in the aftermath of Morton's execution, once they no longer shared a political goal. Arran had then become jealous when Esmé was given the honor of carrying the crown at the opening of Parliament, and a greater strain arose from James's intention to make Esmé his heir presumptive. Arran, backed by various nobles, mounted a campaign at court that persuaded James and Esmé to shelve their proposal. Nominating Esmé as "second person" of

Scotland had always been a safeguard, rather than an imperative. The frustration of their plans for the succession did not therefore greatly worry James, or Esmé, who continued planning to bring his wife, Catherine, and their children to live with him in Scotland.[6] Esmé also pressed ahead with plans for the King's marriage.

Despite Esmé's hope to be reunited with his family, rumors started that there was an unnatural component to his relationship with the King. The question of whether there was a sexual element to their dynamic, and that Esmé therefore perpetrated what we would now recognize as grooming, continues to provoke debate among historians of James's reign.[7] The weight of evidence suggests that Esmé should be seen as the last in a line of older relatives and mentors onto whom James latched as an adolescent. The Lennox and Darnley titles that Esmé was assigned indicate that James saw him as a father figure, and even Esmé's growing number of enemies at court never intimated that they thought there was anything sexually inappropriate between the cousins.

This was not the conclusion reached in the arena of public opinion, where Esmé became a figure of almost cartoonish wickedness. The temporary cease-fire bought by his conversion to Presbyterianism eventually gave way to suspicions that the conversion had been insincere, which in turn prompted sermons criticizing him. Some of these sermons compared Esmé's vices to those of Sodom and Gomorrah, two biblical cities destroyed by the wrath of God for their sins, chief among which, in Sodom's case, was their sexual deviance in attempting to rape two human-appearing angels sent to Sodom to speak to a holy man.[8] Sodom, and its derivative "sodomy," were typically used in the early modern period as a coded reference to penetrative sex between men. Many figures in similar roles to Esmé's had been identified by Edinburgh's rumor mill as dwelling in "beastly buggery Sodom," including James's stepfather, Bothwell.[9] Less frequently, sodomy could cover a multiplicity of sins, including male masturbation, oral sex, rape, bestiality, blasphemy, pedophilia, or any form of heterosexual intercourse through which there was no chance of a conception.[10]

There was a long history of foreign favorites being inaccurately accused of sexual intimacy with their royal patrons, and Esmé's nationality was exploited by his critics, as David Riccio's had been before him. Suspicion was widespread that the king Esmé had served in France, Henri III, had sex with men.[11] Historians again remain divided.[12] There seems little reason to doubt that Henri deeply loved his wife, Louise of Lorraine-Vaudémont, and it is equally impossible to deny that he had strong attachments to several favorite male courtiers, nicknamed his "mignons,"* who were compared to "whores in a brothel" by an unimpressed Parisian.[13] The term "mignon," or its English translation "minion," had been a mocking term in the previous generation, when it was used at the French and English courts to describe gentlemen—typically young upper-class men of much brawn, little brain, and great expenditure—who served Kings François I and Henry VIII. Its later association with Henri III had shifted its connotations to imply sexual relationships. Even in Henri III's triumphs—such as when his mignon led a successful frontal attack on a rebel force commanded by Louis de Bussy d'Amboise—his critics could not resist linking it to the King's private life, with poems like:

> . . . If he'd taken Bussy from behind,
> He'd really have stuffed it to him.[14]

While the most persuasive guess is that he was bisexual, a detailed examination of Henri III's love affairs is beyond the purview of this book. What mattered in the context of James's life and Esmé's service to both kings is that there was a general belief in the 1580s that Henri III had male lovers. In Scottish Protestant circles, to describe something as "French" and specifically as "of the French court" might imply homosexual activity, but it was also a dog whistle for any number of turpitudes—sexual promiscuity, financial extravagance, alcoholism, anti-Protestantism, or effeminacy. When clergymen accused Esmé of introducing the "fruits of the French court" to Scotland, they specified vices like "prodigality and vanity" but could leave open to interpretation what they meant by the catchall "other fruits."[15]

---

* Esmé does not seem to have been high enough in Henri III's favor to be considered a mignon.

The "otherness" of sodomy was a recurring theme in early modern European reactions to it. In the same decade, there was a scandal in the Venetian embassy to Constantinople,* when the ambassador discovered that two of his staff—the embassy's barber and a dragoman called Gianesino—were having an affair.[16] Other employees were questioned and confirmed that "the barber was in love with Gianesino and Gianesino with him."[17] Gianesino was fired and the barber was packed off across the Aegean to work at the Venetian colony in Crete. Throughout the investigation, the ambassador was fixated on ascertaining if information about the romance had spread beyond the embassy's walls. Homosexual liaisons were tolerated, to a degree, in Venetian society and, before he met Gianesino, the barber had a short-lived affair with the embassy's butler, who kept his job even after it was discovered. From the ambassador's perspective, the problem was not what had happened but who knew about it. In many of the Italian states, sex between two men was stereotypically depicted as being more prevalent in Muslim societies, particularly in the Ottoman Empire; as the representative of a Christian republic to a Muslim empire, the Venetian ambassador was concerned that Gianesino and the barber's love for one another would provoke gossip in Constantinople that would lower his country's prestige. Just as Venetians associated homosexuality with the Ottoman Empire, the French called it "the Italian vice," German scholars at the time claimed that it was Japanese, and the Scottish characterized it as French.[18]

Thus, while there were rumors that Esmé had initiated a sexually exploitative relationship with James VI, it is telling that the accusations came generally from those outside the royal household and usually as part of an attack in which his critics claimed that the French-born Esmé was guilty of numerous other sins. The claims included that Esmé had encouraged heterosexual "carnal lust" at court with the "deflowering of dames and virgins," that he had turned his estate at Dalkeith into a cross between a center for Catholicism and a brothel, that he was a Catholic spy or an atheist, a kidnapper, and that, on his wedding night, he had pleasured himself

* Officially renamed Istanbul in 1930.

as he watched his wife losing her virginity to another man because he was too "feeble" to perform the act himself.[19]

Esmé's standing with the Scottish public was further damaged by the behavior of his erstwhile friend Lord Arran. When he had still been Captain Stewart, Arran had started an affair with the Countess of March, wife of James's great-uncle and Esmé's uncle, Robert. Lady March was about thirty-two years younger than her husband, who divorced her when she became pregnant. Having struggled with impotence in recent years, Robert knew the child could not be his. The breakdown of the Marches' marriage caused a scandal that grew larger when the pregnant ex-countess married her lover, Arran. James's admiration for Arran might explain his unwise decision to attend the christening of their son and to allow it to be conducted at Holyroodhouse. An outraged public saw it as further proof that Esmé had corrupted king and court by introducing "French" morals, conveniently forgetting the parade of mistresses and illegitimate children produced by previous kings and regents.

It was ironic that Esmé was blamed by the public for the behavior of Arran, who was among those at the Scottish court who resented him. He was also losing support in France, where his Protestantism cost him the trust of Henri III. The French king was at that time experiencing a deepening of his own Catholic faith: he and his wife went on frequent pilgrimages to pray for an heir, and he created a new chivalric order, dedicated to veneration of the Holy Spirit. In England, the ex-queen Mary had ceased to regard Esmé as a friend. In that case, the disenchantment was mutual. A chill had settled over their relationship after Mary wrote to James with the remarkable news that Elizabeth had agreed to let her leave England and come home, where she would assume joint rule with her son. This plan, known as the Association, was supported by Mary's Guise relatives, who set out to foster James's goodwill through expensive gifts—as James excitedly told his mother in one of his letters, "My horses that Monsieur de Guise my cousin was to send me have arrived which are exceedingly beautiful, and I know by his letters that he bears me a very affectionate goodwill which he will find reciprocated in me."[20]

When news of the proposed Association leaked in Scotland, there was uproar. James, who had been ambivalent about the Association, subsequently discovered that his mother had lied to him. Not only had Elizabeth never agreed to the proposal, but Mary had tried to use one to bounce the other into acquiescence by writing to Elizabeth with the insinuation that the Association was James's idea. With her Guise cousins, Mary had apparently approved the use of force to turn the Association into reality, if coercion proved necessary once she was back in Scotland.[21] Some wondered whether, if the Association had been successful, Mary would have abided by its terms, or if its implementation was the first step to demoting James to prince and then sending him to France to live with her family, until he was reeducated and converted to Catholicism. Given that, when James was a child, Mary had seriously considered offering him as a hostage to the English in exchange for her own liberty, those fears seemed credible to her critics.[22] Esmé was accused of being the principal agent in this Guise plot to kidnap James to France.

However, Esmé's loyalties had shifted from Mary to James and, even if they had not, sensible self-preservation encouraged him to put as much distance as possible between himself, Queen Mary, and Catholicism. He signed a declaration that referred to the Pope as the Anti-Christ, called Catholic theology with respect to Holy Communion "blasphemous" and prayers for the departed "a profane sacrifice for the sins of the dead," attacked the Church's teachings on marriage, specifically its "cruelty against the innocent divorced," and characterized contemporary Catholic teaching that children must be baptized to achieve Heaven as its "cruel judgement against infants departing without the sacrament."[23] James, whose letters to his mother remained respectful while losing their warmth, also signed the declaration. Yet its publication failed to dispel rumors in Scotland that Esmé remained in league either with Mary or the House of Guise.[24]

Scandal and suspicion were inescapable aspects of a successful political career, as was the dissatisfaction of allies who felt they had not been sufficiently rewarded. Among the discontented were several of the staff who had raised James at Stirling. Having expected a windfall when James came into his powers, they were jealous at the favor shown to Esmé and resentful that Esmé did not seem inclined to share his good fortune with them.

Despite this opposition, Esmé retained a base in the aristocracy, with several prominent families serving as the backbone of his political faction. Buoyed by such support, he continued to carry out his policies, one of which was to negotiate a marriage for James—the Protestant Catherine of Bourbon remained the front-runner. Esmé felt sufficiently confident in the future that his political difficulties were sometimes even good for a giggle. James could not control his laughter when they heard that Esmé's unpopular candidate for the archbishopric of Glasgow had been pelted with rotten eggs when he tried to preach a sermon.[25] James knew the egg-besmirched preacher, Robert Montgomerie, who had previously been the local church minister in Stirling.

The King spent most of summer 1582 hunting while Esmé remained near Edinburgh as caretaker of the government. With a small entourage, James rode into Stirlingshire, then northeast toward Perth, where he was invited to stay by the Earl of Gowrie. Gowrie's late father had been the Lord Ruthven who led the group that murdered David Riccio.[26] The younger William Ruthven had been created earl of Gowrie in recognition of his support for the plot that deposed Lord Morton, and he lived primarily at Ruthven Castle, where James arrived after a day's hunting.

The next morning, James was isolated from his attendants and surrounded by Gowrie and his men, who refused to let him leave. James burst into tears when he realized he was trapped. This was the opening incident in an event later called the Raid of Ruthven. Gowrie took the King under guard to the town of Perth, where sixteen-year-old James discovered who else had supported his kidnapping. The group included some former Morton supporters, such as Thomas Lyon, acting head of one of the oldest aristocratic families in Scotland. More distressingly, James saw his governess's son and his former schoolmate John Erskine, 18th Earl of Mar, and two of their former tutors, Adam and David Erskine, who had overseen James's physical education when he was a child. They were joined by several lords, members of the gentry, including the Laird of Drumquhassle, who had been James's Master of the Household at Stirling and chief of those at Stirling who had never forgiven Esmé for prospering without them.

Known as the Lords Enterpriser, this formidable alliance had coalesced with the aim of ousting Esmé. They maintained the fiction that they had brought James there for his own safety and urged him to banish his favorite. James resisted, even after they showed him forged letters masquerading as proof that Esmé was a spy. Security tightened around the King, who was humiliated and frightened, and the gossamer of respect lifted as his detention lengthened. When James tried to leave his bedroom without permission, Thomas Lyon threw his leg across the doorway and mocked him as "a bairn" when he wept.[27]

Hearing of the King's detention, Arran returned to his previous support of Esmé and rode to Ruthven Castle to free James, boasting that he would scatter the rebel lords into hiding like frightened mice.[28] Instead, Arran himself was taken prisoner by the Lords Enterpriser, who moved James back to Stirling. They promised they would free him if he publicly denounced, then exiled, Esmé. Insisting that they were protecting the King from a corrupt adviser, the plotters took control of James's government. Forty-year-old Lord Gowrie became the most powerful man in Scotland, and Esmé's authority collapsed. Gowrie sensibly made overtures to the Kirk that, at its next General Assembly, endorsed his actions as those of a "good and Godly cause."[29]

One evening, James scratched on his chamber walls the words "A prisoner I am/And liberty would have." The next morning, one of his captors had carved a response: "A papist you are, and friend to a slave,/A rope you deserve, and that you shall have."[30] Unless he abandoned Esmé, James faced mirroring his mother's fate of years upon years in genteel imprisonment or, if the graffiti were to be taken seriously, his father's fate of being strangled by his enemies. The long-term goal of the Lords Enterpriser is unclear and may have been so to several of the lords themselves. Despite the threat carved on his walls, it is unlikely that the conspirators planned to kill James. If so, why not stage an accident rather than leave him alive for months? In defense of James's fears, it would take only one to break rank and stab him, strangle him, or push him out a window. Gowrie certainly did not want James dead, but he did want him cowed into quiescence.[31] Some of the Lords Enterpriser shared a desire to turn James into a puppet king. Others simply wanted to pull him into the orbit of a Presbyterian faction that was supportive of the Kirk and led by Gowrie. Whatever differences separated their definitions of long-term success, the Lords Enterpriser were united on their short-term objective—Esmé's downfall.

After four months, James surrendered by ordering Esmé's removal from the council and his banishment from Scotland. Before he could be intercepted by enemies who might do to him what he had done to Morton, Esmé dispatched a letter to James in which he protested his loyalty and promised "whatever may befall, I shall always be your very faithful servant."[32] He then fled across the border to England, where he was summoned to an audience with Elizabeth I. She believed many of the rumors about Esmé, especially those which accused him of being a spy, and she quizzed him about them "greatly."[33] Impressed and convinced by Esmé's rebuttals, Elizabeth not only let him continue his journey but provided him with a ship to take him across the Channel to France. When he landed, he was a pariah among former friends who shunned him for his apostasy. Despite the damage it did to his reputation in France, Esmé remained a practicing Protestant, to the distress of his wife.[34]

In Scotland, James seemed to experience a change of heart so complete that he expressed gratitude to his captors for showing him the truth about his cousin Esmé's avarice. It was a testament to James's learned ability to hate-and-wait that the Lords Enterpriser believed his performance. With the King obedient, they continued their domination of government while allowing James more freedom within his palaces.[35] He was back in Edinburgh, around the week of his seventeenth birthday, when Esmé's embalmed heart arrived in a box.[36] He had died in Paris during an influenza epidemic, and his widow had sent his heart as a testament of his devotion to the dynasty.* She had been unable to bring herself to bury Esmé

* The burial of a heart in the ancestral home, or heartlands, of a dynasty was a relatively common practice among the European elite at the time.

in a Protestant ceremony, despite Esmé confirming his Presbyterianism on his deathbed and refusing to receive the last rites from a Catholic priest. Some of Esmé's enemies had lost none of their enthusiasm for the fight and insisted that the cause of his death was gonorrhea.[37]

In private, James worked on a poem to memorialize his cousin, in which Esmé was allegorized as a phoenix, an asexual creature from myth who symbolized purity, growth, and regeneration and who, in James's poem, was hounded to exile, then death, by jealous lesser birds, including a vicious raven, a pun on Ruthven's correct pronunciation as *riven.* James admitted in the marginalia of "Metaphorical Invention of a Tragedy Called Phoenix" that he had written it to make sense of his bereavement or, as he put it, "that I might live in a lesser grief."[38]

Due to the political nature of his downfall, impartial contemporary assessments of Esmé Stuart are difficult to find. Perhaps the most judicious comes from Queen Mary's former confidant Sir James Melville, who remained at court during James VI's reign. He served as a Gentleman of the Chamber alongside Esmé, of whom he wrote later:

> The duke [of Lennox] was of nature upright, just and gentle, but lacked experience in the state of this country. At first, he was most guided by [Captain] James Stewart and his wife; who both began secretly to envy him and see how they might cast him off, that they might attain to the sole management of affairs; and for this end they gave him wrong advice, and sinister informations against sundry . . . moving him to sudden wrath . . . It is certain the Duke of Lennox was led by evil councillors and wrong informations . . . He loved both the king and commonwealth,* but he [lacked] experience, and was not versed in the affairs of state.

Melville also believed that England's enmity had undermined Esmé, when England "by their ambassador [to Scotland] stirred up sun-

* The political community and public well-being.

dry against him, alleging him to be a papist, altogether at the Duke of Guise's devotion, and therefore a dangerous man to be about His Majesty. But his chiefest fault was that, being true to the King, he was thought unwinnable to [England's] behoof."*[39]

Melville loathed Arran, whom he summarized as a man who could "wreck king, kirk, and country" with his arrogance and greed. His recollections, in which Arran and his wife deliberately supplied Esmé with bad advice, may have been an expression of personal animus. Arran was not the only advice-dispensing ally whom Esmé had in Scotland. Broadly, however, Melville's assessment of Esmé as a man who was loyal to his Stewart family, badly advised, a victim of xenophobia and sectarianism, yet also of his own poor decisions, hubris, ambition, avarice, and political myopia, seems the fairest assessment of the cousin who became James VI's chief minister and last mentor.

James had been kidnapped in August 1582. Esmé left Scotland that December and died on May 26, 1583. Between December and June, James bided his time and rebuilt his network of supporters. The easily swayed Lord Mar had come to regret his involvement in the Raid of Ruthven, as had Thomas Lyon, who had initially been among the rudest of the Lords Enterpriser. This was a welcome development to James, but he could not trust them. Instead, he spoke to his Gentlemen of the Chamber, including Sir James Melville, about his intention "to liberate himself fully or die in the attempt."[40] Melville, nervous at the risks James was asking the gentlemen to take on his behalf, was exhausted after years at court, describing himself as "tired and wearied with the many [political] alterations I had seen, both at home and in foreign countries, and had got great trouble and damage by them for other men's causes. Therefore I was determined and inclined to lead a quiet, contemplative life the rest of my days, which this purpose of my prince and master was like to put me from."[41] Loyalty to James eventually won out over fatigue and fear—Melville prayed about it and felt God wanted him to obey his king.[42] Melville joined with the other Gentlemen of the Chamber to smuggle James's letters to noblemen

* Control.

on whom he could rely for help. They included several lords and earls, among them Lord Crawford, recruited by his brother Alexander Lindsay, who was one of the young men in James's service. Another was the reliable Lord Montrose, whose comparative lack of men and money was almost offset by the depth of his disapproval of Gowrie.[43]

Three other earls signed a secret bond whereby they pledged themselves to free James. All either twenty or twenty-one years old at the time, they were the earls of Atholl, Bothwell, and Huntly, some of the most powerful figures in the Scottish nobility. The new Earl of Atholl was the son of James's late mentor whose suspicious death at the Stirling banquet in 1579 had caused such political fallout; he was strong, courageous, and, since he was married to one of Lord Gowrie's daughters, likely to be above suspicion to the Lords Enterpriser. Francis Stewart, the latest Earl of Bothwell, was James's cousin on his father's side* and, on his mother's, a nephew of James's unpopular stepfather; he was less pleasant than Atholl but no less skilled in fighting, and, in his time as Lord Bothwell, he had established firm control over the family's lands in central Scotland. George Gordon, 6th Earl of Huntly, was the most powerful aristocrat in the Highlands. He was as ruthless as Bothwell, as brave as Atholl, and more charismatic than either of them.[44]

Their most important ally, for the time being, was James's great-uncle Robert, Earl of March. While the others prepared the arms necessary and discreetly recruited allies, Robert would be the bait to get James away from the Lords Enterpriser.

James's loyalists agreed to convene at St. Andrews Castle in June, where the King would join them. With his plans in motion, James announced that he wished to spend time hunting near Falkland Palace, which nestled at the foot of East Lomond Hill. Built to replace an older castle on the orders of James IV, Falkland's interiors and courtyards had been renovated by James V to suit the tastes of his French wife Queen Marie. His alterations also included planting

* John Stewart, Commendator of Coldingham (1531–63), an illegitimate son of King James V and his mistress Elizabeth Carmichael; he had married the 4th Earl of Bothwell's sister, Jean Hepburn, Mistress of Caithness (d. 1599).

some of the finest gardens in northern Europe and one of the best hunting demesnes in Scotland.

James informed the council that during his Falkland hunting trip, he hoped to dine with his great-uncle March, who lived nearby. The Lords Enterpriser evidently saw no reason to distrust either the young king or the elderly earl. James set off from Falkland for a summer hunt; he was joined by his great-uncle March and the Provost of St. Andrews, who took James to St. Andrews Castle, where he was united with his supporters. En route to St. Andrews, one of James's gentlemen observed that "His Majesty thought himself at liberty, with great joy and exclamation, like a bird flown out of a cage."[45]

His new captain of the guard, Arran's cousin, then took one hundred armed men to surround Lord Gowrie's house in the small hours of the morning. After a twelve-hour standoff, Gowrie surrendered and was taken to St. Andrews. Ushered into James's presence, he fell to his knees and "in all humility asked pardon of the King's Majesty," which James granted.[46]

Some of the Lords Enterpriser later regrouped at Stirling, where James arrived on horseback in command of thousands of loyalist soldiers. The castle surrendered and James ordered the hanging of the garrison's captain. A few of the rebels escaped. James's former tutors, Adam and David Erskine, rode to the western coast, from where they sailed to Carrickfergus in the north of Ireland. Others fled south to England or to the eastern ports for a ship to France. Some of those who had backed the Gowrie coup were pardoned by James, including Thomas Lyon, whom James came to respect, calling him "the boldest and hardiest man" in Scotland—qualities that stood Lyon in good stead, as, in time, he would become the captain of James's guard.[47] Lord Mar also initially fled to Carrickfergus and then later to England, where he stayed until he was granted a pardon. On his return to Scotland, he never again deviated from loyalty to James. However, James's forgiveness of Gowrie had been a fiction maintained until his supporters were neutralized. A few months later, Gowrie was accused of sorcery and treason. Condemned, he was beheaded on May 3, 1584.

With the plot defeated, James gave vent to the feelings it had engendered. Seething with hatred, he disinherited Gowrie's fourteen children, abolished their new earldom, and divided the family's estates among those who had remained faithful to him. Ruthven Castle, where he had first been taken prisoner by the Lords Enterpriser, was seized for the Crown. Gowrie's widow, Dorothea, waited outside Edinburgh Castle to see the King. When James rode past, she threw herself on her knees in front of him to beg that he spare something of her husband's fortune for her children. Lord Arran kicked Dorothea to one side, apparently with such force that she injured her back and hand as she fell, and the royal party rode on, leaving her lying in the streets.[48]

When the English ambassador arrived at Holyroodhouse to congratulate James on his victory, James replied that he would never again be in his subjects' power. The English government did not quite grasp the extent of James's new confidence. During the same audience, the ambassador delivered Queen Elizabeth's instructions, disguised as advice, about whom she would like to see installed as James's advisers now that Gowrie had fallen. James laughed and told the ambassador to send a message back to Elizabeth informing her "that your Highness should be no more curious to examine the affection of his Councillors than he is of yours."[49] Elizabeth was told that, henceforth, James intended to rule as an absolute monarch.

5

THE MASTER OF GRAY

'Twas in the month of sweet July
Before the sun had pierced the sky;
Down between two rigs of rye
I heard two lovers talking.

—Anonymous, "The Rigs o' Rye"
(Scottish traditional)

James's triumph against the Gowrie administration coincided with a period of romantic, political, and emotional confidence on the part of the King. He invited Esmé's widow to Scotland. Catherine, Dowager Duchess of Lennox, arrived with three of her five children—nine-year-old Ludovic and his sisters Lady Henrietta Stuart, aged ten, and seven-year-old Lady Marie Stuart. Two siblings—four-year-old Esmé and the toddler Gabrielle—were too young for the long voyage and remained in France in the care of relatives.

The family met James for the first time at Kinneil House, Lord Arran's residence in Borrowstounness,* about twenty miles from Edinburgh; the King was staying there as a guest when they arrived on November 14, 1583, after James's victory over the Lords Enterpriser but before Gowrie's execution. After a successful sojourn during which James promised her that he would pay her daughters' dowries when the time came, Catherine returned to France with Henrietta and Marie, while Ludovic stayed in Scotland to be raised as duke of Lennox and a possible heir to the throne. The King treated his second cousin more like a younger brother, planning his education, keeping him safe at court, and entrusting his welfare to the King's physician, Gilbert Moncreiff.

* More commonly called Bo'ness.

Among those who accompanied Ludovic and Catherine to Kinneil House in November 1583 was Patrick Gray, who can, credibly if tentatively, be identified as James's first romantic or sexual partner.[1] He was styled the Master of Gray as the eldest son and heir to Lord Gray, head of an aristocratic family with estates in eastern Scotland, and he was returning from several years in France.[2] As a diplomatic arrangement, the Auld Alliance had been dead for just over two decades and, as the late Esmé's career had shown, had been replaced by a potent strain of anti-French sentiment. Culturally, however, the ties fostered during the era of the alliance between the two countries' nobilities endured long after its dissolution. Many members of the Scottish aristocracy undertook part of their education in France, fought in its armies, or even protected its kings: among the companies of the royal bodyguard was the *Garde Écossaises.*[3] When these young men and, less frequently, young women also residing at the French court traveled between Scotland and France, they tended to do so in groups to allay the cost and mitigate the dangers of long journeys, which was why Patrick Gray traveled home in Catherine Stuart's party.

During his time abroad, Patrick had expressed an interest in Catholicism, which could have counted against him in Scotland, as could his relationship as a first cousin to the disgraced Lord Gowrie. Every point to Patrick's demerit was, however, negated by his "pre-eminently beautiful" appearance.[4] James evidently did not share the conclusion of a later observer, who judged Patrick Gray's beauty "too feminine to please some tastes."[5] James was dazzled, and Patrick was invited to join his household, where one of his new colleagues, Sir James Melville, observed Patrick's sudden rise to "great favour and familiarity with His Majesty."[6]

When they first met in 1583, James was seventeen and Patrick was about twenty-four. Some genealogies give Patrick's year of birth as 1565, which would have made him seventeen or eighteen; however, given Patrick's wedding in about 1575 to Lord Glamis's daughter Elizabeth Lyon, 1565 seems implausibly late.[7] A much later account claimed he was born as early as 1555, although it is contradicted by contemporary sources dating his parents' wedding to January 1557.[8] While a definitive year of birth remains elusive, the best evidence we have indicates that Patrick Gray was born sometime between 1558 and 1560.

Patrick's flair, wit, and manners won him some admirers at court, including Melville, who came to consider him "my great friend." "He was a proper gentleman," Melville recalled, "of a trim spirit and fair speech."[9] Such admiration was the exception for Patrick rather than the rule. A more common assessment was summarized in a history of the Scottish nobility—"He possessed all the talents of a courtier, a graceful person, an insinuating address, a boundless ambition, and a restless and intriguing spirit."[10]

James spent most of the weeks after he turned eighteen hunting from Falkland Palace and, that summer, Patrick's prominence in his household became obvious to nearly everybody at court.[11] Patrick was appointed Master of the Wardrobe, and James intervened to settle his debts.

A few weeks after hunting at Falkland, James was back in Edinburgh. He hosted a French diplomat, Albert Fontenay, who left a thorough pen portrait of the King. Fontenay's doomed mission was to resurrect the Association, the plan for joint rule between herself and her son on which the former queen Mary continued to pin her dwindling hopes.[12] As the widow of a French monarch, Mary drew a substantial private income from her dower estates there, which were partly administered for her by Fontenay.[13] She trusted him enough to send him to James on her behalf. Devotion to the former Queen of Scots was a family affair—Fontenay's kinsman* Claude Nau had joined Mary in exile to serve as her secretary and it was for Claude that Fontenay wrote his frank assessment of James VI, with the strict caveat that "the letter which follows will remain secret between you and me."[14]

Early modern ambassadors or delegations were often expected to find and fund their own accommodation, for which, theoretically, they would be reimbursed when they returned home. In practice, patrons often took a long time to settle ambassadors' expenses

* The familial relationship between Fontenay and Claude Nau remains unclear. Based on the way they addressed one another in their correspondence, brothers, half-brothers, stepbrothers, or brothers-in-law have all been suggested.

or did not pay them at all. Fontenay was therefore grateful when James offered him accommodation and food at court, which also gave him more opportunities to observe the King at close quarters.

He was impressed by James's "marvellous mind," telling Claude that he "apprehends and understands everything. He judges reasonably. He carries much in his memory and for a long time. In his questions, he is lively and perceptive, and sound in his answers. In any matter which is being debated, be it Religion or any other thing, he believes and always maintains what seems to him to be true and just. He is learned in many tongues, sciences and affairs of state."

Fontenay characterized James as a man with a "heart so big" but who had been "nurtured in fear" by his upbringing. His big heart did not extend to his imprisoned mother, which may have been one of the reasons for Fontenay's insistence to Claude that his letter remain secret. Despite the reasons for Fontenay's visit and knowing that he worked for Mary, James did not ask a single question about his mother's living conditions in England. "I am astonished," Fontenay told Claude, "that he has never asked anything about the Queen, neither of her health, nor of the way she is treated, nor of her servants, nor of what she eats or drinks, nor of her recreation, nor any similar matter."

James at eighteen was oddly competitive. When a courtier mentioned that he had gone two days and nights without sleeping, James stayed awake for three so that he could best these achievements in insomnia. He hated boredom, and he was open about what that entailed. He disliked dancing, had little interest in music and even less in fashion. He had no interest in women, and he swore like a sailor. Fontenay disapproved of the way James would not moderate his language even in the presence of ladies and, like his compatriot Esmé before him, was shocked by James's indifference to etiquette. He wrote, "His manners, as a result of the failure to instruct him properly [in childhood], are aggressive and very uncivil, both in speaking, eating, clothes, games, and conversation in the company of women."

Some traits noticed by Fontenay lend credence to the modern theory that James may have had attention deficit hyperactivity disorder (ADHD).[15] "He never sits still in one place," Fontenay told Claude, "taking a singular pleasure in walking up and down... he cannot work for a long time at [government] business, though when he puts himself to it, he will achieve more than six other men together." James's slender build suggested a fragility that was belied by his activities at the hunt when he was "in the saddle for six hours on end, running up hills and down dales with loosened bridle." The amount of time he spent hunting was one of the three defects Fontenay detected. Another was the way James's subpar arithmetic as a child had produced an adult who did not seem to have any understanding of the straitened finances of the Scottish monarchy after nearly two decades of unrest.

Fontenay's residency at the Scottish court in 1584 coincided with speculation in the royal household about Patrick Gray's rise to prominence as the King's favorite.[16] This inspired the third of James's defects in Fontenay's eyes, who concluded that the King "loves indiscreetly and obstinately, despite the disapprobation of his subjects." It is around this time that "minion" is used in relation to James's favorite, a word that was not used to describe previous favorites like Esmé or Arran and one that, for contemporaries, drew unavoidable and intentional comparisons with the alleged male lovers, or *mignons*, of King Henri III of France.[17] While this is revealing, it is worth issuing a caveat with the note that it is the only firm piece of evidence suggesting that James and Patrick were lovers.[18] The rest should more accurately be categorized as circumstantial—including Patrick's rapid rise in the hierarchy of James's household, something previously experienced only by the King's relatives, the attention paid to the relationship by various courtiers, and the remarks of Melville and Fontenay, the latter of whom felt the matter was of sufficient importance that he ranked James's indiscreet love as a trait "which may possibly be harmful to the conservation of his estate* and government."

Patrick's behavior encouraged suspicions that the King's interest in him had passed beyond the platonic. He did everything in his power to frustrate Esmé's policy of finding a wife for James.

* Position.

Admittedly, Patrick found a willing participant in James, who as Fontenay observed hated "amorous talk" about women. Another contemporary characterized James as "a cold wooer."[19] In 1584 and 1585, discussions about James's potential marriage stalled, which was unusual for a young, childless, healthy early modern monarch.

Confusion persists about Patrick's own marriages. His parents had arranged a marriage for him with Elizabeth Lyon in May 1575, when Patrick was about sixteen years old. Accounts differ on whether Patrick and Elizabeth's divorce occurred before or after Patrick went to France. The uncertainty is caused by the couple's separation not long after their wedding, followed by Patrick's departure abroad. Elizabeth did not, however, legally sue him for divorce until May 1585. She then remarried to another nobleman, and Patrick, keen to make proverbial hay, married Lady Mary Stewart within two months of his divorce from Elizabeth. His new wife was technically James's cousin as the eldest daughter of the 1st Earl of Orkney, another illegitimate son of James V. It did not create the most edifying spectacle for Patrick to be discouraging talk of James's marriage while pursuing one of supreme social advantage to himself. Neither his marriage to Lady Mary in July 1585 nor the birth of their first child in 1586 coincided with any suggestion that Patrick's bond with the King had weakened.

He was sworn in as one of James's councillors and, while this gave him a political role, it was one whereby he acted as a colleague, rather than rising to the role of the dominant voice in the council like Morton or Esmé.

James was determined to hold on to the power he had wrested from Gowrie. While he could not entirely overturn the latter's legacy—the country's economic problems had both led to and been exacerbated by Gowrie's policy of debasing the coinage, which James felt he had no choice but to continue—1584–85 otherwise saw a period of sustained political triumph for James, the benefits of which were felt by those who had helped him assert control over his government. The Earl of Huntly became a councillor, and the Earl of Bothwell was appointed Lord High Admiral.[20] Arran became the most influential of James's councillors as Lord Chancellor of Scotland, and a gentleman called John Maitland became Secretary to the Council.* Arran had lost none of his flair for scheming, and he speedily recruited Patrick, himself hardly a novice when it came to intrigue, as an ally on the council. It was, however, the sober-minded and industrious Maitland who became the adviser James relied upon the most.

An amicable working relationship emerged between Crown and Parliament in Scotland. The Scottish parliament was a single chamber that met infrequently, usually in short sessions of a few weeks or less, with representatives sent by the clergy, landed classes, and burghs. In a rush of loyal enthusiasm for James, the Parliament of 1584 supported his push against the Kirk by voting through legislation that gave the King the right to appoint all Scotland's bishops, abolished the independence of individual congregations, threatened the church with heavy taxation if it did not obey, and outlawed Presbyterian General Assemblies unless they were convened with the monarch's permission. Led by Andrew Melvill, who had succeeded the late John Knox as Presbyterianism's most influential cleric, about twenty Presbyterian preachers emigrated to England rather than accept the new laws or "the Black Acts," as they dubbed them. One of the exiles lambasted Parliament as "traitors to Christ."[21] When a Presbyterian clergyman preached at court against the increase of secular control over the Kirk, James told him, "I give not a steaming turd for thy preaching!"[22]

James ordered the suppression of political works authored by his tutor George Buchanan, who had died two years earlier.[23] In 1584, another of his former attendants from the days at Stirling, Drumquhassle, was arrested and convicted for involvement in a further political plot. This time, James signed Drumquhassle's death warrant, which was enacted with a public hanging in February 1585.

James's expansion of the monarchy's power, his love of a dirty joke, his coarse language, and his infatuation with Patrick Gray were the antithesis of what the king George Buchanan had hoped to create. However, in three important aspects Buchanan's influence

* Brother of William Maitland of Lethington, Mary, Queen of Scots' Secretary of State who took his own life at the siege of Edinburgh Castle in 1573.

endured into James's adulthood. The first, as noticed by Fontenay, was the breadth and depth of James's intellect. The second was his sincere Protestant faith, the theology of which was to remain a passion for the rest of his life. Third was his misogyny, which was strong enough to be remarked upon even in the sixteenth century. His lack of sexual interest in women extended to his lack of interest in them socially and intellectually, with one or two exceptions, such as his fellow poet Christian Lindsay. In one of his own poems, James wrote "all women are of nature vain/and can keep no secret unrevealed . . . They are fulfilled by gossip without worth; They let the smallest crime consume their earth."[24] Buchanan had fed him a diet of history in which women were presented as monsters or morons and, while James's prejudices toward women were to ameliorate substantially as he grew, they never entirely went away.

In August 1584, the same month as Fontenay's mission to Scotland, which ended in failure as James refused to implement the Association, Scotland entered negotiations for a new alliance with England. This would replace the Treaty of Edinburgh from twenty-four years earlier and hopefully draw a line under England's tendency to back troublemaking factions within the Scottish aristocracy. James regarded the potential treaty as a priority. He told Elizabeth in a letter that a stable peace between their two kingdoms was the "most likely grounds for our mutual sureties to be built on."[25]

Arran was sent to represent James at the first stage of discussions, which took place in northern England. Perhaps to convey more respect for James than she had shown previously, Queen Elizabeth's emissary was her cousin and friend Lord Hunsdon.* Negotiations were overshadowed by Arran's strongly—and vocally—anti-English views.† This may have been strategic on

* Henry Carey, 1st Baron Hunsdon (1526–96), son of Elizabeth's late aunt Lady Mary Carey (née Boleyn).

† Among tactics previously deployed by Arran were to hire Kate, the "Scold of Stirling," to stand outside the gates of Stirling Castle and hurl insults at the English ambassador on arrival, and to intercept a ring sent by James as a token of amity, popping out its diamond and replacing it with a crystal.

James's part. In his foreign policy, he made use of the skills in subterfuge that he had acquired while biding his time against Morton and Gowrie. James approached his goals from multiple angles, sometimes using aggression and, at other times, charm and conciliation. While Arran played the role of proverbial vinegar in the official negotiations, Patrick would take the role of honey in secret, unofficial discussions. In October, James sent Patrick south to London in his name. The pair said farewell on October 14 at Holyroodhouse, where James gave Patrick a letter to deliver to Elizabeth's chief minister, Lord Burghley. In the letter, James wrote of Patrick that he had "directed this bearer with more special and secret commission than any I ever directed before."[26]

He sent no letters for his mother. That autumn, James stopped writing to her. Having heard from Fontenay of Patrick Gray's ascendancy, Mary blamed him for turning her son against her. She and Patrick exchanged a tense series of letters, in which Patrick bluntly told Mary to accept the reality of her demoted situation and try to make the best of it, while she fired back that "whoever" was encouraging James in his colder attitude to her was "nothing but a fool and a traitor."[27] This was likely overestimating Patrick's influence and ignoring the complexity of James's attitude to his mother. His childhood education had been directed at convincing him that Mary was emotionally, politically, and sexually corrupt. As his relief at the Bothwell Testament's apparent exoneration of her had shown when he was eleven, James had been eager to read a convincing defense of Mary. Encouraged initially by Esmé and by gifts from the Duke of Guise, a period had followed in which James and Mary wrote to one another more frequently and even with palpable affection. Mary's dishonesty over Elizabeth's role in the Association had soured that.

Two other less emotional factors also shaped James's decision to distance himself from his mother in 1584. The first, which made it easier for him to do, was that he almost certainly had no memory of her. The last time he had seen Mary was when he was ten months old. Even before that, they had been together on only a handful of occasions, due to the contemporary custom for royal infants to be brought up away from court, cities, and crowds.

The second was a more pragmatic, cold, and arguably callous reason. Politically, his mother was his rival for Scotland and his liability in England. Even if the Scottish public had shown any enthusiasm for the Association, which most of them had not, James could not bring her back to Scotland without renouncing half his power. Elizabeth had not yet named an heir to her thrones and, while her Scottish kin were strong candidates, James worried that if Mary became too great a threat to Elizabeth, then the latter might respond by pushing through legislation that barred any Stewart from succeeding her. Persuading Elizabeth to publicly recognize him as her heir was one of James's main objectives for his new treaty with England and, while we will never know precisely what the message was that James entrusted to Patrick for Burghley, it is overwhelmingly likely that it had something to do with Mary or the succession.

James's relationship with his mother disintegrated, and the Anglo-Scottish treaty talks took place as the international climate darkened, especially when it came to the intersection of politics with religion. The two forces were never far from one another in the sixteenth century, but 1584 and 1585 saw mounting worry about their combined impact. In 1584, another sectarian civil war broke out in France,* with King Philip II of Spain intervening to back one of the factions, a worrying precedent whereby religion motivated the great powers to directly intervene in one another's internal politics. In the same year, a man loyal to Philip II shot and killed Prince William of Orange. Sometimes known as William the Silent or William the Taciturn, William had helped lead the Protestant Dutch rebellion against Spanish rule, and his assassination alarmed Protestant Europe. In 1585, Gregory XIII died and Cardinal Montalto was elected his successor as pope. He took the regnal name Sixtus V and initially gave every indicator, at least to worried or hostile Protestants, that he would be more militant than his predecessor. He reissued a previous pope's sentence of excommunication against Elizabeth I and issued his own against the King of Navarre.

---

* Known as "the Eighth War of Religion" or the "War of the Three Henris" (1584/5–88).

In and of itself, excommunication—under which an individual was denied access to the sacraments and was, while the sentence lasted, de facto outside the Catholic Church—was unlikely to distress either the Queen of England or the King of Navarre, both of whom were Protestants. The danger lay in its religious-political consequences. Assassinating an excommunicated sovereign was not a sin—Pius V had gone so far as to bless attempts to kill Elizabeth—and, following the assassination of William the Silent in 1584 and Sixtus V's royal excommunications in 1585, fear mushroomed over Catholic plots to murder any Protestant leader whom they regarded as sinful, inconvenient, tyrannical, or all three. Many English and Welsh Catholics had been aghast at Pope Pius V's initial decision to excommunicate their queen in 1570. They knew that his actions had made them suspects in their own country, and it was they who paid a terrible price as the English government retaliated by introducing punitive anti-Catholic legislation.

In March 1585, James publicly and definitively rejected the Association, stating his intention to remain as Scotland's sole monarch for as long as he lived. In the same month, Patrick returned from England. They were together when an outbreak of plague forced them to leave Edinburgh for Dirleton Castle, where Patrick entertained the King and the court by organizing a series of plays and feasts for them. Patrick fell out with Lord Arran, who resented his former friend's sympathy for the mooted alliance with England. Arran did not know, yet, how far Patrick's betrayal of him had extended.[28] During his mission to England, the ambitious Patrick had ingratiated himself with Elizabeth's government to the extent that he had become an English spy. Utilizing the knowledge he had acquired from his time in France, Patrick told them that Mary was still finding a way to smuggle letters to and from her Guise cousins and her former brother-in-law King Henri III.[29] Among other useful information he passed on to the English was to confirm their suspicion that the main obstacle to the treaty with Scotland was his erstwhile friend Lord Arran. An English opportunity to strike against Arran was provided through the murder of an English aristocrat, Lord Francis Russell, by one of Arran's underlings, Sir Thomas Kerr. Both Kerr and Lord Francis, son of the former

English ambassador to Scotland, had been members of English and Scottish groups who met near the border to discuss the extradition of various petty criminals, who frequently escaped the law in one country by crossing the border to the other. We do not know what made Sir Thomas angry enough to shoot Lord Francis.[30] Whatever the cause, it proved fatal.

James was staying at St. Andrews when he was informed of the murder. Immediately appreciating the risk this posed to the alliance and knowing that he must separate himself from his chancellor's men, he sent a short, sincere letter to Queen Elizabeth: "Since haste, anger, and extraordinary sorrow will not permit any longer letter, this present [letter] shall only serve to assure you of my honest innocence in this late mischief."[31] It was hyperbolic, but likely honest—a diplomat who saw James just after he heard about the murder said that the King was horrified.[32] Nor is there any reason to doubt the sincerity of Elizabeth I's outrage at Lord Francis's murder. Equally, her government seldom missed an opportunity.

The killer was under the protection, and married to a niece, of Lord Arran, who was suspected of having encouraged some act of violence against an English noble to scupper the treaty negotiations.[33] We do not know if that suspicion was correct. Arran was certainly capable of it. On the other hand, personality is not proof.

The English made clear to James that they wanted Arran's downfall in retaliation for Lord Francis's death. Patrick kept London informed about James's diminishing confidence in his Lord Chancellor, which emboldened the English to maintain the pressure.[34] Patrick advised that the English allow to return to Scotland certain lords who had previously emigrated there thanks to various feuds with Arran.[35] They heeded his advice, and the number of Arran's enemies in Scotland sharply increased. With loud cries to dismiss Arran coming from both foreign and domestic sources, James ordered his arrest while they were both staying at Stirling Castle. Belatedly seeing Patrick for the enemy he had become, Arran was so furious that he lunged at Patrick and tried to kill him. He was pulled away by others in the room and escaped on horseback before the castle gates could be closed.[36]

James may have hoped for his former mentor to escape. While he had proven his capacity for ruthlessness toward enemies such as Lord Gowrie, he did not share the trait of his English kinsman Henry VIII, who specialized in the annihilation of former loved ones and favorites. Arran was no longer useful to James, he no longer revered him as he had in childhood, and Arran's actions had jeopardized James's foreign policy. He was dismissed from government and his earldom was taken from him. As far as James was concerned, that was enough and he firmly resisted pressure from Arran's enemies, including the Queen of England, to punish Arran further.[37] The former earl of Arran retired to his manor in Ayrshire, and was left in comfortable obscurity until, ten years later, he was surprised, attacked, and killed by one of Lord Morton's nephews, who had waited fourteen years until he could settle the blood debt he felt was owed for Arran's role in Morton's execution.[38]

Arran's disgrace not only pacified the English, it allowed James to mend bridges with the Kirk. No monarch wanted a feud with the Church, if it could be avoided, and so the departed Arran was retrospectively blamed for the Black Acts of 1584, which was laughable in light of James's assessment of the Kirk's agenda as a "steaming turd." Everybody involved politely pretended to believe otherwise. Andrew Melvill and the other exiled preachers returned to Scotland, which went a long way to establishing harmonious relations between Church and state. The General Assemblies no longer required royal permission to convene, which enabled the custom that persists to the present in Scottish and Irish Presbyterianism of annual assemblies. Reconciliation was not surrender, however. James made clear who would remain the dominant authority by dispatching Melvill on a holy mission to preach and hunt down Jesuit spies in the Highlands.[39] There was no evidence that any Jesuits had been spotted in the Highlands, as James well knew when he sent Melvill there.

On July 6, 1586, the Treaty of Berwick was signed between Scotland and England. Named after the northern English town where negotiations concluded, James achieved much, but not all, that he had intended. His greatest failure was Elizabeth's refusal to name him as her heir. This was not meant as a personal insult on her part. From the age of twenty-one to twenty-five, during the reign of her sister, Elizabeth had been heiress to the throne. Plots against her sister had used Elizabeth as a figurehead, for which she had been imprisoned in the Tower of London, come close to execution, and subsequently endured months of house arrest in the countryside. As her sister lay dying, Elizabeth had witnessed the useful but unappealing sight of courtiers making their way to her palace to curry favor with her before the old monarch had expired. Elizabeth had emerged from that time in her life with an almost pathological aversion to naming her own heir and compared it to weaving her shroud. She likewise rejected James's request that he be awarded a dukedom in the English peerage. An English dukedom, when combined with his royal blood, would have positioned James as heir in spirit if not quite in title. Instead, Elizabeth offered, from the English perspective, a brilliant compromise. She guaranteed James's future cooperation with a promise that she would make no pronouncements against him being a possible heir unless she felt forced to do so "by the said King's unkind usage towards her Majesty which, God forbid."[40]

These were not minor losses for James. However, there were prominent successes. The two governments promised better cooperation in the future on criminal extraditions, and they entered into a pact of mutual defense if either was attacked by a Catholic power. The English government committed itself to paying an annuity to James of £3,000, which was £2,000 less than he had asked but nonetheless immediately increased his yearly income by about 20 percent.[41] Its payment was simultaneously a tribute to James's proximity to the English line of succession, and another useful tool to encourage him to maintain peace with England.

Less than two months after he had signed the treaty, James was informed that his mother had committed treason against Elizabeth. After eighteen years in custody, Mary had reached a nadir of spirits and a peak of frustration. She was accused of complicity in a plot led by an English Catholic landowner called Sir Anthony Babington. Babington's plan was to free her from captivity, murder Queen Elizabeth, and replace her with Mary. Letters between Mary and the plotters had been intercepted by Elizabeth's spymaster and adviser Sir Francis Walsingham, who for years had labored in vain to persuade Elizabeth to execute Mary. When the damning correspondence was presented to Mary, she protested her innocence and accused Walsingham of forgery.

How far Mary was involved in the Babington Plot is unknowable. It seems improbable that she was wholly innocent. A plausible explanation is that Walsingham, who monitored Mary's every move and was fixated on the necessity of her destruction, allowed her to become deeply involved with the plotters until he had enough to persuade Elizabeth to order a trial.[42] In support of this scenario is the activity of Gilbert Gifford, a double agent from a Catholic family who was recruited by Walsingham. Mary was so delighted by her jailers' unexpected kindness in permitting her a Catholic visitor that she took Gifford into her confidence. He not only passed on information about her plots to Walsingham but actively encouraged Mary to participate in them. Somebody later played Gifford at his own game by alerting Mary's French friends to his activities. They waited until he was next in Paris and tracked him down to a brothel, where he was caught in a ménage à trois with a female prostitute and another Englishman.[43] On King Henri III's orders, Gifford was imprisoned in the Bastille for betraying the Catholic cause. He died three years later.

James, initially, was irritated but unalarmed by news of his mother's involvement in the Babington Plot. He said she had brewed this beer and now she must drink it, a contemporary version of making one's bed and lying in it. He told Patrick that he was confident in "her life being safe" because the whole thing was a gambit by Elizabeth to provide her with a reason to remove Mary from the line of succession.[44] After the farce of a trial, James believed that Mary would be left alone to devote her life to prayer.[45] He did not realize that Queen Elizabeth was horrified, convinced, and trapped by Walsingham's evidence. She did not want to execute a fellow sovereign, even a deposed one, but London and the English parliament were gripped by anti-Mary and anti-Catholic fury, which Elizabeth could no longer control. The pressure on Elizabeth to sanction the harshest measures against the former Queen of Scots was sustained and substantial. Belatedly understanding that he had been wrong and that his mother's impending trial was far more serious than he had surmised, James sent several courtiers to England to negotiate with Elizabeth. He, Patrick, and the household moved to Falkland Palace for most of September. In October, Mary was tried by members of the English nobility. She denied that any English authority had the right to try her as if she were one of Elizabeth's subjects. Only subjects could commit treason. She was found guilty nevertheless and sentenced to death.

The winter was dominated by James's attempts to save his mother's life. He even made a bizarre marriage proposal to Elizabeth, which was likely nothing more than a futile ploy to distract the English from their prosecution of Mary.[46] He sent more envoys south in his name. Patrick desperately did not want to be included in their number, sensing that such a mission would be a poisoned chalice.[47] Having worked for them as their spy, he was under no illusions about the dogged determination of Mary's enemies, particularly Walsingham. Perhaps Patrick was also recalling and regretting his brutal, ill-judged quip to Queen Elizabeth the last time he was in London when, discussing the problem posed by Mary, Patrick said, "Mortui non mordent."[48] ("The dead do not bite.") If James discovered what he had said, forgiveness was unlikely. When he heard that one of his envoys had subtly tipped off the English government that executing Mary would not be too widely mourned by the Scottish people, James sent a letter to the gentleman in question, telling him that if he ever set foot in Scotland again, James would have him hanged before he had time to take off his boots.

From Holyroodhouse in December, James wrote to Elizabeth's favorite Robert Dudley, Earl of Leicester, warning that if Mary's execution proceeded, Elizabeth would "be hated by all good Christians." From threats, James pivoted to pleading, asking that Leicester use his influence with Elizabeth on Mary's behalf: "I pray you once again, as ever ye would do me any pleasure or honour, so to behave yourself in fulfilling my expectation in this matter . . . I commit you . . . to the holy protection of the Most High. From my palace of Holyroodhouse the 4th day of December, 1586. Your most loving and assured friend, James R."[49] In another letter to

Lord Leicester, James came close to a rare moment of candor about his confused and confusing attitudes to Mary. "My religion ever moved me to hate her course," he admitted, "although my honour constrains me to insist for her life."[50]

When in a foul temper, James's arrogance grew and his tact diminished, as he proved when he fired off a letter to one of his representatives in England in which he gave full vent to sarcasm, incredulity, snobbery, and rage. He began by agreeing with his mother that no English authority had any legal right to try her: "I perceive by your last letter the Queen my mother continueth still in that miserable strait that the pretended condemnation of that parliament has put her in. A strange example indeed and so very rare, as for my part I never read nor heard of the like practice in such case." He moved on to faux disbelief at Elizabeth's actions: "I am sorry [that] the Queen hath suffered this to proceed so far to my dishonour, and so contrary to her good fame as . . . to condemn a sovereign prince descended on all hands of the best blood of Europe."

What he was thinking when he composed the next part of the letter is anybody's guess. He dredged up the most painful moment of Elizabeth's childhood, when her father, Henry VIII, had signed the death warrant of her mother, Anne Boleyn. "King Henry the Eighth's reputation was never prejudged in anything," James proclaimed, which was not an especially accurate assessment of Henry's standing with contemporaries, "but in the beheading of his bedfellow. But yet that tragedy was far inferior to this."

In two sentences, James had managed to reference the execution of Elizabeth's mother, then simultaneously to insult her dead father for authorizing it and her mother by failing to refer to her as Henry's wife but simply as "his bedfellow."* James did not personally consider "bedfellow" an insulting term, but he should have known how Elizabeth would interpret it.[51] Having summoned the ghost of Anne Boleyn, he then lobbed one final insult at her daughter by

* James could, far less probably, have been referring to Henry VIII's fifth wife, Queen Catherine Howard, who was also beheaded on his orders. The context of the letter makes Anne Boleyn by far the more likely subject. It cannot be ruled out that he was alluding to both executed queens.

describing Anne's beheading as a tragedy, but one "far inferior" to anything that might befall *his* mother.

To add insult and then idiocy to injury, James ordered his representatives to show the letter directly to Elizabeth. "Fail not to let her see all this letter," he commanded. "And would God she might see the inward parts of my heart where she should see a great jewel of honesty toward her locked up in a coffer of perplexity."[52] The diplomatic fallout caused by Elizabeth's rage when she read the letter was sufficient that a chastened James apologized.[53]

Patrick's silver-tongued charm had been used before in England. Just before Christmas, his attempts to avoid involvement in the attempt to save Mary failed when, on James's orders, Patrick set off on the Great North Road that linked Edinburgh with London, at the head of another delegation. His lack of faith in his own mission was shown when Patrick begged James to judge him by his efforts rather than his results. James warned Patrick that no amount of flattery, charm, or fair words would help "if her life be lost . . . if ye look for the continuance of my favour, spare no pains nor plainness in this case . . . Let me reap the fruits of your great credit there, either now or never. Farewell, James R."[54]

In Patrick's defense, he tried his best to obey James, even begging Elizabeth to at least delay the death sentence. She refused. As one of Patrick's companions observed, Mary may as well have been dead by the time they got there. After several fruitless meetings with Elizabeth I and her advisers, Patrick's colleague Sir Robert Melville, brother of the more famous Sir James, lost his temper and, in his brother's words, "spoke brave and stout language to the council of England." Elizabeth was so incensed that she threatened to imprison him.[55] Patrick won the Melville family's lasting gratitude for utilizing "the credit he had" with the English to save Robert from Elizabeth's threats.[56] Dejected, Patrick led their team home where, on February 8, they received the begrudging thanks of the council for their efforts.

They did not know yet that, on that same morning, Mary had been beheaded at Fotheringhay Castle. She met death with courage and dignity. It had taken three swings of the ax to end her life—the first missed entirely, the second missed and swung into the back of her head. Her pet terrier had been hiding in her robes, saw her decapitated head, refused all food, and died a few days later. Mary's body had been taken for burial at nearby Peterborough Cathedral, where it was interred near the high altar.[57] James was in residence at Holyroodhouse when the news reached Edinburgh a few days later.

Some of James's Presbyterian critics, who had never forgiven him for the Black Acts, claimed that he was secretly delighted when he discovered that his mother was dead because he no longer had a rival for the throne.[58] This is refuted by his actions. James stood stock-still when he heard, went to bed without eating, ordered court mourning, and retreated to Morton's former countryside estate at Dalkeith.[59] He left orders that Patrick "especially" was not permitted to return to court and that he wanted time alone for "two or three days" during which the council should "retain all folks . . . from coming to trouble" him.[60] He left Edinburgh engulfed in protests by crowds calling Elizabeth "that Jezebel, the English whore" who deserved a noose for a necklace.[61] Patrick observed with withering disdain, "They that hated most her prosperity regret her adversity."[62] He was right. Many of the people rioting were those who had made it explicitly clear when Mary lived that they did not want her returning to Scotland. However, for a foreign government to behead a Scottish royal was regarded as an unforgivable insult. Elizabeth sent Robert Carey, another of her Boleyn kinsmen, north with a private letter for James, trying to justify what she had done. Carey had been to Scotland before on Elizabeth's behalf and James liked him, which was allegedly why he was chosen in 1587.[63] On James's command, Carey was turned away at the border.

Unlike her advisers, some of whom were euphoric at Mary's death, Elizabeth knew what the international reaction would be and what damage it would inflict on her reputation.[64] Before the execution, she agonized to a delegation from Parliament, "What will my enemies not say, that for the safety of her life a maiden queen could be content to spill the blood even of her own kinswoman?"[65] When the deed was done, Elizabeth lost her appetite, she wept, she could not sleep, and she blamed everyone and anyone but herself. She even ordered the brief imprisonment in the Tower of London of the messenger who delivered the death warrant that she had signed.

After his isolation at Dalkeith, James decided that he could not jeopardize the alliance or, more selfishly, his chance to one day succeed Elizabeth. He allowed Robert Carey to come to Edinburgh and received Elizabeth's exculpatory epistle, which included the mind-boggling request that James should appreciate "how innocent I am in this case."[66] For diplomacy's sake, James pretended to believe her, but there was a veiled threat in his reply that "I wish that your honourable behaviour in all times hereafter may fully persuade the whole world of the same."[67] Elizabeth was sufficiently piqued at his tone that, despite having lamented the "extreme dolour that overwhelmeth my mind" after ordering his mother's execution, she complained to Lord Burghley that she would not write to James again until he adopted a more respectful tone.[68]

Patrick was allowed to return to James's household, but whatever intimacy had existed between them had been destroyed by the failure of his embassy to England. James's resentment was understandable yet unfair. Nothing that Patrick could have done would have saved Mary. James either believed otherwise, or his feelings for Patrick may have been ailing even before the English mission that killed them. In May 1587, three months after Mary's execution, Patrick was accused of espionage and sedition, dismissed from the council and the household, and spent a week under arrest at Edinburgh Castle. He accepted his downfall with good grace.[69]

Given the intrigues in which he had involved himself, Patrick may have counted himself lucky to escape so lightly. Outside his family and a few friends, nobody mourned his departure—Catholics resented him for his failure to save the former queen, Protestants for his alleged sympathy for Catholicism.[70] He returned to France, where he supported himself as a mercenary soldier for two years until he was granted permission to come home.[71] He was eventually accepted back at court, where he occasionally dabbled in palace intrigues without much success and was admired for his ability to plan parties. Never again was there any suggestion of closeness between him and the King, who would subsequently describe Patrick as proud and ambitious, with a flexible conscience and a flair for lying.[72]

6

NIGHTLY BEDFELLOWS

I felt that Love all sudden took
Me captive in his wards.
—Anonymous Scottish court poem
(late sixteenth century)

In the months following Patrick's fall from grace, twenty-one-year-old James seems to have had a liaison with the twenty-five-year-old Earl of Huntly. The chronology of his bond with Huntly is among the more difficult of James's relationships. They had met each other infrequently when they were children but, when Huntly was fourteen, his father, the previous earl, had died of a heart attack while playing a game of soccer. After, Huntly spent more time on his family's estates as earl and then several years completing his education in France. He and James did not see more of one another until Huntly was in his early twenties. Huntly had been one of the earls who came to James's aid during his countercoup against Gowrie in 1583, and it may be that James had an unreciprocated crush on him at that time.[1] In 1587, there is firm evidence of sustained closeness between the two. In June, just after Patrick was rusticated from court, the King transferred a lucrative commendatorship from Patrick to Huntly. James had strong feelings for the earl, including a physical attraction, which seemed obvious to mutual acquaintances.[2] One courtier wrote, "The King hath a strange, extraordinary affection to Huntly."[3] Even in the context of the sixteenth century, when aristocrats often wrote to one another in emotional language, some of James's letters to Huntly exceed the credibly platonic. During one of Huntly's absences from court, James wrote to him, "I may on my soul swear unto you, that since your parting from here I was never one hour unthinking upon you, but when I was sleeping and scarcely then."[4] His feelings toward Huntly frequently overrode James's good sense, which was noticed by Huntly's colleagues on the council.

When, or if, James and Huntly became lovers is less clear. In October 1587, Huntly is mentioned as regularly lying in the King's chamber at Holyroodhouse, followed by numerous observations of James's affection for him.[5] Whether Huntly reciprocated James's feelings, or simply encouraged them, is debatable. Huntly had no shortage of enemies willing to claim that he had deliberately set out to manipulate the King to his own advantage.

Huntly's personal attractions were obvious. He was charismatic, strong, handsome, athletic, and a capable warrior.[6] He was also explosively temperamental—"hot and hardy"—and confident enough that, while he wanted James's favor, he often acted as if he did not.[7] Once, upon arriving at court from his estates, he forgot to bow to James and only half apologized by saying he had just come from a place where everybody bowed to him.[8] Politically, he was far more significant than Patrick, which worried many of James's advisers. As the Chief of Clan Gordon, Huntly was one of the most powerful Scottish lords. In the Highlands, where the Huntly earldom had held sway for centuries, his ancestors had been nicknamed "the kings of the North."[9] Like most of his fellow Highlanders, Huntly was a Catholic who resented the Protestantism emanating from the Kirk and the Lowlands.

Huntly's Catholicism was woven into courtiers' concerns about his relationship with the King. It also brought him to the attention of Elizabeth I, who knew that Huntly was ambivalent about Scotland's alliance with England and in contact with Catholic nobles in France and Spain. He had been among the most outspoken critics of Elizabeth following Mary's execution. The English government ordered their spies to keep an eye on him, after which one of them wrote to Sir Francis Walsingham, "My Lord of Huntly is indeed a great courtier and knows more of the King's secrets [than] any man in this present doth."[10]

The culture of seeing sodomy as a great "other" had persisted but evolved. Where previously its otherness had been geographical, from about the 1580s until the 1650s the focus became confessional, with many Protestant Europeans insisting that homosexual intercourse was a Catholic vice. In 1587, Presbyterian courtiers took this attitude to an extreme with their fear that Huntly was using his personal appeal to trick James into converting to Catholicism, which would certainly have been a novel approach to proselytization.[11] A Protestant courtier insinuated that, in the intimacy of the King's chamber, Huntly was cynically capitalizing on James's feelings for him, when, left to his own devices, Huntly might prefer to be conducting similar activities with a woman; the courtier archly noted that the earl was a "papist, but not so precise* as he had not rather [be] lying in a fair gentlewoman's chamber."[12]

Huntly divided his time between court and his estates in the Highlands, to which he returned for several months in November 1587. At some point between Huntly's departure for the north and March of the following year, James fell in love.

Like Patrick Gray before him, Alexander Lindsay served as one of James's Gentlemen of the Chamber, and he too was part of an old aristocratic family, but when it came to their personalities, he and Patrick had little in common.

He was called Alexander Lindsay of Sandyford, after the family manor near Glasgow where he was born in 1563 or early 1564.[13] This likely helped inspire James's private nickname for him of "Sandy."[14] He was one of five sons. His eldest brother had succeeded their father as the Earl of Crawford, married, and had a family of his own. Sandy had come to court with his brothers John, James, and Henry—known to nearly everyone as Harry—all of whom were to have long careers in royal service. Sandy and the King had been hunting together since they were teenagers, and Sandy had been unwaveringly loyal to him throughout the difficult years that followed. During James's plot to free himself from Gowrie, Sandy had, at risk to himself, carried messages to prominent nobles whom James hoped to recruit, including his brother Lord Crawford.

The Lindsay brothers had been well educated by a series of private tutors commissioned by their Catholic mother and had been taught to fight by their Protestant father. Confessional ambiguity

* Devout or observant to its teachings.

surrounded the family. Sandy was a Protestant, but there was uncertainty in court circles about the religious affiliation of his eldest brother, Lord Crawford, and these concerns were exacerbated by Crawford's friendship with Huntly.[15] Their two families had been allies in the north for centuries, fueling an English fear that Sandy had been planted at James's side to further Huntly's agenda during the months when Huntly was absent from court.

Ascertaining when James's friendship with Sandy turned into something deeper is difficult in terms of precision, but possible in general. There had been comments before about James's attachment to other men, summarized by the diplomat in Edinburgh who recorded a feeling at court "that this King is too much carried by young men that lie in his chamber and his minions."[16] By the spring of 1588, that speculation had narrowed to Sandy. In March, the courtier Lord Home, who was the same age as James, liked by him, and friendly with Sandy, was asked by an English friend who Sandy was. Home answered that Sandy was "the King's only minion and conceit—as he termed it—one esteemed of the King most of any man in Scotland, and was his nightly bed-fellow."[17] A "conceit" had two meanings—it referred to a romantic preoccupation and to holding a high opinion of somebody. That November, Sandy was described by separate courtiers as James's "chief favourite" and in December as "the King's minion."[18] This remained the situation four months later in March 1589 when Thomas Fowler, an English lawyer who had served as executor for James's paternal grandmother, returned to live at the Scottish court, where he observed Sandy as "the King's best beloved" and was another to call him James's "minion."[19]

Fowler's assessment is useful because he saw both Sandy and James at close quarters.[20] Knowing of Fowler's devotion to his late grandmother, James showed him favor at court. James either did not know, or did not care, that Fowler was writing private reports for Sir Francis Walsingham and Lord Burghley, which meant that Fowler had the proximity and the motivation to record details about life at James's court. To Burghley, Fowler wrote: "Alexander Lindsay is the King's best beloved minion, a proper man, and Huntly's wholly."[21]

As an idiom, "proper man" had several meanings in the sixteenth century. Not unlike comparable terms such as "manly man," "a real man," or "all man" for modern readers, its multiple meanings were not necessarily mutually exclusive. To late sixteenth-century readers, "proper man" often indicated handsomeness in a man who conformed to contemporary ideals of attractiveness.[22] That was how Shakespeare used it in *Othello*, where Iago refers to Cassio as a "proper man."[23] The "proper man's" attractiveness could include height and strength.[24] It could mean a man whose character was worthy of respect.[25] Finally, it was a euphemism for a man who was sexually capable, which is the most common contemporary usage of "proper man" in discussions of marriages, questions of sexual performance, or references to it in records from ecclesiastical morality cases.[26]

The other terms used to describe Sandy—"nightly bedfellow," "minion," and even references to lying in the King's chamber—have an interesting context. As shown by the courtier's quip about Huntly lying in the King's bedchamber when he would rather be "lying in a fair gentlewoman's chamber," "lying in" had a double meaning at the time, comparable to the way in which "sleeping with" has double meanings as an idiom in modern English. In regard to "bedfellow," beds were expensive in the early modern and medieval periods in Europe. It was not therefore uncommon for members of the elite to share a bedroom with several servants, some of whom would sleep on trestle beds. To share a bed was a sign of favor, which was misinterpreted by some twentieth-century writers who assumed the only reason for bed-sharing would be romantic or erotic.[27]

As a corrective to this, twenty-first-century interpretations have tended to conclude that two men or two women sharing a bed was such a common practice among the elite that "bed-fellow" never had any erotic connotations or subtext. This is equally misleading. Rather, the sharing of beds or of bedrooms was so common that commenting upon it was unusual. An imperfect comparison to today might be if an observer felt a need to mention that somebody was wearing underwear. Identifying a bedfellow seems to have occurred in atypical scenarios, not all of which were homoerotic but many of which contained sexual innuendo or subtext. In 1541, an English courtier called Thomas Culpepper sometimes shared the bedroom of his master, King Henry VIII. There is no hint that this was because Culpepper was suspected of being Henry's lover. We know that Culpepper occasionally was on bedroom duty because of a contemporary joke made after he was arrested on suspicion of adultery with Henry's wife—the quip being that Culpepper had shared the King's bed before he decided he would prefer to share the Queen's.

There are many examples of the use of "bedfellow" as a romantic pun in the sixteenth century, both between married couples and, more ambiguously, by same-sex pairs. The 6th Earl of Northumberland wrote to his friend Sir Thomas Arundell as "my dearest bedfellow" for years after they had ceased to share a bed when they both served in the household of the English Lord Chancellor.[28] The 1st Baron Cromwell wrote letters to his wife in which he saluted her as "my right, loving bed-fellow."[29] Most relevantly in Sandy's case, James would later refer to his own wife as "my bedfellow."[30] The identification of Sandy as James's nightly bedfellow appeared alongside descriptions of him as James's minion. With the potential sexual subtext of "minion," it is stretching credulity to conclude that courtiers who were using it with phrases like "best beloved" and "nightly bedfellow" were describing a relationship that they believed to be platonic. Bedfellow duties were typically conducted on a kind of rota and there was nearly always more than one bedfellow on duty at the time. For courtiers such as Thomas Fowler and Lord Home to specify that Sandy had become James's "nightly bed-fellow" is unusual, and likely deliberately so.

Concerns that Sandy was Huntly's pawn faded the longer his relationship with James lasted.[31] Sandy was devoted to him, as he had been when they were friends, and his loyalty did not falter as Sandy rose higher in James's estimation. Some of Sandy's kin were known for their temper, but there was another trait that ran in his family, which was a cheerfulness that earned those who possessed it the nickname of "the lightsome Lindsays." Fortunately for James, Sandy had seemingly inherited the latter. In April 1588, they were together at Holyroodhouse, from where they left for a civic visit to the southern Scottish town of Jedburgh then a hunting trip from Falkland in May.[32] James's twenty-second birthday passed in June. He continued writing poetry and started work on his first piece of theology—a commentary on the Bible's last book, Revelation, followed a few months later by his meditation on the Ark of the Covenant.[33] He augmented the prestige of his court by inviting Scottish and foreign artists to serve there and, within a few years, the royal household employed Dutch painters, Irish poets, and English musicians. There were less cerebral pursuits, too. James's sense of humor was filthy. If a joke was scatological or sexual, he loved it. He and Sandy drank together with their friends and sometimes snuck out into the streets of Edinburgh or Dunfermline, incognito.

Royal favor brought out green-eyed hatred in many, and it is a reflection on Sandy's personality that he was never loathed in the way most of James's favorites were, nor even simply disliked, as Patrick Gray had been. The exceptions were members of the Lyon family, but, as his family's ancestral enemies, they had hated Sandy on principle even before he became the King's favorite.[34] There were several arguments and even physical altercations between Sandy and James's captain of the guard, Thomas Lyon.[35]

Sandy's brother Harry held his wedding at court to Beatrix Charteris, which James had helped negotiate for the family. As Beatrix was the sole heiress to her family's fortune, Harry took her name on marriage.[36] There was no discussion yet of a wife for Sandy, but there was renewed pressure on James.

Jérôme Groslot, one of James's former classmates from Stirling, returned to Scotland as a member of a delegation to revive talks on marriage between James and Catherine of Bourbon, Princess of Navarre.[37] James's adviser John Maitland, who had replaced Arran as Lord Chancellor, supported the idea in the face of increasing opposition from some of his colleagues on the council.[38] Princess Catherine's age counted against her—she turned thirty in 1589—and there was concern at the Scottish court that this would be too late to produce an heir.[39] Maitland disagreed. Catherine's late mother, Queen Jeanne, had been thirty when she gave birth to Catherine, who was Protestant, intelligent, and virtuous. At Maitland's urging, James wrote a letter to Catherine, in which he may have labored too hard in his pose as a lovestruck wooer. She thought it was a bit much with "too much care and remembrance of me from so far away."[40]

From those councillors skeptical of the Navarre match, there was a countersuggestion that James consider marriage with fifteen-year-old Princess Elisabeth of Denmark.[41] James listened to their advice but did little to pursue negotiations with either princess. A nobleman observed that James "never regards the company of women, not so much as in any dalliance," while the French ambassador noticed that James "scoffs at all men who pay women honour."[42]

He did not scoff at Esmé's eldest daughter, Lady Henrietta Stuart, who came to live in Scotland with her sister Marie in 1588. As James's cousins, the Stuart sisters brought a feminine presence to his court, which hitherto had been an almost exclusively male establishment. In most early modern courts, there was at least one household that had a majority of female staff serving a dowager, consort, or royal daughter, sister, niece, or cousin. In that regard, James VI's court was unusual. Clever, charming, well-mannered, and considered a great beauty, Henrietta Stuart declined to follow in her father's footsteps by converting to Presbyterianism, although, when she first arrived in Edinburgh, she was willing to go along with some Protestant stipulations, including attendance at their services. In time, Henrietta was to become one of the most prominent and effective Catholic voices in the Scottish elite; it may be that her early flexibility over Presbyterian services was either a consequence of her lack of confidence to say no in her new homeland, of a genuine but then fading interest in the faith to which her father had converted, or of being less stalwart in her Catholicism than she was to become. Whatever the case, as much as James might personally have liked to see Henrietta become a Protestant, he did not pressure her into doing so once her Catholicism became politically useful to him.

Among James's councillors, there were deep and growing concerns about Huntly's ties to Catholic powers abroad and corresponding worries that, if it proved necessary, James's feelings for him would prevent him from moving against Huntly with the requisite severity.[43] A marriage between James's former favorite and his cousin seemed the perfect means of binding Huntly, and through him the Highlands, closer in obedience to the Crown. Henrietta's status and religion made her an attractive candidate to Huntly. Whereas he had opposed previous suggestions for Huntly to marry, James paid Henrietta's dowry and hosted the couple's three-day wedding celebrations at Holyroodhouse. Among the many gifts Henrietta received from her husband's allies were jewels from the Lord High Admiral for her to wear in her hair, and she, along with most of the guests, dressed in French fashion for the ceremony. After the festivities, which also included jousts and a banquet at which venison was the main dish, Huntly returned to his estates. He and Henrietta made an impressive political team, and she, as he did, henceforth divided her time between the Highlands and court, where Sandy remained at James's side. Even those serving in the palace, like clerk David Moysie, who were not so close to the King as members of his household, could see that Sandy remained "a great courtier" and James's "chief favourite."[44]

What were the contemporary attitudes to a relationship like James and Sandy's? Unlike England, where sex between two men had been made a capital crime by the Buggery Act of 1533, or Wales, where the same statute was applied after 1536, Scotland had no laws specifically dealing with homosexual intercourse.[45] In James's childhood, when the Kirk had been at one of the zeniths of its influence in government, this had not proved an impediment to the imposition of the death penalty. Citing the fact that sex between two men is forbidden in the twentieth chapter of the Bible's book of Leviticus, the Kirk contended that there was no need for secular legislation.[46] In 1570, this belief was the net that caught two men, John Litster and John Shaw, who are described in the legal records as "smiths and servants to Robert Hannay."[47] Hannay was a minor landowner and a member of the Blacksmiths' Guild in Edinburgh.[48] When their relationship was discovered, the two blacksmiths were imprisoned for eight days on a diet of bread and water. After that, their sins were written upon their foreheads, and they were taken to be displayed in that condition in the marketplace. Over the next three Sundays, Litster and Shaw were brought to their local kirk to perform public penance in front of the congregation. The next stage of their punishment was to be taken to the nearest river, into which they were repeatedly "ducked."* Lastly, the couple were brought to Castle Hill, in sight of Edinburgh Castle, where they were "bound to a stake and fire kindled about them where their bodies were burned to ashes to the death."[49]

For a variety of reasons, this level of punishment proved difficult to sustain. The first was that it required a complicity from the public that seems to have been lacking. Litster and Shaw were unlikely to be the only two men having sex with each other in Scotland in 1570. They were, however, the only two who paid for it by burning on Castle Hill. The couple's affair was perhaps obvious enough to be noticed by the Kirk; far more likely, someone who knew them betrayed their secret. It may have been that Litster and Shaw's master, Robert Hannay, or somebody else who worked in his household, was deeply devout and, on discovering what the two men were doing, reported it to the Kirk. Either that, or they hated the couple and wished to see them suffer. This level of cooperation does not seem to have been widely replicated across Scottish society; the situation was similar in England, where there were fewer than a dozen executions for homosexual activity between 1533 and 1660.[50] The same attitude was mirrored in the emerging English, then British, colonies overseas, where, even in those which chose to specifically reaffirm the death penalty for buggery, executions for it were rare.[51]

A second reason for a relative lack of executions following the burning of Litster and Shaw was that it was hard to justify applying one of Leviticus's teachings while ignoring the others. The same chapter of the Bible used to condemn men to death for same-sex intercourse mandates the death penalty for both parties who commit adultery, but only public shunning for siblings who committed incest.[52] Unpopular fines were levied by the Kirk on parishioners found guilty of fornication or adultery, but these fell far short of the penalties mandated in Leviticus.[53] Similarly, despite the requirements of Leviticus, executions were not handed down in sixteenth-

* Full bodily immersion beneath the water.

century Scotland to those who cursed their parents, trained as fortune tellers, or had sex during a woman's menstrual cycle.

Despite his Presbyterian faith, James's last regent, Lord Morton, ensured that the Kirk never won the right to override the kingdom's laws based on their interpretation of Scripture. His purpose was to ensure the Kirk did not become the government in all but name—he did not do it to save more men like Litster and Shaw. However, such was an unintended consequence of Morton's opposition to the political idea of "the Two Kingdoms," promoted by some in the Kirk. "The Two Kingdoms" was their ideal society in which the Kirk was completely independent from the government, which would not itself be independent from the Kirk.

Another problem facing anti-sodomy initiatives in the early modern British Isles was ambiguity about what sodomy entailed. It has already been mentioned that sodomy had a multiplicity of moral meanings, and this confusion extended into its legal definitions.[54] Many of James's contemporaries believed that sodomy covered any form of sexual act through which there was no possibility of a pregnancy and that buggery—the contemporary legal term used for both consensual and forced sex between men, as well as anal intercourse between opposite-sex partners—was merely one kind of sodomy. In England, the judge and future Lord Chief Justice Sir Edward Coke went further in his opinion that the Buggery Act of 1533 applied only in cases of full anal sex, by which he meant penetration and ejaculation by at least one partner.[55] Otherwise, in Coke's opinion, it did not count, and the mandated death sentence need not therefore be applied. This left a wide number of alternative forms of sexual contact between two men that were not illegal, even if they were widely regarded as immoral. There is some evidence to suggest that early modern male couples who practiced mutual masturbation or interfemoral intercourse did not consider their activities to be sodomitical.[56]

Here too, however, there was inconsistency in definition and reaction. One's fate very much depended on the attitude of the local authorities, which differed even between countries that shared the same religion. When it came to other expressions of male sexuality, any form of masturbation was illegal in sixteenth-century Portugal—there are no recorded cases of prosecutions. In the Republic of Venice, mutual masturbation was illegal, yet solo masturbation, which included cases in which more than one man masturbated in the same room without touching the other participants, was legal. In 1579, two seventeen-year-old Spanish males were publicly burned to death in their native city of Seville after confessing to mutual masturbation when they shared a bed.[57]

Private uncertainty was mirrored in public discourse. Sodomy was invoked in some sermons as a great evil, but many of the clergy hesitated to specify what they meant by these "things fearful to name," lest it encourage lustful thoughts in their congregation or because the term itself had so many applications. When invoked in the political sphere, sodomy could often be a blanket term for inappropriate or depraved behavior.[58] Depending on whom you listened to in James's lifetime, you could believe that denunciations against sodomy dealt with bestiality, blasphemy, corruption, cruelty to refugees, foreplay, homosexuality, masturbation, pedophilia, rape, tyranny, or a violation of hospitality.[59] James himself never seems to have considered what he was doing as sodomy, which according to him was "a sin which ye are bound in conscience never to forgive."[60] This has been cited as an example of his hypocrisy, which is more than possible, or as an indicator that James subscribed to a different definition of sodomy, or that the intercourse James had with other men was limited to the forms of intimacy that stopped short of anal sex.[61]

Acting against the fear of sodomy, albeit often feebly, were mutating ideas toward same-sex intimacy across western Europe. As the mockery of Henri III and his *mignons* in France showed, it provoked teasing and disrespect, not all of it distinct from loathing. Some of it, however, was simply ribald. When King Henri walked in a religious procession, flagellating his back and followed by his *mignons*, a Parisian quipped that they might prefer the whip a little lower, on their buttocks. During the Renaissance, it became far more common for European authors to explore the limits of what they could get away with in their writings on homoeroticism. There was a wide spectrum of moral responses to same-sex intimacy. In 1581, one of George Buchanan's former students, Michel de Montaigne, was visiting Rome.

He recorded an incident in which eleven men were burned and sixteen escaped out of a group of twenty-seven Spanish and Portuguese sailors, who were identified for having snuck in after-hours to the Church of San Giovanni a Porta Latina.[62] Montaigne wrote that, having broken into the church, the group conducted weddings for various male couples in their ranks: "They married one another, male to male, at Mass, with the same ceremonies with which we perform our marriages."[63] While the authorities cracked down with arrests and the stake, Montaigne recorded that some in Rome thought, or joked, that since the men had undergone a religious wedding service and then consummated it, it should stand as legally valid. "The Roman wits," he wrote, "said that because in the other conjunction, of male and female, this circumstance of marriage alone makes it legitimate, it had seemed to these sharp folk that this other action should become equally legitimate if they authorised it with [the] ceremonies and mysteries of the Church."[64]

There is no reasonable doubt that many of those who knew James VI believed that he had male lovers, a suspicion that was subsequently widespread in public opinion. Their reactions to James's private life mirrored society's heterogenous attitudes to homosexual intimacy. Some were disgusted. A few pretended they did not notice. Others tolerated it in the way they had kings' mistresses in the past, and some objected only if the lover moved from the bedroom to the council chamber. However, unlike the blacksmiths in Edinburgh, the Spanish teenagers, or the eleven sailors in Rome, James's life was never at risk because of his sexuality. His social position insulated him from those dangers, even as it exposed him to others, such as the perennial threat of kidnapping that had haunted his teenage years. It could even credibly be argued that James's gender allowed him to behave in ways that would never have been permissible to a female monarch, especially a heterosexual one. His mother had fatefully lost support through the public's reaction to an alleged extramarital liaison, which may not have been consensual. Had Elizabeth I or any of the other great female heads of state in sixteenth-century Europe behaved with a man in the way James did with Patrick Gray, Huntly, or Sandy Lindsay, they may have been deposed. Their regime certainly would have been less secure.

James's sexuality nonetheless created difficulties for him, and his inability, or refusal, to sublimate his feelings would eventually damage his reputation, particularly when his love affairs became more political or more publicly known than his romance with Sandy. That, however, was some time off. With Sandy spending his days at his side and nights in his bedchamber, 1588 was a happy time in James's private life, even if it was a more checkered period for him politically.

He received an encouraging tribute to how popular he had become with the people when they rallied behind him after he was criticized in a sermon. James had gone to church with a local laird who was hosting him around Christmastime in 1587, and the preacher, worrying that James's behavior would encourage the people to slide back into reviving the old festivities associated with "this idolatrous day," rebuked the King for a visit that would inspire "the people [to] follow the same." James was offended for himself and embarrassed for his host. When the sermon was finished James "very coldly said to the minister, 'I am very sorry that ye reproved this gentleman for my coming to his house. Ye take the matter wrong to judge me either to favour any papistry or raise superstition.' " When news of the sermon circulated in Edinburgh, James was vocally defended by many of his subjects. According to an English spy in the city, "many that are good Protestants" were "very angry with the ministry that they should meddle with his majesty with so sharp reproofs in open audience, he being so well inclined to religion as any prince in Europe."

With regard to his relations with the aristocracy, James was enjoying similar success. Personally he considered many of his nobles to be "feckless [and] arrogant," but he was pragmatic and socially conservative when it came to their role, accepting that they were the bedrock upon which Scottish society was built.[65] He continued with his policy of preventing destabilizing new quarrels between the great houses and reconciling the old ones, and thereby won admiring praise from King Henri III of France, whose reign was beleaguered by sectarian civil war on one hand and overmighty aristocratic families on the other.[66] The Scottish economy was recovering, but with neither sufficient speed nor consistency to justify ending the debasement of the coinage. More tensions arose with the Kirk over the issue of bishoprics, the abolition of which the Kirk desired and James prevented.

In foreign affairs, the alliance between Scotland and England was put under further strain by the threat of England's invasion by Spain. There had been tensions between the latter two countries for some time over trade, religion, colonialism, and espionage. Both had interfered with the other's politics. Philip II of Spain funded Catholic plots in England and Ireland; Elizabeth did the same for anti-Spanish Protestants in the Netherlands. Thus far, Protestant Scotland had maintained cold yet polite diplomatic relations with Catholic Spain, which might collapse due to the mutual defense clauses in the Treaty of Berwick. The execution of James's mother had inflamed anti-English sentiment in most Catholic countries, where Mary was regarded as a martyr. Her death inspired some beautiful poetry, including a lament by the Jesuit priest and future Catholic saint Father Robert Southwell:

> . . . It is not death to me but to my woe;
> The bud was opened to let out the rose,
> The chain was loosed to let the captive go.[67]

In the initial aftermath of the execution, some feared that an attack on England might come from France, but Elizabeth's chief minister had predicted correctly that Henri III was too distracted by his own civil war to risk one against England. Instead, Mary's tragedy provided Philip II with an excuse to justify an invasion, its goal being to overthrow Elizabeth and replace her with a Habsburg.

Most assumed that the candidate would be Philip himself. He was descended from two English medieval princesses—on his father's side, from King Edward III's granddaughter Catherine of Lancaster, Queen of Castile, and, on his mother's side, from her sister Philippa of Lancaster, Queen of Portugal. This was a tenuous connection—it made him the five-times-great-grandson of an English king. Through his English great-grandmother, James had a far stronger claim than Philip. The latter dealt with this complication by revealing that, shortly before her death, Mary had disinherited

James. If her son remained a Protestant at the time of her death, Mary wished for her claim to the English crown to devolve instead to Philip.[68]

Philip explained this in a letter to his ambassador to the Vatican:

> My claim, as you are aware, rests upon my descent from the House of Lancaster, and upon the Will made by the Queen of Scotland . . . I cannot undertake a war in England for the purpose merely of placing upon that throne a young heretic like the King of Scotland, who, indeed, is by his heresy incapacitated to succeed. His Holiness must, however, be assured that I have no intention of adding England to my own domains, but to settle the crown upon my daughter.[69]

To prevent accusations that he was exploiting Mary's execution in order to conquer England and Wales for himself, Philip passed his claim to his eldest daughter, Isabella-Clara-Eugenia, who had been born in the same year as James and who, like him, was admired for her intelligence.[70]

Philip's Spanish Armada sailed against England in July 1588. If they had landed, it would have placed James under great pressure to honor the Treaty of Berwick by sending military assistance to England, which he claimed he was prepared to do.[71] Some wondered if he would be quite so enthusiastic when it came time to translate words into action. In the end, that was not necessary after a storm blew the Armada off course and left its stragglers easy prey for the English navy. For centuries, patriotic British histories celebrated the navy's bravery and brilliance in defeating the Spanish Armada. More recently, the revisionist pendulum has swung in the opposite direction, to the extent that the English victory is attributed solely to the weather. The truth lies somewhere in the middle. The Armada was a formidable force, yet so too was Elizabeth's fleet, which, with just over two hundred vessels, outnumbered Spain's 117. The English used to great effect unusual strategies such as fire ships: in a predawn attack, they set fire to some of their older craft and guided them toward the at-anchor Armada. The gale also played a huge role, as Elizabeth's government acknowledged with celebratory medals bearing the inscription *Flavit Deus et Dissipati Sunt* ("God blew his winds and they were scattered"), in which the tempests were depicted as God speaking His will through nature.

James shared this conviction that the weather was an expression of God's wrath. He wrote a sonnet on how the Spanish fleet "forward came in monstrous array" until:

> the winds began to toss them here and there
> The seas began in foaming waves to swell:
> The number that escap'd, it fell them fair:
> The rest were swallowed up in gulfs of hell.[72]

Parts of the scattered Armada fled past the eastern English coastline and then north. Elizabeth wrote to James to inform him that "the winds have carried them to your coasts."[73]

Despite his alliance with England and his relief that the Armada had failed, James treated humanely any of its survivors who sought refuge in Scotland. In October, after their ships were wrecked in Scottish waters, forty-six survivors "in a most miserable state" were brought to Edinburgh, where James allowed them to rest, provided them with clothes, food for "their hungry bellies," and passports to board Scottish merchant ships trading with Europe "that they might safely pass to their native countries."[74] The most prominent survivors to receive James's aid were invited to spend winter at court as his guests, including Juan Gómez de Medina, nephew of the Armada's commander. Medina had captained the warship *El Gran Grifón,* until it was wrecked in a storm as it passed the Shetland Islands. When the weather improved, Medina and his men were given all requisite assistance to return unharmed to Spain.

In total, it is estimated that about four hundred Armada survivors were saved by James's policy toward them.[75] Unfortunately, it soon became clear that Huntly's response to the Armada had been even more friendly.[76]

7

TO BE YOUR FELLOW, YOU MAY DENY ME

O loyal soul, is this the Fates' decree?
May I not have your presence as before?
—Sir Robert Ayton, "Queen Diophantus Knew"
(late sixteenth century)

In the months after the Armada's failure, Huntly seemed to distance himself from the Catholic cause by announcing his intention to convert to Presbyterianism. James was delighted, and Huntly's prominence at court looked set to increase when he became captain of the King's guard. James had initially wanted to transfer the post to Sandy.[1] This was taken as an insult by the incumbent captain, Thomas Lyon. The Lyons' and Lindsays' dislike of one another was so long-standing that there were tales of a previous earl of Crawford selling his soul to Satan rather than face the prospect of losing to a Lyon. The most recent casualty of their feud had been Thomas Lyon's brother, who had been killed in a brawl with Sandy's brother Lord Crawford.*[2]

With Sandy "in so great favour with His Majesty," James ignored Lyon's objections and transferred the captaincy to him.[3] For Sandy, it was a rare foray into palace intrigue. James's decision had annoyed not only the Lyons but every family allied with, or loyal to, them. It made Sandy a target for the discontented, whose retribution was likely to be far more brutal than the earlier punch-ups

* Lyon's brother was the 8th Lord Glamis, whose murder at Stirling was mentioned in Chapter 3. Lord Crawford had since been acquitted of manslaughter on questionable grounds and released.

between him and Thomas Lyon. Realizing his mistake, James proffered a compromise whereby Sandy would voluntarily relinquish the captaincy to Huntly.[4] The proposal was accepted by Thomas Lyon and his allies who, while not exactly enamored of Huntly, would have preferred almost anyone to take the post, rather than a Lindsay. Sandy accepted the compromise to restore peace to palace life. It also pacified Clan Lindsay, because at least the captaincy was going to their friend Huntly rather than back to their enemy. Huntly's famous skills in combat had the additional benefit of preventing his appointment being interpreted as a poor reflection on Sandy. Nobody doubted that Huntly was physically capable of the job, even if many in the royal household found him insufferable.[5]

For a few months after his appointment in November 1588, Huntly's position as captain seemed secure. Rumors then began to percolate about his views on the Spanish Armada. In February 1589, the English ambassador passed on to James information gathered by their spies, which proved that Huntly had been in secret correspondence with the Spanish government for most of the previous year. In the event of a successful Spanish invasion of the British Isles, Huntly had promised his support. He had even urged Philip II to consider using Scotland as a launching pad for any future attacks on England. Huntly's lands included deep-water ports, which made his sympathy for the Armada doubly concerning. Two other Catholic nobles had added their name to this letter, and James was convinced there must be others. It seemed that Huntly's conversion to Presbyterianism had been a sham, perhaps embarked upon to preemptively secure more favor with James when Huntly suspected his communications with Spain were about to see the light of day.

Evidently fully recovered from her self-loathing malaise after Mary's execution, Elizabeth I was apoplectic.* She made clear to James in her letters that she wanted Huntly punished, a position

---

* Having previously warned James to avoid a friendship with Huntly, Elizabeth also allowed herself to enjoy the pleasure of being proved right. She told James that Huntly's behavior was "the true portraiture of my late warning," a polite yet unambiguous told-you-so.

seconded by James's chancellor, Maitland, who threatened to resign from government if firm steps were not taken against Huntly. There was no love lost between Huntly and the chancellor. Huntly, like many nobles, resented the common-born Maitland's political prominence, which they claimed he used to undermine any noble who might rival him in government. For his part, Maitland had never liked Huntly, despaired of James's fondness for him and insisted that Huntly had betrayed Scotland in his correspondence with Spain.

The question of whether Huntly had committed treason was vexed. The Armada had threatened England, not Scotland. However, both the Treaty of Berwick and Philip II's views on how James was "by his heresy incapacitated" to succeed to the English throne meant that it was at best naïve to believe that the Armada's impact would have been confined to England and Wales.

Huntly was detained for ten days at Edinburgh Castle, from where he begged for an audience with the King to justify himself in person. James replied by letter that Huntly's actions had hurt him as both a man and a monarch: "What, then, is the remedy of all this? Nothing but this: as ye have offended two persons in me, a particular* friend and a general Christian king, so must ye make amends to both."[6] Rehabilitation with James the King was possible only if Huntly promised that he would "conceal nothing" in identifying any fellow plotters.[7] When it came to reconciliation with James the man, there was an odd phrase in the letter. The subsequent interpretation of it as sexual in its subtext is plausible, yet not definitive. James seems to be referencing some form of mutual satisfaction when next they meet. The two relevant sentences are: "As for my satisfaction as a particular man, willingly (without irking) to be content with whatsoever form I shall please to use you in. To remit fully to my discretion for your contentment in all things."[8]

Although James drew a clear distinction elsewhere in the letter between himself as a man and as a king, it has been suggested that "satisfaction" may have political undertones, by implying an acceptable resolution to a problem.[9] This therefore may have been

* Close, intimate, special.

James writing as a monarch who was reminding a subject that his best hope for happiness lay in obedience. It could also have been synthesizing the kingly role with friendship by asking Huntly to obey James's government, because this would bring both men more contentment in the future.

James summoned Huntly to his apartments at Edinburgh Castle, and there, according to an astonished Thomas Fowler, "kissed him many times to the amazement of many."[10] Kissing could be a sign of social respect or friendship, in the way it is in some circles today. Repeatedly kissing a man detained on suspicion of treason was a tad more unusual, as was James's invitation for Huntly to join him for dinner, then to visit him every day during his imprisonment, before finally, on March 7, inviting him to sleep in his bedchamber.[11] Huntly accepted, the unquantifiable enigmas of affection or attraction exerted their influence, and James announced to an incredulous Maitland that he was now convinced that Huntly was innocent.[12]

Huntly overplayed his hand when he clumsily attempted a counterstrike by urging James to dismiss Maitland as chancellor. James refused and Huntly retreated to the Highlands in a magisterial strop. Despite his upset at Huntly's departure, James still would not dismiss his chancellor. Huntly rallied his men in the north, where he was joined by, among others, Sandy's brother Lord Crawford, who shared Huntly's animus toward Maitland. They captured Thomas Lyon, humiliating him by parading him as their prisoner past his family's castle at Glamis, which James considered appalling behavior on their part.[13] As their combined forces moved south through eastern Scotland, Huntly wrote to James to insist that their actions were not a rebellion against him, but rather a plea from his devoted subjects to separate him from a corrupt adviser. James had heard that excuse before from others. His unhappiness deepened and in his response to Huntly, he forlornly asked, "What further trust can I have in your promises?"[14]

Despite his brother's presence at Huntly's side, Sandy remained loyal to James, whom he accompanied as they marched on Aberdeen with an army to face Huntly's. On the evening before they were due to intercept Huntly's forces, James walked through the camp to talk with his men; as one of them recalled, "His Majesty would not so much as lie down on his bed that night but went about like a good captain encouraging us."[15] At the eleventh hour, Huntly had a change of heart before the two armies clashed at Brig o' Dee, the bridge crossing the River Dee near Aberdeen. Huntly surrendered, as did his aristocratic allies, including Crawford, all of whom were pardoned in return for surrender. Huntly was detained at a royal castle until autumn, after which he reunited with his wife. They devoted themselves to a series of ambitious architectural projects, including the building of three manor houses and a new hunting lodge, and commissioning maintenance on two of their existing castles. At court, the captaincy of James's guard was returned to Thomas Lyon, and Sandy settled back into his apolitical role as the "King's best beloved minion."[16] Courtiers observed that James and Sandy remained inseparable, but James's foot-dragging over his marriage caught the public's attention.[17]

There was a revival of sermons criticizing the King, which James insisted were a consequence not of his own behavior but of crypto-republicanism within the Kirk. "I was oftentimes calumniated in their popular sermons," he would recall, "not for any evil or vice in me, but because I was a King, which they thought the highest evil."[18] While there was truth in his conclusion, it was not the whole truth. It had been eight years since discussions first took place about a wedding between James and Catherine of Bourbon. What Esmé had pushed, Patrick had stalled, and James was, by his own admission, quite content to let the situation lag.[19]

James retreated to the countryside for two weeks, where he daily prayed for guidance from God on what to do about his marriage.[20] He knew that he must one day take a wife, an inevitable dénouement that loomed over his time with Sandy. When pressed, James stipulated that he would not marry a Scotswoman. He contended that it was beneath the dignity of a monarch to wed a subject. This may have been an intentional insult to both his mother and the English royal family, among whom marrying a subject rather than a foreign princess had become the rule rather than the exception over the past century.[21] The Kirk added their criterion that Catholics should be excluded. Between James and the Kirk, the two principal candidates were a princess of Denmark and Catherine of Bourbon.

Of the two, the former was the more popular in Scotland. It was hoped that such a marriage would resolve historical tensions between the two monarchies over the sovereignty of the Orkney and Shetland Islands, which had been annexed by King James III of Scots in the previous century. Norway and Denmark, both of which were ruled by the same king, had strong trading links with Scotland.[22] A possible outcome of the royal marriage was that Scottish merchants would be granted favorable concessions by the Danish government. In May, there were protests in Edinburgh in support of the Danish match and against James marrying Catherine of Bourbon.[23]

Events in France combined with those in Scotland to euthanize the possibility of a marriage with Catherine. In August 1589, King Henri III was assassinated and his death brought Catherine's brother to the French throne as Henri IV. To secure the loyalty of the majority, he converted to Catholicism but, to end the persecution of the Protestant minority to which he had once belonged, he introduced religious toleration in France.[24] The country's generation-long cycle of sectarian civil wars, which had snuffed out an estimated three million lives, stuttered to its exhausted end.[25] His accession also meant that Navarre and France were ruled by the same monarch. Princess Catherine served as her brother's regent in Navarre, and his political reliance on her grew as he attempted to secure his new throne while ending the Wars of Religion. Although there were further discussions of Catherine's marriage to James, they faded as James listened more to councillors urging a younger bride and at the same time Catherine's importance in France increased. She remained one of her brother's most capable and influential advisers until her death in 1604.

As he contemplated his marriage, James was determined to maintain peace within his aristocracy, rather than lose control of it, as Henri III had done in France. The tensions between the great landowning families, and even the minor ones, had repeatedly proved their capacity for menace. Ambitiously but sensibly, James hoped to bury the feud between the Lindsays and the Lyons with a wedding. He proposed a marriage between Sandy and Thomas Lyon's recently widowed niece Jean Lyon, Dowager Countess of Angus.

James wrote to Jean directly, in more ways than one, to inform her of the good news that he hoped she would marry Sandy, "whom I have out of my own bed been willing to bestow upon yours."[26]

In one of the less surprising developments in James's reign, Jean Lyon was not exactly head over heels at this proposal by proxy. James had to write several times pushing the suit for Sandy; he felt Jean should appreciate acquiring a husband "whose affection, and whose credit with me" were so high.[27] James was determined that Sandy, as a younger son with no inheritance of his own, would be well provided for. "I am resolute to advance this man of mine," he wrote in another letter to Jean.[28] An advantageous marriage that bought peace between two of the kingdom's great families would also keep Sandy safe in the future from the one serious source of opposition he had faced in his career: the Lyons themselves. To judge from their later correspondence, James seems to have broached the subject with Sandy, along with his plan to ennoble him in his own right, but Sandy demurred or hesitated.[29]

Meanwhile, James's negotiations to marry Princess Elisabeth of Denmark had encountered their own difficulties. The Princess's father, King Frederik II, suggested that James consider Elisabeth's younger sister Anna. James and his advisers felt it was more in keeping with a king's status to marry the eldest daughter. Discussions were ongoing when Frederik II died. One of his last decisions had been to negotiate Elisabeth's marriage to a German nobleman, Heinrich Julius von Welf, Duke of Brunswick-Lüneburg and heir to the principality of Brunswick-Wolfenbüttel. Heinrich Julius was not a king; nonetheless, he controlled important territory near Denmark, which made it an excellent match from the Danish perspective. Following Frederik's death, neither his widow, his son, nor the Danish government wished to violate his wishes concerning Elisabeth's future.[30]

Edinburgh accepted that Princess Anna would be the next queen of Scots.[31] On the issue of Anna's dowry, Denmark agreed to accept the existing reality of Scottish sovereignty over the Orkney and Shetland Islands. Scotland's merchants received their hoped-for trading concessions for Norway and Denmark, which was then one of the economic powerhouses of Europe. James entered with a request for a cash dowry payment of one million Scottish pounds. This was absurdly or tactically high, perhaps both, and his future mother-in-law negotiated him down to one hundred and fifty thousand pounds. James indulged in some well-timed amnesia and cheerful snobbery, by glibly proclaiming that he had no intention of haggling like a merchant for his bride. One hundred and fifty thousand pounds was acceptable.

On August 20, 1589, James's marriage was celebrated at the Kronborg, a Danish palace that had the largest reception room in northern Europe. James was not present. It was a proxy service, with a Scottish nobleman standing in for his king. James's choice for his proxy was Lord Marischal, whose embonpoint won him the somewhat tactless endearment from James of "my little fat pork."[32] A necessary precaution for transnational upper-class brides, proxy services had arisen in the Middle Ages, when they were introduced to counter the risk of kidnapping as a princess traveled from her homeland to her husband's. If she was unmarried, she might be sexually assaulted and forced into marriage by a rival lord or imprisoned to prevent a diplomatically inconvenient marriage. With the marriage solemnized, albeit not yet consummated, it rendered attempts to kidnap the bride redundant. There was usually a second, in-person wedding ceremony when the princess arrived at her husband's court.

After the proxy ceremony at the Kronborg, there was a ball, the sumptuousness of which dazzled the guests. Two weeks later, with a trousseau and wardrobe so lavish it had employed three hundred tailors, Anna—now legally Queen of Scots—bid a tearful farewell to her family and set sail for Scotland.[33]

While he waited for her, James spent two weeks in September as a guest of Lord and Lady Seton at Seton Palace. Regarded by contemporaries as one of the most beautiful private homes in Scotland, it had wonderful, clear views over the sea approaching Leith harbor, where Anna was expected to disembark. Lord Seton, a former Scottish ambassador to France, had been devoted to James's mother, who had spent her honeymoon with Darnley at Seton Palace. Lady Seton accepted James's invitation to join Anna's household as a lady-in-waiting. The emerging Queen's Household was already down a senior member when, that same month, Lady Janet Kennedy, who had been appointed First Lady of the Queen's Chamber, drowned with dozens of other passengers in a storm that sank a ferry crossing the Firth of Forth from Edinburgh. The same terrible weather that claimed Lady Kennedy's life delayed Anna's arrival. A Scottish councillor, who had been in Denmark negotiating the King's marriage, made it home safely and informed James that the larger ships, including the one carrying the Queen, had been forced to turn back by adverse winds.[34]

James left Seton Palace to go hunting from Craigmillar Castle, the fifteenth-century country residence of the aristocratic Preston family on the outskirts of Edinburgh. The winds remained strong and the weather was poor, which marred his sport.[35] A Danish diplomat arrived with news that Anna's flotilla had been engulfed in a storm so severe that "the said Queen was in extreme danger of drowning; in her own ship, a cannon brake and slew eight men afore* her, and shook the ship that hardly could keep her above water, but with extreme labour; and being ten huge ships, they were all bruised and weather-beaten."[36] Peder Munk of Estvadgård, traveling to Scotland as the admiral in command of Anna's flotilla, claimed that in all his years at sea he had never seen worse storms.[37] Three times, the Queen's ships had tried to reach shore safely. Eventually, some turned back to Denmark and a few of their fleet-mates, including the vessel in which Anna was a passenger, had limped east to the safety of a Norwegian harbor. Anna and her traumatized attendants had been put ashore, where they were taken south to Oslo to stay as guests of the governor. Anna wrote to James to tell him that "now winter is hastening down on us," she must "make no further attempt at present, but to defer the voyage until the spring."[38]

James decided that he would bring Anna to Scotland.[39] Rebuffing advice from his chancellor, Maitland, and Esmé's son Ludovic, Duke of Lennox, both of whom begged him not to put his life at risk with an autumn voyage, he also rejected Maitland's offer to go instead, although he briefly considered sending Lord Bothwell in his capacity

* In front of.

as Lord High Admiral, before returning to his original intent to go in person. He carefully balanced the council between different factions to prevent unrest in his absence and issued a proclamation to explain to the public why he was sailing to Norway to retrieve "the Queen my bedfellow."[40] He obliquely acknowledged that this was his wish, rather than his councillors', when he explained that "the place where I resolved this was Craigmillar, not one of the whole Council being present there. And as I take this resolution only of myself, as I am a true Prince, so advised with myself only."

Elsewhere in his proclamation, James admitted that he had been stung by public speculation over his apparent lack of interest in marriage:

> I doubt not that it is manifestly known to all, how far I was generally found fault with by all men for delaying so long of my marriage . . . [This] made me to be weak and my enemies strong . . . These reasons, and immeasurable others hourly objected, moved me to hasten the treaty of my marriage; for as to my own nature, God is my witness how I could have abstained longer.[41]

He ended with an order for peace and obedience in his absence:

> [let] no man grudge or murmur at these my proceedings, but let every man lead a peaceable and quiet life without offending . . . whomsoever contraries my directions in my absence I will it think a sufficient proof that he bears no love towards me in my heart; and by the contrary, these will I only have respect to at my return that reverences my commandment and will in my absence. Farewell, James Rex.*[42]

He set sail with an entourage of about three hundred people from the port of Leith on October 22. Sandy joined him on board the

* "James the King." James would often sign his private letters more informally as "J.R." Queens signed with their name, also followed by *R* for *Regina*, "the Queen."

largest of their five ships, which had names such as the *James Royal* and *Falcon of Leith*. Knowing of the resentment that the chancellor had inspired in some of the nobles, James wisely ordered Maitland to accompany him. It would keep Maitland safe from any enemy who, on the assumption that it was better to ask for forgiveness than permission, might be tempted to take advantage of James's departure by ridding themselves of the chancellor. Not all the guests invited by James accepted. His grandmother's executor Thomas Fowler declined swiftly with the regret that his poor health did not permit him to "venture to sea in this cold time of year."[43] This may have been true. The speed with which he proffered his regrets nonetheless suggests that Fowler was not too distressed to miss the journey.

For four days as they crossed the North Sea, James's fleet enjoyed a breeze in their favor and clear skies. The calls of the cattle and fowl brought to provide fresh milk, eggs, and meat mixed with the groaning of the timber, the conversation of James's retinue, the bark of a few of the hunting dogs he had brought with him, and the flap of the sails. On the fifth day, all were sublimated to the sounds of the storm that pummeled the Scottish ships for the last day and a half of the voyage, which ended when they passed between the tree-covered hills of Flekkefjord in southwest Norway.

James disembarked and spent the night in a local farmhouse. He was soon greeted by dignitaries, who arranged his onward journey to the nearest city, Tønsberg. Founded by a Norwegian king in the ninth century, Tønsberg was the country's oldest city, with a busy harbor in the summer months. Accommodation was found for his men in the city, while James was welcomed, with his favorite attendants, to the home of alderman Jørgen Lauritsen, the mayor's brother, where they rested for six days.[44]

On his Sunday in Tønsberg, James attended religious service at St. Mary's Church, where his chaplain, who had accompanied him from Scotland, was invited to preach a two-hour sermon.[45] Early on the Monday morning, James, Sandy, and their entourage set off east from Tønsberg for Oslo.[46] They traveled slowly, battered by snow, ice, and wind as the temperature plummeted and Norway faced one of its harshest winters in living memory. They reached the capital on November 19, one month after they had set sail from Leith and three weeks since they had landed in Flekkefjord.

Oslo, which from 1624 to 1925 was renamed Christiania in honor of Anna's brother King Christian, was a small city with several impressive castles. One was the impregnable Akershus, the official residence of the Stattholder of Norway, who ruled as governor during the King's absences in Denmark; another, the Old Bishop's Palace, where Anna was staying, had been secularized during the Reformation when it was converted into a home for the mayor. The Danish retinue accompanying the princess had already taken up most of the accommodation in Oslo's castles and inns. When he arrived, James was hurriedly provided with rooms at the local Shoemakers' Guild. He was so impatient to meet his bride that he set off for the Old Bishop's Palace, still—according to one courtier—wearing his riding boots, but otherwise elegantly dressed in red velvet with gold details and a sable-lined black velvet cloak.[47]

Shown into Anna's rooms, he tried to kiss her, which was customary in Scotland.[48] She recoiled and explained that this was not the custom in Denmark.[49] The kiss of an impetuous husband was a recurring etiquette minefield when it came to royal spouses' first meetings. At least James had not come in disguise, as had two kings of England, Henry VI and Henry VIII, whose brides understandably not only refused to kiss them but were horrified when somebody masquerading as a messenger launched themselves at them.[50] The issue of the first kiss was complicated by the fact that, thanks to the proxy wedding service, the couple were legally husband and wife, yet Anna of Denmark was correct when she reminded James that Danish ladies did not kiss men they did not know. After a brief discussion and the citation of the proxy wedding, there was a polite kiss between the couple, followed by conversation in French, their mutual language.

James spent the night at the Shoemakers' Guild. The next morning, he returned to the palace for breakfast with Anna. Three days later, on November 23, dressed in a blue velvet suit and accompanied by six pages dressed in red velvet with sable-lined cloaks, James went in procession to the palace's Great Hall, where he was joined by Anna and her retinue for their second wedding ceremony.

The service between James, who was twenty-three, and fourteen-year-old Anna, was conducted in French by James's chaplain and followed by a feast, at which James and Anna were hosted by Axel Gyldenstierne, her brother's governor in Norway.

"It is hard for men in drink, at which they are continually kept, long to agree," explained one of the guests, after James had to intervene to calm a quarrel between Chancellor Maitland and "my little fat pork" Lord Marischal. Having served as James's proxy at the wedding in Denmark, Marischal felt that he should take precedence over the chancellor at the wedding banquet.[51] Maitland was inclined to disagree and, in his cups, disinclined to do so quietly.

The weather put paid to James's hope of a swift return to Scotland. A November voyage in the North Sea was ill-advised under the best of circumstances. It was impossible given the weather in 1589. Even the fjords had frozen, and so James and Anna stayed in Oslo, which, as Anna had suspected when she first arrived there, could not be accessed by sea until spring. An invitation arrived from James's mother-in-law, the Dowager Queen Sophia, for him to bring Anna home for the winter and meet her family. Sandy announced that he was too ill to accompany them any further and asked for permission to recuperate in Oslo, which James granted.[52] He and Anna left Oslo by sledge on December 22, usually lodging at the homes of local clergy en route. They spent Christmas at Båhus, a clifftop fourteenth-century fortress near what was then the border between Norway and Sweden. It was the first time that James could remember keeping Christmas with celebrations and present-giving. He made Anna a lifetime gift of his palace at Dunfermline, as well as the right to collect the rents generated by its sizeable estate.

When they entered Swedish territory, they were provided with a military escort of three hundred soldiers as a courtesy by King Johan III, who was occupied with a political dispute in Stockholm and sent his brother Prince Carl, Duke of Södermanland,* as his deputy to welcome the newlyweds.[53] A devout Protestant, Prince Carl was more popular than his brother with the Swedish people, including the clergy and nobility. Johan III had married a Polish

* Later King Carl IX of Sweden (r. 1604–11).

princess, Katarzyna Jagiellonka, and the complications that had arisen from his decision to allow her to raise their son as a Catholic had been one of the specific examples cited by the Kirk in Scotland when they urged James to marry a Protestant.[54]

In James and Anna's honor, Prince Carl threw an Old Year's Night banquet which culminated with a nocturnal display of cannon fire from the palace parapets. At the Øresund, the narrowest point between Sweden and Denmark,* the water—as it sometimes did—had frozen into a bridge of ice; once there was a lull in the blizzard, James and Anna crossed in horse-drawn sledges. Cannons roared in welcome as the Queen of Scots returned to Denmark. Her family were waiting for her at the Kronborg, their palace overlooking the Øresund, which James and Anna reached on January 21.

Anna of Denmark was the second child, and second daughter, of King Frederik II and his wife, Sophia of Mecklenburg-Güstrow. Born in December 1574 at Skanderborg Castle, a royal hunting lodge in eastern Denmark rebuilt at great cost in the Renaissance style on her father's orders, Anna had spent most of her infancy, along with her elder sister Elisabeth, in the care of their German grandparents, the Duke and Duchess of Mecklenburg-Güstrow. Anna stayed there until she was four and Elisabeth was six. The decision to send the princesses to live with their grandparents in Güstrow had been motivated by the children's best interests. Frederik II was constantly on the move at this stage in his reign. Until an heir was born, Queen Sophia felt her place was by his side and she wanted her daughters to be safe until they were old enough to travel more often.[55] The Duke and Duchess were affectionate grandparents and Anna adored them. There were frequent visits after 1579, when Anna and Elisabeth left their care and returned to Denmark on their father's orders.

She had five younger siblings—the princes Christian, Ulric, and Johan and the princesses Augusta and Hedwig. The youngest, Johan, was born when Anna was eight. Their mother, Queen

* Now the site of the five-mile Øresund Bridge, linking the two countries by rail and road.

Sophia—described by an English diplomat in Denmark as "a right virtuous and godly princess which with motherly care and great wisdom ruleth her children"—was more involved in her children's daily lives than were many other royal and noble mothers at the time, and was a formative influence on Anna's personality.[56] Anna shared Sophia's preoccupation with status, tenacity, devotion to family, and titanic ability to hold a grudge.

The Danish royal family were lovers of the arts, especially theater, with itinerant companies of actors often arriving at their palaces to entertain the court. Anna spoke German to her mother, Danish to her father, and she later became fluent in French. She idolized her larger-than-life father, who was popular with the Danish people, in part because of his personality and his role as a patron of the arts, education, and the sciences, but also because his economic policies had helped turn Denmark into one of the wealthiest countries in Europe. He had achieved this principally by increasing tolls on trading ships, the state income from which he tripled.[57] It is unclear how much young Anna knew about her father's frequent adulteries or his drinking.

She could not be shielded from the impact of her father's alcoholism when it was mentioned at Frederik's funeral in 1588 by an honest if tactless clergyman, who included in the eulogy his belief that "had the King drunk a little less, he might have lived."[58] Frederik had fallen ill with severe abdominal pains during a sailing trip and was rushed ashore; he died at Antvorskov Castle, when he was fifty-three and Anna was thirteen. Her brother succeeded as King Christian IV. Their mother, frustrated in her hopes of becoming Christian's regent when a council instead took power, channeled her energies into founding her own bank, through which she became one of the richest individuals in Europe.

Sophia encouraged James to allow Anna to continue to worship by the rites of the Lutheran denomination, even after she returned to Presbyterian Scotland. Following the start of the Protestant Reformation—usually dated to Martin Luther's protests at the German city of Wittenberg in 1517—Protestantism's emphasis on personal interpretation of Scripture rendered possible a plurality of conclusions as to its meanings. The result was many new denominations that differed not only from Catholicism but from previous iterations of Protestantism. The closer a denomination's origin was to 1517, the more likely it was to share similarities with Catholicism. This was especially obvious in the contrasts between Lutheranism, one of the first Protestant denominations to form after 1517, and Presbyterianism, which emerged several decades later. James promised that Anna could worship as a Lutheran in Scotland and that she could bring Lutheran chaplains with her to serve in her household.

Anna's late father had sunk a fortune into transforming the Kronborg, located in the northeastern Danish town of Helsingør, into one of the most magnificent palaces in Europe. Cocooned from blizzards in Kronborg's warmth and luxury, James was entertained with comedies and plays, which, since he could not speak Danish, were tactfully performed in French or Latin. There were feasts, balls, and a lot of drinking. Sir James Melville, whose hopes of a peaceful fireside middle age continued to be dashed by his service to the Stewarts, recorded how James enjoyed the plentiful liquor. Drinking was encouraged at the Danish court, where the royal family's physician lamented that it was seen as a sign of manliness.[59] Freed from censorious eyes, James had a marvelous time in Denmark and "drank stoutly."

He liked Anna's family. He saw the least of her youngest siblings—six-year-old Johan, eight-year-old Hedwig, and nine-year-old Augusta—who spent most of their time in the nursery. He was impressed with their brother Ulric, who turned eleven during James's visit, and liked to discuss religion with his Scottish brother-in-law. Ulric's interest was fortunate, given that his mother had already earmarked him for a vocation in the Church.

Along with attending the many parties arranged by the Dowager Queen Sophia and her household, James met some of the scholars who had benefited from King Frederik's patronage of academia. Sophia arranged for James to go to the island of Hveen, which her late husband had presented to the astronomer Tycho Brahe. Sophia was also a patron of Brahe's research, which he conducted from an underground observatory and an aboveground study constructed for him on his island. Like James, Brahe was unassailably convinced of his own genius. He greeted James and Anna wearing a metal nose strapped to his face in replacement of what he had lost in a duel with his cousin over who was the better mathematician. For James, the nose may have been of gold or silver, as those were reserved by Brahe for special occasions; brass was his everyday nasal wear. James found Brahe fascinating, as he told him in a note following his visit to the island: "I have learnt from your very agreeable and learned discourses, things which still occupy my mind to such a degree that it is difficult to say whether I recollect them with greater pleasure or admiration."[60] Among other topics, we know that they discussed Copernicus's theories of a heliocentric galaxy. As a thank-you, James made the lonely scholar a gift of two dogs for company. James was also invited to deliver a lecture in Latin to the Faculty of Theology at Copenhagen University and visited the Danish philosopher Niels Hemmingsen at his home in the city of Roskilde, where they debated Christian teachings on salvation.

The weather improved enough for James to go hawking. He preferred hunting with hounds, though he and twelve-year-old King Christian, also an enthusiastic hunter, were unable to do so until the snows melted.[61] Voyages to Scotland, though no longer impossible, remained ill-advised. One of James's attendants took messages back to his council in Edinburgh, including James's orders that they start preparing for Anna's coronation as queen consort.[62] He called Anna "my new rib," in a nod to the biblical story of how Eve, the first woman, was created from the rib of the first man, Adam.[63]

Sandy remained in Oslo, from where he seemed to be avoiding James's questions on how he could best be rewarded by his king. James decided that, along with arranging his marriage to Jean Lyon, he would make Sandy a noble in his own right with estates in the Highlands, near those of his eldest brother. He wrote to him from the Kronborg to inform him of his decision:

> Sandy,
>
> Till your good hap furnish me some better occasion to recompense your honest and faithful service, uttered by your diligent and careful attendance upon me, specially at this time, let this assure [you] in the inviolable word of your own prince and master that, when God renders me in Scotland, I

> shall irrevocably and with consent of Parliament erect you the temporality of Murray in a temporal lordship with all honours thereto pertaining. And let this serve for cure to your present disease.
>
> From the castle of Kronborg, where we are drinking and driving o'er* in the old manner.
>
> J.R.[64]

The Dowager Queen Sophia persuaded James to let Anna stay in Denmark for her sister's wedding at Easter. Elisabeth had been betrothed to Heinrich-Julius as her father had wished, but her dowry negotiations took even longer than had Anna's with Scotland. James stayed with Anna—"my Annie," as he affectionately nicknamed her—until shortly after the wedding. It too took place at "the stately castle" of Kronborg, as James dubbed it in a letter to one of his ambassadors.[65]

Where Anna resembled their mother, with her blue eyes and blond hair, brunette and dark-eyed Elisabeth was closer in appearance to their late father. The groom was already a widower, having lost his first wife in childbed. Two years James's senior, Heinrich-Julius was tall with red hair, a polyglot, a patron of the arts, autocratic, occasionally brusque, and clever. He and Elisabeth were married on April 19, 1590, and Anna's widowed grandfather, the Duke of Mecklenburg-Güstrow, made it to Kronborg for the ceremony. He had been kept away from Anna's nuptials by the weather and, if a duke could now travel safely, so could a king.

Two days after Elisabeth and Heinrich-Julius's wedding, Anna said a second farewell to her mother, siblings, and grandfather. With a retinue of two hundred Danish courtiers and servants, she and James boarded a convoy for Scotland. The King and Queen traveled on board the *Gideon*, a ship once again under the command of Admiral Peder Munk, who was determined that, this time, he would get Anna safely across the North Sea. Storms again nearly scuppered Munk's plans. The *Gideon* tossed in the swell over the nine days it took to reach its journey's end in Scotland.

---

* Killing time.

8

THE DAMNABLE LIFE AND DEATH OF A NOTABLE SORCERER

Thou shalt not suffer a witch to live.

—Exodus 22:18

Cannon fired from Leith and large crowds gathered when the fleet came into view through the unseasonable May mists. Once docked, the *Gideon* was boarded by representatives from the government, including fifteen-year-old Ludovic Stuart, Duke of Lennox, who had served as President of the Council during James's absence, and the Lord High Admiral, Lord Bothwell. Despite his support for him against Gowrie, James had never liked Bothwell. He resented the legacy of their mutual grandfather, James V, whose numerous illegitimate children had produced far too many grandchildren with royal blood in their veins. Their prominence proved a headache to James VI, and he was convinced that part of a good king's duty was to sire no bastards who might plague the lives or reigns of legitimate children. Of all his cousins from the illegitimate line, popular and ambitious Bothwell was the one James trusted the least. However, to James's chagrin, he was too powerful an aristocrat to ignore.

With Bothwell and Lennox heading the delegation, a representative from the Courts of Justice in Edinburgh delivered a welcome speech to Queen Anna. Along with Bothwell and Lennox, two of the people formally introduced to Anna at Leith were the Earl of Mar and his mother, James's former governess, who had already been appointed as one of Anna's ladies-in-waiting. There were still many vacancies in Anna's household; to prevent the Queen feeling overwhelmed on arrival, James had ordered other aristocrats not to come to Leith if their intention was to petition for a place in her service. The command was politely yet sedulously ignored, so while James dealt with the petitioning nobles, he allowed Anna to go ashore to a nearby government building to rest.[1] Later that day, James went to South Leith parish church, where a service of thanksgiving was offered for his safe return.

There had been no new queen consort in Scotland since the arrival of James's grandmother fifty-two years earlier, which explained both the intensity of aristocratic jockeying for a place in the household and the work that was necessary on several of the palaces. While James's rooms were comfortable, the English ambassador to Scotland did not consider any of the residences ready for a queen consort or her household. James agreed. After seeing the luxury in which Anna had been raised in Denmark, he was anxious about her quarters in Scotland, which were not ready when he and Anna reached Leith. James wrote to Sandy, who was still in Norway, confessing his fear of embarrassment for himself and Scotland if Anna's entourage judged her rooms at Holyroodhouse to be deficient, in which case "we be all shamed before strangers."[2] Finding the funds in the short term was proving difficult—Queen Sophia had ensured that part of her daughter's dowry had been legally ring-fenced to provide for her household wages, while much was draining away to meet the staggering cost of entertaining in style the large retinue who had accompanied Anna from Denmark, and more would be needed for her impending coronation. To ameliorate James's worries, Sandy discreetly loaned him the money to redecorate the Queen's apartments.

After five days in Leith, while the last-minute improvements were made to Holyroodhouse, James and Anna left for Edinburgh. James rode on horseback and, accompanied by some of her Danish ladies, Anna traveled in her carriage, upholstered in velvet decorated with silver thread and drawn by eight horses. Commissioned as a gift by Anna's mother, dismantled for shipping, and reassembled in Leith, the carriage passed cheering crowds who lined the roadside to see the new Queen. When they arrived at Holyroodhouse, Anna was shown into her lavishly decorated apartments, including a bedchamber hung with cloth of gold and silver.[3]

Anna brought to the monarchy an indefinable quality of glamour that had been absent since Queen Mary's downfall. She arrived in Scotland with a wardrobe that was designed to impress.[4] Her mother had sent tailors, seamstresses, and milliners to Paris to research the latest fashions before work began on Anna's trousseau. The Kirk fidgeted at the ostentation.

With the public, Anna was a sensation. She smiled, she waved, she dazzled. She looked like the archetypal fairy-tale princess of contemporary European popular culture and the similarities were heightened by the romantic appeal of her survival of terrible storms as she traveled to unite with her intended. Her fairy-tale image blinded many people in Scotland, including James, to the steel in Anna's personality. She was determined to make a success of her queenship. Less than a week after her arrival at Holyroodhouse, she sent a delegation of Danish advisers, including Admiral Munk, to inspect her newly acquired property at Dunfermline, which James had gifted to her at Christmas. Having arrived, Munk was handed a fistful of earth. This was a symbolic gesture of sasine, the transferral of ownership from James, represented by a lawyer, to Queen Anna, represented by Munk. The palace itself was small but comfortable, and its surrounding grounds would generate a tidy income for Anna as landowner.

In the countdown to Anna's coronation, feather mattresses were rented for high-ranking guests, who were also provided with candles and coal at the royal household's expense. Its main events—the coronation and the Queen's ceremonial entry to Edinburgh—were split over two days. The bifurcation was in response to the Kirk's concerns that Anna's entry would involve alcohol and dancing. To prevent a violation of the Sabbath, the crowning would take place on Sunday, May 17, and the ceremonial entry to the capital two days later, on Tuesday, May 19. There were strenuous objections from the Kirk over the content of the coronation, which, as the first of a queen consort in Scotland since 1540, would also be the first since the country's repudiation of Catholicism. They wanted the coronation drastically pared back by stripping it of any ritual that they regarded as "papist," their principal objection being to the act of anointing with holy oil. James countered with biblical examples of anointing at coronations of kings of Israel and Samaria in the

Old Testament, which prompted the Kirk to reply that they did not want any ceremony "borrowed from the Jews."[5] Having been flexible on the Sabbath, James refused to compromise on anointing. To remove the holy oil would dilute his wife's standing and diminish the status of royalty in Scotland.

Anna was anointed during the seven-hour ceremony at the Abbey of the Holy Rood, adjacent to the palace. Proceedings ended with cries from the congregation of "God Save the Queen!"[6] Andrew Melvill delivered a sermon that impressed both the foreign guests and the King, who thanked Melvill for how he "had honoured him and his country that day."[7] Afterward, followed by some of her ladies and by pages and footmen in red velvet, Anna walked back to the palace, wearing her crown and a taffeta-lined purple robe. She was accompanied by James, who was also in regal purple, trimmed with ermine.

Two days later, Anna's silver-decorated carriage carried her through the packed streets of Edinburgh. Her route was lined with crowds, singing maidens, performances by choirs, presentations by city officials, allegorical tableaux; sermons were preached, speeches were delivered in Scots and Latin, and, as the Kirk had feared, the fountains ran with wine. Among the displays was an artificial tree that showed the genealogy of Anna's Danish family, the House of Oldenburg. Afterward, there was a banquet in her honour at Holyroodhouse, where she, James, and the court watched a performance of Highland sword-dancing. It was customary for a new batch of titles to accompany a coronation, and among those honored by James VI in 1590 were his chancellor, who became Lord Maitland of Thirlestane, and Thomas Lyon, who was knighted.

On the following Tuesday, James and Anna returned to Leith to bid farewell to most of the Danish contingent. However, James broke with tradition in allowing Anna to keep with her several of her favorite Danish maids and ladies, some of whom would remain in her service for the rest of her life.

As Admiral Munk led many of the Danes home, Sandy crossed the North Sea in the opposite direction. He had landed in Scotland by the end of May and had married Jean Lyon by June 14. She had been widowed twice before—her first husband had drowned, while her second, the 8th Earl of Angus, had died in 1588 of dysentery that was attributed to witchcraft. Jean's year of birth is unknown. Evidence from her family indicates that she was roughly the same age as Sandy, who was born in about 1563–64—her parents married in April 1561, she had an elder sister, Elizabeth (Patrick Gray's first wife), and both sisters are mentioned in a family document from October 1571, by which point they had been joined by their youngest sister, Sybilla.[8]

James had kept his promise to ennoble Sandy. To judge by the surviving evidence, it must have been among his first actions upon returning to Edinburgh on May 6.[9] On the same day, James issued a charter that granted Sandy the barony of Spynie with lands in the northeast of Scotland, near his family's ancestral home. The paperwork was turned into reality over the summer and, by November, Sandy appears in the records for the first time as Lord Spynie.[10] His barony may have been intended to solace Sandy for his sudden irrelevance, yet it also fulfilled James's intention to "make something of this man of mine" by rendering him safe and giving him prominence as the head of his own household.[11] Sandy and Jean retreated across the Firth to her castle at Aberdour, which she had inherited from her second husband. Sandy's marriage was not initially a happy one, and Jean allegedly had an affair with their neighbor, John Lumsden, Laird of Airdrie.[12]

Cynics claimed later that James's marriage had also and always been a sham. Yet it seems as if he entered it with a determination that it should work, personally as well as politically. The affection and admiration he had felt for Anna during their "honeymoon" period in Scandinavia continued when they returned to Scotland. She loved her home at Dunfermline, particularly because its scenery reminded her so much of Denmark.[13] There were rumors that Queen Anna suffered a miscarriage in the early stages of pregnancy at the end of her first summer in Scotland. She spent much of the subsequent autumn recuperating at Dunfermline, from where she returned to Edinburgh for Christmas. However, most of her pregnancies seem to have come later, and it may be that she was unwell, a state of affairs that public gossip attributed to a miscarriage.

The events of 1589–90 were a tribute to James's success as king in the six years since his wresting of power from Lord Gowrie. Earlier in his reign, it would have been unthinkable for him to leave his realm for six months. It is unlikely that he would have had a throne to return to, much less for the country to have functioned peacefully for months under the command of his deputies. There were still substantial challenges, not least with the economy. However, James had broken the cycle of coups and subdued the Kirk without provoking rebellion. He had balanced court faction as well as an early modern monarch could, he had navigated, quelled, and prevented some serious feuds within the nobility, presided over an important new peace treaty with England, resolved a century-long sovereignty dispute with Denmark-Norway, and established himself as king rather than pawn at the heart of his government. There was no greater testament to James's success than in the enemies he attracted. In 1590, the Devil appeared in Scotland, where he urged his followers to murder the King.

In the town of Tranent, south of Edinburgh and on the eastern coast, Geillis Duncan, known by her nickname Gillie, worked as a maid in the house of a local bailie* called David Seton. Like many servants at the time, Gillie lived in her employer's home. She had a reputation in Tranent as a healer. To prepare some of her medicines, she would leave the house at night to gather ingredients by moonlight. David Seton and his teenage son, who shared his father's name and views, were suspicious of Gillie's craft. When she resisted their questions, they refused to let her leave the house. Subsequently, they beat her and locked her in her room, where their abuse escalated to stripping her naked in search of a witch's mark, depriving her of sleep, and, allegedly, subjecting her to thumbscrews. After sustained psychological and physical torture, Gillie confessed that she was a witch and named various other locals as her partners in sin.

The torture of Gillie Duncan was one of the principal early tragedies in what was later known as the North Berwick witch trials. Their first incident had been in July 1590 with the burning in Denmark of Anna Koldings, who had testified under duress

* Magistrate.

that she belonged to a coven that had conjured a storm to wreck Queen Anna's ships on their journey to Scotland. Koldings named five women, who were arrested and questioned. Some were tortured, and all confessed that there had been a cabal of witches who worked to turn the weather against Queen Anna's fleet. The two "chief witches" from the Danish searches were taken to burn at Helsingør, the town where the Kronborg palace was located. The Danish government ordered that the inquiry be extended to Norway, where a coven of five men and four women was discovered near Oslo.

The storms that nearly drowned Anna and later James had been unusual. Even Admiral Munk, who observed they were like nothing he had seen in his decades at sea, had wondered if they were a consequence of sorcery, a suspicion shared by the Governor of Copenhagen. There was a precedent for Danish society attributing similar events to magic; after a sudden summer storm twenty-four years earlier that had sunk fourteen ships of the Danish navy, with the loss of nearly six thousand men, it was generally accepted in Denmark that it had been caused by witches in the pay of their enemy, King Erik XIV of Sweden.

The late sixteenth and early to mid-seventeenth century saw a spike in the number of witch hunts in western Europe. Prior to the late sixteenth century, no mass witch trials were recorded anywhere in the British Isles. In England, medieval accusations of witchcraft were typically yet infrequently levied against powerful, or inconveniently wealthy, women, such as Edward IV's mother-in-law, Jacquetta of Luxembourg, Henry VI's aunt Eleanor, Duchess of Gloucester, and Henry IV's widow, Joanna of Navarre. A similar situation existed in medieval Scotland, where accusations of witchcraft often ran alongside a belief that someone in the elite had treasonous intent. This had motivated the notorious incident in 1537 when James V had tortured the servants of Lady Glamis to provide testimonies against their mistress, before burning her to death outside Edinburgh Castle with her son in enforced attendance. In James VI's childhood, the Moray regency had executed a knight for using divination to encompass Moray's death.[14] In contrast to these infamous examples, most medieval witch trials in Scotland ended with public humiliation, brief imprisonment, social rustication, or acquittal.

In the late sixteenth century, this changed. Witch hunts condemned far higher numbers across the social spectrum. It does not seem coincidental that this occurred after the Protestant Reformation. For over a millennium, a constant in the lives of most western Europeans had been their religion. One might argue over who was the rightful king, why a plague had come, how best to plant crops or build castles; you could even criticize clerical corruption, query the validity of an alleged miracle, or back a different candidate as pope. But through everything, Christianity, "the one true Faith," remained a coherent, inviolate whole. Depending on where one lived and at what point in the Middle Ages, there might be Jewish or Muslim communities nearby, many of whom later suffered terribly, particularly in Spain and Portugal. What Christianity was, however, did not change as far as most of its believers were concerned. Schism with the eastern branch of the Church in 1054 made little practical difference to the lives of most western Christians, nor did the heresies that intermittently rose, fell, flourished, or festered. In the space of a generation after 1517, this status quo fell apart. No longer an unquestioned adjective, "Christian" became a word whose meaning was ferociously contested. What had once been axiomatic became explosive.

The schism that followed 1517 was not even a dichotomy. Protestantism kept splitting in an ongoing quest to rediscover and define truth. Catholicism remained, officially, a unified faith. In reality, for most of the latter half of the sixteenth century it too suffered under tremendous internal strains as to how best to counter the Reformation. There were tensions between those who pushed for a militant response and voices who advocated for a more compassionate proselytization. As the pursuit of the truth became more passionate, so did fears that the forces of darkness were walking the earth to frustrate that quest by infesting the new denominations or corrupting the old.

The shattering of certainty is often when a society is at its most unstable. The consequences are seldom edifying and often horrific. The most ferocious and sustained witch hunts took place in

Switzerland, Poland, and the German states. In comparison, British witch hunts remained smaller in scale and frequency, even at their zenith.[15] In the period between 1563 and 1727, Scotland tried about 1,500 suspected witches, compared to the ten thousand estimated for Switzerland.[16] There was also more skepticism about them. Staple claims of the witchcraft panics in Europe—infanticide, secret conspiracies of evildoers kidnapping children, sex rings, cannibalism—did not enjoy widespread belief in the British Isles. Some contemporaries, like the English author Reginald Scott in *A Discovery of Witchcraft*, published in 1584, even mocked the witch hunts as ludicrous.

Of all the witch hunts that took place in the British Isles, the largest tended to occur in Scotland. In the days before the Reformation, the task of dealing with Scottish witchcraft had been left to ecclesiastical tribunals, whose authority had gone into decline with Catholicism after the 1540s.[17] In 1563, witchcraft had been transferred to the jurisdiction of secular courts, who sanctioned execution only if a witch or wizard had cast spells that ended somebody's life. From the 1570s, there were more regular, and brutal, outbreaks of witch-hunting.

Various reasons have been postulated for this and for why the scope of Scottish witch hunts exceeded England's. Factoring in the disparity in population size, witch executions per head of the population in early modern Scotland may have been as high as ten times the English equivalent.[18] One theory identifies how the English state tried to preserve torture as a state prerogative for use only in cases of suspected treason.[19] Another difference between the two jurisdictions was that English trials required unanimity among the jury for witchcraft convictions, whereas Scottish law required only a majority. Cultural differences, created or influenced by language, have also been suggested. None of Scotland's witch panics took place in the Gaelic-speaking Highlands. They occurred in the Lowlands or the Northern Isles.[20]

In the North Berwick witch trials, these long-term and short-term factors reacted with one another. The dreadful weather of the late 1580s and 1590s, with feeble summers and brutal winters, the failed harvests, the tempests that had nearly drowned James and

Anna, the Danish and Norwegian witch hunts, religious tension, economic stagnation, and political unrest seemed to be evidence, rather than the cause, of a besieged society, undermined by a shadowy conspiracy that sought to destroy it.[21] The final factor was James.

One of those named by Gillie Duncan was a local woman called Agnes Sampson, who, before she discovered her talent for healing, had been so poor that she and her children had to huddle together at night to stay alive during winter. She was a devout Christian, who believed a holy being, possibly an angel, had warned her in time to prevent the suicide of a local aristocrat. Agnes was regularly invited to pray over people who had taken to their beds or seemed unable to work.[22] But what if the spirit advising her had been a demon instead? Agnes could allegedly transfer pain, which was a skill associated with dark magic.

Following Gillie Duncan's claims, the local authorities put Agnes to the thumbscrews, which did not alter her claims of innocence. To check her for the Devil's mark, all the hair on her body was shaved. A rope was then tightened around her forehead to keep her still. Agnes's tragedy reinforces in brutal detail how several of the interrogation tactics used on female suspects were sexual assault. When the investigators digitally penetrated her genitals by force under the guise of searching for satanic marks, Agnes broke. She agreed that she was a witch and named others in her coven.[23] More arrests were made.

As an older woman—her age is unknown, but it was between fifty and seventy—a traditional healer, widowed, and among the poorest in the community, Agnes Sampson fits the stereotypical victim of the early modern European witch hunts. Another of her co-accused, Euphemia MacCalzean, marked a return to the older tradition of accusing rich women. Euphemia too had been named during Gillie Duncan's interrogation. In her mid-thirties, she was a member of an affluent Edinburgh family and had recently been made even wealthier when her mother-in-law left her six times more than she left her daughter and son-in-law—the latter being David Seton, Gillie Duncan's employer, questioner, and torturer.[24] Seton gleefully reported to the authorities how Gillie had told him about Euphemia's communion with malevolent spirits, whom she conjured against him. Once she had been taken into state custody and away from her torturers, Gillie admitted that she had identified Euphemia only at the urging of David Seton, who stood to gain financially and substantially if Euphemia was out of the way.[25] It was too late. Euphemia was already answering questions in prison. Barbara Napier, the wealthy widow of an Edinburgh bookseller and a sister-in-law of a laird, came from a similar background and was of a similar age to Euphemia MacCalzean. She too was named and imprisoned.

In prison, Agnes kept testifying. She claimed that six men and ninety-four women, including Gillie, Euphemia, and Barbara, had met in the coastal town of North Berwick, where they had broken into the church to desecrate it. They lit their black candles while Gillie played a musical instrument, then the Devil appeared in front of them—"his body was hard like iron . . . his face was terrible."[26] He mounted the pulpit, while the local schoolmaster took attendance. Each of the coven answered with "Here, master!" The Devil preached a sermon calling on the witches to destroy King James. When they asked why, Satan answered that it was because James VI was the greatest enemy that he had in the world. James's defense of a Protestant Scotland and the wisdom of his rule had marked him out as a threat. The coven then lined up to kiss the Devil's buttocks, in a profane inversion of Holy Communion; afterward they went to the graveyard, where they dug up bones to grind them into powders for their spells.

Agnes's adult daughter Bessie Thompson was arrested, as was John Fian, the schoolmaster who Agnes claimed had taken attendance at the satanic service in North Berwick. Fian had enjoyed casting horoscopes in his spare time; after Agnes's testimony, he had his fingernails ripped out while knotted cords were tightened around his head and hammers taken to his legs. Among other admissions forced from the prisoners was of their exhuming corpses from consecrated ground, dismembering them, and tying some of their muscles to each limb of a black cat in sacrifice to evil, before the cat and limbs were tossed into the sea at night.

James was intrigued yet skeptical at these reports. Andrew Melvill, representing the Kirk at court, urged him to take the threat more seriously, and when James went to church, he was exhorted in sermons to do more in the crusade against witchcraft. In discussing the sinking of the Edinburgh ferry on which Anna's attendant, Lady Janet Kennedy, had been a passenger, Melvill told James that Kennedy had been killed by witches "who, in conjunction with their sisterhood in Norway, had brewed the storm to drown the harmless young Queen, but when that failed, their malice fell upon her lady-in-waiting."

James remained unconvinced. It was not that he doubted the existence of witchcraft, the study of which he regarded as a branch of theology, but he thought that, under torture, the suspects were likely to have lied.[27] A turning point came when Agnes Sampson was brought to testify in front of James. She, apparently, whispered in his ear "the very words which passed between the King's Majesty and his Queen at Upslo* in Norway on the first night of marriage . . . whereat the King's Majesty wondered greatly, and swore by the living God, that he believed all the devils in hell could not have discovered the same, acknowledging her words to be most true, and therefore gave the more credit to the rest" of the accusations.[28] James was fatefully and fully convinced.

Agnes claimed that a merchant called Richard Graham was a member of the coven. Arrested, questioned, and tortured, he stated they had all worked as underlings for a nobleman who wished to kill the King; he identified the man as the Lord High Admiral, James's cousin Lord Bothwell. Richard, too, was questioned in person by James, who believed his claims.[29] A link existed between Richard and Bothwell; Richard was a friend of Bothwell's manservant, who was thus suddenly cast as an intermediary between Bothwell and the coven.[30] The servant managed to escape north before he became another victim of the trials.[31]

When Richard's testimony was recounted to Agnes, she corroborated it with the additional detail that they had conducted a ritual in the town of Prestonpans. There, ten of the coven had summoned the Devil as they passed around a wax image, made by Agnes, and

---

* Oslo.

chanted, "This is King James the Sixth, ordered to be consumed at the instance of a nobleman Francis, Earl [of] Bothwell."[32] Agnes Sampson was convicted at trial and publicly strangled to death on January 27, 1591. Her corpse was burned.

Richard claimed that Bothwell's plan had been for James's bride to drown, to attack the childless King afterward, and then to seize the throne for himself. Bothwell's family had been suspected of sorcery for generations. As far as James was concerned, such suspicions had been confirmed by the previous Earl of Bothwell on his deathbed in Denmark in 1578, when he confessed in the Bothwell Testament that he had used witchcraft to manipulate Queen Mary and hoped to use it against the infant James. One of the North Berwick accused, Barbara Napier, was an acquaintance of Bothwell; in the febrile atmosphere of a conspiracy where coincidences became clues, this seemingly added further validity to the charge that Bothwell had controlled the coven through several proxies.

Bothwell was brought after sunset to a meeting of the council at Edinburgh Castle, where James presided over his questioning. Bothwell denied any involvement in witchcraft, and the King refused his request that he be allowed to prove his innocence with trial by combat. He ordered Bothwell detained in the castle until a proper trial could be arranged. Through sheer ingenuity and strength, Bothwell overpowered a guard and escaped. The council issued a proclamation denouncing Bothwell for "consultation with necromancers, witches and other wicked and ungodly persons, both without and within his country, for bereaving* of his Highness's life," through which he had placed himself "in the hands of Satan, heaping treason upon treason against God, his Majesty, and this his native country."[33]

The witch trials continued, the panic grew, hundreds were questioned, and dozens were executed. *News from Scotland: The Damnable Life and Death of a Notable Sorcerer,* a book detailing the interrogation and execution of Richard Graham, was read in great numbers in the Lowlands and England. For months, witchcraft and Lord Bothwell's role in it was the primary matter that occupied

---

* In this context, meaning to bring about a troubled ending of.

James, who had been transformed from dubious spectator to obsessively vindictive participant. As he informed the English ambassador, "I have been occupied these three quarters of the year for the sifting out of them that are guilty." Furious when Barbara Napier was acquitted at her trial, albeit on the technicality that she was pregnant, James rode roughshod over the law by ordering Maitland to discover "if Barbara be with bairn" and, if she was not, to proceed with her public execution by burning and disemboweling. She was indeed pregnant, and her fate remains unknown.[34] If Barbara was burned after her child's birth, there is no account of it and, while it is unlikely that she died in such a manner with no record of it, it cannot be ruled out.[35] She may have died of disease in prison or in childbed. She seems to have been dead by 1594, when a second escheat for her estate was issued, and she certainly was by 1600, when one of her daughters tried to establish her right to her mother's pension. In correspondence with Barbara's jury, James insisted, "I am innocent of all injustice in these behalfs, and for my part my conscience doth set me clear, as did the conscience of Samuel."*[36] However, in the unlikely event that Barbara Napier did burn to death at some point in 1591, it is an act for which James bears close to full responsibility, since she had been acquitted until he intervened.

Euphemia MacCalzean continued to hold out against incriminating herself or others, so she was taken to witness public floggings for "two or three days" in the hope that it would frighten her into confessing.[37] It did not. Euphemia burned on June 15, 1591. Gillie Duncan and Agnes Sampson's daughter Bessie Thompson met a similar fate on December 4.

Meanwhile, Bothwell remained at large. James suspected "that vile man" had fled to England, and he wrote to Elizabeth to request that she honor the Treaty of Berwick by extraditing him if he was apprehended.[38] Bothwell was in fact hiding in southern Scotland, moving between the homes of sympathetic aristocrats who sheltered him while he pondered his next move. He also had friends at

* A prophet in the Bible, noted for his self-critical conscience through which he examined himself in the fear that he had contravened justice or morality.

court, the most important of whom was Queen Anna. After greeting the Queen at Leith, Bothwell set out to charm her. Their nascent friendship was encouraged by Bothwell's fluency in French, which meant they could converse easily while Anna was still learning Scots.[39] She found him witty and charismatic. Ludovic, Duke of Lennox was another friend of Bothwell's who was unconvinced by the North Berwick confessions.

Sandy, who had officially remained part of the royal household despite spending more time away from court, came to James's side and urged him to abandon his vendetta against Bothwell. His efforts were rewarded with a tirade in which James accused him of disloyalty. When James discovered that one of his Gentlemen of the Chamber, John Wemyss, was in league with Bothwell, he detained him in the palace. Wemyss's lover was Margrethe Vinstarr, a maid who had accompanied Anna from Denmark. One night, Margrethe helped Wemyss escape. When James discovered what she had done, he was incandescent. He went to Anna and screamed at her until both he and she were weeping. Tears notwithstanding, Anna refused James's demands that she punish Margrethe or send her back to Denmark.[40] James eventually backed down and Margrethe remained in royal service. Anna did, however, abandon her own inclination to intercede for Bothwell, as did a chastened Sandy, who retreated to his estates.[41]

James and Anna were back at Holyroodhouse in December when the King heard screams from the palace corridors of "Justice! Justice! For Bothwell, for Bothwell!" The fugitive earl had crept into the palace after sunset with about fifty armed supporters. Queen Anna's shrieks of terror were soon added to the cacophony of straining wood as the invaders tried to batter down the doors to her apartments, incorrectly believing that Chancellor Maitland was hiding there. Bothwell was convinced that Maitland had manipulated the witches' and sorcerers' testimonies to frame him. James's attendants surrounded their king and rushed him into the most secure part of his chambers, where they were soon battling with smoke inhalation as Bothwell's men set fire to the door. They were saved by the quick response of Harry Charteris, Sandy's brother, who arrived to battle hand to hand with Bothwell as another courtier ran to raise the city alarm.[42] The warning bells of Edinburgh pealed and the plotters fled, killing John Shaw, James's Master of the Stable, who tried to stop them as they went. Bothwell escaped for a second time, while the King and Queen were evacuated to shelter at a merchant's home before they could be moved to Linlithgow Palace, which would be harder to breach as one side bordered a loch. Funerals were organized for the seven royal attendants killed in the raid. James wrote a poem for John Shaw's epitaph, promising to protect his loved ones, socially and financially, in gratitude for Shaw's loyalty.[43]

As 1592 dawned, the fervor necessary to sustain a witch hunt yielded inch by inch to the voices of the skeptical. Having kept quiet when the moral panic was at its height, they now felt sufficiently emboldened to ask questions about what they had all so willingly gone along with. After ending the lives of seventy people, the North Berwick witch trials ebbed into oblivion. Their last unresolved case was the missing Earl of Bothwell, who, with the help of a friend at court, the Countess of Atholl, was smuggled into Holyroodhouse on a July morning in 1593. James was being dressed by his servants when Bothwell burst in and threw himself at his feet. James shouted, "Treason!" and ran toward Anna's bedchamber, where the door was bolted because the Queen, who had recently discovered that she was pregnant, was still asleep.[44] James turned back to face Bothwell. He told him that he might take his life but, unlike Satan with Bothwell's, he would not be able to take his soul. Bothwell shed tears as he promised that "We came not to murder Your Majesty, nor to do you any harm. I come but as a loyal subject. I swear it by this sword." He offered his weapon to James, telling him that he could use it to kill him if he truly believed him to be in league with the Devil. James was so moved by this that he too wept "and compassion came so fast upon his Majesty that he granted unto my Lord Bothwell a pardon."[45]

Even to some of his closest friends, James maintained the fiction that he suddenly believed in Bothwell's innocence.[46] As with his pardon for Lord Gowrie a decade before, it was a charade until he was strong enough to strike back. After Bothwell involved himself in another series of plots, he fled into exile, perhaps correctly guessing that he had provided James with the excuse he had been waiting for. With dwindling friends and fortune, Bothwell wandered Europe and died years later in 1612 in Naples, where he was "famous for suspected necromancy."[47]

9

THESE RUMORS SET DANGEROUS FIRES

As on the wings of your enchanting fame
I was transported o'er the stormy seas . . .
Your smiling is an antidote against
The melancholy that oppresses me
And when a raging wrath into me reigns
Your loving looks may make me calm to be.
How oft you see me have a heavy heart
Remember then sweet Doctor on your art.

—A poem by James VI to Anna of Denmark
(c. 1591)

In the two years following the North Berwick witch trials, James's popularity faded as attacks on his leadership and personality increased. Anonymous pamphlets revived the claim that the King's biological father was David Riccio. As Queen Mary had feared in 1566, Lord Darnley's accusations had taken a second to utter and a lifetime to dispel; this was not the first time James had been publicly taunted by the rumor. In government literature and in the tableaux that accompanied his civic entries, James was often compared to the Bible's King Solomon, who was famed for his wisdom. Unfortunately for James, Solomon's father, King David, shared a first name with Riccio; this had led to several incidents when he was mocked by anonymous voices in the crowd crying out a welcome to "the son of David!"

The pamphlets were joined in circulation by others claiming that James was an enthusiastic "buggerer" who had such a preference for men that he had been unable to consummate his marriage with the Queen. It was ironic that the pamphlets appeared at a time when James seems to have had no male favorite. They upset James far more than had the Riccio libels, and he ordered the Kirk to preach sermons refuting the claims. The Kirk refused and James's panic grew. His reaction to them, the Kirk's refusal to refute, and speculation about James's private life confirmed the assessment of courtier John Colville that "*Haec sunt incendia malorum.*"[1] ("These rumors set dangerous fires.")

A resurgence in support for the Kirk emboldened several preachers to upbraid James in their sermons, as they had when he was younger. They sometimes did so when James was seated in the congregation. After another embarrassing sermon in which the reverend reprimanded James's leadership, the King felt the need to defend himself, but when he took to the pulpit, he faced the further embarrassment of half the congregation walking out in protest and the other half heckling him. There was little sympathy from the public when the King narrowly escaped drowning, having fallen off his horse while fording a river and been trapped until a servant rushed forward to pull him out of the water by his neck.

In his private life, James knew that he had become a nightmare to live with, oscillating between "a melancholy that oppresses me" and a foul temper "when a raging wrath into me reigns," as he put it in apologetic poetry to his wife. The confidence and bonhomie of the late 1580s had been replaced by maudlin self-pity, deep unhappiness, and aggressive mood swings.

With its Saturnian tendency to devour those it once nurtured, public opinion also turned on the Queen, who soon became almost as unpopular as her husband. Her Lutheranism was attacked in sermons by clergy who, while relieved James had heeded their advice to avoid marriage with a Catholic, were offended by the Queen's refusal to embrace Presbyterianism.[2] One reverend went so far as to encourage his congregation to stop praying for Queen Anna, who was also criticized for her partying or her "night walking and balling."[3] The sneering sobriquet "our dancing queen" was used in sermons, with the implication that dancing was a sign of moral laxity.

Within the court, there was resentment of Anna's continued

preference for her Danish retainers over their Scottish counterparts, who were aggrieved at their exclusion from the most prominent positions in her household. To help his wife, James decided to give her an adviser whom he trusted and who knew the ways of the Scottish court. He chose poor Sir James Melville, who, having only just received royal permission to retire, was summoned back for an audience with the King at Falkland. James asked him to accept the post of First Gentleman of the Queen's Chamber.

"I know," said the King, "that you would fain* live at home in your own house, with contentment of mind; but you know that a man is not born for himself only, but also for the weal† of his prince and country." He outlined Anna's current difficulties and her mistakes, for which James blamed his own failure to help her sooner. He explained to Melville that he needed to "place about the Queen, his bedfellow, good and discreet company; which he had left too long undone, until at length, having advised with himself, he thought me the fittest man to commit that charge to; desiring me not to refuse the just calling of my prince . . . I answered that, as His Majesty's most humble servant and subject, I never refused to obey his commandment."[4]

Melville's first few weeks in the Queen's Household were made difficult by Anna's obvious dislike of him. Eventually, she gave voice to her suspicion by asking Melville if he had been sent to spy on her by her husband. Melville replied, truthfully, that he had been sent to help, an explanation that Anna accepted. Later, she privately apologized to Melville with the accompanying explanation that several of her staff had jealously tried to poison her against Melville and that she, to her regret, had listened to them.

After that, Anna became more wary of palace politics.[5] To listen in on what her staff were saying about her when they thought she could not understand them, the Queen downplayed her grasp of Scots with frequent complaints about how much she was struggling with the language, long after she had in fact acquired fluency.

---

* Rather.

† Well-being.

This was how she caught the Dowager Countess of Mar and the chancellor's wife, Lady Maitland, lamenting to one another in Scots that James had not married Catherine of Bourbon. From that point, she considered both women her enemies.

Anna, who turned eighteen in December 1592, transformed herself into one of the most powerful political forces in Scotland. She formed a faction of her own, recruiting more Scots to her household, as per Sir James Melville's advice. She formed friendships with these ladies and, through them, made alliances with their houses. Anna had no intention of crawling to public opinion. In fact, she seemed to take criticism as a challenge. If the Kirk was offended by Anna's Lutheranism, then she would befriend prominent Catholics, such as Henrietta, Countess of Huntly, whom she took as her guest to watch a debate in Parliament, where Anna was spotted cheering and applauding in the gallery at legislation opposed by the Kirk. When representatives of the clergy arrived at Edinburgh Castle one evening, asking permission to deliver a sermon to their queen in person, she replied through a messenger that she was having too much fun dancing.

Understanding money's relationship to power, Anna was assiduous in defending and expanding her property portfolio. She was displeased to discover that although her estate at Dunfermline had hitherto incorporated the adjoining lordship of Musselburgh, James had excluded Musselburgh, and its rents, from her. This was because, a few years before he met her, he had detached Musselburgh from Dunfermline to award that part of the estate to Maitland in recompense for his diligence as Lord Chancellor. Anna insisted on somewhat questionable grounds that Musselburgh was hers by right, and she recruited the Danish government to weigh in on her behalf. Already irked by what she had overheard about Catherine of Bourbon, Anna retaliated by dismissing Lady Maitland as one of her ladies-in-waiting and by making life as difficult as possible for Lord Maitland, who resigned as Lord Chancellor and left court.

The Kirk, Queen Elizabeth, and King James urged Anna to reconcile with the former chancellor, who had respectively won their admiration by his Protestantism, Anglophilia, and competence.

Correctly guessing that their worries proved that she held the upper hand, Anna held out for total victory. If Maitland wanted to return to court and the chancellorship, then Musselburgh was the price he would have to pay. Exasperated but impressed by his wife's tenacity, James went to visit the Maitlands at their estate, where he asked Maitland to help him by burying the hatchet with the Queen. From a king, this was somewhere between a request and a command, to which Maitland yielded by writing a fulsome apology to Anna. A solution that was a clear triumph for the Queen was reached and politely called a compromise. Parliament ratified the lordship of Musselburgh as Anna's while she lived, after which it would return to the Maitland family.[6]

During their feud over Musselburgh, Anna had suspected that Maitland was responsible for rumors in Edinburgh that she was an adulteress. The Kirk's constant insinuations about her late-night dancing had more probably birthed those lies, and they continued even after Anna's reconciliation with the chancellor. Whom she was having an affair with depended on whom you were gossiping with or in which tavern you were drinking. Some claimed the Queen was sleeping with her friend Lord Bothwell, and those rumors grew stronger when she had tried to intercede on Bothwell's behalf in the early stages of the North Berwick witch hunts. Other gossips insisted that the Queen had started an affair with James's kinsman Ludovic, Duke of Lennox.

The most popular rumor identified her lover as the Earl of Moray, son-in-law of James's first regent. Moray's good looks were proverbial—he was considered the most handsome man in the Scottish aristocracy, which in Edinburgh earned him the nickname the "bonny Earl of Moray."[7] Their imagined relationship inspired poetry and song after Moray was murdered by James's former favorite Lord Huntly, who returned to politics with a flair melodramatic even by his own standards.[8]

The two earls had never liked one another. In years gone by, their families had fought over everything from faith to fishing rights. Moray was among the most prominent of the Protestant lords, and Huntly was his Catholic equivalent. The short-term countdown to their fatal encounter began when Moray granted protection to two Protestant families, the Grants and the Mackintoshes, who had been sworn to Huntly's house before rebelling against him. Huntly vowed revenge for Moray's involvement in his affairs by protecting "the said malefactors."[9] He tracked Moray down to Donibristle, a castle on the southeastern coast where Moray was visiting his recently widowed mother. Huntly's men set fire to Donibristle, killed the local sheriff, and smoked Moray out. Giving chase on horseback, Huntly caught Moray at the shore. Accounts diverge over whether it was Huntly who fired the fatal shot, but legend soon insisted that he had and that Moray, the best-looking man in the Scottish nobility facing death at the hands of the second, departed with an immortal putdown: "Huntly, you have spoiled a far fairer face than your own!"[10]

Once again, James could not bring himself to punish Huntly. He was so lackluster in his condemnations that it led to speculation that he had secretly ordered the killing. This in turn fueled gossip that Anna had been sleeping with Moray, a version of events popularized in the ballad "The Bonnie Earl o' Moray." In response to the public outcry, James issued a proclamation denying complicity in Moray's death. The scandal persisted.[11] Moray's embalmed corpse was brought to Edinburgh by his devastated mother, who extracted the bullets from his body with her own hands and presented them to supporters as a memento mori. She refused to bury her son until Huntly was brought to justice; his body remained unburied until her own death six years later in 1598. On her deathbed, she apparently cursed King James's name for leaving her son's killer at liberty. It was another five years before the feud was buried with a peace agreement between the two families.

The sordid impression created by the murder of the Queen's alleged favorite by the King's was augmented when Huntly again made a fool of James's leniency. Evidence emerged that Huntly was still in clandestine correspondence with the Spanish government. Then his feud with another noble family led to serious unrest in the Highlands. When Huntly clashed with the Earl of Argyll, the Chief of Clan Campbell, Argyll called his banners, attracting support from most of the Protestant clans in the north and west; Huntly was backed by the Catholic clans of the north and east.

Huntly scored a victory over Argyll at the Battle of Glenlivet in October 1594. Under pressure from the Kirk, James set off north with an army to support Argyll and the Protestants. He was away from the court for over two months but failed to track down Huntly or any of his prominent allies; most of them had retreated far north, into lands it proved difficult for James's forces to access as winter set in. "These papist lords have retired alone into some hiding-places," James explained in a December letter to Anna. "Nobody knows where, at this hour I am proceeding to make secret enquiry concerning them and their associates in order to strike at them."[12] As before, Huntly decided eventually to surrender to James, who exiled him and a fellow Catholic nobleman. The sentence of exile was lifted a year later; the King had, however, made a more confident and ruthless response. This time, he had the homes of several prominent rebel families burned or razed—including parts of Huntly's great castle at Strathbogie—until Huntly bent the knee.

On February 19, 1594, Queen Anna gave birth to a boy at Stirling Castle. James wrote to Queen Elizabeth with the announcement, "God has blessed us in the birth of a young son."[13] In an instant, the public's recent criticism of the royal couple was dispelled. Bonfires were lit to celebrate the birth of an heir, cannons fired from all the major castles and palaces, and villages and towns hosted dances as the country seemed "daft for mirth."[14] Among those assigned to care for the new prince were James's trusted physician, Gilbert Moncreiff, the Dowager Countess of Mar, the Earl of Mar, and his new wife, James's cousin Marie Stuart.* James trusted the Dowager Countess, whom he still called by his childhood nickname for her, "Lady Minny"; he had forgiven Mar for his involvement in the Raid of Ruthven, and he was delighted that a cousin whom he regarded as being more like a sister would run the prince's household in conjunction with her mother-in-law. Anna, who had never forgiven the Dowager Countess for regretting that Catherine of Bourbon was not queen instead, was displeased. Remembering the

* A younger daughter of Esmé Stuart, 1st Duke of Lennox, sister of Henrietta, Countess of Huntly and Ludovic, Duke of Lennox, she had married Lord Mar in 1592.

numerous attempts made to kidnap him in his youth, James ordered the establishment at Stirling that they were never to hand the prince over to anyone else's care unless "I command you with my own mouth."[15] This included representatives of Parliament or the Queen herself, a stipulation that shocked and offended Anna.

A new chapel, its measurements matching those recorded in the Bible for the main chamber of Solomon's Temple but its interior plainly decorated to advertise James's devotion to Protestantism, was constructed at Stirling for the baptism, at which the Bishop of Aberdeen officiated.[16] French, Dutch, and German ambassadors descended on Stirling for the service. They were joined by Robert Radclyffe, 5th Earl of Sussex, who had come to stand as proxy for Queen Elizabeth, one of the godparents. She sent a silver-inlaid cupboard and golden goblets as christening gifts, which were delivered to Queen Anna, with Sir James Melville at her side, taking inventory.[17] The prince was christened with the names Frederick and Henry after his grandfathers—"Henry Frederick, Frederick Henry," cried the herald, and it was by Henry that he was known. He was given an heir's titles of Duke of Rothesay, Earl of Carrick, Cunningham, and Kyle, Baron of Renfrew, and Lord of the Isles.

Queen Anna's vision for the post-christening celebrations did not lack aplomb. In fact, they might have shown excessive zeal in their flair. Her staff had to talk her out of her original plan for a pet lion to enter the Great Hall, pulling a chariot. They labored long and hard to convince her that there was a wide margin of error as to how the lion might behave when surrounded by a crowd, loud noises, and flaming torches. The Kirk was dismayed by the Queen's decision to dance in some of the entertainments herself and by a ball at which Amazonian warriors were played by men in female costume. The banquet's lobster, clams, and crabs were delivered to guests on a six-meter-long replica ship that was wheeled into the hall, with thirty-six brass guns firing blanks. Some of the parties continued until three o'clock in the morning. James competed in the tourneys, and gold coins were tossed to the celebrating crowds in Stirling.[18] Financial want being friend to neither conservation nor sentiment, the golden goblets sent by Queen Elizabeth were melted down to foot the bill, to the regret of Sir James Melville, who thought they were so beautiful that they "should have been kept in store to posterity."[19]

The sequestering of their son at Stirling under the care of a woman whom she disliked was intolerable to Anna and caused the first serious strain in her marriage. At court, an eavesdropping diplomat heard Anna tell James that "it is a cruel response to refuse her suit, which is founded on reason and nature, and to prefer instead giving the care of her babe to a subject, who neither in rank nor character is deserving." James responded, "though he doubts nothing of the Queen's good intentions, yet he fear that if some faction get strong enough, she could not be strong enough to hinder his boy being taken from her to be used against him, as he himself was used against his own unfortunate mother."

Thwarted, Anna widened her dislike from the Dowager Countess of Mar to her entire family. When James defended them by reminding Anna of their years of loyal service to him, she laughed and sarcastically said that was an odd way to describe Lord Mar's involvement in the Raid of Ruthven.

Between March and August 1595, the tensions within the royal marriage intensified. "The Queen speaks more plainly than before and will not cease till she has her son," observed a courtier in May. In July, a diplomat concluded that "No good* can come between the King and Queen till she be satisfied" about Prince Henry.[20] Anna even faked an illness. When James rushed to her side, she announced that she would feel better if the Mars were dismissed and the prince's household entrusted to her. James told her, "My heart, I am sorry you should be persuaded to move me to that which will be the destruction of me and my blood." It was a rare moment of gentleness from the King, who more often than not was angry at his wife. A clergyman at court observed, "There is nothing but lurking hatred disguised as cunning dissimulation between the King and the Queen. Each intending by slight to overcome the other."[21]

Around the same time, James allegedly had affairs with two of his wife's ladies-in-waiting—Anne Murray of Tullibardine and Euphemia Douglas. One of the Queen's favorite ladies, Euphemia was

* Happiness.

the second of the Earl and Countess of Morton's* seven daughters, who were collectively nicknamed "the Seven Pearls of Lochleven" for their beauty and their family seat at Lochleven Castle. Both she and Anne Murray later married into the Lyon family—Euphemia to courtier Sir Thomas Lyon and Anne to his nephew, the 9th Lord Glamis. Confusion over their respective titles after marriage resulted in the claim that James and Euphemia Douglas were lovers in 1595. There is no other evidence linking the two. In 1598, the English ambassador identified Euphemia as a favorite of the Queen. In contrast, Anna's former fondness for Anne Murray, which had extended to buying her bodices, sleeves, and silver thread in 1594, degenerated into open loathing in 1595.

James knew Anne Murray's family—her grandfather, Sir William Murray of Tullibardine, had been comptroller of his childhood household at Stirling—and she was described as "fair" in contemporary accounts, indicating that she was considered attractive. Evidence is scarce, but her affair with James seems to have lasted from April or May 1595 until June or July of the same year, when Anne married. An English visitor to the Scottish court described her as "the King's mistress" in two letters, one dated to May 1595 and the other to June.[22] In terms of other evidence, one of James's poems, which is almost certainly about Anne Murray, contains overt sexual imagery, most obviously with James's description of how wonderful it felt to have Anne's "silken hands" clasped around his neck while they were in bed and when his "earthly parts" were inflamed by her presence.

Queen Anna found common cause with her former enemy, Lord Chancellor Maitland, in her quest to stop Anne Murray's wedding to Lord Glamis. Maitland worried that an alliance between the two families would not be to his political benefit; the Queen despised Anne and her grandfather's family, especially his sister, the Dowager Countess of Mar. They failed to stop Anne becoming the new Lady Glamis, but Anna did prevent Anne from returning to court as a lady-in-waiting.[23]

---

* William Douglas, 6th Earl of Morton (c. 1540–1606), cousin of James's last regent, and his wife, Agnes Leslie, Countess of Morton (c. 1541–c. 1606).

10

EXPECTATIONS

Hope doth lead from day to day.
—Anne Boleyn, Queen of England
(d. 1536)

On October 3, 1595, Lord Chancellor Maitland died, in his early sixties, at his newly renovated home of Thirlestane Castle. On his deathbed, he allegedly expressed regret that he had not used the money spent on Thirlestane to found a hospital.[1] He had been chancellor for nine years and one of James's trusted advisers for eleven. After Maitland's death, James retreated to Linlithgow Palace to escape the politicking from different court factions as they tried to persuade him to install one of their own as Maitland's successor. To maintain them in balance by keeping them in competition, James delayed appointing a new Lord Chancellor, a policy that he continued for four years.

Despite the strains in their marriage, the King and Queen continued to sleep together. On August 19, 1596, Anna gave birth to their first daughter, who was christened Elizabeth in honor of the English queen who stood as her godmother. In his personal life, James remained circumspect. There is no surviving evidence from this period indicating that he had either male or female lovers.

The years from 1596 to 1600 were, politically, a time of success for James. The Scottish economy stabilized to the extent that, in 1596, he was finally able to end the policy of debasing the coinage that had persisted since the Gowrie administration. Financial reform of the royal household was less successful. At the start of the 1590s, several of the kitchen staff had walked out over arrears in their wages. In 1594 and again in 1596, there were attempts to strengthen the monarchy's income and reduce its spending.[2] A cabal of eight advisers was appointed to help Queen Anna with her household expenditure. Their number earned them the collective nickname "The Octavians" and, at the start of 1596, Anna presented James with a thousand marks in gold coins, the amount she had managed to save since the Octavians became her accountants. Sir James Melville told the King that spending beyond his means was one of four ways how "a prince soonest wrecks himself"; the other three were laziness, listening to bad advice, and generosity to flatterers.[3] James VI had good intentions when it came to his finances, but the periods in which he adhered to a budget, or at least attempted to, repeatedly gave way to a surge of overspending.

In 1597, another witch-hunting panic swept Scotland, after two consecutive years of terrible harvests throughout the British Isles. This time, James was less involved, more skeptical, and, eventually, in opposition to it. The key witness was an early victim, Margaret Aitken, who was nicknamed "the Great Witch of Balwearie" after her hometown. She had been subjected to torture there and confessed not only to being a witch herself but to the existence of over two thousand more, whom she alone could identify by looking into their eyes. The witch-hunters paraded Aitken from village to village, corralling women in front of her and leaving bodies in their wake as Aitken pronounced them "innocent" or "guilty." Some local clergymen helped with the detention and torture of suspects. At the start of August, the hunt collapsed after a suspecting lawyer held back a few whom Aitken had identified as witches the day before. He included them in the crowd brought to her the next day. Not recognizing them, Aitken declared them innocent. A woman called Marion Walker made it her mission to print and disseminate the details of Aitken's exposure as a fraud, which detonated the credibility of the 1597 witch hunts. It did not save Aitken's life—she was burned to death for perjury instead.

Like many people who read the details of Aitken's real experiences, it was not that James no longer believed in witchcraft or the impact of satanic influences in politics. In the same year, he published his book *Daemonologie*, which he had likely been working at, on and off, since the North Berwick trials six years earlier. In *Daemonologie*, James warned his "beloved reader" that witchcraft was most "certainly practiced" by witches, sorcerers, and necromancers, whom he described as "these detestable slaves of the Devil." However, the King had reverted to his previous concerns that the brutality meted out against suspects might induce false confessions.[4] He would later tell his son Prince Henry that, when the time came, his duty as a king would be to discern the innocent from the guilty, even when all around him assumed guilt. In August, James abolished the standing committees that had been established to permanently investigate witchcraft after the North Berwick trials.[5]

He was determined too to ameliorate the Kirk's recent resurgence. In this, he was at first unsuccessful. He ordered the arrest for sedition of a clergyman who told his congregation that all royalty were "the Devil's bairns," but the Kirk remained confident that, in any competition with the Crown, they were the stronger party.[6] At Falkland Palace in September 1596, during a discussion of the Two Kingdoms theory, Andrew Melvill grabbed the King and told him that royalty was nothing more than "God's silly* vassal."[7] In December 1596, Edinburgh erupted with pro-Presbyterian riots, whose participants presented themselves as the living embodiment of "the Sword of Gideon"—Gideon was a general, mentioned in the Bible, who dedicated his victories to a holy cause. The protesters claimed that they were acting to preempt a Catholic coup that, almost certainly, existed only as a conspiracy theory. The damage that the rioters caused in the city was such that James left Edinburgh, taking the law courts and council with him as he relocated to Linlithgow Palace. He invited loyal Lowlanders to join him, and many answered his call. With these supporters, the government, and the judiciary at his side, James refused to return to Edinburgh until the civic authorities punished the rioters and paid him a fine of twenty thousand marks.[8] This subdued the capital and added much-needed funds to the royal coffers. Perhaps most importantly, the Kirk's alleged role in encouraging the riots dealt a blow from which it would take political Presbyterianism years to recover. With the Kirk clipped, James turned his attention south of the border.

---

* Weak.

It was one of the great frustrations of James's Scottish reign that he could not persuade Elizabeth I to officially declare him her heir. Throughout the 1590s, James remained watchful of events in England to see which worked in his favor and which against.

The roots of James's claim to the English throne lay earlier in the century with Henry VII, King of England from 1485 to 1509, who had eight children, of whom three lived long enough to have children of their own. From those three siblings alive at the start of the sixteenth century had descended nearly all the claimants alive by the century's end. The eldest of the three, Margaret, who had married the King of Scots in 1503, was James's great-grandmother. The youngest, Mary, and her second husband Charles Brandon, 1st Duke of Suffolk, had two sons together who died in childhood and two daughters, both of whom later had children of their own. The middle of Henry VII's surviving children succeeded their father as Henry VIII, reigning from 1509 until his death in 1547. In those thirty-eight years, Henry VIII married six times; the consequences of his marriages played a large role in paving James's path to the Tudors' throne.

Henry VIII's first marriage—to the Spanish princess Katherine of Aragon—produced a prince, Henry, Duke of Cornwall, who was born and died in 1511. It also resulted in a daughter, Mary, who survived to adulthood. After eighteen years of marriage, King Henry petitioned the Vatican for an annulment, at the same time as the new Protestant religion was spreading across western Europe. When the Pope dithered on a decision for seven years—largely through fear of offending Queen Katherine's Habsburg relatives—Henry's mind proved fertile soil for Protestant sympathizers in England who, in the early 1530s, supported him when he severed the country's loyalty to the papacy and created a separate Church of England.

Intending initially to lead a church that would not be too different theologically from the Roman Catholicism it had left, Henry married the Earl of Ormond's daughter Anne Boleyn, with whom he fathered James's future godmother, Elizabeth.[9] Exerting significant influence at the heart of government did not save Queen Anne from being framed on charges of adultery, incest, and treason, for which she was executed after a show trial in 1536. Before the month was out, Henry had married courtier Jane Seymour, who died the following year from postnatal complications caused by the birth of their son, Edward.

Henry's three subsequent marriages all had diplomatic, social, or political significance at the time. Dynastically, however, they had no long-term consequences after Henry's death in 1547. His will left the crown to Prince Edward and any heirs he might father. If that line became extinct, the crown would pass to Edward's elder sister, Mary, and her descendants, and failing that to the youngest sister, Elizabeth. In the unlikely event of all three siblings dying childless, Henry VIII stipulated that the crowns of England and Ireland should pass to the descendants of his youngest sister, Mary, Duchess of Suffolk. She had been Henry VIII's favorite sibling, and some have suspected that Henry's will sentimentally reflects that, but his decision to violate primogeniture by prioritizing Mary's descendants over those of their elder sister Margaret was, however, likely motivated more by Mary's marriage to an English duke and the subsequent marriages of both their daughters to English aristocrats.[10] The descendants of thrice-married Margaret in contrast either were members of the Scottish royal family or had married Scottish aristocrats—and there were many in England, including Henry himself, who did not want to see the throne pass to a foreign dynasty. What followed was a dubious argument on the part of some English experts that their crown could be inherited only by somebody born in England or Wales.[11]

The Stewarts never accepted that Henry VIII had any right to elevate nationality as a criterion over primogeniture. Historically, half a dozen kings of England had been born in lands that were neither in England or Wales, nor controlled by its crown.[12] However, Scottish objections to the English line of succession seemed more academic than relevant until the lingering uncertainty caused by Henry VIII's private life fused with the sectarian tensions created by the Reformation and the mercilessness of early modern diseases to cut like a scythe through the Stewarts' competition.

In 1553, Henry VIII's unmarried Protestant son, Edward VI, died aged fifteen, likely of bronchopneumonia.[13] Edward's reign had moved the Church of England in a much more Protestant direction and, piously fretting at the thought of his reforms being overturned by his Catholic sister, Mary, the dying King tried to void their father's will by skipping over the surviving Tudor line altogether to go straight to Lady Jane Grey, the fervently Protestant granddaughter of Henry VIII's favorite sister.* Jane lasted nine days on the throne before the people rallied behind the disinherited Mary, who became the country's first crowned female monarch and subsequently had Jane executed for treason. Queen Mary married the future King Philip II of Spain, with whom she had no children by the time she died in 1558. The throne passed to Elizabeth, the last of Henry VIII's children.

Elizabeth kept the two remaining Grey sisters at arm's length, trusting them no more than had her late sister. In diluting the threat posed by their royal ancestry, the Greys did much of Elizabeth's work for her by eloping without her permission, which, as potential heiresses to the throne, they were expected to seek. The elder surviving sister, Katherine, married a member of the influential Seymour family; for this, she and her husband were later imprisoned in the Tower of London by an irate Queen Elizabeth, who declared both their infant sons to be bastards. The youngest sister, Lady Mary Grey, fell in love and eloped with a palace servant. She was spared the Tower when the Queen discovered what she had done, but she was separated from her husband and sent in disgrace to the countryside, where she died of the plague in 1578, ten years after a combination of tuberculosis and an eating disorder had ended the life of her equally unhappy sister Katherine.[14]

With the alternatives vanishing, the Stewarts emerged as the clear front-runners to succeed Elizabeth. Mary, Queen of Scots' claim

---

* Despite her Protestant faith, Edward's youngest sister, Elizabeth, was collateral damage of her brother's plan in 1553. Edward was disinheriting Mary on religious grounds, but that was not yet a legally acceptable criterion to remove someone from the English line of succession. It did not become so until 1689. In 1553, Edward and his advisers therefore cited the dissolution of the marriage between Henry VIII and Mary's mother, Katherine of Aragon, as their justification for demoting her. As the same thing had happened between Henry and Elizabeth's mother, Anne Boleyn, Edward also removed Elizabeth from the line of succession.

to be Elizabeth's rightful heir had been strong even before that, but James's was stronger, thanks to his parents' marriage. Of his English great-grandmother's three marriages, two had produced children. With her first husband, King James IV, she was the parent of the future James V. After James IV's death in battle, Margaret had married a Scottish nobleman, the Earl of Angus, who became the father of her daughter, Lady Margaret Douglas. The latter also married a Scottish aristocrat—in her case, James VI's future regent the Earl of Lennox—but they spent most of their married life in England, where their sons, including the future Lord Darnley, were born. Darnley's claim to the English throne via their shared grandmother could have been a threat to that of Mary, Queen of Scots, especially since he had the legal advantage of English birth. Their competing claims were instead combined by the cousins' wedding in 1565, which, disastrous as it was in nearly every other aspect, meant that the senior bloodlines from both sides of Margaret Tudor's grandchildren merged in one candidate—James.

Following his mother's beheading, James's main competitor for Elizabeth's crown was a member of the English court called Ferdinando Stanley, 5th Earl of Derby.* Under the terms of Henry VIII's will, Lord Derby took precedence over James as heir to the throne, but in the half century since Henry's death his will had been questioned so many times, not least by his own son Edward VI, that James had reason to be confident that it could be ignored, in his favor, a final time. Confidence, however, was not certainty, and James worried that the anti-Scottish lobby in England would promote Derby after Elizabeth's death.

Plots multiplied as Elizabeth aged, and each faction hoped to have their candidate positioned as next in line when the Queen died. One such intrigue may have cost Derby his life. He had been discreetly contacted by an illegal Catholic group, led by a Jesuit priest, who promised Derby support if he would guarantee to reign as a Catholic king.[15] Although rumored to be sympathetic to what

* Henry VIII's great-great-nephew, as the son of Margaret Stanley, Countess of Derby. Margaret was the daughter of Eleanor Clifford, Countess of Cumberland, the younger daughter of Mary Tudor the Elder, Henry VIII's sister.

was, by then, referred to as "the Old Religion" in England, Derby had no intention of risking his life by scheming against Elizabeth's Protestant regime. He reported the Jesuit padre's words to Elizabeth's chief minister, Lord Burghley, who sanctioned arrests and executions against the group. In revenge, one of the plotters allegedly slipped poison into Derby's food and he died on April 16, 1594.[16] (Stomach cancer has also been suggested as the cause of death.[17]) Whatever brought it about, the death of the thirty-three-year-old earl removed James's last serious potential rival for the English crown. Derby's surviving younger brother swiftly distanced himself from their family's claim to the throne, and Derby's three young daughters, thanks to their youth and the popular preference for a male heir, presented a negligible risk to James.

Derby's daughters and their uncle were four of nine other claimants whom James could henceforth regard as minor threats.[18] The others included Philip II of Spain and his daughter Isabella-Clara-Eugenia. Philip's death in 1598 removed him and weakened the chances for Isabella-Clara-Eugenia, whose brother Philip III seemed less dazzled by dreams of England than had their father. In truth, Isabella-Clara-Eugenia was not particularly enthusiastic about it either. James did, however, worry from time to time that the Catholic minority in England and Wales might gravitate toward a Habsburg queen if they feared that, as a Protestant, he would sustain the anti-Catholic initiatives passed by Elizabeth.[19]

Another possible rival was James's cousin Lady Arbella Stuart, the only surviving child of his father's younger brother, whose claim as an English-born descendant of Henry VII was undermined by the lack of enthusiasm for her claim at Elizabeth's court. Last were Edward and Thomas Seymour, Lady Katherine Grey's sons. As mentioned, the brothers had been bastardized by Elizabeth, but then so too had Elizabeth and her sister, Mary I, by their own father, a detail that had prevented neither sister from succeeding to the throne. Bastardy aside, Edward Seymour united in one person the five preferred contemporary qualities for a future monarch by being an adult Protestant English male in good health. Although he had married a political nonentity from a minor family of the Dorset gentry, Edward could have proved a challenge to

James if Queen Elizabeth made some kind of step to rehabilitate him as a member of her family or if Edward tried to recruit a faction of supporters. While James maintained friendly relations with Elizabeth, neither made any move to do so, and James's hope to become the next king of England and Ireland grew.

Time isolated Elizabeth, robbing her, one by one, of her confidants. Her favorite, the Earl of Leicester, died in 1588, followed by Sir Francis Walsingham in 1590 and Lord Burghley eight years later. Elizabeth sat by Burghley's bedside and served him soup during his final days. Aside from grief, these bereavements left Elizabeth surrounded by those who lacked the devotion of the previous generation. Leicester's stepson, the Earl of Essex, became the darling of those who wanted to see England take her place as a militant Protestant power with a commensurately aggressive foreign policy. Burghley's son Sir Robert Cecil rose to take his father's place as the Queen's chief political adviser, where he promoted an anti-war agenda that earned him Essex's hatred. With no memory of Elizabeth in her prime, this younger generation of the English elite saw her as an anxious, melancholy, ineffectual queen presiding over the diplomatic and economic decline of her kingdom.

James entered into discreet communication with some of these influential members of the English court, whom he hoped would support him as king when the time came. The Scottish ambassador to England, Edward Bruce, later ennobled as Lord Kinloss for his efforts, was tasked with facilitating this epistolary espionage. The correspondents' careers, and quite probably their liberty, would have been forfeited had Elizabeth discovered what they were doing. However, participating in the intrigue was in their best interests, despite its risks. It would stand them in good stead if James did succeed Elizabeth, and several, including Sir Robert Cecil, feared a civil war if a clear successor was not presented to the public immediately upon Elizabeth's passing. To keep themselves safe until that day, the conspirators wrote to one another in code and by numbers, instead of names—James was *30.*[20]

From his new correspondents, James received conflicting advice. Essex encouraged him to recruit enough men in England to add military heft to his claim, sufficient to coerce Elizabeth into legally recognizing him as her heir. Robert Cecil suggested James bide his time and avoid anything that might antagonize Elizabeth. The Earl of Mar had previously spent time in England and, from what he had seen, advised James that Cecil would prove a more beneficial ally than Essex.[21] The accuracy of Mar's assessment was proved when an attempted uprising led by Essex against Elizabeth's government collapsed for lack of popular support and ended with his execution for treason. Fortunately for James, Essex had burned their letters before he was arrested. With Cecil, James agreed to a plan whereby, if Elizabeth was truly dead, Cecil would send him word via a messenger, whom James would know he could trust because of a particular ring the messenger brought with him.

James agreed with Cecil that maintaining good relations with Elizabeth was paramount in order to prevent any possibility of her punishing him by endorsing a rival heir. In 1596, Elizabeth heard rumors that Anna had secretly converted to Catholicism thanks to the evangelizing efforts of her friend Henrietta, Countess of Huntly. Elizabeth wrote to Anna, asking her to clarify that it was not true.[22] Anna responded with charming denials and proclamations of Protestant piety, and she sent repeated flattering requests to London for a portrait of Elizabeth to decorate her apartments at Dunfermline. Whatever private matters strained their marriage, when it came to foreign policy, James and Anna were united as a force with which to be reckoned.

James's evolving political beliefs, however, weakened his cause in England in some quarters. After *Daemonologie* in 1597, his next two books, *The True Law of Free Monarchies* in 1598 and *Basilikon Doron* ("Royal Gift") in 1599, were political. The latter was ostensibly couched as a manual for James's son to consult as he prepared to "become a perfect King." It reads almost as James's political memoir of his reign, specifically "the particular diseases of this kingdom, with the best remedies for the same," by which he meant the forces that had opposed him. At length, he blamed the Kirk for the chief miseries of his reign. *Basilikon Doron* became one of the best-selling books of the era, with sixteen thousand copies sold internationally and nationally, and the Kirk was furious with how they had been presented in it.[23]

Basilikon Doron warned Prince Henry against reading anything by George Buchanan or John Knox, authors of "infamous invectives," and it contained moral instructions for the prince's private life.[24] If James had slept with Anne Murray in 1595, his warning to Prince Henry to avoid "the filthy vice of adultery" is striking for its hypocrisy, as is James's characterization in the same book of sodomy as an equally unforgivable crime. On the topic of kings' adulteries, James reflected on the challenges he and his mother had faced because of his grandfather's sexual adventures. In Mary's case, her bastard half brother the Earl of Moray had rebelled against her, and in James's, many plots, both real and imagined, had been led by his cousin Lord Bothwell, whose father was another of Mary's illegitimate half brothers. "Have the King my grandfather's example before your eyes," he warned Henry, "who by his adultery, bred the wrack of his lawful daughter and heir; in begetting that bastard, who unnaturally rebelled, and procured the ruin of his own sovereign and sister. And what good her posterity* hath gotten since, of some of that unlawful generation, Bothwell his treacherous attempts can bear witness."[25]

Both books exhibit how nimble was James's grasp of the intellectual philosophies that underpinned the Divine Right of Kings. James's ideal political system was a kingdom modeled on Christianity's interpretation of the Davidic monarchy practiced in the Old Testament, in which a king administered justice, punished the evil, and promoted good. In defending this symbiosis between a strong monarchy and a happy people, James paraphrased the words of the biblical prophet Jeremiah that "through the prince's prosperity, the people's peace may be procured." James depicted monarchy as a contract between ruler and ruled, underpinned by reciprocal obligations, one of which was a king's duty to rule so capably that it helped his subjects "keep their hearts free from such monstrous and unnatural rebellions."

James presented his vision for monarchy as an affirmation of ancient practices, but his belief in the Divine Right of Kings was also a response to more recent cultural and intellectual developments.

* Her heirs and successors.

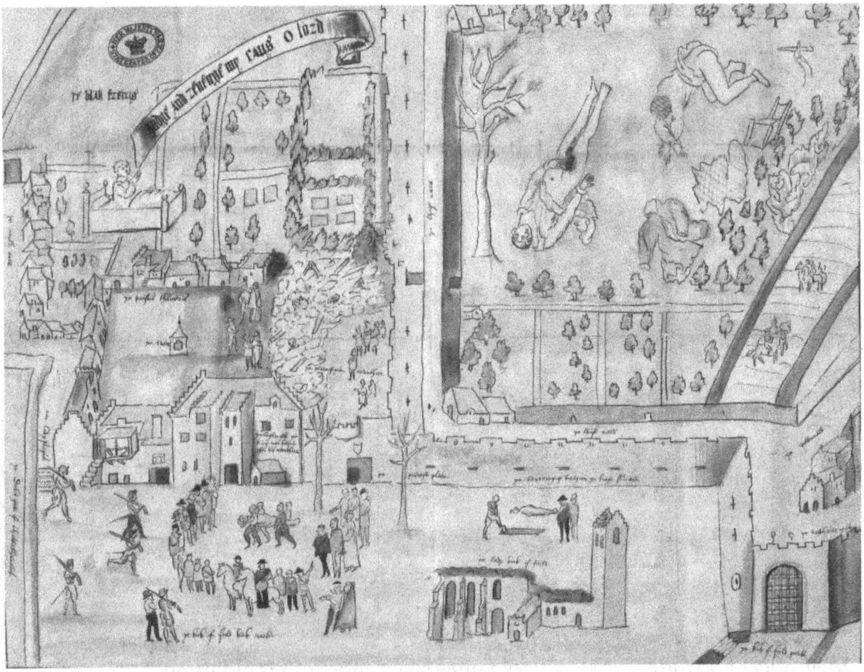

James, aged eight months, in his cradle (*top left*). This propaganda from 1567 also shows the bodies (*top right*) of James's murdered father, Lord Darnley, and his valet, William Taylor. From his cradle, baby James encourages the people to take revenge on his behalf.

James's mother, Mary, Queen of Scots.

Magnificent Stirling Castle, where James spent most of his childhood.

A man of many words but few kind ones—James's tutor George Buchanan.

Grim but clever Lord Morton, who ruled Scotland in young James's name.

James's elegant and unpopular French cousin Esmé Stuart, Duke of Lennox.

James as a teenager. He was about seventeen in this portrait.

Ruthven Castle, where sixteen-year-old James was kidnapped in 1582.

James's godmother, Queen Elizabeth I of England, who signed his mother's death warrant in 1587.

A coven receives wax images from the Devil to kill James.

James personally interrogates some of the North Berwick witches in 1590—including Agnes Sampson, whose testimony was to have enormous and tragic consequences.

James's remarkable wife, Anna of Denmark.

Gowrie House, 1600—the murdered body of Alexander Ruthven lies beneath the feet of his killer, John Ramsay. Both Ruthven and Ramsay were subsequently suspected of being James's lovers.

James in his early thirties.

A sketch with costume ideas for courtiers cast as knights in the royal masques. Philip Herbert and George Villiers both excelled in the role.

The Habsburg Archduchess Isabella-Clara-Eugenia, one of James's rivals for the English throne. She sent him this portrait of herself to assure him of her friendship.

James, painted around 1606, the year he turned forty.

In the Middle Ages, western European monarchies had wielded substantial power in tandem with the Church and with the aristocracy, to whom were devolved many issues of justice and local government. Aristocracy and Church often kept monarchy in check, as it did them. In the sixteenth century, this imperfect consensus yielded to competing ideologies. Some, such as those put forward by George Buchanan, John Knox, or Andrew Melvill, sought to further limit monarchies' power in favor of other authorities, be they the proto-democracy of Buchanan's "lawful resistance" or the implicit theocracy of Melvill and Knox's "Two Kingdoms." In opposition to this, the Divine Right of Kings elevated monarchies far beyond the status they had enjoyed in the Middle Ages, by preaching that monarchs were subject to no earthly authority, including church hierarchy or parliaments. Monarchy mirrored Heaven and monarchs were answerable to God alone, who, in the next life, would call the monarch to account for how he or she had ruled their domains. This belief could engender a confidence that evolved to megalomania in some sovereigns. It could also pose a very real threat to the mental equilibrium of devout monarchs. Absolute power brought with it absolute responsibility. For those who truly believed that they would one day be held to account by God for everything that had gone wrong in their realms, the Divine Right of Kings could push them into a nervous breakdown; it very likely did so with Henri III of France, whose last years were spent in self-flagellating panic, penitential processions through the streets of Paris, and health-destroying fasts, as he sought to atone for whatever it was he had done that had made God send him four civil wars and no children.

James was not afflicted by Henri III's self-doubt. His belief in the Divine Right of Kings was to become one of the mainstays of the latter half of his life. Perhaps that is unsurprising when looked at in the light of what he had endured in George Buchanan's classroom and the humiliations he had suffered at the hands of Morton, Gowrie, Bothwell, and the Kirk. More concretely, the Divine Right of Kings reflected where monarchy was moving ideologically, principally in favor of more centralized absolutism and away from the de facto federalism through feudalism that had hitherto existed in many western European societies. In a European context, James's political writings in 1598 and 1599 provoked little controversy. In England, what he wrote ruffled feathers, particularly his bold claim in *The True Law of Free Monarchies* that "the King is above the law."* That royalty was not regarded as being above the law in England had been brutally advertised by the executions, within living memory, of Lady Jane Grey, James's mother, and two of Henry VIII's wives.[26]

Support for the Divine Right of Kings had not exactly been lacking in James's English relatives. Elizabeth's mother, Anne Boleyn, had been an early and unambiguous proponent of it. In conversation with one of her chaplains, she came as close as anyone ever did to succinctly articulating the philosophical foundations of the Divine Right as a flawed but deliberate mirror for Heaven: "the royal estate of princes," she said, "for the excellency thereof doth far pass and excel all other estates and degrees of life, which doth represent and outwardly shadow unto us the glorious and celestial monarchy which God, the governor of all things, doth exercise in the firmament."[27] Some who knew him well had suspected that James's great-great-grandfather Henry VII would have ruled as an autocrat, if he had been able to get away with it.[28] Therein, however, lay the rub—he would not have been able to get away with it. Rebellions in the thirteenth century had forced England's King John to sign a great charter, better known by its Latin name of Magna Carta, under which he, with supreme reluctance, promised that the monarch would never again place themselves above the law, specifically but not exclusively with the clauses that no English sovereign could arbitrarily tamper with his subjects' property, freedom, or right to a trial by their peers. In the reign of John's son Henry III, parliaments had emerged as a feature of English government, a role that endured and expanded after Henry's death in 1272. Monarchs could disband parliaments if their members, who were chosen from and by a constituency's landowners, became too

* He argued that monarchs should obey the law because that was the morally right thing to do, but that they were under no other obligation than their conscience to do so.

obstreperous. However, the lower chamber—which in the fourteenth century acquired the name of the House of Commons—had the right to vote extra funds to the Crown, a function that meant parliaments could not be in abeyance for very long by any sovereign who hoped to pursue a strong foreign policy.

In the centuries between Henry III and Elizabeth I, parliaments' fiscal role grew with their political utility, as the monarchy turned to Parliament to help deal with the intermittent crises of the fourteenth, fifteenth, and sixteenth centuries. By the later years of Elizabeth's reign, English government without Parliament bordered on the unthinkable, and James's political tracts thus gave many in the English elite cause for concern.

On Christmas Eve 1598, James welcomed the arrival of his second daughter, Princess Margaret, who was born at Dalkeith. As with most winters in the 1590s, the weather that December was horrible and so James postponed "the baptism of our dearest daughter" until the following April.[29] To the surprise of few and the delight of fewer, Huntly was invited back to court to participate in the jousts celebrating the princess's baptism. He was the last Earl of Huntly as James elevated his title in the aristocratic hierarchy by making him the 1st Marquess of Huntly.

After the christening, Princess Margaret was sent to join her sister, Elizabeth, in a nursery household at Linlithgow Palace under the control of Helenor Hay, Lady Livingstone. Compared to her hatred for her son's household at Stirling, the Queen had a good relationship with Lady Livingstone, whom she came to regard as a friend. Anna was often able to visit her daughters at Linlithgow, where she watched as Princess Elizabeth grew to resemble her Stewart forebears with her red hair and hazel eyes, and baby Margaret was entertained for hours playing with strings of Florentine ribbon. Shortly after her first birthday, Princess Margaret fell ill. Apothecarists failed to cure her, as did the German doctor who specialized in infant ailments. She died in March 1600, aged sixteen months, and was buried in a shroud wrapped with Florentine ribbon.

11

CROCK OF GOLD

And if I [a] Rebel prove
Against my will, I do it
Yet I can hate, as well as love
When reason binds me to it.

—Sir Robert Ayton and John Wilson,
"Shall Fear to Seem Untrue"
(seventeenth century)

The question of how much Anna knew about James's attraction to men and, more specifically, when she knew, is interesting. She certainly knew by the early 1610s, and an often-overlooked piece of evidence strongly suggests that she knew by the middle of 1603.[1] A credible case can be made for the summer of 1600 as the point of realization. Whether this came as a shock or confirmed longer-held suspicions on Anna's part is less clear.

At various points in the 1590s, Anna had friendly interactions with two of James's previous favorites, Patrick Gray and Sandy Lindsay. Like many at court, she warmed to Sandy's personality. His brother Harry served as Anna's Master of the Household, and both she and Sandy had been concerned by James's obsession with Lord Bothwell during the North Berwick witch trials. In the first half of the decade, she had occasionally recruited Patrick to help organize her parties, including one to welcome the incoming French ambassador and his wife.* She also developed a close friendship

* In 1596, Patrick successfully applied for a passport from the council to go traveling in Europe. His wife opted to stay in Scotland and Patrick stayed away for over a year, before returning when his father's health collapsed. A devoted son, Patrick helped care for his father and gradually took over the running of their estates.

with Huntly's wife, Henrietta, bonding over their shared fluency in French and interest in the arts.

However, Anna had come to Scotland after Patrick and Sandy's ascendancy. It seems doubtful that either would have been in a rush to share details with her of their previous bond with her husband. On several occasions, the Queen's Household had acquired a reputation as a place where gossip flourished. Anna felt it merited the reputation, although she tried to warn James that the King's Household was equally adept at incubating rumors.[2] It cannot therefore be ruled out that, at some point between 1590 and 1600, Anna may have heard anything from an insinuation to an admission about her husband's premarital private life. The uncertainty over what she might have heard in the 1590s against the certainty of what she knew in the 1610s returns us to 1600 as the most likely watershed date in James and Anna's marriage.

It is credible that Anna either did not hear, or may not have believed, rumors about her husband prior to that point. If James did have any lovers apart from Anne Murray in the first ten years of his marriage, there are no traces of them in the primary sources, unlike their predecessors. James's actions from the time of his wedding to Anna until the spring or summer of 1600 strongly suggest that he was attempting to distance himself from the same-sex love affairs he had enjoyed in his late teens and early twenties.

There was a cultural precedent for him to do so. Among those who tolerated such relationships, there was a belief in the late sixteenth century that homosexual encounters were a product of youth, which would be left behind at marriage. In support of this, justificatory examples from ancient history were often cited by James's contemporaries, most commonly Alexander the Great's premarital romance with his general Hephaestion and Julius Caesar's alleged affair, aged nineteen, with Nicomedes IV, King of Bithynia, for which Caesar was nicknamed, much to his chagrin, "the Queen of Bithynia."[3] This was one of the reasons why moralists in the Renaissance had objected to young men's study of classical civilizations, as they feared it normalized and encouraged sodomy.

In 1600, James became close to Alexander Ruthven, one of his Gentlemen of the Chamber. The rehabilitation of the Ruthven family over the course of the 1590s was one of the most remarkable aristocratic comebacks of the century. Alexander had been a child of four when his father, Lord Gowrie, was beheaded for treason and sorcery. It had been followed by the humiliating incident in which his mother, Dorothea, was kicked to one side by Lord Arran as she begged the King for mercy outside Edinburgh Castle. Alexander's childhood had been overshadowed by disgrace and his adulthood shaped by the pursuit of restoration, a goal shared by his twelve surviving siblings.*

Regretting the family's hardship because of their father's misdeeds, James allowed the earldom of Gowrie to be revived for Alexander's eldest brother, another James, "a youth of great hopes, and sweet disposition" who tragically died of an unknown disease, possibly cancer, as a teenager.[4] The title passed to John Ruthven, the brother born between him and Alexander.

Three years after his eldest brother's death, when Alexander was about eleven years old, the King's kinsman Ludovic, Duke of Lennox, fell in love with Alexander's sister Sophia. While James did not want to see the family suffer, he nonetheless worried at a marriage between a Ruthven and the second cousin who, in 1591, was his heir presumptive. Ruthvens and royals did not have a history of mixing well. In the hope that absence would make the heart forgetful, James dismissed Sophia Ruthven from court and sent her to his castle at Wemyss in Fife. Seventeen-year-old Ludovic rode to Wemyss Castle, from where he rescued sixteen-year-old Sophia. They eloped the following morning and James was in foul form for ten days, until he agreed to hear Ludovic's explanation. Accepting that love made people behave unusually, James forgave the couple and received them back at court, the mercy of which seemed doubly fortunate when, only a year later, the new Duchess of Lennox died, leaving Ludovic heartbroken.[5]

The division of their father's estates among his enemies meant that the Ruthvens faced an impossible task in recapturing everything taken from them in the 1580s. However, James did return

* A thirteenth sibling, Lilias Ruthven, died in childhood, shortly after their father's execution.

some of the properties requisitioned for the Crown, and the family's financial stability increased as rapidly as their rebuilt social prominence. John Ruthven, the new Earl of Gowrie, went abroad to study at the University of Padua, while Alexander remained in Scotland, where he graduated from the University of Edinburgh. He then went to court to climb diligently on his family's behalf.

By the time his brother John came home from Italy in 1599, the Ruthvens were once again a great house. An exception was their mother, Dorothea, who, after remarrying to her late husband's cousin,* lived quietly with her younger children in the countryside. Otherwise, there were Ruthvens everywhere one looked in the Scottish elite. In 1599, James had finally chosen Maitland's successor as chancellor in the dependable Earl of Montrose, who had married his son, with James's blessing, to one of Alexander's sisters.

Their eldest sister, Mary Ruthven, Countess of Atholl, was a power in the land, as women whose convictions she successfully pushed for during the witch hunts of 1597 discovered to their cost. Three of the four she accused—Bessie Ireland, Marion MacCouss, and Janet Robertson—burned in September 1597 in Perth, a town traditionally dominated by the Ruthvens.[6] Two more Ruthven sisters, Barbara and Beatrix, served as ladies-in-waiting to the Queen. Beatrix Ruthven had a cruel sense of humor—she had once mocked a Protestant pastor for his clubfoot—but she had become close friends with, and a political ally of, Queen Anna.[7] The Ruthvens had guarded their restored fortune wisely, protecting it and growing it, and young Lord Gowrie even discreetly loaned King James substantial sums of money to fund the always over-budget royal household.

Twenty-two-year-old Alexander was the linchpin of the Ruthvens' dominance of court life. As the next in line to the earldom until such time as his elder brother married and had children, Alexander carried the title of Master of Ruthven; he was unmarried, intelligent, strong, and considered handsome.[8] He was one of James's frequent hunting companions and was in regular attendance on

* Andrew Kerr of Fawdonside, who had pointed his loaded pistol at a pregnant Queen Mary on the night of David Riccio's assassination.

him as a Gentleman of his Chamber, where his colleagues included his two younger brothers and two of their brothers-in-law.

Queen Anna's pregnancy in 1600 was difficult, and James visited her in her bedchamber at Falkland Palace on the morning of August 5 to see how she was. He mentioned that he was looking forward to the day's hunt and that he hoped to have killed a buck by noon. Anna remained in her apartments at the palace, while James set off with his men. Alexander, who had been visiting his elder brother at their nearby home of Gowrie House, joined the hunting party later that morning.

During the hunt, James accepted Alexander's invitation to spend some time at Gowrie House. James and his entourage rode in under the stone gateway to the courtyard, where they were greeted by Alexander's brother Lord Gowrie, who seemed surprised to see the royal hunting party landing on his doorstep. He had to rustle together a lunch for them, which included cold mutton and venison. After a dessert of strawberries, Alexander invited James to see a different part of the castle, with nobody but himself for company. As they went, Alexander increased their privacy by locking each door after they passed through.

The rest of James's entourage, about sixteen in number, moved out to the courtyard. They were chatting among themselves when, above them, a window in one of the towers was flung open, from which James shouted, "Treason! Treason! Treason!" until Alexander dragged him back inside.

The King's men swarmed into the house, where Lord Gowrie told them that the King had ridden off somewhere with Alexander. Knowing that he was lying, they demanded hammers to break open the locked doors. In the tower, James had managed to extricate himself from Alexander's grasp, then used his hunting knife to keep him at bay.[9] They continued in this desperate struggle until the room was breached by James's gentlemen.

The first through was a nineteen-year-old page called John Ramsay. James, by then hysterical, screamed at Ramsay, "I am murdered!"

Ramsay drew his sword and killed Alexander. He was joined by his colleagues who had followed him up the stairs; they turned back to face Lord Gowrie and his armed eight supporters, who were hot on their heels. Within moments, the Earl of Gowrie had joined his brother in death. His body was left on the stairs where he was killed, and Alexander's lay in the top room of the tower.

News of the violence at Gowrie House spread quickly. At Falkland Palace, the Queen burst into tears when she heard. She was extremely relieved that James was not more seriously wounded. It was not long, however, before she, and many other people in Scotland, had questions. The tides near Edinburgh were behaving unusually that week, which some took as a sign from nature that a great person had committed an unnatural act.[10] Anna's response was to ask why her husband, who was notoriously alert to the risk of assassination, treason, and, above all, kidnapping, had willingly gone into a difficult to access part of another man's house without any attendants and complacently watched Alexander lock each door, one by one, as they went.

James announced that Alexander had told him that he had discovered a crock of gold, which he had hidden in the tower and wished to share with his king.[11] For such an adept liar, it was not James's best work. The joke that the story was a crock of something else entirely was not far from anyone's mind. Nobody believed James's version of events, least of all his wife. When James suddenly claimed that there had in fact been another man waiting in the room to help Alexander with the murder, and had swiftly produced that man as a witness—but then pardoned him—it looked as if James was fabricating details and potentially committing perjury so that it would no longer look as if he had been alone with Alexander.

When James asked the Kirk to preach sermons disseminating his account, they hesitated on the grounds that they could not recount so dubious a story. James invited prominent Presbyterian clergy to discuss their doubts with him at Edinburgh Castle. After he had recounted his narrative again for them, James asked one of the doubters: "Are ye fully persuaded?"

"I shall speak nothing to the contrary, sir," was the best he could offer.

"But are ye not persuaded?"

"Not yet, sir."[12]

James retaliated by banning any recalcitrant reverends from preaching in Edinburgh until they promised to obey his instructions about their sermons' content.[13] He ordered that the anniversary of the plot's failure be kept as a national day of thanksgiving in Scotland; since it had been a Tuesday, for the rest of his life James attended sermons on Tuesdays as well as Sundays in gratitude to God for saving his life at Gowrie House.

There seems little reason to doubt that James sincerely believed Alexander Ruthven had intended to kill him and had come close to doing so. The ferocity of his reaction further confirms how seriously he took what had happened. He had Alexander's and Lord Gowrie's corpses brought to Edinburgh for hanging and public dismemberment. Some of their quartered limbs were sent for display in the Ruthven family's former heartlands at Perth. Alexander's two surviving brothers fled abroad. Parliament expelled the men of the family from the ranks of the aristocracy so "as the name of Ruthven should be extinguished in all time thereafter."[14] James abolished the Gowrie earldom, reseized all their properties, renamed any building in Scotland that had Gowrie or Ruthven as part of their name, and banished their sisters from court. Anna pleaded with James to let Barbara and Beatrix remain in her service. He refused, they were expelled, and Anna locked herself away from James for days. His attempt to cheer her up with a performance by a troupe of traveling acrobats was inventive but futile.

What happened in that room at the top of the tower in Gowrie House on August 5, 1600, remains a mystery, perhaps the greatest of James's life. Given its dramatic and bloody consequences, there have been many attempts at explanation.

The first is that it was a feint by James. Alexander's brother Lord Gowrie had been a staunch Protestant whose death was regretted by many of his fellow Presbyterians, some of whom suggested that James had staged the whole thing, possibly to procure the death of Gowrie, to whom he owed a great deal of money.[15] However, debt was never something that seemed to worry James, unduly or otherwise. Had he been planning to murder everyone to whom he owed money in 1600, he would have had to embark upon a killing frenzy that started with Anna's jeweler, George Heriot.

A variation on that argument was that James resented Gowrie's popularity with the Kirk and the people, and hence hoped to neutralize the threat by destroying Gowrie with violence that could be presented to the public as self-defense. However, this leaves many unanswered questions about the central role of Gowrie's brother Alexander in the day's events.

The second theory was that Queen Anna had pulled the strings of the plot in order to kill her husband, after which she would reclaim custody of their son and seize control of the Scottish government as regent.[16] She had used her friendships with Alexander's sisters to arrange the details with Alexander and his brother, who could expect prominent positions in the regime that followed James's death. If this is correct, Lord Gowrie's surprise when James arrived at Gowrie House is odd. Had he been trying to lull James into a false sense of security, surely, Gowrie would have made a greater show of hospitality? Anna's alleged motives are likewise unconvincing. To have embarked upon such a plan when she was enduring a difficult pregnancy would have been extremely unwise, something that Anna cannot be accused of. She had only to look at the fate of most dowager queens in Scotland to know that she was even less likely to secure her son's custody as a widow. It was not the custom in Scotland for a dowager queen to assume the regency—Marie of Guise's service as regent for her daughter Mary, Queen of Scots had been an anomaly. Instead, the regency went by tradition to one of the King's male relatives. It would probably have been Ludovic who became regent if James died in 1600. Furthermore, Anna's shock at what happened seems to have been sincere, as was her happiness that James was safe.[17] It was only when she noticed the manifest inconsistencies in her husband's recollections that her sympathy waned.

The third and least convincing hypothesis argues that James lured Alexander away and tried to force himself on him, whereupon Alexander overpowered him and James panicked.[18] This does not correlate with most of the details preserved in the sources. It was Alexander, not James, who suggested going upstairs, and it was he who locked the doors as they went, nor was James likely to start screaming "Treason!" out a window if he was trying to hush up a sexual rejection.

The fourth and most popular theory is that James was the intended victim of assassination by Alexander, who had played a long game of masking his hatred for the King until he could one day exact revenge for his father's execution on James's orders. Once they were in the room, Alexander tried to kill him, but James moved too quickly and reached the window in time to raise the alarm. At best, Alexander had hoped to kidnap James and establish himself as head of government, as his father once had.[19]

What, then, did Alexander use as bait to get James to the tower? That James may have been telling the truth about the crock of gold has been suggested. He had recently accepted loans from the family, so he had no reason to be suspicious when Alexander informed him that the Ruthvens were willing to part with more of their money, which was kept behind locked doors to prevent its theft. However, why was it Alexander who took James to see the gold, rather than Lord Gowrie as head of the family? Nor does it answer why Gowrie appeared surprised by the King's arrival that day. Most importantly, it does not explain why James went alone with Alexander. If he was taking a crock or chest full of gold, somebody would have been needed to bring it down.

Even the French and English courts laughed at James's account of what had happened at Gowrie House, the manifest plot holes in which had become the punch line of the moment.[20] Elizabeth I apparently found it hilarious.[21] It remained a favorite joke with the Scottish public; according to contemporary writer Francis Osborne, thirty years later, James's claim about the crock of gold was still considered so deliciously ludicrous that "no Scotch man when they encounter one another abroad does not but laugh about it when they meet together."[22]

For many of those laughing at the King's claims, there was an obvious reason why he had gone alone to a tower with locked doors in the company of his favorite. If accepted, this version of events presents Alexander Ruthven as someone who had used intimacy, or held out the promise of it, to lure the King away from his men and kill him.

There is a fifth and final possibility, which is arguably the most tragic of them all. This explanation fits with the key pieces of evidence. However, it should fairly be understood as circumstantial or logical, rather than definitive.

James and Alexander had been, or were about to be, physically intimate with one another. During the hunt, Alexander impulsively invited James to spend some time with him at Gowrie House. James accepted and went with his entourage to the house, where Lord Gowrie was surprised to see them but quickly ordered lunch for them. Afterward, Alexander invited James to come with him. James, again, accepted. The rest of his entourage, either knowing from past experience what this meant or explicitly told to stay behind by the King, finished their meal or went out into the courtyard, while James and Alexander went up to the tower, with Alexander locking the doors to guarantee privacy. They reached a small room at the top, which had apparently once been used as a study by the family. Gowrie House was one of the few homes that had not been confiscated from the Ruthvens when Alexander's father fell from power. As a result, it had never been stripped of decorations in the way their other properties had, and a portrait of Alexander's father still hung in the room. Either Alexander had forgotten that it was there, or he had seen it so many times that he had ceased to take notice of it. One account mentions that James spotted it the moment he walked into the room and, unable to help himself, made an extremely insulting remark about the late earl. In a flash of temper, Alexander punched, shoved, or attacked James.

As he grew older, there were more and more moments in which, when confronted by danger that might indicate violence against him, James suffered a temporary shattering of logic. One such incident, at a colliery in 1617, forms the prologue to this book. All he needed then was an unexpected sight of some water. Is it possible that the old earl's portrait, followed by Alexander lunging at him, sent James into a tailspin of panic in which he ran to the window in terror, screaming "Treason!" to those in the courtyard below? When, in fact, Alexander had simply momentarily lost his temper?

Even allowing for the adrenaline produced by fear and the fact that James had his hunting knife with him, Alexander was exceptionally strong, much more so than James—"thrice as strong," said a contemporary.[23] According to their own testimonies, James's men did not reach him quickly. They could not find the keys to the doors leading to the tower and had to smash them with hammers. If Alexander was intent on harming James, he had time and capability to do so. Yet James was not seriously hurt by the time he was rescued. Did Alexander try to restrain him, stop him from screaming "Treason!" and fail to calm him? All his gentlemen saw when they breached the room was a hysterical James, screaming that he was the victim of attempted murder. Acting on this, John Ramsay killed Alexander. Lord Gowrie, realizing his brother was in danger, rushed upstairs with his own men and was himself killed in the melee. Unlike the later incident at the colliery, there was nobody at Gowrie House to calm James or disabuse him of his paranoia.

This is offered as a possible conclusion, which explains most and contradicts little. However, the aforementioned caveat remains. The chief inconsistency that it fails to resolve is the existence of the witness-participant, who was allegedly in the room to assist with regicide but was then pardoned by James. Considering how terrible James's anger was to those whom he believed had plotted to harm him, the acquittal of Alexander's alleged accomplice is highly suspicious, justifying the widespread contemporary belief that the man had never been there. The "participant" was likely a product of James's ham-fisted lies to obfuscate why he had gone there with Alexander in the first place. Likewise unanswered is why Lord Gowrie lied to James's men by saying he and Alexander had ridden off together. Did he suspect a tryst might be happening upstairs and wanted to protect his brother and the King from discovery? Did he genuinely think they had left? Was he lying for some more nefarious, political reason?

The horrible events at Gowrie House have remained a mystery with many unanswered questions. While the five main theories are not all equally credible, none can be proved.

The royal marriage was severely strained in the aftermath of the Gowrie House killings. The Queen retired to her palace at Dunfermline, where she gave birth to their son Prince Charles on November 19. She and the child, who was created Duke of Albany by his father, were unwell. James went to Dunfermline and sought out the midwife, Janet Kinloch, to thank her in person for her care and give her twenty-six pounds and thirteen shillings. His generosity to his wife was lavish even by his standards. Knowing of her love for jewelry, James gave Anna a diamond worth £1,333, about a tenth of his annual income.

Prince Charles was given his own establishment, with Lord and Lady Fyvie for his governor and governess. It had hitherto been the custom for Stewart princes to be raised together, but James's decision to separate his sons may have been motivated by a tragedy in 1541 when his uncles, the princes James and Arthur, died within a day of one another.[24] If sickness entered a household, it spread quickly. Prince Henry thus remained at Stirling under the auspices of Lord and Lady Mar, while Prince Charles stayed at Holyroodhouse in the care of Lord and Lady Fyvie, a friend of the Queen.[25] The choices of Lady Fyvie and Holyroodhouse for Prince Charles were clearly intended as recompense to the Queen for the pain James had caused her over Henry's upbringing, but it did not distract Anna from her campaign to end Lord Mar's governorship at Stirling.

Another few years in which we read of no male or female favorites followed the Gowrie House scandal. The relationship between James and Anna became less fraught in 1601. On January 18, 1602, their third son, Prince Robert, was born, also at Dunfermline Palace. He was proclaimed Duke of Kintyre at his christening a few months later, the celebrations for which were overshadowed by the murder of one guest by another. The killer, an English merchant called Humphrey Dethick, slit the throat of courtier James Chambers while the latter was being shaved by his barber.[26] Dethick was taken into custody, and there were suspicions that he had come to Scotland with the intention of assassinating the King. Queen Elizabeth wrote to James to assure him that, were this to be proved true, he need not feel obligated to spare Dethick's life on account of his nationality.

James hesitated because he was convinced that Dethick was mad, and he worried that it was immoral to execute the insane. Dethick insisted that he was not mad, an assessment confirmed by two doctors sent to examine him. Dethick's version of events was that he had attacked Chambers when he was paranoid with drink, but he also kept muttering about a prophecy. His trial was postponed after a virulent outbreak of the measles in the Lowlands, which affected James's six-year-old daughter, Princess Elizabeth, who recovered, and her infant brother Prince Robert, who died on May 27. Anna was grief-stricken and confessed to James that, in the aftermath of Robert's death, she had prayed often for God to send them another child to replace the one they had lost.

Like Barbara Napier during the North Berwick witch trials eleven years earlier, Humphrey Dethick vanishes from the records. His most likely fate was either that James released him, or he died in prison. Had Dethick been executed, there likely would have been some record of it.

In 1602, the English diplomat Henry Wotton came to Scotland under the pseudonym of Ottavio Baldi, which he had adopted since leaving Florence. Wotton, who had served as the English ambassador there, had been entrusted with a warning for James. It was sent by the Grand Duke of Tuscany, who had uncovered a plot among certain Catholic groups in Florence who claimed one of their number had set off to Scotland to poison its heretic king. The solidarity of crowns counted for more to the Grand Duke than religious affinity, and he sent Wotton to Scotland with antidotes for any Italian poisons that might be slipped into James's food.

Wotton—who is most famous for his observation that "an ambassador is an honest gentleman sent abroad to lie for the good of his country"—stayed in Scotland for three months as James's guest. As with Albert Fontenay's observations eighteen years earlier, Wotton earned historians' gratitude for committing his thoughts on James to paper for an English friend.

James turned thirty-six that year, but Wotton thought he looked no older than twenty-eight. He had a trimmed ginger beard and, according to Wotton,

> He is of medium stature, of vigorous constitution, his shoulders broad, the remainder of his person below somewhat slender. In his eyes and in the outward expression of his face, there appears a certain natural goodness verging on modesty. He discusses literary matters, and especially Theology, willingly . . . He wears his hair short, in imitation of his

> grandfather James the Fifth . . . [He is] patient of hard work, and little interested in either food or clothes.

He thought that James was capable of great hatred, but only in the most extreme cases. Otherwise, his instinct was to be merciful. There was no whisper of a favorite during Wotton's time at court. "Among his good qualities none shines more brightly than the chasteness of his life," Wotton wrote, "which he has preserved without stain down to the present time, contrary to the example of almost all his ancestors, who disturbed [the peace of] their kingdom with the great number of bastards which they left."

After dinner every night, James liked to relax with his friends "listening to jests and pleasantries, in which he takes great pleasure." Wotton thought this was a little too relaxed for a king and that the Scottish court was not run with the same commendable, rigid etiquette as England's. He noticed, however, that the men of James's court were watchful of strangers, perhaps in consequence of the near miss at Gowrie House two years earlier:

> His Court contains a large number of gentlemen for the size of the country; amongst whom it is very difficult for a foreigner to pass unnoticed, because immediately a new face arrives, they ask, either out of natural curiosity or out of concern for the safety of the person of their King, who he is, and what is his business. In the sum, they all show great zeal towards their Master.[27]

The Queen's twenty-eighth birthday was on December 19. Her blond hair had darkened to a light chestnut as she grew older. She was elegant, a beautiful dresser, dignified, and charming, but she never recovered her earlier popularity. There had been too many rumors about her love for other men—Lord Bothwell, the Duke of Lennox, the "bonny" Earl of Moray—which, false as they were, were kept alive by speculation resting on the adage of smoke's relationship to fire. Her friendships with prominent Catholic families did nothing to aid her in the Presbyterian Lowlands and, as shown by Queen Elizabeth's worried letter to her in 1596, the rumors that she had secretly converted had spread as far as England. Some suspected that James and Anna let tales of her Catholic sympathies leak in a Machiavellian manipulation of Catholic sentiment in England—which, they hoped, would be less tempted by the prospects of a Habsburg as their next monarch if they thought the King of Scots had a Catholic wife. It is possible. Nonetheless, Anna's interest in Catholicism appears genuine, as does James's discomfiture over it. Anna's friend Henrietta, Lady Huntly, had made her a gift of the Catholic catechism in French, which stretched even James's normally invincible tolerance for the Huntlys to the extent that he briefly banished Henrietta from court.

Whether the Queen went as far as conversion is unclear. Letters between her and Clement VIII, pope from 1592 to 1605, strongly indicate that she had become a Catholic, but later, Pope Paul V admitted that he had no idea what Anna's religion was.[28] She avoided Protestant communion and remained close to Catholic landed families, but she also continued to employ a Danish Lutheran as her chaplain, commissioned sermons from Protestant clergymen, and failed to speak out for Catholic priests arrested by the Scottish or English governments. A reasonable conclusion may be that she was interested in the Catholic faith, that she had a happier relationship with it than she did with Presbyterianism, and that at some point she found it sufficiently appealing to worry James, who briefly dismissed Lady Huntly from court to neutralize a Catholic influence close to the Queen. Anna remained sympathetic to Catholicism for most of her adult life, but it seems unlikely that she ever went through with a formal conversion.

Understandably, Anna had developed a fear of the ocean. However, although she never again braved the North Sea, she was at times tempted. During moments of low spirits, her ladies-in-waiting had seen Anna weeping for how much she missed her mother.[29] When her brother Christian IV turned eighteen in 1596, she had considered going home for his coronation, which by custom in Denmark did not take place until a king, even one who inherited as a child, reached his majority. Her plans had been scuppered by her pregnancy with her daughter Margaret. Two years later, her younger brother Prince Ulric, Duke of Holstein, had come to Scotland.

When they had first met at the Kronborg, eleven-year-old Ulric had shared James's interest in Scripture. On a visit to his sister in Scotland in 1598, nineteen-year-old Ulric shared another of James's interests—hard-drinking merriment. As a Scottish courtier put it, they all enjoyed "great carousing with the drunken Duke of Holstein."[30]

Anna remained close to her Danish family, writing to them all and often, particularly her mother. 1602 was a year of emotional peaks and troughs for the Danish royals. In September, Sophia informed Anna of her sister Hedwig's diplomatically advantageous marriage to the ruler of Saxony, followed only a few weeks later by the death of the youngest of Sophia's children, Anna's nineteen-year-old brother Prince Johan. Anna was pregnant again in the middle of March 1603 when more sad news arrived from Denmark—her grandfather who had cared for her in her childhood, the Duke of Mecklenburg-Güstrow, had died—and Anna went into mourning.

James had been told to expect another royal death. His informants at the English court had warned him that Elizabeth I's reign was drawing to its close. She had been listless throughout the Christmas celebrations in London. At the end of February, her cousin and closest friend, the Countess of Nottingham, had died, plunging an already unwell Elizabeth into a depressed state. Her physical ailments multiplied, until it was a painful struggle for her to swallow.

Twelve days after the Duke of Mecklenburg-Güstrow's death, James had just gone to bed at Holyroodhouse when his men told him that a messenger had arrived from London. James walked into his audience chamber to see a blood- and mud-stained man on his knees, who told him that Queen Elizabeth had died in her bed.

Sir Robert Carey apparently made a habit of reporting the deaths of queens to the Scottish court. He had last been there sixteen years earlier to convey Elizabeth's apology for the execution of James's mother. A grandson of Elizabeth's aunt Mary Boleyn, Carey had been dispatched by Sir Robert Cecil from Richmond Palace, where Elizabeth had died. To present a fait accompli for the succession, speed was of the essence. The pre-agreed-upon ring that was to serve as proof to James that Elizabeth was dead was dropped out a palace window to a waiting Carey, who had then ridden to Scotland in such haste that he had not stopped to tend to his wounds after he fell off his horse, which kicked him in the face. He was the first to kiss the hand of King James I of England.[31]

Looking at the ring proffered by Carey, James said, "It is enough: I know by this you are a true messenger."[32]

12

UNION JACK

More men prefer the rising sun, than the one that sets.
—Elizabeth I, Queen of England and Ireland
(d. 1603)

The days after James joyfully raised Robert Carey to his feet were dominated by activity. James's allies—now his subjects—in London assured him that the situation was proceeding better than he could have hoped. In the days immediately after Queen Elizabeth's death, the public's mood had been so unsettled that food prices quadrupled.[1] However, the plans laid by James and his correspondents came to fruition as the latter moved with lightning speed to secure a bloodless transfer of power. When heralds proclaimed him king at ceremonies in London, the announcement was greeted with celebratory bonfires throughout the city.[2] The Church of England proclaimed their loyalty, and all his potential rivals put distance between themselves and their claims. Edward Seymour, Lord Beauchamp went into his nearest town, Bristol, where he publicly acknowledged James as his king.[3] James's cousin Lady Arbella Stuart, who had been miserable in the final years of Elizabeth's rule, likewise declined to press her suit and instead hoped for better days when James came to England.[4] From the Netherlands, which she had ruled for the last five years as governor for her brother, Isabella-Clara-Eugenia and her husband, Archduke Albrecht, dispatched a message to James in which the Archduchess disavowed her claim to the English throne. As a gesture of her goodwill toward them, she sent James and Anna a portrait of herself posing with her favorite courtier, who had dwarfism. With James's peaceful accession, an English judge observed, "The contentment of the people is unspeakable, seeing all things proceed so quietly, whereas they expected in the interim their houses should have been spoiled and sacked."[5]

In Edinburgh, it was decided that James would go south at the first opportunity and that Anna, who was pregnant, should follow later with two of their three children. Prince Henry would remain at Stirling to complete his education, while six-year-old Princess Elizabeth and two-year-old Prince Charles, Duke of Albany, accompanied their mother. Anna's decision to stay in Scotland until the birth helped smooth over a logistical difficulty about her new ladies-in-waiting in England. They could not attend on her until they had completed their last duty to their former mistress, Queen Elizabeth, by playing a ceremonial role at her funeral and, until then, keeping vigil on a rota beside her coffin. It was an English custom that monarchs did not attend their predecessor's funeral. James authorized an expensive, respectful ceremony for Elizabeth, who would be buried at Westminster Abbey just over a week before his arrival in London.

There would be no time for James to go to Stirling to say goodbye to his eldest son in person. Instead, he wrote to Henry, urging him never to be arrogant because of his exalted position as heir to three crowns:

> Be merry, but not insolent, keep a greatness, but *sine fastu;** be resolute but not wilful, be kind but in honourable sort. Choose none to be your playfellows but of honourable birth; and, above all things, never give any countenance to any, but as ye are informed that they are in estimation with me.† Look upon all Englishmen that shall come to visit you as your loving subjects, not with ceremoniousness as towards strangers, but with that heartiness which at this time they deserve.[6]

A week to the day after Elizabeth's death, crowds gathered to hear James become the first king of England to be proclaimed

* Without pride/arrogance.

† Do not trust or show favor to anyone unless you are certain they have found favor with me.

at Edinburgh's Mercat Cross. Loud cheers were heard from those who were proud that their king would rule over England, but there were groans from those who worried about what this would mean for Scotland's good government. Sir Thomas Craig, a lawyer in Edinburgh, did not agree with his countrymen who thought James's accession to the English throne was one of the greatest triumphs in Scottish history, through which the southern kingdom had yielded to the northern. Craig feared that the English would triumph by stealth, swallowing up the Stewarts, or the Stuarts as they would be known there, until future generations of the dynasty no longer thought of themselves as Scottish. "Our kings will be Englishmen, born in England," Craig predicted.[7] Anxiety in the face of the new was the dominant emotion by Sunday, April 3, when James and Anna attended church at St. Giles's. Many in the congregation wept when the King's departure was mentioned.

James thought both segments of public opinion had it wrong in seeing the new relationship with England as a competition. During the service at St. Giles's, he gave a speech to the congregation, to whom he presented the union between Scotland and England as in everyone's best interests:

> One country has wealth, and the other has a multitude of men, so ye may part the gifts, and one do as they may to help the other . . . There is no more difference betwixt London and Edinburgh, yea, not so much as betwixt Inverness or Aberdeen and Edinburgh . . . my course must be betwixt both, to establish peace, and religion, and wealth, betwixt both the countries. And as God has joined the right of both kingdoms in my person, so ye may be joined in wealth, in religion, in hearts, and affections . . . I have a body as able as any king in Europe, whereby I am able to travel, so I shall vissie* ye every three year at the least, or ofter, as I shall occasion . . . Think not of me as a king going from one part to another; but as a king lawfully called, going from one

* Visit.

> part of the isle to the other, that so your comfort may be the greater.[8]

James once compared ruling Scotland, especially its nobility, to riding "a wild unruly colt."[9] The riding was difficult, but being thrown off and trampled was even worse. He believed the English aristocracy possessed an instinctive fidelity to their monarchs; there had been only three serious English aristocratic plots against the sovereign in the last century.[10] Yet despite the problems that had faced James since childhood and the pain those problems had caused him, he was among the most successful kings in Scottish history. The economy had stabilized. He had clipped the Kirk without alienating too many of his Presbyterian subjects. There had been no sectarian persecutions or war during his reign. He had survived and crushed every aristocratic plot against his power. He had maintained social order in the localities that was dependent on the nobility, while promoting peace among the great families by encouraging feud-mitigating weddings. He had resolved in Scotland's favor a century-long sovereignty dispute over the Orkney and Shetland Islands. He had balanced political factions at his court after the 1st Earl of Gowrie's downfall, and his was the first reign in centuries during which there had not been an invasion by, or of, England. In the context of the interaction between monarchy and aristocracy throughout Scottish history, to say nothing of how that dynamic was altered by the emergence of the Presbyterian Kirk, it was unreasonable to expect that any sovereign in post-Reformation Scotland would enjoy a tranquil or easy reign. Ruling successfully meant engaging with, and surviving, difficulties. This James had done.

There had been mistakes. His popularity had ebbed and flowed. People laughed for decades about his "crock of gold" story concerning Alexander Ruthven. Despite his revivified skepticism about their validity, he had failed to halt the witch-hunting panic of 1597 and had been an integral factor in the savagery of the same phenomena in 1591. Relations with the leaders of the Kirk were, at best, coldly cooperative and, more often, acrimonious, and his leniency toward Huntly had cost James respect, in and out of court.

On Tuesday, April 5, two days after his speech at St. Giles's,

James kissed Anna goodbye at Holyroodhouse and set off for England. Among those who accompanied him were Ludovic, Duke of Lennox; the Earl of Mar, who had delegated the running of Prince Henry's household at Stirling to his wife and mother until his return; the captain of James's guard, Sir Thomas Erskine, and the King's treasurer and confidant, Sir George Home. Lord Montrose stayed behind as Lord Chancellor. During James's time in England, Montrose would liaise between the King and the council, headed by Montrose himself, which would continue to oversee Scotland's daily government. James made it clear to Montrose that he wanted to be kept abreast of all developments and that he intended to be as involved from England as he was when on one of his extended hunting trips.

After riding out from Edinburgh, the King spent the night at Dunglass Castle, the ancestral home of his accompanying treasurer, Sir George. The next day, James VI left Dunglass with his entourage and James I crossed into England.

On Wednesday the sixth, the King entered Berwick, site of the negotiations for the treaty between his government and Elizabeth's seventeen years earlier. The town's authorities provided a warm welcome that was dampened by heavy rain. James toured the fortifications and, at the governor's invitation, fired a blank from a cannon. He was pleased to hear an apology during a sermon preached by the Bishop of Durham, one of those who had queried if England's crown could be inherited by a foreigner. After the service, James told the bishop that he held no grudge for his former opinions. Impressed by his eloquence, acumen, and contrition, James later even promoted him to the archbishopric of York. He was less magnanimous upon receiving a letter from the council in London declining his request, or rather his order, that they send much of Elizabeth's jewelry north so that he could forward it on to Anna, who was now its rightful owner. Elizabeth's Master of the Great Wardrobe, Sir John Fortescue, claimed that they could not send any royal jewel out of the country, a quibble that James interpreted as xenophobia ill-disguised by protocol. He had Fortescue dismissed from office.

After Berwick, James and his men continued to the port of Newcastle upon Tyne, where over the two nights of his sojourn James was impressed by the town's wealth and how "all things were in such plenty."[11] This was followed by more travel and a night's rest at Widdrington Castle, the ancestral seat and namesake of a local gentry family. The pattern was set for James's path to London, of civic entries into important towns where he would stay for a few nights, see the people and meet the town's authorities, punctuated as he traveled by stays at the homes of the elite. Between Newcastle upon Tyne and his official entry to Durham, one of the places at which James lodged was Lumley Castle, home of Lord Lumley, an urbane seventy-year-old art collector with Catholic sympathies and a very grand sense of himself. As James was shown the castle's treasures, he could not contain his sarcasm at a tapestry depicting Lord Lumley's ancestry all the way back to Adam and Eve.

"Let me digest the knowledge I have gained," he said, interrupting his guide, "for I did na ken* Adam's name was Lumley."[12]

James's brusque way of speaking and his relaxed manners fascinated those whom they did not offend. The scholar and courtier Sir Francis Bacon, one of many who arrived to join James as he traveled south, wrote to a local nobleman that their new king was "rather like a prince of the ancient form than of the latter time. His speech is swift and cursory, and in the full dialect of his country; and in point of business, short; in point of discourse, loud."[13] For those exasperated by the late Elizabeth's conservatism in policy and protocol, this was another point in James's favor. "Few wished the Queen alive again," concluded Sir Roger Wilbraham, the former Solicitor-General of Ireland who also came to pay homage during James's journey to London.[14]

After puncturing the pretensions of his host at Lumley Castle, James stayed at Durham, where he attended a service in its extraordinary twelfth-century cathedral. Following his departure from Durham, James spurred on his horse to ride ahead of his retinue. The weather had improved, and it was apparently a glorious spring afternoon when James dismounted at a quiet spot called Haughton-le-Side, where he stood and gazed over the fertile fields of his kingdom.

---

* Not know.

It was a rare moment's quietude for James, who was feeling overwhelmed by the intensity of the English public's interest in him. Farmers were making a tiny fortune by renting out their carts for onlookers to climb up and get a better look as James rode by. The crowds were so dense "that they covered the beauty of the fields; and so greedy were they to behold the King that they injured and hurt one another."[15] After more cheers at seeing the new monarch's face, James turned to one of his Scottish courtiers and said, "By God's wounds! I will pull down my breeches and they shall also see my arse!"[16] At another stopping point, James seemed so overwhelmed that he locked himself away for a few hours in a quiet room. It was only with difficulty that he was persuaded to return to a top-floor window to acknowledge the people's acclamation.

His mood had lifted by the time he made his ceremonial entry into York on Saturday, April 16, arriving from nearby High Walworth Manor, where he had spent the previous two nights as a guest of the widowed Lady Elizabeth Jennison. He knighted her son-in-law in thanks to the family for their hospitality. "Using no great majesty nor solemnity," James refused a coach at York and instead walked through the crowds toward the Minster.[17] A cathedral had existed on the site since the early seventh century; the building in which James worshipped, and which survives to the present, had been completed in 1472 after 242 years of intermittent construction. From its famous stained-glass windows, emerald, purple, and blue light fell on the cathedral's stone floors. James prayed in the carved company of other kings of England who stared unseeing at their latest successor—statues of every ruler of England from William the Conqueror, king from 1066 until 1087, to the fifteenth century's Henry V, loomed on York Minster's choir screens. The last living royals to worship beneath the Minster's white-and-gold vaulted ceiling had been Henry VIII and his wife Queen Catherine Howard; their visit in 1541 was also the last royal visit to York until James's over half a century later, a snub that the city felt keenly.

Encircled by two miles of walls accessed by five fortified gateways, York was the home of England's only other archdiocese, apart from the country's senior archiepiscopacy at Canterbury. It also housed the King's Council in the Northern Parts, which made it both the religious and administrative heart of the north of England. Late in Elizabeth's reign, a visitor had described it as "the second city of England, the finest of this region and indeed of the whole North, as well as its principal fortress. It is pleasant, large, and strongly fortified, adorned with private as well as public buildings, crammed with riches and with people, and famous as the seat of the archbishop."[18]

It was at York that James first met Sir Robert Cecil, the ally who had helped make him king so peacefully. His arrival at James's side had been delayed because Cecil's rotund horse was no great enthusiast for speed.[19] While thirty-nine-year-old Cecil was mocked by his enemies, who seemed to think he had the charisma of a lettuce, he was a political genius who spoke six languages, commanded one of the most sophisticated systems of spies and informants in Europe, and was indefatigably hardworking. His scoliosis, hunched back, and short stature had earned him the nicknames "my pigmy" from Elizabeth I and "my little beagle" from James. With his passion for hunting, James's sobriquet for Cecil was more affectionate than Elizabeth's, and the nickname may have been a nod to Cecil's diligence in flushing out James's enemies. Cecil's elder brother had inherited their father's title as Lord Burghley, while Robert inherited his political talents. James was deeply grateful to Cecil and, as always, he respected intelligence. Before Cecil arrived at York, somebody had already tried to discredit him to James, by insulting both his integrity and his appearance, particularly his height. Cecil was relieved to hear from a fellow courtier that James was not swayed by this attempt at manipulation, remarking that although he had "heard you were but a little man, but he would shortly load your shoulders with business."[20] He intended to keep Cecil in place as chief minister of his new kingdom.

England in 1603 had a population of about four million, an increase of approximately 45 percent on what it had been at the end of Henry VIII's reign in 1547.[21] There had been serious setbacks to such growth due to harvest failures in 1555 and 1556, followed immediately by influenza epidemics in 1557 and 1558, but there was a sustained expansion of the population between 1561 and 1586, which continued, if more slowly, from 1586 to the turn of the century.[22] As in Scotland, the English population was not evenly distributed. About half lived in the southern third, a third in the Midlands, and about a sixth in the north. In a further similarity to Scotland, approximately 90 percent lived in the countryside, which included isolated farmsteads, hamlets, villages, and small towns.[23] Huge amounts of money had been generated since the Middle Ages by the country's wool trade and, in terms both of feeding the nation and its exports, farming remained the bedrock of English society. For the 7 percent who lived neither in the countryside nor in London, there were about seventy towns with a population between two and four thousand, and fifteen towns or cities with four to twelve thousand residents.[24] Of those, the largest were Newcastle upon Tyne and York in the north, Bristol, Exeter, and Salisbury in the south, Coventry in the Midlands, and Norwich in the east. The last was England's second-largest city with about twelve thousand living there, a distant silver medalist in population compared to the 190,000 people living in London (which will be discussed in more detail later).

The average age for marriage was twenty-five, and average life expectancy was thirty-seven. The latter figure is impacted significantly by high levels of infant mortality. If somebody lived past their dangerous first five years, of which the first was the most perilous, then we would expect a generally higher typical life span. Literacy levels in England exceeded the European average, especially in London, where about 70 percent of men and 20 percent of women were fully literate; the numbers who could read but not write were higher still, if harder to quantify.[25]

English, with many dialects, was the majority language, with a few prominent exceptions. Cornish was spoken in Cornwall, Manx in the Isle of Man, and French in the Channel Islands. The latter two were within the English royal inheritance but separate from English government. The Isle of Man was thirty-one miles from England and ninety miles from the north of Ireland. Its lordship was hereditary within the aristocratic Stanley family, who were themselves subjects of the English Crown, and it had the High Court of Tynwald as its legislature, the oldest parliament in continuous existence, a record that holds to the present. The Channel Islands were closer geographically to France than England, but they had been politically attached to the latter after England was conquered by the dukes of Normandy in the eleventh century. They too had their own legislatures and—like the Isle of Wight, which had emerged as a major naval base during Tudor rule—governors, who were usually chosen from local or English noble families.[26]

The English nobility had more money but less power than their Scottish equivalents. They could exert significant political influence at a national level, either at court or through hereditary membership of Parliament's upper chamber, the House of Lords, which they shared with the twenty-four bishops and two archbishops of the Anglican Church. In the counties, matters of local government were increasingly dominated by ambitious "new" gentry families who, as a class, had prospered under the Tudors. Merchant families, the progenitors of an emerging middle class, had meanwhile flourished in commercial centers such as London, Norwich, and Bristol. This middle class was often literate, financially comfortable, and interested in new ideas about politics and religion.

As regards religion, England by the end of Elizabeth I's reign was overwhelmingly Protestant. Judaism had been illegal since 1290 and would remain so until 1656, and populist anti-Catholicism was potent. Weekly attendances at the services of the state religion, the Church of England, were mandatory, and heavy fines were levied on "recusants," those Catholics who refused to attend. Small, and diminishing, pockets of Catholicism existed in the north, the west, on the island of Guernsey, and in certain elite families.

Diplomatically, England remained in a state of war with Spain and of a cold war with the Vatican. Friendly-to-cordial relations existed with most of the other western European powers. Under Elizabeth, ties had been forged with countries farther afield, including an alliance between Elizabeth and Sultan Murad III of the Ottoman Empire in 1579, and embassies to the Safavid Empire,* Morocco, and Russia. The last of these had been a valuable trading partner, particularly for fur, until the massive economic disruption caused by a civil war that broke out five years before James succeeded Elizabeth.

---

* Iran, also known contemporaneously as Persia.

Despite trying his best hitherto to keep himself informed of English matters, there was a great deal for James to learn, and nuances to discern, after he moved to England in 1603, especially as he sought to unite it with Scotland. James had erroneously assumed that a political union was automatically achieved the moment he became king of England, a title that he thought should be replaced with "king of Great Britain." A huge amount of legislative work would in fact be required to unify two independent countries, which both kingdoms' parliaments would need to approve. James discussed proposals for creating a single currency, mutual laws, and free trade, and he was very interested in plans for a new flag that merged Scotland's Saltire—the blue and white cross of Saint Andrew the Apostle—and England's red and white Cross of Saint George. The Latin for James, *Jacobus*, gave its name to the new Jacobean era in England and also to the flag of the hoped-for Union. Knowing of King James's enthusiasm for it, the flag, the design of which was decided upon in 1606, was nicknamed "the Union Jac," or "Union Jack," a shortening of *Jacobus.*[27]

As James embarked upon ruling his new kingdoms, a man with Sir Robert Cecil's skills and experience was invaluable. James expressed his gratitude by leaving Cecil's power as chief minister intact, and he subsequently raised him to a peerage in his own right. Moving rapidly through the ranks of the aristocracy, Cecil was made Baron Cecil in 1603, Viscount Cranborne in 1604, and Earl of Salisbury in 1605.

Distributing titles seemed a sensible way to reward those who aided or celebrated James's accession. Aristocratic positions—in ascending order in England, Wales, and Ireland, these were baron, viscount, earl, marquess, and duke—were more complicated and expensive, as they typically came with a grant of land. Knighthoods were accompanied by no such expectation, and James dubbed many knights on his way to London. He knew that his Scottish attendants were taking bribes from English families to get knighthoods for their sons and was amused by it. Supportive of his friends whom he had not always been able to generously remunerate before, he gamely knighted those who had paid them for the privilege. For James personally, money was no longer a worry. For the first time in his life, it seemed in almost limitless supply. All he needed to do was ask for it and it was forwarded, from one town to the next.

The affluence of those who hosted him confirmed James's appreciation for England's prosperity. After York, he continued south, but there was no gentry or noble household nearby to accommodate him that night, so he lodged at the Sun and Bear Inn in Doncaster. Even this comparatively humble venue impressed James, for England at the time was considered to have some of the finest inns in Europe, with a reputation as the cleanest with the best food.[28]

After that, it was another run of grand households and hosts. At Worksop, his host was the Earl of Waterford and Shrewsbury, whose late father had been entrusted with guarding James's mother in England until he was dismissed after Elizabeth's councillors feared he had become too sympathetic to Mary, perhaps even to the extent of having fallen in love with her. Shrewsbury laid on a great feast to welcome James—no small task, given that James's retinue had swelled to about five hundred people, as more and more Englishmen swarmed to ingratiate themselves with the new regime. Shrewsbury had written to his neighbors beforehand with the understated plea that "I will not refuse any fat capons and hens, partridges and the like." For his guests' entertainment, he arranged for the "most excellent soul-ravishing music" to be played by local musicians. Even James, who was usually indifferent to music, was moved.[29]

Shrewsbury was Arbella Stuart's uncle, on the other side of her family, and he nervously put in a good word for her with James. Although Arbella could have been a rival for James's new crown, Shrewsbury wondered if James might be moved to help her by ordering that she could leave the household of her redoubtable grandmother and his mother-in-law, to which Arbella had been rusticated when she earned Elizabeth I's displeasure.* Arbella's

* Arbella felt strongly that she had been treated badly by Elizabeth, enough so that she refused the government's request that she serve as chief mourner at Elizabeth's funeral, saying that since Elizabeth had not wanted her company when she was alive, she did not see much point in attending her when she was dead.

grandmother, known as Bess of Hardwick,* was one of many figures in history far more enjoyable to read about than to live with. Arbella was miserable. James assured Shrewsbury that he bore Arbella no ill will; it was hardly her fault that they shared a set of grandparents or were both descended from Henry VII. He wrote, "We are desirous to free our cousin the Lady Arbella Stuart from that unpleasant life which she hath led in the house of her grandmother with whose severity and age she, being a young lady, could hardly agree."[30] Twenty-eight-year-old Arbella left Bess's household and accepted James's invitation to come to court, where she would live with honor as his cousin.

When he reached the county of Northamptonshire, James's hostess at Apethorpe Hall, Lady Grace Mildmay, was admired in English high society for her skills as a confectioner, crafting the new import of sugar into gilded castles, heraldic animals, or figures from myth. These were served to guests who picked them apart, experiencing what we must assume was an intense sugar high before crashing to satiety by the banquet's end. A courtier who attended James's reception at Apethorpe noted, "Everything that was most delicious for taste, proved more delicate, by the art that made it seem beauteous to the eye." His next host was Sir Oliver Cromwell,† who gave James gifts of golden goblets, hunting horses, hounds, hawks "of excellent wing," and £50 to share among his Scottish entourage when he left the Cromwells' estate at Hinchingbrooke, the grounds of which had been transformed from grass to muck by the tents erected to house James's followers.

Burghley House, where James arrived in time for Easter, was so magnificent that it was said to be more like the home of an emperor. Owned by Sir Robert Cecil's brother, its many towers, windows, expansive grounds, and sumptuous interiors were a testament to

---

* Elizabeth Hardwick (c. 1527–1608), prominent aristocrat and businesswoman. Through her first three marriages, Elizabeth Barley, Cavendish, then St. Loe. Through her fourth, she became Elizabeth Talbot, Countess of Waterford and Shrewsbury.

† Sir Oliver Cromwell (c. 1562–1655), MP for Huntingdonshire, uncle and namesake of the more famous general.

the vast wealth that their family had acquired through their service to Queen Elizabeth. Before Elizabeth's accession in 1558, they had been a minor family of diligent career courtiers. Since then, they had become the best example of the "new" families who had risen to greatness under the Tudors.

James broke his collarbone at Burghley when he came off his horse during a hunt. He evidently had so much adrenaline—"his blood yet hot" was how a fellow hunter put it—that he did not acknowledge the pain until later.[31] His arm was in a sling by the time he reached Cecil's residence at Theobalds* in the county of Hertfordshire on Tuesday, May 3. Theobalds was James's favorite of the houses that he had seen thus far in England. Accessed through a large gateway, it was built around two courtyards. There was a white marble fountain at the center of the inner courtyard and another one in the middle of nine low mazes that covered the first of the house's three gardens. Another property built by Sir Robert Cecil's father, who had left it to his younger son, Theobalds's sybaritic splendor included an indoor garden for walks on rainy afternoons and a large hall that boasted a moving planetarium in its ceiling, with a mechanical sun that crossed during the day and stars that twinkled at night.†

During his four-day stay at Theobalds, James met most of his Privy Council for the first time. Like their counterparts in Scotland, the Privy Council's members were appointed by the monarch, often traveled with them from residence to residence as their principal body of advisers, and were still, as of 1603, the principal body of daily government for England and Wales. The late Elizabethan regime had been dogged by justified accusations of corruption, since many government officials, assuming that they would be out of a job when the Queen died, took the opportunity to line their pockets.[32] In his quest for stability during a historically unprecedented transferral of power—the accession to the throne of the first Scottish king of England—James announced that he would

---

* Pronounced *Tibbollds.*

† Unfortunately, we do not know how this was achieved. The original Theobalds House was demolished in 1650, after the fall of the monarchy.

maintain in their positions all thirteen of Elizabeth's privy councillors. He added five Scots to their ranks: his kinsman the Duke of Lennox; his son's governor, the Earl of Mar; Sir James Elphinstone, a former "Octavian," as one of Queen Anna's financial advisers; James's treasurer Sir George Home; and the former Scottish ambassador to England, Lord Kinloss.

With the Privy Council weighted in England's favor, James ensured that his Gentlemen of the Privy Chamber were drawn half from England and half from Scotland. The English equivalent of Scotland's Gentlemen of the Chamber, the Gentlemen of the Privy Chamber oversaw access to the King's apartments, including the public rooms where he granted audiences, as well as his more private spaces, such as his library, withdrawing chamber, and personal dining room, where he might receive particularly esteemed guests like close advisers or those with more sensitive messages to deliver. This gave the Gentlemen of the Privy Chamber great influence through access to the King. Since the post had been in abeyance since the death of the last king, Edward VI, fifty years earlier, the prestige of securing a place was correspondingly high. Forty-eight Gentlemen were chosen, twelve of whom would be on duty for three months at a time, and always with an equal division between the number of English and Scottish attendants.

When it came to the Gentlemen of the Bedchamber, James asked that politics stop at the threshold. This was an office James brought with him from Scotland, dividing the staff of the Bedchamber from those of the Privy Chamber. The tasks of sharing his room, helping him dress, and maintaining his accommodation were highly personal and, at this stage, he decided that it was to remain staffed solely by those he had known for years in Scotland. The Gentlemen of the Bedchamber included twenty-three-year-old Sir John Ramsay, who had earned James's lasting gratitude for killing Alexander Ruthven in 1600; John Murray, a nephew of James's old governess; middle-aged Sir Roger Aston, who was said to be one of the best huntsmen in Scotland; devoted Sir George Home, who, along with his other duties, was placed in charge of James's wardrobe; and Ludovic's younger brother, Lord Esmé Stuart, named after their late father, a patron of poetry and theater, and who had come to join James's service earlier that year after completing his education in France.[33]

James dismissed Sir Walter Raleigh from his post as Captain of the Guard, which he had exercised for Elizabeth, and replaced him with his Scottish counterpart, Sir Thomas Erskine. Raleigh had been among those who queried the validity of a Scottish succession in England. Even if Raleigh's loyalty had not been suspect, James likely and understandably would have preferred as captain a man whom he knew: in Erskine's case, for years following their shared childhood at Stirling.

Receptions were held at Theobalds for James to meet the rest of the English court. Many of them accompanied him on Saturday, May 7 when he rode to Stamford Hill, four miles from the capital's boundary, to be escorted into London by its Lord Mayor. Cannons fired in greeting above the cheers of the twelve thousand Londoners who had come to see James on his journey to Greenwich, the first property that he stayed in which he owned as King of England.[34]

A riverside palace in red brick and with a private covered wharf for use by the royal family, Greenwich had been built in the fifteenth century and expanded in the sixteenth. Three Tudor monarchs, including Elizabeth I, had been born there. The Queen's Apartments overlooked the west side of the palace's inner courtyard and the King's faced east, with views of the palace's tiltyard and octagonal towers.

James's journey from Edinburgh to London had been, from his perspective at least, a triumph. There had been no protests against him as the new monarch. Instead, as a relieved English eyewitness recorded, "He was met with great troops of horse and waited on by the sheriff and gents of each shire [and] joyfully received in every city and town, presented with orations and gifts: entertained royally all the way by noblemen and gentlemen in their houses."[35] In London itself, "the streets seemed to be paved with men" and their families, who turned out to cheer him.[36] Many of those who saw him at close quarters in the first two months of his English reign were impressed. Sir Roger Wilbraham wrote, "The King is of the sharpest wit and invention, ready and pithy in speech, an exceeding good memory; of the sweetest, pleasantest and best nature that ever I knew . . . he is a man of letters and business, fond of the chase and of riding, sometimes indulging in play. These qualities attract men to him and render him acceptable to the aristocracy. Besides English, he speaks Latin and French perfectly and understands Italian quite well. He is capable of governing, being a Prince of culture and intelligence."[37]

At Greenwich, it was time for the diplomatic corps to get their first look at him. Giovanni Scaramelli, who accompanied the Venetian ambassador as his secretary, was a little surprised to see the King's arm in a sling and even more taken aback by the simplicity of his outfit. Simplicity in a monarchical setting is comparative—James wore a chain of diamonds around his neck and a huge diamond in his hat—but to Scaramelli, who was used to the enormous ruffs then en vogue, the pendulous ear studs and ropes of pearls in which young English noblemen liked to bedeck themselves, James's plain gray silk suit with a black cloak, lined with scarlet, was the soul of understatement. He, too, was impressed by James's intellect, and touched both by his attempts to speak Italian and his apology for not speaking it as fluently as he would have liked.

Language came with less difficulty in James's private rooms at Greenwich, where he was heard cursing like a sailor one evening as he read a letter from Scotland.[38] Anna had waited until he was across the border and then gone to Stirling to fetch her son.

James was not an indulgent father—he expected much from his children, especially in their academic achievements—but he was an affectionate one. When Prince Henry, who had turned nine only a few weeks before his father's accession to the English throne, realized that his father would be hundreds of miles away in England and there would be no more frequent visits from him to Stirling, he wrote to Queen Anna with the observation that it seemed cruel to be denied his mother's company as well as his father's.

Anna set out to rectify the situation by riding to Stirling with a few ladies-in-waiting and an armed escort of supporters drawn from the network of allies she had established among Scotland's great families. She was greeted at the gate by the new Countess of Mar—Ludovic's sister and James's kinswoman Marie—who refused to allow the armor-clad men into the castle and had enough guards of her own to enforce that decision. She could not, however, think of any good reason for turning away the Queen. Anna and her ladies were conducted to the Great Hall, where she was hosted to a meal by Lady Mar and her mother-in-law, the Dowager Countess of Mar, whose longevity was, as far as Anna was concerned, one of her most insufferable qualities. Marie would not let Prince Henry leave with the Queen. Marie's loyalty was entirely to James, whose instructions had been clear since the day of Henry's christening: the child was to be handed over to no one, including the Queen or a delegation from Parliament, unless "I command you with my own mouth."[39] The King had given no such instructions and Marie would not therefore surrender the heir to his mother.

Anna became so upset that she collapsed. She was taken to one of the castle bedchambers, where she suffered a miscarriage on May 10.[40] She spent days in seclusion with her women. Concluding that a royal woman might want privacy only if she had something to hide, Anna's detractors in Scotland spread the rumor that she had either fabricated her pregnancy to manipulate their sympathy for her own ends or, when she could not get her own way at Stirling, had taken a potion that "had hastened her [to] abort."[41]

From England, James sent an order to transfer Henry's custody to his mother. He was distressed by news of Anna's miscarriage and then by a letter he received from her, in which she accused him of never having loved her and of marrying her only because of who her father was. Given the reason most royals married in the sixteenth century, that seems an accurate yet unfair charge. In the same letter, Anna claimed that Lord Mar, his wife, and his mother were the origins of gossip that she was secretly a Catholic, as well as of the latest conspiracy theory that she was plotting with the King of Spain to foment another Armada.[42] James replied:

> My heart,
>
> . . . I wonder that neither your long knowledge of my nature, nor of my latest purgation to you can cure you of that rooted error that anyone living dare speak or inform me in any ways to your prejudice . . .

> I can say no more but protest upon peril of my salvation and damnation that neither the Earl of Mar nor any flesh living ever informed me that ye was upon any papist or Spanish course, or that ye had any other thought but a wrong conceived opinion that he had more interest in your son and would not deliver him unto you.
>
> God is my witness that I ever preferred you to all my bairns, much more than to any subject; but if you will ever give place to the reports of every flattering sycophant that will persuade you . . . then neither you nor I be ever at rest or peace. Praying God, my heart, to preserve you and all the bairns, send me a blithe meeting with you and a couple of them.
>
> Your own,
> James R.[43]

James sent Ludovic north with the letter, along with some suggestions for the composition of Anna's household when she came to England. Lord Fyvie, governor to their son Prince Charles, politely yet firmly suggested that the latter be kept from the Queen until she recovered. He advised, "Medicine requireth a greater place with her Majesty at present than lectures on economics and politics."[44]

With Prince Henry at her side, and after refusing to allow the Mars to say goodbye, Anna set off from Stirling for Edinburgh. She decided to leave Prince Charles in the Fyvies' care, as he was unwell, and the long journey might exacerbate his illness. Somebody else remained behind too: the half-reluctant Figaro of the Stewart court, Sir James Melville, was at last allowed to retire to his fireside, rather than follow his king and queen south.*

Wounded by the cruel gossip about her miscarriage, Anna had the body of the child she had lost at Stirling embalmed and placed in an infant's coffin, which followed her in the new coach she had commissioned as she, Henry, and Elizabeth set off from Edinburgh on June 1. Few wept to see her depart, but in the three and a half weeks that it took her and the children to reach James, Anna

* Melville retired to his manor at Halhill, where he died fourteen years later.

captured with the English public all the popularity she had lost in Scotland.

With her hairdresser, Blanche Swansted, never too far from her side, Anna appeared before the English people with a towering coiffure and shimmering from head to toe. Elizabeth's jewelry had at last been handed over to her—a gold and diamond brooch in the shape of a crossbow became one of her favorite pieces. Sir Robert Cecil's brother thought Anna was "magnificent" when he hosted her at Burghley House, where she hugged his nervous son when he was presented to her.[45] The English public agreed. At several stops along the way, those cheering her were so boisterous that most of the authorities could not be heard. Some mayors gave up entirely, abandoned their speeches, and stepped back silently while Anna waved at the crowds. When she bowed to them as a gesture of thanks for their welcome, dozens of people apparently burst into tears.[46] She sent Ludovic on to Greenwich with her reply to James's suggestions for her household; she had scored them out and replaced them with her own choices.[47]

On their way she and the children stayed at Althorp, whose owner, Sir Robert Spencer, was one of the richest men in England. As Anna was guided through the estate's sprawling park, pipers hidden in the trees serenaded her and her children. To create the illusion that the royals were moving through a fairy realm, actors jumped in and out of the shrubbery reciting lines from a new play commissioned by Spencer from the author Ben Jonson. The spectacle culminated with an actor playing a faerie queen who presented Queen Anna with a huge emerald, a gift from the Spencer family.*

Althorp was the Queen's last stop before she reunited with the King at Easton Nestor, a manor house that the King reached with his entourage before the Queen arrived with hers. The Earl of Southampton, a patron of the arts with a densely populated love life, was with the King as the Queen arrived, along with Prince

---

* As thanks for his lavish hospitality, Anna suggested to James that Sir Robert be included among those ennobled for their forthcoming coronation. He agreed, and Sir Robert was created Baron Spencer of Wormleighton, thereby launching the Spencer family into the aristocracy. Sir Robert was a direct ancestor of Diana (née Spencer), Princess of Wales (1961-97).

Henry and Princess Elizabeth, the latter of whom James called "my little Bessy."[48] Southampton heard James refer to his wife as "my Annie" and tell those around him how wonderful she looked.[49] Another large crowd had gathered; their cheers became deafening when, after the long years of uncertainty over the succession under Elizabeth, James stepped forward with his elegant queen and their two healthy children—a perfect royal family for a new era.

13

PHILIP

Cursing the time, the place, the sense, the sin;
I came, I saw, I viewed, I slipped in.
. . . If it be a sin to love a lovely lad,
Oh then sin I . . .

—Richard Barnfield, *The Affectionate Shepherd* (1594)

Among the courtiers whom James met in 1603 was Lord Philip Herbert, who was handsome as Adonis and as stupid as a tree stump.[1] Philip minded neither and acknowledged both. He cheerfully admitted that he knew little about anything except dogs, horses, and hunting.[2] Nineteen years old in 1603, he was tall and energetic, with blond hair and blue eyes, and he was clean-shaven at this point in his life—he chose to grow his beard several years later. He was the second and younger son of the 2nd Earl of Pembroke, who had died two years earlier, and brother of the 3rd Earl. Their family was part of the Welsh aristocracy, where their earldom was based.

About 317,000 of James's new subjects lived in Wales.[3] In the 1480s, Henry VII, England's Welsh-born king, had repealed the anti-Welsh legislation introduced and upheld by the previous monarchs of the fifteenth century. Under his grandson Edward VI, a dozen new towns had been built in Wales, although, like England, it remained a predominantly rural society. Some of the best grain in the kingdom was produced by farms in South Pembrokeshire. Its ports facilitated lucrative trade with Ireland and France and, according to tax returns, its wealthiest county was Glamorganshire in the south, where many of those ports were located.[4]

Wales was absent from James's list of titles. He was never referred to as king of Wales in the way he was as king of England or Ireland. Wales and England had been ruled by the same monarchy since a series of wars in the late thirteenth century that culminated with the English conquest of Wales. The preconquest title, prince of Wales, was thereafter accorded by tradition, but not automatically, to the heir to the English throne. For two centuries following the conquest, Wales and England operated under different legal codes until the reign of Henry VIII, when a series of laws were passed that subdivided Wales into English-style counties, empowered to send representatives to Parliament in London. Welsh jurisprudence was abolished and its laws unified with those of England.[5] The speaking of English alongside, or in preference to, Welsh was also encouraged but met with limited success, and Welsh would remain the majority language until the nineteenth century.[6] To all intents and purposes, the laws passed by Henry VIII politically and legislatively unified Wales with England, and the two ceased to be referred to as separate national entities.[7]

Like most members of the Welsh elite, the Herbert family also had homes in England, including a London residence and palatial Wilton House, their estate in Wiltshire, where Philip was born. His English mother, Lady Mary Sidney, was admired for her intellect, and his father's family was notorious for their temper.[8] Philip inherited none of the former and some of the latter. He had briefly been at court during Elizabeth's reign and, after the accession of James in 1603, hoped to make that a more regular occurrence, using his looks to advance himself.

He was not the only one. That much of the contemporary evidence about James's private life has not survived to the present is indicated by just how many members of the English aristocracy tried to use it to their advantage and the fact that they already knew, before he left Scotland, that his tastes lay with men. The Countess of Suffolk, who schemed as naturally as other people breathed, advised Sir Robert Cecil to find a handsome man either to join James's household or to ally with one already there. A man of Cecil's intellect knew that it was unwise to act without insurance in politics. He was King James's most trusted adviser in England, for the moment, but rivals would come in time to try to turn James against him, as they had tried with Queen Elizabeth. Lady Suffolk sought a candidate from among the court's "choice young men, whom she daily curled and perfum[ed]" in the hope that they would catch James's eye.[9] She had done her research. She knew that, whomever they picked, their breath must be pleasing, as James could not abide bad breath.[10]

Cecil found their ally in Sir James Hay, a twenty-three-year-old Scotsman. The nephew of a law professor whose works James admired, Hay had been educated in France. He was outgoing, friendly, a good dancer, and a better hunter. Anna became an unlikely sponsor of Hay's career, reflective of the alliance she formed with Cecil shortly after her arrival in England.[11] If James was going to have a male favorite, it might as well at least be someone who owed his position to the Queen and the chief minister. Hay's nationality meant that the King could have no theoretical objection to Anna and Cecil's suggestion that he serve as a Gentleman of the Bedchamber, to which post Hay was admitted in October 1603. Hay was soon described as the King's "prime favourite," and Cecil observed in a letter to his brother that a handsome man was "an excellent good instrument to conserve his Majesty's good opinions."[12]

After reuniting, the royal family had decamped to Windsor Castle for a few days before going to Hampton Court Palace. Fifteen miles outside the capital and, like Greenwich, located on the banks of the Thames, it was a former ecclesiastical estate that had been transformed into Crown property by the Tudors. Henry VIII had spent a fortune on it. Four years before James first lived there, a visitor from Switzerland on a tour of Europe had described Hampton Court as "the finest and most magnificent royal edifice to be found in England, or for that matter in other countries."[13] Its demesne had expanded substantially when the monarchy requisitioned many nearby Church lands during the Reformation, and these were used to create the Hampton Court Chase, a private hunting ground encircling the palace and so extensive that it was dotted with several smaller residences.

Hampton Court became a favorite home for both James and Anna. The Chase, with its subsidiary residences, was useful to them. One of its smaller homes was Oatlands Palace, a retreat built for Henry VIII with terraced gardens, two courtyards, and an orchard. It was close to the main palace, luxurious, and sequestered deep enough in the countryside to keep its occupants isolated from any outbreaks of plague in the city. Freed from his fears of kidnapping, James, to his wife's joy, allowed Prince Henry and Princess Elizabeth to be raised together at Oatlands and other country residences.

The Chase also enabled James to indulge his passion for hunting. One of his wife's ladies remembered that James's language was particularly colorful when hunting.[14] Others were more amazed by his physical endurance during the chase. Sir Roger Wilbraham wrote to a friend that James "ventures to hazard his own body in hunting especially and [he is] most patient of labour, cold and heat." From his tailors, the King commissioned several new hunting habits, including one "as green as the grass he trod on, with a feather in his cap, and a horn."[15]

It was from his hunting trips that speculation arose about the King and two courtiers—Cecil and the Queen's new ally, Sir James Hay, and Lord Philip Herbert. During their days in the Chase, Philip's looks and "his skill, and indefatigable industry in hunting" brought him to James's attention.[16] He could make James laugh and, apart from a disastrous attempt to have him perform secretarial work, a task at which Philip himself admitted he was woeful, James enjoyed his company.[17] He was much more talented at the gaming tables—gambling hovered somewhere between a favorite pastime and an addiction for many Jacobean courtiers. During one Christmas, Philip offered to play on the King's side during a game of cards and won for James the hefty sum of £750.

The period between 1603 and 1607 is another in James's life to feature a complicated chronology of romantic affairs, and it may be that this was a time when he had more than one sexual partner. A few things can be said with certainty. The first is that in the initial few months of James's time in England, Hay and Herbert were identified by other courtiers as the King's favorites. The second is that there was a suspicion that these affairs were conducted during James's hunting trips away from court with the group of men referred to as his "hunting crew."[18]

There was speculation, albeit later, about the King and two other courtiers. The first was Sir John Ramsay, who was about the same age as Herbert and Hay. James was certainly very fond of him—one Sunday, Ramsay dozed off during a long sermon and talked so loudly in his sleep that it startled the preacher; James "laughed heartily."[19] He was made a viscount by James in 1606 and, sixteen years after that, was elevated to the earldom of Holderness. Apart from his position as a Gentleman of the Bedchamber, Ramsay's titles are the only evidence we have for a romance. As with the "hunting crew," while each of James's lovers was likely a Gentleman of the Bedchamber, not every member was his lover.[20] In Ramsay's case, there are other more convincing explanations for the favor he received from the King. After his killing of Alexander Ruthven in 1600, James believed that he owed his life to Ramsay, who never deviated from fealty to him throughout a long career. Furthermore, Ramsay's earldom comes far too late for it to credibly serve as proof of a romantic liaison. While it is possible that Ramsay and the King were lovers in 1603 and that they managed to keep it more discreet than James's attraction to Philip Herbert or James Hay, it begs the question of why James would feel the need for discretion with Ramsay yet none, or less, with Philip and Hay. James remained nervous to the point of paranoia about the general public's views on his private life. However, he moved through the cloud of witnesses at court with no meaningful attempt to disguise his affections.

Equally tenuous is the evidence for an alleged affair between James and Richard Preston, a Scotsman whom James knighted in the summer of 1603. James had known Richard's family for years—they owned Craigmillar Castle on the outskirts of Edinburgh, from where James had occasionally gone hunting—and Richard had infrequently come to court with his relatives when he was a teenager in Scotland. He sometimes filled in as a page during banquets, but never for very long. It was not until his early to mid-twenties, in 1603–4, that Richard rose to any kind of prominence. He had "an agreeable and winning deportment" and was a talented jouster.[21] Like Ramsay, Richard was subsequently to become an earl, in his case in the Irish peerage as earl of Desmond, when he married

Lady Elizabeth Butler, a member by birth of one of the oldest and wealthiest families in the Irish aristocracy. However, this took place in 1614, again years after his alleged romance with James. Despite his prowess in the tiltyard, Richard was not considered a member of the King's "hunting crew," and he was never a Gentleman of the Bedchamber, serving instead in the prestigious yet less intimate role of a Gentleman of the Privy Chamber. None of this is sufficient to reach a satisfactory conclusion as to whether either Richard Preston or John Ramsay was romantically or sexually involved with James, but on the balance of probability, in both cases it seems unlikely.

Throughout June 1603, preparations continued for the coronation. At the same time, James would also be crowned king of France, a practical absurdity with no more tangible impact than if he had been crowned king of the planet Mars. Long ago, the title had been of great importance. Due to their descent from the dukes of Normandy and Aquitaine and the counts of Anjou, for most of the Middle Ages the English royal family had controlled more of France than their French counterparts. In the fourteenth century, the claim by Edward III, King of England, that he was rightful heir to his childless uncle, the King of France, was rebutted by the French, who proclaimed a rival cousin of male-line descent as their new monarch. This launched a conflict that lasted on and off for 116 years, later called, for reasons of elegance rather than accuracy, the Hundred Years' War. Its battles acquired a totemic importance in English nostalgia, which presented the war as the apogee of chivalry. In 1431, young King Henry VI of England was crowned king of France at Notre Dame. It was both zenith and tipping point. In the decades that followed, England lost not only the French claim but most of the land they had previously held. Despite this catalogue of defeats, Henry VI's successors maintained that they were the rightful heirs to the French throne, even after the last chunk of their European empire, the Pale of Calais, was conquered by France in 1558. James went along with it, as would, incredibly, each of his successors until George III retired it in the early nineteenth century.

James and Anna were crowned as king and queen of England, France, and Ireland at Westminster Abbey on July 25, 1603. Protestants did not generally keep saints' days; however, since James's patron saint had been one of the Twelve Apostles, none but the most devout Puritans objected to the coronation being held on his feast day. It was customary in England that a king would be crowned and anointed first and, if he was married at the time of his coronation, his wife would be crowned as his queen consort later in the same ceremony. If he married after his accession, the Queen might receive her own coronation as consort at some point after her wedding. The last coronation of a king and a consort in London had taken place in 1509, before the Reformation, but, as at Anna's coronation as queen of Scots in 1590, James wished to retain as many of the ancient traditions as possible, regardless of how "papist" they seemed to his critics.

With the sound of heavy rain falling outside, the crown of Saint Edward, an eleventh-century English king noted for his piety, was placed on James's head by John Whitgift, Archbishop of Canterbury. He was assisted by Thomas Bilson, Bishop of Winchester,* for the anointing of James's chest, arm, and hands with holy oil. The rituals were then repeated for Queen Anna, after which commenced the long process of accepting the homage of the peers. When his turn came, Philip stepped forward and knelt. Having sworn before the congregation to serve as James's "liege man of life and limb," a vow of fealty that all the nobles had pledged, he stood and disregarded protocol by leaning in to kiss James on the cheek. Only male members of the royal family were supposed to do that. James, who playfully tapped Philip's cheek after the kiss, was delighted and, before summer was out, Philip was the only Englishman who had been sworn in as a Gentleman of the Bedchamber.[22]

It was not a relaxed summer. An unusually potent strain of plague killed a hundred Londoners in the week of the coronation alone. As those present returned home, they took the disease with them, as they had after Elizabeth's funeral in April. The trade networks

* Each of the English bishoprics was under the ecclesiastical province of one of the two archdioceses, Canterbury and York. Winchester was part of the Province of Canterbury, also known as the Southern Province. Canterbury was senior in rank to York, as it was the first Christian archbishopric created in the British Isles for Saint Augustine, known as "the Apostle to the English," when he began his evangelizing mission to re-Christianize southern Britain in 597.

in and out of London had also played their part in spreading the contagion, which swept into the countryside with such virulence that Oatlands Palace was no longer judged safe; Prince Henry and Princess Elizabeth were evacuated to a smaller royal residence farther from London. As the court moved to more obscure residences, accommodation provisions thinned, until even Sir Robert Cecil was sleeping in a tent. He wrote to his brother, "It is uneaseful, for only the King and Queen, with the privy chamber ladies, and some three or four Scottish Council, are lodged in the house, and neither Chamberlain, nor one English Councillor have a room."[23]

Discomfort notwithstanding, Cecil worked on whatever government business he could while the court remained in perpetual panicked motion. This included Queen Anna's jointure—her own properties, residences, and sources of income. Her Danish family leaned through their ambassador to ensure there was no repeat of what had happened with Maitland and Musselburgh. James gave Anna Greenwich Palace and Somerset House in London, a Tudor-era palace that she renamed Denmark House.[24] The logistics were managed by Cecil. In terms of her other lesser properties that could be rented out by the Queen's Household, he went digging in the archives to see what had been allocated to Henry VIII's first wife, Katherine of Aragon, the most recent queen of England to have been, like Anna, a king's daughter. When Anna's brother King Christian wrote from Denmark, she replied thanking him for his care for her and informing him that she had been given what "King Henry the Eighth, King of England, gave to Queen Katherine, daughter of Spain, in which we have not only our desire to imitate her that was born a king's daughter, but his Majesty hath ordained in all other things thereunto belonging so as we are satisfied in the point of honour."[25] While the Queen's jointure could be decided on within the royal household in that chaotic summer and autumn, James delayed several of his other political, ecclesiastical, and diplomatic projects until the winter frosts buried the plague or, at the very least, rendered it supine until summer.

Peace was, as always, James's priority. Diplomatic channels were opened discreetly with the Vatican in an attempt to avoid the lethal animus that had dominated Elizabeth's last three decades in power. Whispers of Queen Anna's sympathy for Catholicism undoubtedly helped, as did James's promise not to rigorously enforce the country's anti-Catholic laws and, perhaps, to consider repealing them altogether. Communicating through an emissary, Pope Clement VIII made it known that he would ensure "as far as humanly possible that no harm befalls you from Catholics . . . He has already ordered all Catholics to revere and obey you."[26] Almost as remarkable was the conclusion of peace between England and Spain; James offered to host negotiations to which Philip III sent representatives, the outcome being the Treaty of London in 1604. He also invited to court the north Irish aristocrat Hugh O'Neill, Earl of Tyrone. In his early sixties, O'Neill was short in height, strong in build, brave, and with a personality that a contemporary described as "affable and of profound wit."[27] For a thousand years, the O'Neills had been the most powerful noble family in Ulster, the northernmost of Ireland's four provinces.[28] Tyrone had led the largest uprising against Elizabeth I, the scale of which was so vast that it occupied more of her men, money, and resources than her wars against Spain.[29] Tyrone's Catholicism and friendly overtures from both the Pope and the King of Spain, so soon after the Armada, had aggravated English fears that Spain might use Ireland as a base from which to launch a second invasion attempt; their attitude was best summarized in the contemporary rhyme, "He who would England hope to win/Must with Ireland [he] begin."[30] Known as Tyrone's Rebellion or the Nine Years' War, the uprising ended with the Treaty of Mellifont in 1603, under which Tyrone, accepting that victory was unlikely to be won on the battlefield, surrendered on condition of further parlay. The English public hated him almost as much as had the late Queen Elizabeth, who called him an "author of misery," and he was nicknamed "the Monster of the North" by the people of London, some of whom pelted him with stones and mud when he came at King James's request.[31] James ordered that "no man abuse the Earl of Tyrone," who accepted the King's invitation to join the royal family at Hampton Court for Christmas 1603.[32]

As the protesters had shown, this was not a popular move, especially among the families of English soldiers who had fallen in the Nine Years' War. A veteran was outraged: "I have lived to see that damnable rebel Tyrone brought to England, honoured . . . I adventured perils by sea and land, was near starving, ate horse flesh in Munster,* and all to quell that man, who now smileth in peace at those who did hazard their lives to destroy him."[33] Despite the backlash, James was determined to achieve concord in Ireland and, along with pardons and guarantees of safe conduct, he created Rory O'Donnell, Tyrone's chief ally in the rebellion, the new earl of Tyrconnell.

Beyond the obvious short-term benefits of peace in Ireland, James could see a use for men like Tyrone and Tyrconnell. As king of Scots, he had relied on the great houses for the maintenance of order in their localities, especially in the Highlands. As king of Ireland, he hoped to establish the same kind of relationship with the earls in Ulster.[34]

James's first Christmas as king of England was as different from those of his childhood as day was to night. Every evening of the Twelve Days of Christmas, which ran from Christmas Day on December 25 to the Feast of the Epiphany on January 6, there were festivities at Hampton Court. Anna was in her element watching plays by William Shakespeare and his actors, reminiscent of entertainments she had enjoyed as a child in Denmark. Both parts of Shakespeare's *Henry IV*, his *Henry V*, *Troilus and Cressida*, *Twelfth Night*, *A Midsummer Night's Dream*, and *Hamlet*, set in the Queen's homeland, were performed. James was bored, even after Shakespeare set out to charm by locating most of *Hamlet*'s drama in Elsinore, the anglicized name of Helsingør, where James and Anna had spent their first months as husband and wife. James was, however, canny enough to become patron of Shakespeare's company, henceforth known as the King's Men, once he appreciated the influence plays had over London's mood.

Casting herself in the role of the goddess Athena, Queen Anna ransacked Elizabeth I's famous state gowns for costumes and distributed them among her eleven favorite ladies-in-waiting, whom she cast as other goddesses for a masque performed in the palace's

---

* The most southern Irish province.

Great Hall. *The Vision of the Twelve Goddesses,* written on commission for the Queen by playwright Samuel Daniels, was, like many early masques, light on story and heavy on cost. Dazzling costumes for the participants, who would act, declaim, dance, or combinations of the three, were set off by elaborate sets, most of which were dismantled after use. For *The Vision of the Twelve Goddesses,* the court's page boys were provided with white satin jackets, embroidered with gold, that glittered as they held candles to light the way for the queen-goddess when she entered a Great Hall transformed into a mythical realm with artificial caves and temples. Anna and her ladies danced before the assembled courtiers, including King James, who had never shed his lack of interest in dancing.

He perked up for a masque on another evening that Christmas, when Philip Herbert was cast in the role of a knight. Philip's steps commenced with greater confidence than they concluded. Forgetting the first rule of theater, Philip had not rehearsed in his costume, which was decorated with so many jewels that after a few moments even his strength was struggling. As Philip and his fellow dancing warriors slowly buckled under the weight of their costumes, the court looked on by candlelight.

The Cecil faction's changed attitude to Philip indicated that, in 1604, he eclipsed Hay as James's "prime favourite."[35] They negotiated a marriage between Philip and Sir Robert Cecil's niece Lady Susan de Vere, an erudite lady-in-waiting to the Queen. James accepted that his favorites should marry. With Philip, he did not regard it as a point of separation, in the way that he had with Sandy Lindsay's marriage and his own when he was younger. Philip's marriage was solemnized in the Hampton Court chapel, and James enthusiastically helped arrange the wedding celebrations that followed. Around the same time, James Hay was sent on a diplomatic mission to France. After his return, he remained a man whom the King trusted and liked. He settled his debts for him—Hay loved to entertain and to do so in style—and James supported his prestigious marriage in 1607 to Honora Denny, only daughter and heiress of a wealthy nobleman. Hay served in the royal household for the rest of his life and on frequent embassies, most often to France, where he had been educated. James always regarded Hay as a friend, but the only time we read of Hay as his "prime favourite" is in 1603.

Politics resumed after Christmas. Along with Spain, the Vatican, and Ireland, James was determined upon peace within the Church of England, whose hereditary position as Supreme Governor he had also inherited from Elizabeth. The Church, founded by Henry VIII, had maintained many Catholic features for its first fourteen years, until Edward VI's reign, when it was given a more unambiguously Protestant nature, including a Book of Common Prayer, which was to be used in every service. The Church of England had been abolished in 1554 by Queen Mary I and the See of Rome Act, which reunified the English Church with Roman Catholicism. Five years later, an independent Church of England was reestablished by Elizabeth I, who devoted a huge amount of energy to her religious policy in the first two years after becoming queen as she sought initially to balance the legacy left by her siblings' competing devotion to Protestantism and Catholicism. Her *via media* ("middle road") on religion aimed to make the revived Church of England acceptable to the majority of English and Welsh Catholics, by maintaining certain parts of the traditional liturgy, and also to the Protestant community, by restoring the Book of Common Prayer, preaching Protestant theology on Holy Communion, permitting clerical marriages, and diminishing certain parts of Catholic theology—principally Marianism, prayers for the departed, the intercession of the saints, and fidelity to the papacy.

Elizabeth I's compromise solution was a success in winning over to the state religion many people who, like her, were sincere but not fanatical Christians, but there was an obvious and mountingly tragic problem for those Catholics who, in good conscience, felt they could not support a church that was in schism with Rome, nor one that preached against Transubstantiation, veneration of the Blessèd Virgin Mary, or several of the ancient sacraments. These spiritual objections had acquired a political hue, and a higher body count, after Elizabeth I's excommunication, first by Pope Pius V in 1570 and again by Pope Sixtus V in 1585.

On Elizabeth's death, the greatest threat to the Church of England was, however, internal. She had been keen to prevent English and Welsh Protestantism splitting into multiple denominations as it had in Europe. Whatever her intentions, as of 1603 that was the reality in all but name. There were two loose but determined factions within the Church, which in modern parlance we might refer to as its "High" and "Low" branches. The "High" had various names in the 1600s, and its adherents tended to support more traditional worship to the extent that their critics characterized them as crypto-Catholics. Many in the High Anglican wing were in fact sincere in their objections to what they regarded as the errors that had crept into Roman Catholicism over the centuries, but they were equally opposed to the "Low" wing, more often called the Puritans, who felt the Reformation had not gone far enough. When asked how he would summarize the differences between his cause and that of the Puritans, a High Anglican theologian replied, "A Puritan is a Protestant frayed out of his wits."[36]

For Puritans, it was necessary that English churches be gutted of their decorations, just as much as the liturgy and the prayer books should be of any theology that smacked of Catholicism. One of several major points of contention was the Church's organization: the High Anglicans championed the hierarchy of bishops, while the Puritans wanted their abolition in favor of a more democratic structure similar to that of Scottish Presbyterianism, with congregations that met occasionally to discuss doctrine at general assemblies under the watchful eye, but not the authority, of a Moderator.

The Church of England in 1603 was thus supported by most and loved by few. Petitions from clergymen begging him to restore unity had been submitted to James within days of his arrival in England. Due to the plague, he had pushed back his planned ecclesiastical conference to convene after Christmas at Hampton Court. In preparation, James read the two factions' rival translations of the Bible. The High Anglicans preferred the English-language translation known as "the Bishop's Bible," which had been sanctioned by Queen Elizabeth for use throughout the Church of England in 1568. The Puritan wing preferred their own translation, popularly called the "Geneva Bible." It had been written in Switzerland, where many English Protestants had fled in the 1550s during Queen Mary I's crackdown on Protestantism. Translated to provide their fellow refugees with access to Scripture in English, the Geneva Bible reflected the time and place in which it was produced, among a community of exiles who were victims of royal authority and living in a Calvinist theocratic republic.

James found little to object to in the Bishop's Bible, except that its translations were not quite up to his standards. When he went through the Geneva Bible, he was concerned and then angry at the marginalia—commentary designed to explain what certain verses meant. James felt the Geneva translators had gone far beyond what was exegetically permissible. He was personally offended by the commentary on the Bible's Second Book of Chronicles, chapter 15, verse 16, which narrated how King Asa of Judah refused to execute his idolatrous mother, Queen Maachah. The verse read:

> And King Asa deposed Maachah his mother from her regency, because she had made an idol in a grove: and Asa brake down her idol, and stamped it, and burnt it . . .

The accompanying marginalia informed readers that Asa had failed in his duty, because he ought to have pursued his mother to death for her sins, but instead "herein he showed that he lacked zeal, for she ought to have died both by the covenant, as [in] verse 13, and by the Law of God: but he gave place to foolish pity."[37] This addendum had been included in the edition published in 1599, and James wondered if the Puritans were alluding to him as Asa and his mother as Maachah.

He had spotted what he considered another overreach in the first chapter of the book of Exodus, when the pharaoh of Egypt summoned the chief midwives of his kingdom to obey an evil law. Rather than carry out the pharaoh's orders, the midwives lied.[38] The Geneva Bible's commentary informed its readers, "Their disobedience herein was lawful" but did not qualify that this was because the pharaoh's law was a moral monstrosity. Rather it seemed, to James, to imply that disobedience to any monarch was permissible.[39]

On Thursday, January 10, 1604, James opened the ecclesiastical council later called the Hampton Court Conference. He brought

Prince Henry to some of the ceremonies; James wanted to educate him early about the public aspects of monarchy, something he had lacked in his own upbringing. The archbishops and bishops were invited, along with most of the leading clergymen and professors of theology from England's two universities, Oxford and Cambridge. A few in the High Anglican wing had encouraged James not to hold the conference at all, since it would provide a platform for a Puritan lobby that they preferred to silence. When the Bishop of Winchester carried on with the point a little longer than was necessary one evening, James shut down the conversation with, "Content yourself, my Lord, we know better than you what belongeth to these matters."[40] At least Winchester complained in private, unlike the Bishop of London, who caused tempers to fray when he interrupted somebody else's speech to throw himself on his knees before the King, entreating him not to listen to the Puritans.

James thought the Bishop of London's tirade was irritating and pointless. He did not need to be warned about Puritanism. He disliked what he had read in the Geneva Bible and thought Puritanism was far too close to Presbyterianism for him to trust it. He expressed as much in a private conversation with the Bishop of Norwich, whom he told "that his Mother and he, from their cradles, had been haunted by the Puritan devil, which he feared would not leave him [until] his grave."[41] James claimed to another group of bishops at Hampton Court that the Kirk agreed with monarchy as much as the Devil did with God—"How they dealt with me in my minority, you all know; it was not done secretly."[42]

He did, however, let the Puritans speak in the hope that the principal disagreements would be resolved and unity within the Church of England restored. "Jerusalem was not built in a day," he joked.[43] One of the most prominent Puritan delegates was Dr. John Rainolds, President of Corpus Christi College at the University of Oxford. Rainolds was a superb orator, however, perhaps he was not the best choice to speak on the Puritans' desire to shorten wedding vows by removing what they considered to be the lewd phrase "with my body I thee worship." Although Protestant clergy were permitted to marry, Rainolds had never married, and James could not resist teasing a celibate man pontificating on sexual subtext. He interjected during Rainolds's speech to joke, "Many a man speaks of Robin Hood, who never shot his bow."[44]

James's temper got the better of him on several occasions—once, quite seriously, when he stormed out of the room shouting, "No bishop, no king!" after an impasse over the proposed abolition of bishoprics. James was convinced that the abolitionist proposal was a Trojan horse for Puritan republicanism to attack all forms of hierarchy. More often, he was simply exasperated. The Puritans wanted to remove Confirmation, the making of the sign of the Cross during worship, and wedding rings, because none of them were mentioned in the Bible. When the High Anglican representatives pushed back with the argument that these were, by now, part of Christian tradition, the Puritans countered that, unless something was specifically mentioned in the Bible, it was un-Christian.

Why not get rid of the Holy Trinity, then, James asked. As a term, "the Trinity" is not mentioned in the Bible. Better yet, why not get rid of shoes, since they had those before the Reformation too? "They used to wear hose and shoes in popery," he said, "therefore, you shall now go barefoot."[45]

James thought that the Puritan reverence for the Early Church, by which they meant the Church that had existed in Christ's earthly lifetime and that of the Apostles, was ridiculous. He preferred accretion theology, whereby the Bible was the foundation but not the totality of Christianity. To cling to *sola scriptura*—the Bible alone, only what was done and said at the time the Bible was written—and to ignore all the developments that had come since was, in James's words, to prefer stranding, not anchoring, Christianity with "things done before a Church be settled and grounded, unto those which are to be performed in a Church [e]stablished and flourishing." God, James believed, had continued to speak in the hearts of the faithful to perfect, grow, and reform the Church as the centuries passed.

With one or two of the points he made, James managed to unite the factions against him. Both were almost unanimous in shooting down his suggestion that women be allowed to administer the Sacrament of Baptism. On a few issues, he agreed with the Puritans. First, in their plea for better funding to provide more thorough education for the clergy. From the reports he had read in his nine months as the Church's Supreme Governor, James knew enough to agree with Rainolds by saying, "In many parts of the realm the parishes are so ill-served with persons not able to instruct in matters of their faith as is very scandalous."[46] Second, he was excited by the request that the Crown resolve the discord created by the competing Bibles with his commissioning of what Rainolds called "one translation of the Bible to be authentical and read in church."

In most areas, the Hampton Court Conference ended in stalemate, and many of the issues it failed to resolve mushroomed in years to come into insuperable barriers that, within a generation, shattered the Church of England and further divided the realm. With clerical education and the commissioning of a new English-language Bible, however, it had substantial and positive outcomes for the Church. Fifty-four translators were chosen from both factions in the Church. They were subdivided into six committees, two of which researched out of Oxford, two from Cambridge, and two at the Church's administrative center at Westminster. Each was assigned a certain number of books from the Bible's canon, which they were to work on together to produce, on James's order, an "exact Translation of the Holy Scriptures into the English tongue."[47]

14

CHILDREN OF WRATH

We all had our conversations in times past in the lusts of our flesh, fulfilling the desire of the flesh and of the mind, and were by nature the children of wrath . . .

—Ephesians 2:3

Seven months after the Hampton Court Conference, James and Anna were reunited with their youngest son, Prince Charles, who was brought south to England once his health was strong enough that he could regularly walk unaided up and down the gallery of his mother's palace at Dunfermline. James appointed as Charles's tutor Peter Young, who had been James's gentler, junior tutor at Stirling. Charles was a quiet child. He had weak ankles, for which his governess provided him with special boots, and he was considered "tongue-tied," meaning that he likely had ankyloglossia. He grew up to physically resemble both sides of his family. With his chestnut hair and brown eyes, he looked like his mother's relatives in the House of Oldenburg, while the shape of his face and eyes recalled his grandmother Mary, Queen of Scots.

The royal family grew with the birth at Greenwich Palace on April 8, 1605, of a princess, who was named in honor of her grandmother. Princess Mary's christening on May 5 was lavish, with "the noble babe carried under a canopy of cloth of gold."[1] Anna's brother Prince Ulric was visiting and was asked to stand as one of the godparents, alongside Lady Arbella Stuart. Princess Mary's was the first birth in the English royal family in sixty-eight years, and the capital celebrated with street parties, bonfires around which revelers danced in the evening, and the peal of church bells to announce the news. Three aristocratic titles were created to mark the princess's birth—

two went to Robert Cecil and his family and the third, the earldom of Montgomery, was granted to Philip.

In August, the King, the Queen, and Prince Henry visited Oxford together. James and Anna were the university's guests at Christ Church College; the thirteen-year-old prince and his entourage were accommodated at nearby Magdalen* College. James attended lectures, one of which encouraged his disgust for the new habit of smoking tobacco, imported from the Americas.† During a reception at St. John's College, the royal family was greeted with an address, delivered in classical Greek by a professor. Knowing how much her husband prided himself on his pronunciation of Greek, the Queen enthused to the professor that she had never heard Greek more perfectly enunciated.

The King and Queen shared a sense of humor, in which they often made fun of each other and other people. They wrote to one another frequently when they were apart, such as during the trip later in 1605 when James hunted in Oxfordshire while Anna went to Basing House to visit her friends the Marquess and Marchioness of Winchester. The septuagenarian Earl of Nottingham had told James privately of his betrothal to the twentysomething Lady Margaret Stewart, so James wrote to Anna to give her advance warning, in case she heard the news in public and burst out laughing.[2] He also told her to keep the news of Nottingham's engagement secret until the two families announced it themselves. Anna replied, "Your Majesty's letter was welcome to me. I have been as glad of the fair weather as yourself and on the last part of your letter, you have guessed right that I would laugh—who would not." As to his request that she keep the news secret, "I humbly desire your Majesty to tell me how it is possible that I should keep this secret that I have already told—and shall tell it—to as many as I speak with, and if I were a poet I would make a song of it and sing it to the tune of . . . *Fools Well Met.*"[3]

---

* Pronounced as *Maudlin*.

† James had recently written an anti-smoking book, *A Counterblast to Tobacco* (1604), in which he described smoking tobacco as a "custom loathsome to the eye, hateful to the Nose, harmful to the brain, dangerous to the Lungs."

Around this time, there was a rumor, impossible either to verify or dismiss, that James went to a brothel with some of his favorites.[4] Theaters and brothels, known as "stews," proliferated on the south bank of the River Thames in Southwark, which contained London's red light district, where the streets had subtle names like Cock Lane. The two halves of London were accessible from one another only by London Bridge or by the dozens of fee-charging ferries that carried the estimated two to three thousand Londoners who crossed the Thames daily. Visible from the south on the opposite side of the bank was Saint Paul's Cathedral, Westminster Abbey, the Palace of Whitehall, the Tower of London, and the riverfront mansions of the wealthy. Centuries earlier, London had been three separate jurisdictions—the City of London, the city of Westminster, and Southwark. The City of London, an economic hub, had expanded, as had the religious and political heart at Westminster, until they were linked in the fourteenth century by the row of palaces and mansions known as the Strand, where Queen Anna's Denmark House was located.

London's size, with about 190,000 residents, was not only enormous in comparison to any other city in the British Isles—its population was nearly twenty times that of its closest rivals, Dublin, Edinburgh, and Norwich—but even in comparison to other European capitals at the time.[5] It was only substantially exceeded by Paris, which was the most populated city in Europe with nearly 300,000 inhabitants. About 97 percent of London's population was Caucasian, and about 3 percent consisted of communities of sailors, merchants, or diplomats, mostly from northern Africa or the Middle East.[6] London's docks, streets, shops, theaters, and palaces never seemed to rest. Both a key to, and a consequence of, this size was London's position as a trading center, with its commercial guilds forming influential political and economic blocs for wealthy Londoners outside the aristocracy.

James never liked London and once referred to it as England's worst feature. Whenever he could, he spent time away from it. In October 1605, James was with Philip and the "hunting crew" at Royston, a new private hunting lodge that he had built on the outskirts of a village in Hertfordshire.[7] Royston was described in a history of the county as "all of brick well-tiled," and with two stories. There was a small garden at the back and kennels for the hounds were built nearby. It was not, by royal or aristocratic standards, a large house—it could accommodate no more than forty. James loved it. He was "exceedingly well pleased with the air of these parts," and it became "his favourite spot of hunting."[8]

At the start of November, James returned from Royston to London for the opening of Parliament, another event, like the Hampton Court Conference, to which he would bring his eldest son to help prepare him to one day reign as king. From the bucolic bliss of Royston, James went to the sprawling magnificence of Whitehall, which was not only the grandest royal residence in England but, by general agreement, the ugliest.[9] Whitehall was another former ecclesiastical property confiscated during the Reformation by Henry VIII, who had died there in 1547 having spent over a decade transforming it into a working palace at the heart of the capital. Its inchoate façade, built as necessity dictated while the palace was expanded, explained its contemporary reputation as an unsightly residence in comparison to Greenwich, Hampton Court, or Windsor. Penned in by the city streets on one side and the brown, busy waters of the River Thames on the other, at twenty-three acres Whitehall functioned more like a small town.[10] The largest royal home in Europe until Louis XIV expanded Versailles later in the century, it had four tennis courts, outdoor preaching auditoriums, orchards, bowling alleys, and a tiltyard for jousting. A gatehouse, straddling a busy London thoroughfare that still bisected Whitehall, connected the two halves of the palace complex, with the gardens on one side and the accommodation, kitchen, chapels, stables, public rooms, and a dilapidated banqueting house on the other. James had the last of these demolished and rebuilt at great cost.

Sir Robert Cecil came to James's Whitehall apartments overlooking the river and requested an audience. When this was granted, he showed the King an anonymous letter passed on by Lord Monteagle, a Catholic aristocrat who was due to be among the nobles attending the opening of Parliament. Monteagle had received the letter on October 26, when it was dropped off at his house by an unknown messenger. Since he was enjoying his dinner at the time, Monteagle had asked a servant to read it aloud for him:

> My lord, out of the love that I bear to some of your friends, I have care of your preservation. Therefore I would advise you, as you tender* your life, to devise your excuse to shift off your attendance of this Parliament. For God and man have concurred to punish the wickedness of this time . . . I say, they shall receive a terrible blow this Parliament, and yet they shall not see who hurts them. This counsel is not to be contemned,† because it may do you good, and can do you no harm, for the danger is past as soon as you have burnt the letter. And I hope God will give you the grace to make good use of it: to Whose holy protection I commend you.[11]

Monteagle took the letter to the palace, where he interrupted Sir Robert Cecil at his evening meal with four fellow privy councillors. The councillors agreed that the cryptic promise that "they shall not see who hurts them" and mention of "a terrible blow" suggested gunpowder, not unlike the plot years earlier at Kirk o' Field that had aimed to kill James's father. The pious hope that "God will give you the grace to make good use of it," the allusion to the plot as a holy enterprise in which "God and man have concurred to punish the wickedness of this time," and the fact that the warning had been sent to Monteagle indicated that the author, like its recipient and likely the author's comrades, were Catholics.

After reading the letter, James approved Cecil's request to authorize a search in, and near, the Palace of Westminster, where Parliament was to convene on November 5. He ordered that the search not take place until the day before, because only then would the culprits have moved into position. James wanted them taken alive. On the evening of November 4, a search discovered a man called John Johnson standing guard over kindling, piled high in one of the

* Value, care, protect.

† Receiving this advice should not make you angry.

cellars for rent in a building adjoining the Palace of Westminster. The news was brought to James at Whitehall, whereupon he ordered a further search and commanded that Johnson be prevented from taking his own life before he could be questioned. Shortly before midnight, the King's men uncovered barrels of gunpowder. The information was relayed back to Whitehall, where the King fell to his knees, thanking God for delivering him and his son from death by traitors.[12]

Under questioning, "John Johnson" admitted that his real name was Guy* Fawkes, that he was originally from York and was an anti-Scottish soldier who had converted to Catholicism and fought for Spain. On his return to England he had liaised with fellow hardline Catholics to kill the King, Prince Henry, and the entire Protestant ruling class who would convene for the official opening of Parliament. They allegedly planned to kidnap nine-year-old Princess Elizabeth, proclaim her queen, and raise her as a Catholic, with a regency of their own choosing until she came of age. What was to happen to Queen Anna, Prince Charles, and Princess Mary was unclear, although if it was true that the plotters planned to install Princess Elizabeth as Queen Elizabeth II, Prince Charles's chances of a long life seemed slender.[13]

The King and Cecil ordered a thorough, swift investigation. Those caught were tortured, including Guy Fawkes, whose sufferings can be gauged by the differences in his signature before and after questioning. Some of his fellow conspirators in what was later dubbed the Gunpowder Plot were ambushed at a safe house, fought back, and were killed. Those taken alive were publicly hanged until they lost consciousness, cut down to be revived, castrated, disemboweled, beheaded, and then posthumously quartered. As with his delivery from the Gowrie House conspiracy five years earlier, the anniversary of James's survival became an annual day of celebration. Unlike the Gowrie commemoration, "the Fifth of November" is a holiday that survives to the present in England, with bonfires on which it is traditional to burn an effigy inspired by Fawkes, known as "the Guy."

---

* Sometimes given as "Guido."

Catholic confidence in James as the man who would deliver them from Elizabeth I's penal laws had been frustrated in the two years since his accession. Most Catholics continued to hope for better days, but some felt so betrayed that they gravitated toward militant solutions like the Gunpowder Plot. Government hunts for priests, whose presence was still illegal in England and Wales, continued, as the priests were moved in secret, often from one Catholic stately home to another. When raids on these homes took place, the priests were hurriedly rushed into "priest hides,"* ingenious hiding spots within the walls, behind the chimneys, or under the stairwells.[14] Many were the work of a physically disabled carpenter, a devout Catholic from Oxford called Nicholas Owen, who was captured by the government in 1606.† Cecil was euphoric when they caught him. As someone with physical disabilities, Owen should have been legally exempt from torture, but he was racked to reveal the identities of the wealthy families whose homes he had equipped with hides. He refused to give their names. One session of torture caused Owen's hernia to rupture, and he died on the rack.[15]

In his two years as king of England, James had been strongly advised by Cecil and other councillors not to relax the Penal Laws, as any attempt to grant toleration to Catholicism would provoke staunch opposition from Parliament. Then and later, some Catholics suspected that the Gunpowder Plot had been a scheme masterminded by Sir Robert Cecil, who planted a double agent to encourage a plot that would frighten James away from his desire for religious toleration. It is more probable that, as with the fatal correspondence used to condemn James's mother to death eighteen years earlier, the government knew that there was a conspiracy brewing. Having managed to penetrate its ranks, they watched to see who else would be revealed as a threat, before swooping in to foil it at the last moment.[16]

There had been two plots against James in the first years of his English rule, the Main and Bye plots—half-baked and eas-

* More often referred to by their later name of "priest holes."

† He was canonized by Pope Paul VI in 1970.

ily thwarted intrigues to put the English Lady Arbella Stuart on the throne. Their motley crews of supporters included a Catholic priest, a few disaffected aristocrats, gentry, and the ousted Captain of the Guard, Sir Walter Raleigh. With a mixture of mercy and masochism, James had reprieved the men as they stood on the scaffold waiting for execution. He bore no ill-will toward Arbella, assuring his cousin that she could not be blamed for malcontents who concocted plots in her name but without her knowledge. The Gunpowder Plot had shown that James could not afford to be so sanguine about intrigues against him.

As the Protestants of London celebrated the Gunpowder Plot's defeat, James went to Parliament on November 9 to express gratitude to both the houses of Lords and Commons for their good wishes to him, and to give thanks where it was due for their mutual survival. Having offered prayers of gratitude to God "for the great and miraculous delivery He hath granted to me, and to you all," he told Parliament of his belief in the Divine Right of Kings, whereby monarchs were God's "lieutenants and vice-regents on earth." He then became more personal, referring to the dangers he had faced over the course of his life in the context of feeling that one day he would "be baptised in blood." He made a very rare reference to the night David Riccio had been murdered in front of his pregnant mother, saying that many kings "being in the higher places [are] like the high Trees . . . most subject to the daily tempests of innumerable dangers; and I amongst all other Kings, have ever been subject unto them, not only ever since my birth, but even as I may justly say, before my birth, and while I was yet in my Mother's belly."[17]

For months after the plot was foiled, James's daughter Elizabeth suffered nightmares. In the day between Fawkes's apprehension and the capture of the other plotters at their safe house, the princess had been in the countryside with her household at Coombe Abbey, an estate on the outskirts of the city of Coventry. To prevent her kidnapping, Elizabeth's governor had, in a panic, ridden with her into Coventry, where they hid her in the house of a merchant. It was only a few hours before they discovered the princess was safe, but for a child of nine it had been terrifying. In January, her governess told a worried Queen Anna that Elizabeth "hath not yet recovered

[from] the surprise and is very ill and troubled."[18] James fared no better and, for a time, his mental equilibrium was shattered. The Venetian ambassador wrote in January, "The King is in terror. He does not appear, nor does he take his meals in public as usual. He lives in his innermost rooms with only Scotsmen about him."[19]

On June 22, 1606, seven months after the Gunpowder Plot, Queen Anna gave birth at Greenwich Palace to their seventh child. It was a long, difficult, and likely a traumatic labor. In the tradition of her sister Princess Mary, who had been christened in honor of a grandmother, the child was named for Anna's mother, Sophia. She died a day after her birth. Three days later, carrying a little coffin, a barge draped in black velvet left Greenwich and sailed to Westminster for Princess Sophia's burial in the Abbey. On her father's orders, Sophia's body was interred in the Henry VII Chapel near the great shrine of Saint Edward the Confessor. Her mother ordered that the King's Master Carver, Maximilian Colt, sculpt a tomb in the shape of a baby sleeping in her cradle, onto which the court artist John de Critz painted the King and Queen's epitaph for Sophia. It is moving by the standards of any time, and especially so for the emotion it showed on a public dynastic memorial in the Jacobean era. Translated from Latin, it reads:

Sophia
A royal rosebud untimely plucked by Fate and snatched
away from her parents
James, King of Great Britain, France and Ireland and
Queen Anna,
to flower again in the rose garden of Christ,
lies here.
23rd June, 4th year of the reign of King James,
In the Year of Our Lord, 1606.

To her grief at Sophia's death, Anna almost certainly had to add the burden of medical agony. Something had happened during the princess's birth that left the Queen with gynecological issues. We do not know what they were—however, a clue as to the pain she endured is provided by the religious literature Anna commissioned for her private worship, which focused on a miracle by Christ recorded in the Gospel according to Saint Mark and referred to, at the time, as "Christ healing the woman with the bloody issue."[20] There were no further pregnancies, and it seems that Anna and James's sexual relations with one another ceased after the tragedies of 1606.

The Queen was still recovering when her brother King Christian IV came to England. Christian, who had just turned thirty, arrived by ship with a large retinue of "courtiers [who], according to their country's fashion, were richly decked in silk with chains of rare estimation."[21] He was blond, strong, tall—"of goodly person in stature," according to an English courtier, who added that Christian IV was "in face so like his sister that he who hath seen the one may paint in his fancy* the other."[22] He was greeted at the dock by King James and Prince Henry, who escorted Christian to Anna's palace at Greenwich. On arriving, he rushed up the stairs to his sister's rooms and wrapped her in a hug for the first time since she had sailed from Copenhagen sixteen years earlier.[23]

Christian IV's time in England was a diplomatic failure. He had come to persuade James to enter an alliance of Protestant rulers opposing Habsburg hegemony in Europe. To avoid military entanglements, especially any that might jeopardize his treaty with Spain, James demurred. There was an argument between the two kings, but it was over Anna, not politics—Christian accused James of neglecting her. On other occasions, James and Christian enjoyed one another's company. Both loved hunting and were strong drinkers. During a banquet at Theobalds, Christian spoke with a lady dressed as the Queen of Sheba, who accidentally spilled a tray on him when she tripped. Servants rushed forward to wipe up the mess. Rather the worse for wear, King Christian waved them away, asked the lady to dance, slipped in the puddle, landed on his face, and had to be carried to bed with his outfit still sporting the party's detritus or, as English courtier Sir John Harington put it, with his clothes "not a little defiled with the presents of the Queen [of Sheba] that had been bestowed on his garments; such as wine, cream, jelly, beverages, cakes, spices." Harington did not understand how anybody

* From his imagination.

had remained sober during King Christian's visit. "Our feasts were magnificent," he wrote, "[but even] the ladies abandon their sobriety, and are seen to roll about in toxication."[24] Another observer joked that it was considered "more barbarous to have refused drink, than [a] disgrace to be drunk."[25]

Criticism over the court's decadence was growing. Lady Arbella thought James's indifference to etiquette, heavy drinking, and wild spending had turned the court into a childish, vulgar, ridiculous milieu, where, when it came to good manners, "I see little or none of it but in the Queen."[26] When it came to expenditure, however, Anna was as much to blame as her husband. During one night over Christmas, she lost £400 at the card tables. She had clocks made of tortoiseshell and silver, pear-shaped pearls to wear in her hair, rubies and emeralds studded into the canopy above her throne, and a jewelry collection so dazzling that the Venetian ambassador thought no other royal family could rival it. Before the delivery of her daughter Mary at Greenwich, Anna had insisted that she could not possibly give birth unless in a brand-new canopied bed that cost nearly one thousand pounds.

In the aftermath of Princess Sophia's death, Queen Anna settled into a routine. She and James would spend Christmas in the sumptuous hideousness of Whitehall. Anna might then pass a few weeks at Greenwich with her household, followed by spring at Hampton Court or Oatlands with her children. May or June would often be spent at Greenwich with James. During the summer, she would hunt and tour through her properties in the south of England, sometimes in the West Country,* but never in Scotland. September was typically whiled away back at her favorite home, Hampton Court; October was for Greenwich, and November would either be at her London property, Denmark House, or early to Whitehall for Christmas. In addition to their early summer stay at Greenwich, she and James saw one another at all major events and, when they were apart, they wrote to one another often.

James admitted later that the first few years after he came to England had been like one long Christmas holiday. The Gunpow-

* A popular name for a group of counties in the southwest of England.

der Plot ended the party by confirming and exacerbating James's worst fears, and its aftermath shone an unforgiving light on the problems that had been festering in England and Wales beneath the pomp of James's accession.

Catholics' frustration was not the only source of discontent. Within days of his becoming king of England, there had been ominous signs, had James been prepared to look. He had missed the protests by local people against several of the families who hosted him on his journey from Edinburgh to London, some of whom were encroaching on arable land that had for centuries been held collectively and set aside for the community's use. Not content with the wealth they had accumulated under the Tudors, some English landed families were determined to become richer still under the Stuarts. Consequently, social tensions festered in the countryside.

Money was nowhere near as plentiful as James, his wife, or his entourage first imagined. The funds that appeared, seemingly at will, during his journey south in 1603 had in fact been scraped together by the court's financial officials, who were "much disquieted" by their new king's spending.[27] The English monarchy had an annual income roughly nineteen times that of Scotland's and could be self-funding when it came to its households, which were sustained by rents generated by Crown properties across England and Wales.[28] However, it had accrued significant debts in the sixteenth century. A problem facing the English monarchy was that the work of a frugal monarch could be undone in a decade, while the consequences of a spendthrift lasted for generations. The kings who ruled between 1471 and 1509 had adopted cautious, and often ruthless, financial policies to keep the monarchy solvent. Henry VIII had decimated their legacy with an ambitious foreign policy and an unprecedented expansion of his property portfolio, to the despair of his ministers who begged him to think of the cost of maintaining the fifty-five homes he had acquired for himself by the middle of the 1540s. The upkeep of so many houses had been a golden chain around his children's reigns, all three of whom kept trying to divest themselves of the unwanted properties under the guise of awarding them to deserving aristocrats who could afford to keep them. To further ameliorate the cost of the court, Elizabeth I spent every summer bestowing the honor of a royal visit on wealthy courtiers who, while hosting, had to pay for her, and her household's, food, fuel, and board. James had done the same when he lived in Scotland, but his decision to surround himself in England with those whom he had known for years ensured that it took longer for him to forge friendships with any English nobles, bar his adviser Sir Robert Cecil and his favorite Philip. He did not feel comfortable staying with people whom he did not know and did not yet trust, preferring instead to live in his own homes at his own cost.

The potential difficulties posed by James's personality had flickered in 1603 when it became evident how uncomfortable he felt with the public's attention. James's popular decision to walk through the cheering crowds at York in 1603, rather than ride in a carriage, had been out of character. Far more typical was his joke that he would flash "my arse" to those clamoring for a sight of him, or the incident when he was so overwhelmed by the attention that he retreated to a room, from where he was coaxed with difficulty to wave from a window at the crowds. Even at court, James was increasingly protective of his privacy and resentful at feeling "greatly pressed with the extraordinary company that come into our privy chamber"; he called it a "ready way to make all greatness contemptible."[29] His response was to introduce strict new rules as to when councillors or nobles could see him.[30] An English courtier recalled years later that "He did not love to be looked upon . . . He was not like his predecessor, the late Queen, of famous Memory, that with a well-pleased Affection, met her People's Acclamations, thinking most highly of herself when she was borne upon the Wings of their humble Supplications."[31] Wherever she went and whomever she met, Elizabeth I had the gift of appearing, or being, interested. James never bothered to hide his boredom.

The Venetian ambassador wrote home that the King's avoidance of the crowds had not gone unnoticed: "The people desire to see their sovereign. The discontent has reached such a pitch."[32] James refused to indulge the public's curiosity. As far as he was concerned, kings and queens were God's anointed. Monarchy was not a popularity contest that was subject to the whims of the population. His stubborn reticence on the issue was in sharp contrast to his grasp of Scottish public opinion and the lengths to which he had gone to court it, including mounting pulpits to defend himself.

In a later letter, the same ambassador offered a shrewd assessment of how James's failure to cultivate the public mood had decimated the popularity he enjoyed in 1603. It is also a thoughtful depiction of James in 1606, the year he turned forty:

> He is sufficiently tall, of a noble presence, his physical constitution is robust, and he is at pains to preserve it by taking much exercise at the chase, which he passionately loves, and uses not only as a recreation, but as a medicine. For this, he throws off all business, which he leaves to his Council and to his Ministers . . .
>
> His Majesty is by nature placid, averse from cruelty, a lover of justice . . . no inclination of war, nay is opposed to it, a fact that little pleases many of his subjects . . . He does not caress the people nor make them that good cheer the late Queen did, whereby she won their loves: for the English adore their Sovereigns, and if the King passed through the same street a hundred times a day the people would still run to see him; they like their new King to show pleasure at their devotion, as the late Queen knew well how to do; but this King manifests no taste for them but rather contempt and dislike. The result is he is despised and almost hated.[33]

The public's disenchantment with James was fueled by a decrease in their standards of living. After three years of improved weather and bumper harvests between 1603 and 1606, the country's mood became more unsettled with the first of twelve consecutive years of average harvests. It was not the disaster that had threatened in the final years of Elizabeth I's rule, but the downturn nonetheless undermined the collective optimism that had greeted James's accession.

The two years that followed 1605 were thus difficult for James, who was increasingly fearful of assassination and unpopular with his people. They culminated with the collapse in 1607 of two of his most cherished goals—the Union between England and Scotland

and peace in Ireland—both of which played out against the backdrop of his deteriorating relationship with the English parliament.

James's first parliament as King of England, which met in 1604, had voted him a generous annual subsidy to help meet the spiraling costs of the royal household, but he never succeeded in staying within that subsidy's limits, nor did he give much impression of trying to do so. James, who advised Prince Henry to "hold no Parliaments, but for necessity of new laws, which would be but seldom," was frustrated by how central the institution was to English and Welsh government.[34] England's legal system was shaped by a range of authorities including Parliament, the Equity Court under the aegis of the Lord Chancellor, common-law courts, the Star Chamber that reserved the right to try aristocrats on minor charges, and the ecclesiastical courts of the Church, all slowly grinding against one another like tectonic plates and jealous of their prerogatives. None more so than the House of Commons. James fairly pointed out that its members were more obstreperous with him than they had ever dared to be with his predecessor. He failed to realize, however, that this was in large part because Queen Elizabeth had played to the gallery, deploying regal disdain when she wanted to intimidate the MPs but more often delivering rhetoric to delay, dazzle, and dominate the House. James's speeches, in contrast, were characterized by his aversion to coddling and brevity. One member noted, "the King's Majesty used an Eloquent and very long speech, which continued an hour and a half."[35] James sometimes resorted to threats when he dealt with Parliament. On one occasion he warned them, "I am your King. I am placed to govern you, and shall answer for your errors. I am a man of flesh and blood, and have my passions and affections as other men. I pray you, do not too far move me to do that which my Power may tempt me unto."[36]

The relationship between King and Parliament had enjoyed a happier period following their mutual survival of the Gunpowder Plot, but it had more often decayed between 1603 and 1607 as the House of Commons became disenchanted with James's spending, personality, and policies. Above all, Parliament simmered with suspicion at England's proposed Union with Scotland. There was a variety of reasons motivating their opposition. Nervousness over the economic impact of such a significant constitutional change was not unfounded. Inflation had been a serious problem since Henry VIII, under whom prices had doubled while wages remained stagnant. Its legacy had plagued the reigns of Edward VI and Mary I. Elizabeth had managed to slow, then reverse, inflation in the 1560s.[37] Thereafter, she lost the battle. Food prices were about 67 percent higher at the end of her reign than they had been at its beginning; wages had increased, but at a much slower pace.[38] These long-term strains had reacted with the short-term problems of poor harvests and economic stagnation in the 1590s to leave the Exchequer heavily in debt by 1603.[39] In this context, a change on the scale of the Union seemed a risk.

Members of Parliament (MPs) representing constituencies with a sizable merchant community refused to support the Union, in solidarity with their constituents, who worried that free trade between Scotland and England would be to Scotland's benefit as Scottish merchants undercut England's. Somewhere between patriotism and xenophobia was a worry that the ancient name of England would vanish under James's plans to rename England, Scotland, and Wales as a single country called Great Britain. The House of Commons became a forum for anti-Scottish sentiment. Why would England want a Union that would end up with her as "subject to a needy beggardly nation" like her former enemy Scotland, asked one MP.[40] James was furious when told of a speech delivered by Sir Christopher Piggott, an MP for Buckinghamshire, who railed that the very idea of the Union was obscene: England, he said, was magnificent and Scotland was "poor and barren, and in a manner disgraced by nature . . . There was as much difference between an English and a Scots man as between a judge and a thief."[41] James summoned the whole Privy Council, ordering them to censure Piggott by writing to the Speaker of the House with the reminder that the King "was a Scot himself and that nothing could be applied to the nation [of Scotland] in general in which he had not his share."[42] Anti-Union tales were told in London, where it was claimed that men in the north had seen the ghosts of old armies fighting on the Borders, retracing the English victory over the Scottish invasion in 1513.[43]

James tried desperately to force the Union through. In speeches to Parliament, he extended the metaphor of the Union as a family of nations, asking rhetorically,

> Hath not God first united these two kingdoms both in language, religion, and similitude of manners? Yea, hath He not made us all in one island, compassed with one sea, and of itself by nature so indivisible . . . What God had conjoined then, let no man separate. I am the husband, and all the whole isle is my lawful wife; I am the head, and it is my body; I am the shepherd, and it is my flock. I hope therefore that no man will be so unreasonable as to think that I that am a Christian King under the Gospel, should be a polygamist, and husband to two wives.[44]

Parliament was unmoved. The Union was debated into oblivion, as was the name of "Great Britain," which remained a legal fiction until the reign of James's great-granddaughter a hundred years later. James's achievement was retrospectively called the Union of the Crowns, whereby the two monarchies, but not the two nations, were united in the person of their monarch but not in their laws. England and Scotland would maintain their respective legal, political, religious, and economic systems that had existed before 1603. In James's lifetime, unionism's most substantial achievement was limited to the agreement of both parliaments to rescind any laws prejudicial to citizens of one of James's kingdoms living or traveling in the other.

The anti-Scottish sentiment expressed in Parliament was mirrored at court, with its resentment over James's continued preference for Scottish attendants. "The Scottish monopolise his princely person, standing like mountains betwixt the beams of his grace and us," complained one gentleman of the court.[45] They "hung like horseleeches on him," griped another.[46] The Scottish attendants' selling of knighthoods during their journey in 1603 was loathed by social conservatives, who claimed that the actions of the King and his entourage had made knighthoods "almost [a] prostituted title."[47] Wallowing in snobbish anxiety, another courtier fulminated that the knights from "new" families who had bought their titles through the King's gentlemen were "a scum of such as it would make a man sick to think of them."[48]

In the same year as unionism's defeat, James's Irish policy imploded when Hugh O'Neill, Earl of Tyrone, defected to Spain. Debate continues among historians over what motivated Tyrone's mad horse ride to the northwestern Irish port of Rathmullan, where he boarded ships with his ally the Earl of Tyrconnell and about ninety of their followers. The departure of Tyrone and Tyrconnell was perceived as so devastating to the Catholic cause in the north of Ireland that it was later referred to as "The Flight of the Earls," which inspired songs, poetry, and paintings. Its name was a very loose translation of the title chosen by Tadgh Ó Cianáin, an Irish gentleman who was among Tyrone's entourage, when he later published his own diary of the Flight under the title *Turas na dTaoiseach* ("the Departure of the Lords/Leaders"). What is clear from Ó Cianáin's diary is that neither Tyrone nor Tyrconnell thought their exile would be permanent. They expected to return, with the help either of Spain or Rome, where Tyrone emigrated after he became disillusioned with the grand promises and empty actions he encountered in Madrid. Philip III did not plan to risk his treaty with England. Pope Paul V granted Tyrone a palazzo in Rome, where he died in 1616.

The reasons for the Flight of the Earls likewise remain contested, but Tyrconnell perhaps mistakenly believed he was about to be arrested and convinced Tyrone of the same. They had enough enemies in the government in Ireland to justify their fears; some were veterans of Elizabeth's wars and had assiduously if covertly worked to undermine the peace established between James and Tyrone. Fear of imminent arrest would explain many elements of the Flight; for instance, they departed with such haste that Tyrone's youngest son was left behind. Or why Tyrone was in a cold panic as they rode through the Sperrin Mountains when "the Countess, his wife, being exceedingly weary, slipped down from her horse, and weeping, said she could go no farther; whereupon the Earl drew his sword, and swore with a great oath that he would kill her in her place, if she would not pass with him, and put on a more cheerful countenance withal."[49] Lady Tyrone clambered back onto her horse and left Ireland with her husband.

By fleeing abroad, Tyrone and Tyrconnell had handed a blank check to their enemies in the north of Ireland, especially after James declared the earls' flight to be treason in November 1607. This permitted the legal confiscation of their estates, which were vast. What to do with them inspired many proposals, one of which came from the politician Sir Thomas Shirley the Younger. He had spent time as a sailor abroad and urged James to turn Ulster into a place of refuge for Jewish families fleeing persecution in Europe and the Middle East.[50] A previous king of England, Edward I, had outlawed Judaism and expelled, at terrible human cost, the entire Anglo-Jewish community in the thirteenth century. In the end, and perhaps predictably, the decision was taken to redistribute the exiled earls' lands among Crown loyalists. Similar settlements had already been created in other parts of Ireland by Mary I and Elizabeth I, and James expanded the policy to the north, a process referred to subsequently as the Plantation of Ulster. Most of the families granted land in Ulster were Scottish and English Protestants, although some, especially those offered land in the western county of Fermanagh, were Catholics. The ties between Scotland and the northeast of Ireland had been strong for centuries, but the plantations extended Scottish influence inland and westward, along with the influence of England and Protestantism.

There was significant unrest in Ireland after the Flight of the Earls. A rebel force burned down the northern city of Derry, which was rebuilt only when it attracted investment from guilds of London merchants; in return, the name of the investors' city was merged with that of the investment to form the portmanteau "Londonderry." Years later, it was widely assumed in Ireland that "London" had been added by the British government when, in fact, James had done next to nothing to rebuild the city after it was attacked.[51] He was more proactive in issues that required his approval but not his money, such as the granting of charters to found the port of Belfast in the east or the settler town of Bushmills in the north. The latter subsequently became famous for its whiskey, the distilling of which James also authorized.

At the time of James's accession, Ireland had a population of approximately 1.4 million. About twelve thousand lived in its capital, Dublin, which was part of the Pale, a larger area of ports, towns, and countryside on the eastern coast that was generally loyal to the Crown. Three languages were spoken in Ireland, of which Irish was the most popular, especially in the west and south. A dialect of Scots—Ulster-Scots—was popular in the north-east and English was common in the Pale. Since the twelfth century, the kings of England had held the feudal title Lord of Ireland. Some had visited Ireland in their capacity as lords, but most left government in the hands of the great noble houses. These operated in nominal conjunction with the monarch's representative, known either as his viceroy or lord deputy, and himself often an Irish aristocrat. Beyond the Pale, the aristocratic dynasties of Ireland ruled with a power comparable to their Scottish equivalents.

Throughout the Middle Ages, Ireland had maintained its own bicameral parliament, which met in Dublin. In the 1540s, it had passed the Crown of Ireland Act, which replaced the lordship of Ireland with the title of a kingdom. This theoretically "new" monarchy made Henry VIII the first king of Ireland. Beneath the luster of a fresh royal title, the Crown of Ireland Act had disguised an important legal innovation, whereby Ireland was a monarchy rather than a lordship. Therefore, it was equal in status to any other country with a monarchy—specifically, England. The implications of that shift in national definition were sufficiently significant that, with the benefit of hindsight, it has been referred to by historians as part of the Irish constitutional revolution of the sixteenth century.[52]

As lord and then king of Ireland, Henry VIII undercut the power of the Irish aristocracy with measures that included ending the custom of choosing the lord deputy from the ranks of the Irish nobility and instead sending an Englishman, a policy that was sustained by his children. From the Tudors, James had inherited a fraught situation in Ireland. He had tried his best to ameliorate those problems but, when that failed, he exacerbated them. The consequences of which would come to horrific fruition for Irish Protestants and Catholics later in the century.

In England, James's popularity continued to decline. Private homes across the land again displayed the portraits of their late queen that had gone into storage when Elizabeth died, or when she had endured her own brush with public resentment in the 1590s. Those who had remained Elizabethans in their hearts were gratified, if a little smug, as they saw how many Jacobeans were returning to the fold. Remembering Queen Elizabeth's dignity but her obvious appreciation for the acclaim of a crowd, her godson Sir John Harington, who had privately and severely criticized her in her final years, changed his tune dramatically. "We did all love her," he insisted in 1606.[53] Perhaps the most surprising, and telling, defector to nostalgia was Sir Robert Cecil, who told his brother that after two years of serving James, "I wish I waited now in her presence chamber, with ease at my food, and rest in my bed. I am pushed from the shore of comfort."[54]

London's theaters reflected and fueled the King's declining popularity. In 1606 and 1607, one of the city's most popular plays was *The Isle of Gulls*, a political satire by English playwright John Day. A beautiful fictional land, Arcadia, is taken over by the King of Lacedaemon, Basilius, who neglects his royal duties to go hunting, drains the public treasury with his extravagance, and is far too close to various effeminate male favorites. Basilius's name was almost certainly a nod to James's book *Basilikon Doron* and, while the theater and the play's publishers got cold feet and tried to make the comparison a little less obvious by changing Basilius's title from king to duke, the actors played the Lacedaemonian characters with Scottish accents.

The time James spent hunting was added to the lengthening list of his demerits, but he refused to give it up. He insisted that he found "such felicity in that hunting life, that he hath written to the council, that it is the only means to maintain his health."[55] Providing a glimpse into his state of mind, he explained that he missed the "hard exercise" he had enjoyed in Scotland and was concerned that the gentler pace of life in England "robs him of his appetite and breeds melancholy and a thousand other ills."[56] Sir Robert Cecil, who personally despised hunting, defended James's passion for it by telling another councillor they ought to be grateful that, like the great emperors of ancient Rome, who had also hunted, they too had a monarch "disposed to such manlike and active recreations; so ought it be a joy to us to behold our King of so able a constitution, promising so long life."[57] James, who still referred to him as his "little beagle," appreciated Cecil's defense of him, especially since he knew how much Cecil hated the pastime, teasing him in one letter as "the little beagle who lies at home by the fire."[58]

During his absences from London, James ordered the council to meet where the Queen was in residence. This further increased Anna's standing, as did James's command that she should deputize on his behalf at ambassadorial audiences. Anna's decision to spend a great deal of her time in, or near, London was doubly fortunate, since the court was the highest employer in the capital, after the ports.[59]

Since Cecil would not go hunting, other councillors had to; at least one had to be with James at all times to act as a conduit for matters of state, news of which would be sent to him from wherever the Queen or the council was in residence. The Earl of Worcester drew the proverbial short straw to accompany James on a hunting trip in the freezing December of 1604. He also served as the King's Master of the Horse, which meant his duties continued from sunrise to sunset during the hunting trips. "In the morning we are on horseback by eight," Worcester wrote to a friend, "and so continue in full canter from the death of one hare to another, until four at night;* by that time I find in my lodging sometimes one, most commonly two packets of letters, all of which must be answered before I sleep, for here there are none of the Council but myself."[60]

James's claims that hunting helped preserve his health were undermined by the severe cold he caught in the spring of 1605.[61] Courtiers blamed it on his hunting, because when he was sweaty and "hot with riding a long chase, he sitteth in the open air and drinketh, which cannot but continue, if not increase, a new cold."[62] During a trip to Royston, James's favorite hunting dog, Jowler, disappeared. It returned a day later with an anonymous note tied to its collar, telling the King to spend less time hunting and more time ruling.[63] James laughed, ignored it, and set off for another hunt.†

---

* Four p.m., referred to as nighttime due to the early sunsets.

† Jowler had a tragic end. During a hunting trip at Theobalds, the Queen joined her husband. Taking aim at some deer, she missed and instead shot, and killed, Jowler, who was giving chase. James was initially furious and very upset, but he tried to mask his reaction after witnessing how aghast Anna was. When she realized that she had accidentally killed a pet dog, Anna was devastated. By the next day, she was still so tearful and racked with guilt that her ladies-in-waiting alerted James. He came to her apartments to assure her that what had happened had been nobody's fault.

When he was in London, James seemed miserable and unable to relax. During an audience with the Venetian ambassador, discussing the fate of a pirate popular with the English public but whom the Doge* of Venice wanted hanged for his attacks on Venetian shipping, the ambassador's secretary noticed that James behaved "with extreme impatience, twisting his body about, striking his hands together, and tapping with his foot."[64]

Queen Anna worried about her husband's unhappiness and his drinking. She watched as James, never a slouch when it came to how much alcohol he could put away, consumed so much that some evenings she struggled to understand what he was saying. She feared that it was only a matter of time before it destroyed either his mind or his body.[65] Others, who had known James as long as had Anna, shared her concerns. Some of James's fellow Scots had feared that life in England would not be everything that he had hoped and that it might stunt the acumen that had helped make him successful as king of Scots. Upon meeting James in 1603, the former Solicitor-General for Ireland agreed with these Scottish grandees when he wrote, "I pray unfeigned that his most gracious disposition and heroic mind be not depraved with ill council, and that neither the wealth and peace of England make him forget God, nor the painted flattery of the Court cause him to forget himself."[66]

After the difficulties of 1605–7, those fears had been justified. A diplomat in England concluded, "The King, in spite of all the heroic virtues ascribed to him when he left Scotland and inculcated by him in his books, seems to have sunk into a lethargy of pleasures, and will not take heed of matters of state. He remits everything to the Council, and spends his time in the house alone, or in the country at the chase."[67] Another put it more bluntly: "He seems to have forgotten he is King."[68]

* Head of state for the Venetian republic.

15

ROBERT

Come live with me and be my love,
And we will all the pleasures prove . . .
—Christopher Marlowe,
"The Passionate Shepherd to His Love"
(1599)

In the midst of so many personal and political difficulties, James met a man who would become one of the great loves of his life. On March 24, 1607, James and Anna took their seats at the tiltyard to watch the annual jousts held to celebrate the anniversary of James's English accession. James was forty and Anna was thirty-three. "The Queen is very gracious, moderately good looking," thought the Venetian ambassador:

> She is a Lutheran. The King tried to make her a Protestant;* others a Catholic; to this she was and is much inclined, hence the rumour that she is one. She likes enjoyment and is very fond of dancing and of fêtes. She is intelligent and prudent; and knows the disorders of the government, in which she has no part, though many hold that as the King is most devoted to her, she might play as large a rôle as she wished. But she is young and averse to trouble; she sees that those who govern desire to be left alone, and so she professes indifference. All she ever does is to beg a favour for someone. She is full of kindness for those who support her, but on the other hand she is terrible, proud, unendurable to those she dislikes.[1]

* It is unclear if the ambassador meant an Anglican or a Presbyterian. Likely, the former.

Philip Herbert was also at the Accession Day jousts in 1607. It was two years since James had created him the 1st Earl of Montgomery.

Philip was a younger son and, as with Sandy before him, James wished to see him well provided for. Philip did not attempt to dominate court life through the favor he enjoyed with the King. In another courtier's judgment, he "received the king's bounty with more moderation than other men who succeeded him," and there had been little objection to him as favorite between 1603 and 1607.[2]

Another of James's former favorites, Philip's onetime rival Sir James Hay, competed in the Accession Day joust. He was joined by Scotsman Robert Carr, a member of the Kerr family, whose name had become Carr in England, just as the Stewarts had become the Stuarts. Robert was about twenty-three years old, with blond hair; he was strong, muscular, and of average height. Robert's age in 1607 is sometimes given as twenty; however, his father died in 1585 and Robert was his youngest child, placing his birth in 1584–85 at the latest. Arthur Wilson, who in the next generation would compile the recollections of many of James's courtiers, left a summary of Robert as someone "rather well compacted than tall; his features and favour comely, and handsome, rather than beautiful; the hair of his head flaxen, that of his face tinctured* with yellow, of the Sycambrian† colour: in his own nature, of a gentle mind, and affable disposition."[3] Robert had a strong Scottish Lowlands accent and good manners, and he was unmarried. Despite his skills as an equestrian, at the Accession Day jousts in 1607 he was thrown from his horse and broke his leg. Witnessing the fall, James left the dais to see if the injured rider was all right.

After Robert was carried from the tiltyard, the King visited him to see how he was recuperating. He knew Robert's family—they were prominent landowners in the Lowlands, where Robert's father had been the Laird of Ferniehurst, close to the border with England. Ferniehurst had fought for Queen Mary at the siege of

---

* Slightly imbued with.

† Sycambria was a legendary city, still believed to be historical in James's lifetime, founded by an ancient king on the banks of the river Danube. In the legends, the people of Sycambria had sallow complexions.

Edinburgh Castle in 1573. His estates were occupied by Lord Morton afterward and he was driven into exile in France, where he was among the Marian exiles who first influenced Esmé Stuart against Morton. When he rose to prominence in Scotland, Esmé had facilitated Ferniehurst's return, and he remained loyal to Esmé until the latter's death. Less pleasantly, he had caused a diplomatic incident for James when he shot and killed Lord Francis Russell during the negotiations for the Treaty of Berwick. Ferniehurst died when Robert was an infant and the lairdship passed to Robert's brother, who cared for Robert following the death of his mother, Janet, when Robert was about nine years old.

Despite his family's connections, Robert's career at court in Scotland had never quite taken off. He had been too young to make much of an impact and, when he was a teenager, had apparently embarrassed himself when he tried to deliver to a visiting dignitary an address in Latin, a language he could not speak and did not memorize. He had eventually served as a page to James's treasurer, Sir George Home, a fellow Lowlander. In his late teens, he had accompanied Home to England, where he participated in the court's special occasions, including the Accession Day jousts.

Perhaps Robert told James of his earlier public embarrassment thanks to his subpar Latin. During his visits to Robert's sickbed, which became a daily occurrence, James tried to teach him the language. Hearing of these lessons and recalling Robert's accent, one of the Howard family, who regarded themselves as the bastions of the old English aristocracy, mockingly suggested, "I think someone should teach him English, too."[4]

Robert's Latin lessons were not a success, and the King eventually gave up, but not before strong feelings had developed between the pair. It marked the end of Philip's time as favorite, a development that Philip accepted with equanimity. The future Earl of Clarendon, who knew Philip later in his life and had a high opinion of him, recorded in his memoirs that Philip had remained favorite from James's accession in 1603 until just after the jousts of 1607: "[Philip] had not sat many years in that sunshine, when a new comet appeared in court, Robert Carr, a Scotsman, quickly after declared favourite: upon whom the king no sooner fixed his eyes, but the earl [Philip], without the least murmur or indisposition, left all doors open for his entrance; (a rare temper!)"[5]

James was grateful to Philip for the time they had spent together and for his acceptance of Robert's rise.[6] While their affair was over, a friendship endured for several years. James stepped in to smooth over quarrels caused by Philip's temper and his athletic competitiveness, such as the occasion when he threatened to punch the Earl of Southampton over a contested point in a tennis match.

The rest of 1607 saw Robert Carr's rise at court. The same Howard who made fun of Robert's accent chronicled the ascent of the "Scottish lad" for an unwell friend who, while away from court because of his health, wished to be kept informed of developments. "This fellow is straight-limbed, well-favoured, strong-shouldered, and smooth-faced," he wrote. He thought that Robert's lack of intellectual curiosity did not mean he was without "some sort of cunning" in terms of winning James's favor, evidenced by the fact that he "doth it wondrously in a little time." By year's end, Robert had been knighted and appointed a Gentleman of the Bedchamber. According to Howard's letter, the King "leaneth on his arm, pinches his cheek, smoothes his ruffled garments, and, when he looketh at Carr, directeth discourse to divers others." *[7] The author joked in another letter, "If any misfortune be to be wished, 'tis breaking a leg in the King's presence."[8] News had seeped out into the public arena by December, when Robert was identified as the King's "new favourite" in a letter written by Londoner John Chamberlain.[9]

Like several of James's previous favorites, Robert was kept away from government, but he dominated the court's social life in a way none of his predecessors had. He changed his tailors many times to find clothes that best complemented his appearance. The young gentlemen of the court rushed to imitate his fashion. Howard had a field day making fun of this to his friend, informing him that their fellow courtiers were so assiduous in their sycophancy that they were all one step away from saying "that the stars are bright jewels fit for Carr's ears . . . that his eyes are fire, his tail is Berenice's

---

* Stares/gazes at Robert, even when he's talking to somebody else.

locks* . . . We are almost worn out in our endeavours to keep pace with this fellow in our duty and our labour to gain favour, but all in vain; where it endeth I cannot guess, but honours are talked of speedily for him."[10] James gave Robert a miniature portrait of himself, encircled by diamonds: it was the kind of gift more commonly exchanged between courting or married couples.[11]

As Howard noted, the courtiers' collective obsequiousness was "all in vain," because Robert had no interest in involving himself in court politics. The only person he cared about promoting was his best friend, Thomas Overbury, an Englishman whom he had first met in Edinburgh in 1601 when they were both teenagers, shortly after Overbury's graduation from Oxford.[12] In early 1608, Robert persuaded James to knight Overbury. Robert and Overbury were close enough that a romantic relationship between them has been postulated by some historians.[13] Sir Roger Wilbraham, who knew them both, described Overbury as Robert's "bedfellow, minion, and inward councillor."[14] Equally revealing is James's uncharacteristic jealousy toward Overbury. After knighting Overbury at Robert's urging and granting him an income of his own with the lease to a profitable saltworks on Crown land, James suddenly sent Overbury abroad on a diplomatic mission to the Netherlands.

Howard's letters to his friend in 1607 are invaluable in dating the start of Robert Carr's liaison with James and his rise to prominence. However, further evidence for James's relationship with Robert differs from that for James's other favorites. Although it is substantial, much of it is retrospective; many of the details are provided by a series of arguments the couple had in 1612, when James was upset enough to write down in a letter to Robert his memories of when they had been happy. We know from these recollections that Robert spent many nights sleeping alone with James in his bedchamber, and James referred to Robert's "own infinite privacy with me."[15] The King recalled how much joy he had found in the way "ye never think to hold grip of me but out of mere love."[16]

---

* Berenice II, Queen of Egypt, who was said to have hair so beautiful that when she sacrificed it to the goddesses, they carried it up into the heavens, where it formed the Coma Berenices constellation.

Robert's influence was negligible throughout the great events of 1607—not only unionism's defeat and the Flight of the Earls, but England's expanding colonialism in North America. Jamestown, originally named James Fort, was founded in Virginia in 1607 and named after the King, perhaps in a vain attempt to stimulate greater royal interest in the American colonies. James remained indifferent, and much of his American policy consisted of passing on proposals to the commercial guilds in London, who were encouraged to invest since the Crown had little interest in doing so.

In September 1607, there was another bereavement in the royal family when James's daughter Princess Mary died of pneumonia. Mary's tomb at Westminster Abbey was next to her sister Sophia's and described her as "received into Heaven in early infancy."

Robert remained a private rather than a public force throughout 1608, when James granted him a country estate of his own, Sherborne, which provided him with an income of £1,000 per annum. Sherborne was useful to Robert, but he saw little of it, since he and James were hardly ever apart from one another. They settled into a routine, which did not vary much from one year to the next. Their spring and early summer were often spent at Theobalds. In 1607, after realizing how much the King loved it, Cecil gave the King the house, estate, hunting demesne, and stomach-clenching running costs. In return, James granted Cecil the smaller but impressive Hatfield House, where Elizabeth I had spent much of her childhood.

In early summer, James and Robert often hunted from Eltham Palace, near Greenwich, which had first been used as a royal residence by Edward II, who acquired it in 1305. Several monarchs had since enlarged Eltham, most extensively among them Edward IV, who had commissioned its famous Great Hall. James spent a significant sum restoring Eltham after it had gone a little to seed in Elizabeth I's later years. He and Robert also hunted infrequently in early summer from eleventh-century Windsor Castle, which was never one of James's favorite properties.

When summer stag hunting gave way to hawking and hare hunting in autumn and winter, James and Robert, with a reduced number of the King's entourage, spent much of their time either at Royston or at James's other smaller hunting lodge at Newmarket. Easy to heat, comfortable, and both close to the University of Cambridge, from where James could send for books in which he was interested, Newmarket and Royston, where new quarters were created for Robert, were arguably where James was happiest at this period in his life.[17] He would spend three days of the week out hunting and the other three reading in his rooms, responding to letters, playing chess with Robert, taking care of his new pet armadillo, which he loved, reading government reports, about which he seemed more conscientious than when he first came to England, and working on his own writing. In 1609, he published another book, *Premonition to all Christian Monarchies.* A defense of Protestantism and royal leadership of national churches, its anti-Catholic sentiment was sharp, yet James seemed surprised to learn from his ambassador in Venice how poorly the book had been received in Catholic countries.[18]

James and Robert spent their Christmases at Whitehall, where they were joined by the Queen and her household. Anna knew about her husband's intimacy with Robert and, to judge from later conversations between them, made clear to James that she expected Robert to treat her with every respect to which she was entitled by her position. Robert obeyed and, during their Christmases at Whitehall, Anna remained the cynosure of society. Diplomats, as well as nobles, appreciated her deft handling of etiquette and the effort she expended "to entertain strangers, suitors and her people, with more courtly courtesy and favourable speeches than the king uses."[19] The Venetian ambassador conceded that James was more intellectually accomplished than his wife and perhaps kinder too, but it was the Queen who better understood people and the daily public-facing duties of monarchy.[20]

Anna's sumptuous masques had become part of the Stuart court's celebrations of major events and its Christmas traditions. Their cost remained staggering, and they were increasingly didactic in transmitting a political message. Stories of goddesses or kings bringing unity to disparate fairy-tale kingdoms might be an attempt to revive the unionist dream. Or, with their celebration of obedience and the emergence of order from chaos, the masques could serve as a vehicle for Anna to promote the Divine Right of Kings. Their evidently expensive production costs were used to convince foreign ambassadors, who were nearly always invited to watch as guests of honor, that James's kingdoms were wealthy and powerful. Admiration for the masques' ingenuity and spectacle grew, but so did criticism of their politics. There were other complaints—at one Christmas masque, the costumes worn by the Queen and her women were judged "too light" or revealing.[21] After Christmas, the Queen, with her household of councillors, ladies-in-waiting, chaplains, jesters, seamstresses, cooks, valets, pages, maids, and stable hands, returned to her houses, while James and Robert went to Royston or Newmarket.

This repetition of happy days endured its first interruptions in 1610. In foreign and domestic policy, it was an eventful year. There was more expenditure at court to welcome Queen Anna's German nephew Friedrich Ulrich of Brunswick-Lüneburg for a two-month visit. James and Anna both insisted on entertaining him in royal fashion. More masques, banquets, and jousts were held at court to celebrate sixteen-year-old Prince Henry's formal investiture as Prince of Wales. Along with his mother, Henry was the most popular member of the royal family with the English public, certainly far more so than his father. He was given St. James's Palace, then located on the edge of London, as his principal home, and Richmond Palace, near Hampton Court, as his primary country residence. The Prince of Wales was athletic and loved to "practice tilting, charging on horseback with pistol"; he was interested in anything military, and the Dutch engineer Abraham van Nyvelt came to teach him "all manner of things belonging to the wars."[22] Henry's friends were drawn from those in the aristocracy who favored a more aggressive, expansionist, and pro-Protestant foreign policy. This augmented Prince Henry's standing in London, where such aims were popular.

James worried about his son's mediocre academic achievements. He encouraged Henry to study as hard in the schoolroom as his brother, Prince Charles, did. Henry nodded obediently, but when James returned to his own palace, Henry scoffed to his attendants, "It is not necessary for me to be a professor, but a soldier and a man of this world."[23] When his comment was repeated to James, the King was embarrassed by what his son had said, especially since it seemed to reject his guidance and mock as unkingly his love of learning. Queen Anna's chaplain chose tact when he wrote of Prince Henry, "I think he was a little self-willed."[24]

In May, news arrived from Paris that Louis XIII had acceded to the throne after his father, King Henri IV, was stabbed to death as his carriage drove through the streets. Henri IV's murder intensified anti-Catholic sentiment in England, which had not diminished since the Gunpowder Plot. Like Henri III, his assassinated brother-in-law and predecessor, Henri IV had been killed by a fellow Catholic who felt he lacked zeal for their cause. Henri IV's assassin may have been mentally unwell—he had been rejected from joining the priesthood after claiming he had a series of miraculous visions that sounded to the priests questioning him to be more like hallucinations. As punishment for regicide, incisions were made in his flesh, into which were poured molten lead and burning oil. Each limb was then tied to one of four horses, who were whipped to ride off in unison, tearing the King's killer, quite literally, limb from limb.

A few weeks later, a scandal broke in England when James discovered that his cousin Arbella had secretly married "the selfsame person whom, for many just causes, we had expressly forbidden [her] to marry."[25] James's treatment of Arbella had been lenient by contemporary standards, especially when compared with how his Tudor predecessors had behaved toward their cousin rivals. James had refused to rusticate Arbella when she was the unwitting figurehead of plots against him and had told her that he would grant her permission to marry almost anybody she wanted, so long as that match did not threaten the succession. Arbella unfortunately fell in love with William Seymour, a son of Edward Seymour, Lord Beauchamp, who was the son of Lady Katherine Grey. Edward's claim to the throne could have proved a challenge to James had he chosen to pursue it in 1603. A marriage between Arbella and William Seymour would unite her Tudor-Stuart ancestry with his Grey descent; if combined in any children they might have, that could produce rival claimants to Prince Henry and his descendants. It was through a similar marriage between his parents that James had emerged as the most credible heir to Elizabeth I. Arbella and William, who seem to have been very much in love, begged James for permission to marry. He refused, so they eloped. When he discovered what they had done, James ordered their detention—Seymour was sent to the Tower of London, while Arbella was placed under house arrest at a friend's home in Lambeth, a parish in south London. James's conditions for their imprisonment were so lenient that the couple planned to reunite. When their plan was discovered, James decided to send Arbella north to live in the Bishop of Durham's household. Fearing that they would never meet again, Arbella and William planned their escape on the same night, when they would flee to France. William's ship made it; Arbella's was intercepted by the Navy, who brought her back to England. James ordered her incarceration in the Tower, where she died four years later, aged forty, after refusing food and having suffered a period of illness, likely exacerbated by depression. James ordered her funeral at Westminster Abbey, and her widower was eventually permitted to return home.

Toward the end of the year, Robert took his first steps into politics when he tried to turn James against Cecil. He was helped by the failure of Cecil's Great Contract proposal to Parliament, which would pay off the monarchy's debts and then provide it with an annual income generated by taxation, in return for which the Crown would yield some of its ancient privileges, lands, and prerogatives. James had to be talked into the suggestion by Cecil, who then failed to get it through the House of Commons. James did not dismiss Cecil after this embarrassing defeat, but his trust in his "little beagle" cooled. The process was encouraged by Robert, who aligned himself with those at court urging James to punish Parliament by disbanding it, which James did in February 1611.

James needed little encouragement to disband Parliament, and it would be wrong to see Robert as the brains behind a plot. His friend and possible former lover, Thomas Overbury, is the most likely reason why Robert involved himself in affairs of state. Following Overbury's return from the Netherlands, James allowed Robert to keep him at court. Robert soon asked Overbury to serve as his secretary, a position that the extremely intelligent and equally ambitious Overbury intended to use as a springboard to a political career, preferably as a member of the Privy Council. In furtherance of that goal, Overbury liaised with members of the competing court factions with the offer of serving as their gateway to Robert, who could be their gateway to the King.

Factions in early modern courts were a collection of individuals united sometimes by shared politics, more often by religion, and most often by family. Better understood as loose associations rather than as analogous to an ideological movement or political party, factions could be complicated by marriages between different "opposing" houses, personal quarrels, or religious conversions. At James's English court, there were three broad factions by 1610.

The first was dominated by the aristocratic Howard family, who generally advocated a pro-absolutist policy that encouraged the King to rule without recourse to Parliament as much as possible. They were sympathetic to Catholicism—several of their members continued to practice Catholicism privately in their homes—and, in terms of foreign policy, they wished to see England's 1604 treaty with Spain deepened into an alliance. The Howards were a formidable force in English politics and had been for over a century. Few families were more familiar with the spinning of Fortune's wheel. The heads of the family had been dukes of Norfolk until the 4th Duke was beheaded in 1572 for plotting against Elizabeth I. His father, the Earl of Surrey, had met the same fate under Henry VIII, and the 1st Duke had been killed at the Battle of Bosworth fighting against Henry VII. The two Howard queens of England—Catherine Howard on her father's side and Anne Boleyn on her mother's—had been executed. One of the family's subsidiary titles, the earldom of Arundel, had also been confiscated when the last incumbent died in prison in 1595 after refusing to abandon his Catholic faith.* Perhaps even more remarkable than the Howards' generational lurches from ruin to greatness and back again was their tenacity, which they proved with the overpowering obsequiousness they had deployed to win James's favor once he became King

* St. Philip Howard, 20th Earl of Arundel (1557–95), canonized in 1970 by Pope Paul VI.

of England. When James observed a courtier retreating from the sun on a hot day, a Howard leaped in to suggest that the brightest sunshine he was retreating from was "your resplendent Majesty."[26]

It worked, but only to a degree. Keen to reward the Howards but careful to prevent them becoming too powerful, James declined to revive their dukedom of Norfolk but granted three earldoms to the family—Northampton to one of the elder generation, Arundel and Suffolk to two of his nephews. Arundel had no interest in politics and devoted himself instead to art, becoming one of the greatest collectors and conservationists in English history. Northampton and Suffolk established themselves as leaders of their court faction, whose other most valuable member was Suffolk's wife, considered one of the most beautiful women at court.[27] A confidante of the great and the good, including the Spanish ambassador and Queen Anna—whom she served as a lady-in-waiting—the Countess of Suffolk's political instincts were augmented by her skills in reading people's wants, fears, and desires, as she had shown when she truffled out specific information on the kind of men the King was attracted to.*

The second faction had as its most influential members Henry Wriothesley, 3rd Earl of Southampton, Robert Devereux, 3rd Earl of Essex, and Philip Herbert's brother William, 3rd Earl of Pembroke. They were defenders of Parliament, sympathetic to Puritanism, and supportive of colonialism—particularly in North America. In foreign affairs, they favored an alliance with the United Provinces of the Netherlands, the Protestant Dutch republic that had emerged from rebellion against Spain. The complexity of religious identity in factionalism was exhibited by this group. All its members shared a commitment to the Protestant cause, especially as an influence on foreign policy. However, they did not all share every value that we might associate with Puritanism—Lords Southampton and Pembroke were prominent patrons of the arts and theater, of which Puritanism was suspicious.

---

* Years earlier, there had been rumors of an affair between the Countess of Suffolk and the widowed Sir Robert Cecil, which, if true, may have added a personal element to the Howards' quarrel with Cecil.

Third was the Scottish faction, consisting of Ludovic, Duke of Lennox, and several Gentlemen of the Bedchamber, including Sir George Home,* who were less interested in English religious policy than the other two factions but were keen to see an alliance with France.

Sixteen-year-old Prince Henry's marriage became the focus of the three factions' competing agendas. A royal wedding would be accompanied by an alliance, which would shape how England interacted with the rest of Europe and, depending on the princess's faith, domestic religious policy. The Howard faction wanted a Habsburg. However, since the King of Spain's daughters were both very young, the Howards suggested a marriage between Prince Henry and one of the princesses of Savoy, either Maria-Apollonia, who was the same age as Henry, or her sister Francesca-Caterina, who was a year younger. Their mother was a Spanish princess and their father a Spanish ally. The Scottish faction promoted a wedding to Louis XIII's eldest sister, Princess Elisabeth of France, while the Puritans wanted anyone but a Habsburg and preferably a Protestant—such as Princess Maria-Elizabeth of Sweden, whose father, now King Carl IX, had long ago been the first royal to host James and Anna as a married couple, during their winter journey to Denmark.[28]

None of these factions had definitively won the support of either the King or Cecil, dislike of whom was arguably the only position that united all three in 1610. Most of them felt that they were kept from achieving their goals by Cecil's dominance of government. They were keen to manipulate Robert into allying with them so that they would have direct access to the King. For three years, Robert had resisted, until Overbury decided to use him to advance his own career.

Overbury's price was steep. He demanded £1,000 from Sir Francis Bacon, a brilliant philosopher and courtier with political ambitions, in return for inducing Robert to persuade the King that Bacon deserved to be the next Master of the Court of Wards, a lucrative legal position tied to revenue collection. Bacon did not have £1,000, so Overbury would not speak to Robert on his behalf.

---

* After 1606, the 1st Earl of Dunbar.

The post went instead to Sir George Carew, the former English ambassador to Poland.

Above all, however, Overbury desired power. His sympathies lay with the Puritan faction, partly because he disliked the Howards and had, as a young man, idolized Lord Essex's father, the hawkish Earl of Essex, who had been executed in 1601 for his failed rebellion against Elizabeth I.[29] From his time in the Netherlands, Overbury had also returned with a suspicion of the Habsburg empires, which made him even more predisposed to ally with anti-Catholic aristocrats like Essex, Southampton, and Pembroke. To the Howards' alarm, Overbury steered Robert in the direction of the Puritan faction. He even wrote drafts of flattering letters to Lord Essex's beautiful wife, Frances, who, as a Howard by birth, had made one of the faction-spanning marriages that occasionally defused but never dissipated their rivalries. The drafts were given to Robert, who would copy them out in his own hand, pass them off as his own, and send them to Lady Essex.

In 1611, James's distrust of Overbury was revived, at the same time as Overbury made a dangerous enemy in Queen Anna. Since his university days, Overbury had been noted for his caustic sense of humor and his often needlessly confrontational manners. The court had spent part of May at Greenwich, where the King had gone to visit his wife. A courtier who was present recorded what happened when Robert "and his dear Overbury [were] walking in the garden at Greenwich whither the queen's window openeth, [and] she broke into a sudden and contemptible laughing at them."[30] Overbury and Robert responded by laughing at her with similar contempt and Anna, with tears in her eyes, went to her husband, threatening that she would return to Denmark if he did not protect her honor. James banished Overbury from court for six months. Upon his return in November, he was forbidden from entering the Queen's presence, but he immediately reestablished his close relationship with Robert. Sir Francis Bacon, thwarted in his attempt to ally with Overbury, later told Robert that it seemed as if he and Overbury "made a play* of all the world besides themselves."[31]

---

* Joke.

Along with their numerous private jokes, the pair had code names for the King, the Queen, and the other great personalities at court.[32]

Overbury's bond with Robert was swiftly matched by his reestablishment of his political influence at court, which was furthered by a development in James and Robert's relationship. In the "infinite privacy" of James's apartments, and after four years at one another's side, the King now frequently discussed politics with Robert, who had the self-awareness to know that he understood few of the issues as well as he should. He therefore passed the government documents given to him by James "unto Overbury, who perused them."[33] Overbury reveled in his importance and advertised it to foreign diplomats, who noted that he had grown "very insolent" in his confidence as Robert's "oracle of direction."[34]

The before-and-after signatures of Guido ("Guy") Fawkes give an idea of the torture he had endured when he was arrested for his role in the Gunpowder Plot.

Influential, glamorous, popular but extravagant Queen Anna, shown here in her early thirties.

The tomb of James and Anna's daughter Princess Sophia, carved in the shape of her cradle. Behind that is the tomb of her sister Princess Mary.

Robert Carr, Earl of Somerset, one of James's great loves. Shown here with his well-connected and ambitious wife, Frances. Both are dressed in the lavish fashions of James's court.

The notorious "Bloody Tower" at the Tower of London. Thomas Overbury's mysterious fate here would cause one of the greatest scandals in British royal history.

James's son Henry, Duke of Rothesay and Prince of Wales, aged eighteen.

James, painted in his mid-forties by Nicholas Hilliard.

James's daughter Elizabeth, whose dramatic life earned her the nickname "the Winter Queen."

Queen Anna in hunting attire. This portrait, painted during her later health struggles, is now on display at her former home of Edinburgh Castle.

James's son Prince Charles, aged nineteen.

Robert Carr's rival, George Villiers, Duke of Buckingham, described by more than one courtier as the most handsome man they had ever seen. In private, James addresses him as "sweetheart" and "my darling wife." The King's love turned George into one of the most powerful men in the country.

An exhausted and unwell James, painted in his fifties by Daniel Mytens.

16

PRIVATE COCKS

What secrets have passed betwixt you and me.
—Thomas Overbury to Robert Carr
(1613)

In 1611, James ennobled Robert as Baron Winwick. He made him wealthier still by awarding him seven more country estates in the counties of Durham and Westmorland and, later the same year, elevated him up a rung of the aristocratic pecking order to become Viscount Rochester. While Robert's star continued to rise socially, it had stalled politically. James valued their time together when he could privately discuss with him matters of state, but he showed no intention of dismissing Cecil. If there was to be another powerful force to emerge at the heart of government, it would be Prince Henry, who turned eighteen in February 1612.

Then, on May 24, 1612, Cecil died. The last months of the forty-eight-year-old's life had been agony, with tumors in his stomach, liver, and neck, and weeping sores breaking out all over his body. The men who worked for him were so devoted that they cradled his head in a pillow when, toward the end, he could not get up because he was in so much pain.[1] Their sentiments were not widespread. Like many chief ministers throughout history, Cecil was unpopular and his critics relished his pain. They joked that his actions as a politician had earned him his cancers and his sores, through which everybody "may see by this foul loathsome end,/How fully then they did offend."[2]

The summer that followed Cecil's death was a sweltering one in the south of England, so much so that the Prince of Wales worried he had contracted sunstroke. The heat made Henry irritable, as it did many who sweated through June and July. As part of the heir's growing political influence, James included Henry in the ongoing discussions about his future wife. The preferred Protestant candidate, Princess Maria-Elizabeth of Sweden, had married her cousin, the Duke of Östergötland, at the behest of her mother, who worried that the Duke's claim to the Swedish throne might be a threat to that of Maria-Elizabeth's brother. It may have been just as well for the women of England and Wales that Maria-Elizabeth stayed in Sweden. An avid supporter of witch hunts, she encouraged her husband to introduce them throughout his duchy.

With Maria-Elizabeth married, James and Henry debated whether to proceed with a proposal to the King of Spain's niece Princess Maria-Apollonia of Savoy or the King of France's sister. Elisabeth of France was to be betrothed to a different foreign prince, so Anglo-Scottish attention pivoted to her younger sister, Princess Christine. Henry had no clear preference. However, if he could not have a Protestant wife at the start of his married life, he wanted one not long after. He suggested to his father that the marriage treaty stipulate that the princess come to England to complete her education, as that would provide "a greater likelihood of converting her to our religion."[3] This made Christine of France, who was only six years old, the more obvious choice. However, if Henry was betrothed to her and she was brought to England, it would require waiting, at the very least, eight years until a wedding, and perhaps longer before consummation. Contemporary wisdom held that sixteen or over was the preferred age for safe childbearing. Eighteen-year-old Maria-Apollonia of Savoy was the same age as Henry, but she was also a devout Catholic who was unlikely to change her religion, no matter how much time she spent in England. James knew that no Catholic royal house in Europe would agree to a marriage with the condition that their daughter become a Protestant. Henry grudgingly agreed to his father's suggestion that the future princess of Wales be allowed to practice her faith in the privacy of her own household, provided she made no public comment on the anti-Catholic laws then in place.

In September, when the summer's heat at last broke, plans were finalized for the reburial of Mary, Queen of Scots. One of James's early acts as king of England had been an order for Mary's original tomb to be marked for the first time with a rich velvet pall and her royal coat of arms, until he could build something more appropriate. In October 1612, he had his mother's coffin exhumed from Peterborough Cathedral and brought to Westminster Abbey. She was buried in a magnificent sepulcher that James had commissioned for her; its splendor and cost substantially exceeded that of the nearby tomb of Queen Elizabeth.

At the time of Queen Mary's reinterment, the royal family were still discussing Prince Henry's marriage and preparing for Princess Elizabeth's. Sixteen years old, with the red Stuart hair and dark eyes, Elizabeth was betrothed to Frederick V, a German Protestant prince who ruled over the Palatinate in the Rhineland. Anna, who had previously made it quite clear when it came to her children's marriages that she considered even a Medici to be a bit low-end, was appalled. She told Elizabeth that she might as well be known as Goody* Palatine.[4] On a personal level, the match proved a success. Elizabeth and Frederick liked each other when he came to England in October in preparation for their wedding, and their liking subsequently evolved into love. They were almost exactly the same age—Frederick was seven days younger than Elizabeth—and Frederick got on well with her family, especially Prince Henry, who hosted the betrothed couple to dinners at St. James's Palace, over which the aurora borealis had appeared on October 2. The King invited Frederick to join him on a hunting trip out of Royston, where he took the opportunity to impress upon Frederick that he expected him to treat Elizabeth well.

Whereas Anna saw the comparative diplomatic irrelevance of the Palatinate as an insult to her and her daughter, James regarded it as one of two great points in Frederick's favor. James did not want a marital alliance with any country that had an aggressive, ambitious, expansionist, or complicated foreign policy that might pull him into war. Frederick's family was also noted for the zeal of their Protestant faith, which James correctly guessed would please the Puritan factions in court and Parliament, as well as ameliorating

* "Goodwife," a contemporary equivalent of today's "Mrs.," but also associated in Anna's lifetime with Puritans in the middle class.

some of their frustration at Prince Henry's likely future wedding to a Catholic.

At the end of the month, the Prince of Wales was unwell with diarrhea. He had been overdoing it with three- and four-hour tennis matches, nighttime strolls by the riverside, and long swims in the river when he went to Richmond Palace outside London. Henry knew he was tiring himself out and that it was taking a toll on his appearance—his servants fell back on distracting jokes or unctuous platitudes when he asked them, "How do I look this morning?"[5] The prince had a strong aversion to laziness, which made him unwilling to relax his routine. He had no choice when his illness forced him to pull out of a dinner on October 29 in honor of Elizabeth and Frederick, hosted by the Lord Mayor of London at the Guildhall. Three days later, Henry missed a council meeting, which aimed to resolve whether a proposal of marriage should be sent to the court of France or Savoy. His doctors informed the King and Queen that the prince's condition was more serious than he or they had initially surmised.

The royal family converged on Prince Henry's house at St. James's Palace, where he had slipped into a delirium. Candlelight hurt his eyes. His physicians bled him, applied enemas, and covered his body in a poultice made from freshly slaughtered pigeons and cockerels. Henry likely had typhoid, which he may have contracted swimming in the Thames at Richmond during the heat wave. His parents, his sister, and her fiancé gathered at his bedside. Eleven-year-old Prince Charles arrived to join them, clutching a small bronze equestrian statue from the royal collection that he knew Henry liked. He pressed it into his brother's hands and, crying, whispered to him that he must get better. When he was well again, they would ride the real thing, as they had before.

The next day, James was turned away at the bedchamber door by his son's doctors. Inside, they were slicing open a cockerel on Henry's back. The day after that, the King and Queen missed the annual service of thanksgiving on the anniversary of the Gunpowder Plot. Denied access to his son's rooms, James could not seem to sit still and, "apprehending the worst," rode to Theobalds, where his words seemed garbled and his movements erratic. Those with him thought the King looked so distressed that he was "more like a dead man than a living."[6] The frantic Queen contacted explorers who had been to the Americas and begged them to make a potion with ingredients from the "New World" that might restore Henry's health.

It was too late. Just after eight o'clock in the evening of November 8, the church bells of London began, one after the other, to toll, until they flooded the city with the sound of mourning. While we do not know who told James at Theobalds that Henry was dead, we do know that the King screamed, collapsed, and could not get out of bed for the next three days.[7] When the news was brought to the Queen at Denmark House, she fainted. Upon reviving, she ran into a small room and locked the door behind her. Her ladies hammered on the door, pleading with Anna to let them in to help her, but all they could hear for hours was her sobbing.

In keeping with tradition, neither parent attended Henry's funeral at Westminster Abbey, nor did James ever respond to the rumors concocted by his enemies that, jealous of his popularity, he had poisoned Henry. When he returned to council meetings, James impressed his advisers with his seeming ability to focus on matters of government until, while a councillor was speaking about another matter, the King's eyes suddenly filled with tears and he cried out, "But Henry is dead! Henry is dead!"[8] This continued for months after the Prince of Wales's death, with James sometimes mumbling the phrase in disbelief under his breath.

When Antonio Foscarini, the new Venetian ambassador, came to convey his government's condolences to the Queen, one of Anna's ladies pulled him aside before he was shown in. She told him, as she had told other ambassadors, that he was not to mention Prince Henry. In a letter home, Foscarini explained, "I was advised to act thus, and so have other ambassadors, because she cannot bear to have it mentioned; nor does she ever recall it without abundant tears and sighs."[9] The ladies-in-waiting eventually banned the entire household from so much as mentioning Henry's name, because Anna could not hear it without weeping.

Anna made a last-ditch attempt to prevent Elizabeth's marriage to Frederick on the grounds that Henry's death had made Charles heir and Elizabeth second in line to the throne. Under those circumstances, Elizabeth could not be married off to somebody as low-ranking as Frederick. Neither James nor Elizabeth agreed with her. Father and daughter spent a quiet Christmas in mourning at Whitehall, where they played cards together and talked about the future. Elizabeth's formal betrothal ceremony went ahead in the palace's Banqueting House on December 27; Anna declined to appear on health grounds, but she attended the wedding itself, at which the Archbishop of Canterbury officiated in Whitehall's chapel on February 14. Elizabeth and Frederick were described by a London merchant as "young turtles that were coupled on St. Valentine's Day."[10]

The morning after the wedding night, James bluntly asked Frederick—in negation of spiteful rumors that he was impotent—if the marriage had been consummated. Frederick assured his father-in-law that it had been, which was confirmed by the fact that Elizabeth conceived a few weeks after she said farewell to her family on April 14. Before she embarked on her ship, Elizabeth sent a letter to her father in which she expressed grief at the thought that "I shall, perhaps, never see again the flower of princes, the king of fathers, the best and most amiable father that the Sun will ever see," but promised no matter the geographical distance between them, she would always love him.[11] In his last meeting with Frederick before his departure, James reiterated that he expected Elizabeth to be cherished privately and honored publicly, and that no member of Frederick's court, including his mother, should ever be granted precedence above her.[12]

Henry's death seems to have placed a strain on James's relationship with Robert. They quarreled in the weeks immediately after, until James too fell ill and Robert nursed him back to health. In the middle of December, the diplomat Sir Isaac Wake recorded in a letter to a colleague that Robert "has been in some disgrace but his credit is much increased by his tender attentions to the King during a recent illness."[13]

The unprecedented events of 1612, with the deaths within six months of both the King's chief minister and the heir to the throne, paved the way for Robert to move from the private sphere to the political. The only remaining figure who could have prevented this was the Queen, but she was grieving the loss of her son and had recently been diagnosed with gout. In pursuit of comfort if not a cure, she spent even longer away from court with trips to take the waters at Bath. With Anna distracted by her health, her heartbreak, and her disinclination to involve herself in plots, Overbury, through Robert, could confidently expect to exert great influence in government.

To Overbury's distress, and that of his fair-weather allies in the Puritan faction, victory was snatched from them by the Howards. During Overbury's six-month rustication from court after he mocked the Queen, the Howards had taken advantage of his absence to swoop in and befriend Robert. As they had with the King, they laid on flattery of Robert with a trowel. Their campaign was aided when Robert developed romantic feelings for Frances, Countess of Essex. Her husband was one of the Puritan faction's leaders, and her father, Lord Suffolk, was one of the Howards'. The Essexes had been married when Frances was fourteen and the earl was thirteen. They had grown older but never happy. Twenty-two-year-old Frances soon, apparently, reciprocated Robert's affections, and her family was happy either to encourage or capitalize on the situation.

Overbury was furious when he discovered not only that Robert wanted to marry Frances, but that the Howards had, unsurprisingly, given their blessing. The Howards were unlikely to be under any illusions as to the dynamic between King James and their putative son-in-law. Frances's mother was the Countess of Suffolk, who had once urged her allies to plant handsome men with good breath in the King's household if they wanted to influence him.

For Frances to marry Robert, she would need to be freed from her current husband. Overbury knew that a divorce between the Earl and Countess of Essex would cause a scandal that would infuriate Essex's allies in the Puritan faction, and he tried desperately to persuade Robert to end things with her. He mocked Frances for falling in love with Robert and vice versa, telling him that "you only fell in love with that woman, as soon as you had won her by my letters."[14] "That woman" was among the kinder epithets by which Overbury referred to Frances, whom he insulted to Robert as often and as colorfully as he could. He wrote poems listing the perfect virtues of a woman, every single one of which he strongly insinuated was lacking in Frances. On at least one occasion, he referred to her with a contemporary slur for a prostitute.[15] His attacks on her character had the opposite of their intention, instead inspiring Robert to defend her and gravitate closer to the Howards.

James noticed that Robert seemed distracted, for which he blamed Overbury rather than Frances. Rumors about Overbury's influence wounded James's pride. A courtier wrote of Overbury to a friend in the countryside that the King "hath long had a desire to remove him from about the Lord of Rochester,* as thinking it a dishonour to him that the world should have an opinion that Rochester ruled him and Overbury ruled Rochester."[16] Overbury aggravated the situation by boasting to other courtiers that James's dislike of him was jealousy because of Robert's "loving me better than him"; he also mocked the eighteen-year age gap between James and Robert, by telling Robert that, if James objected to Robert spending time with him, Robert should remind him "you are no old man yet, nor can delight in old company continually."[17]

In early 1613, James tried his old tactic of sending Overbury abroad on a diplomatic mission. He was angry enough to offer Overbury a job as the new English ambassador to Russia, which had just emerged from its fifteen-year civil war, during which 1.2 million had died as the crown changed hands six times following the collapse of the Rurikid dynasty in 1598. On February 21, 1613, a national council, the Zemsky Sobor, elected a Muscovite noble, Mikhail Romanov, as their new tsar. Confidence in sixteen-year-old Mikhail's survival was not exactly vigorous. Overbury declined with regrets James's request that he convey the Stuarts' congratulations to the Romanovs. Sadly, as he explained, he had delicate kidneys. A change of air would do wonders for his health, came the reply. Overbury pointed out he did not know the language. No need to worry about that. After all, Overbury was always telling everybody how clever he was. Surely, there would be no problem in him learning a new tongue.

* Robert, following the award of his viscounty.

To nullify his objections, Moscow was replaced with the offer of Brussels. Overbury finally and flatly refused by saying that he did not want to leave England. James replied that it was an order, not an offer. Overbury again declined, with the reminder to James that "neither in law nor justice" had the King any right to force him to accept the job or leave his country.[18]

James was furious. On April 22, he had Overbury imprisoned in the Tower of London. Given that all Overbury had officially done was to turn down a job, James's retaliation was a significant overstep of the monarch's power in England. Overbury's quarters were in the Bloody Tower, one of the structures within the fortress that was frequently described as among its more comfortable. In the late fifteenth century, it was where Richard III had at one point housed his nephew and ousted king, Edward V. In reality, the Bloody Tower is so close to the river—it directly overlooks the notorious entrance point to the Tower of London known as Traitors' Gate—that its inmates were at constant risk from damp, even in summer when the mist rose off the river every morning.

Overbury asked Robert to secure his release, which he promised but failed to do. The Bloody Tower wreaked havoc on Overbury's health. If Robert could—or would—not secure his swift pardon, Overbury asked if he could persuade the King to lighten the conditions of his imprisonment. He would love to "taste the felicity of the open air" with a walk on the battlement at the Bloody Tower that is now called Raleigh's Walk, after Sir Walter Raleigh, who was also held there in James's reign.[19] Robert again promised and again failed to deliver. In his defense, his task may have been impossible given just how many people at court loathed Overbury.

Overbury had alienated almost everybody.[20] The Queen had never forgiven him. The Howards regarded him as an enemy. The Puritans resented him for failing to prevent Robert's drift toward the Howards. The King "hath a great hatred towards Overbury."[21] Robert remembered the horrible things he had said about Frances. She alone showed magnanimity toward Overbury by sending him mulled wine and tarts baked with her own hands.

Overbury's health continued to decline. His urine stank so potently that the guards could smell it from their corridor. Accepting that he had lost Robert's love, he asked in another letter if his liberty might be Robert's parting gift to him: "All I intreat of you is, that you will free me from this place, and that we may part friends. Drive me not to extremities, lest I should say something that you and I both repent."[22]

Again, however, Overbury's living conditions did not improve. Another, far angrier letter was scribbled in the Bloody Tower. "This Paper comes under Seals," Overbury explained in its accompanying note, "and therefore I shall be bold to speak to you as I used to do."[23] His pleas married affection to threat; he and Robert were men "betwixt whom was nine years [of] Love, and such Secrets of all kinds have passed."[24]

As Overbury's health failed, his rage increased. He explained that "the Bitterness of my Soul cannot conceal itself in Letters." He reminded Robert that he should think of him as the person "to whom you owe more than to any Soul living, both for your Fortune, Understanding, and Reputation."[25] If Robert would not help him win his freedom, then Overbury would take that reputation from him by divulging their secrets to the world—and it would not just be the things he had seen in the state papers Robert had passed to him to read: "They shall know what words have passed betwixt us heretofore of another Nature than these."[26]

After Whitsun, the summer festival that falls seven Sundays after Easter, Overbury wrote to Robert to inform him how he had spent the holiday: "I have all this Vacation wrote the Story betwixt you and me from the first Hour to this Day."[27] Overbury had written down everything that had ever passed between him and Robert, "sealed it up under eight Seals, and sent it by a Friend of mine whom I dare trust," with the instruction that the unnamed friend should, at some point, disseminate it to their acquaintances, "read it to them and take Copies of it, and I vowed to have wrote the Truth." He closed this bombshell letter with the bitter, defiant, and plaintive promise that "whether I live or die, your Nature shall never die, nor leave* to be the most odious Man alive."[28]

A panicked Robert contacted every one of Overbury's corre-

* Cease.

spondents and ransacked any possible place where his testament might be hidden. According to one of Robert's servants, "all places Trunks, Chests, Boxes, Studies, and such like houses wherein he suspected any Letters or other matters that appertained to that mischief lay hid, were broken open, and searched, to the intent that they might bring such writings to my Lord."[29] Writhing from yet another infection, Overbury vowed, "Whether I live or die, your shame shall never die."[30] Sir Francis Bacon, who knew them both, wrote that Overbury's actions had helped turn Robert's love for him into "a mortal malice or hatred, mixed with deep and bottomless fears . . . [a] fear of discovering secrets; secrets (I say) of a high and dangerous nature."[31]

Overbury was out of sight and mind by June 4, when a courtier wrote to a relative that nobody thought about him nor enquired about his welfare.[32] With Overbury out of the way, and to enable her marriage to Robert, the Howards petitioned for an annulment of Frances's marriage to Lord Essex on the grounds of nonconsummation.

Essex countered that the Howards were lying. The Essexes had been married for eight years and lived together for six. The Howards insisted that was irrelevant because Essex was impotent. As the case progressed, relations between Frances's family and her husband degenerated into open hatred. Essex's title of earl was the English equivalent of the European title of count, and the Howards took to referring to him as "the silly count," with a silent "o." When Frances's brother repeated the nickname and jokes about impotence, Essex challenged him to a duel, which prompted the Howards to quip that it was one thing to "draw his sword in defence of a good prick," but another thing altogether to fight for a bad one.[33] Essex became so irate at this perceived attack on his manhood that, during discussions about the annulment, he leaped up in a rage, lifted his nightshirt, and waved his erection in the face of his lawyers to prove that he was capable of arousal. Frances swore to anyone who would listen that she was still a virgin and even offered to undergo a medical test to prove so. Ten nurses and two midwives inspected Frances; all attested that she was a virgin. At the last moment, just before the inspection began, Frances claimed that because of her

Christian modesty and her high birth she could not bring herself to look at the women prodding at her. She was allowed to veil her face throughout. Rumors soon arose that the party of twelve had not inspected Frances, but a substituted teenager called Bridget Monson whose father was a knight in the Howards' service. A ditty did the rounds in London mocking the whole affair—its title was "The Dame was Inspected, but Fraud Interjected." Whatever the truth, the medical consensus that Frances was a virgin was submitted to the law court.

The Archbishop of Canterbury thought this was utter nonsense and said as much to the King, who replied that the Archbishop should "have a kind of faith in my judgement, as well in respect of some skill I have in Divinity."* James intended to honor his promise to Robert that he would have his marriage. The Archbishop was so upset at the King's expectation that the Church annul the Essexes' marriage that he tearfully sank to his knees during an audience. From his spot on the floor, he begged James not to ask him to violate his conscience in this way. James told him "to reverence and follow my judgement and not to contradict it, except when you demonstrate unto me that I am mistaken or wrong informed."[34] The Archbishop repeated his arguments, which James listened to but rejected. The ecclesiastical panel of ten was locked in a five-five split over Frances's petition. When the Archbishop refused to change his vote against the annulment, James appointed two more bishops to the panel who had promised to vote in Frances's favor.

On September 14, James was hunting when a messenger brought word that Overbury had died in the Tower. His birthday is unknown but, as he was baptized on June 18, 1581, he was in his early thirties when he died. In his final days, he had resorted to enemas as fever ravaged his body. He had died alone in the depth of anger and unhappiness in the middle of the night and was buried the next day in the Tower's chapel of Saint Peter ad Vincula. The court took no notice of his death or burial. Ten days later, the Church annulled the Earl and Countess of Essex's marriage.

On November 3, in preparation for his wedding to Frances,

* Theology.

Robert was made earl of Somerset by James. On the twenty-third, he was appointed Treasurer of Scotland, a post he exercised via a deputy in Edinburgh. On December 26, Frances and Robert were married at the Palace of Whitehall. Frances made a point of wearing her long black hair loose, a symbol of virginity, while James, who had discreetly sold two pieces of Crown land to raise £10,000, paid for the wedding, its banquet, gifts, and celebratory masque. The Queen attended and somewhat undercut the pretense of goodwill by scattering invitations to the guests for another wedding—that of Jane Drummond, one of her favorite ladies-in-waiting, and her fellow Scottish noble, the Earl of Roxburghe—which would be held at the end of the Christmas season at Denmark House. Exhausted, James left Whitehall to hunker down at Newmarket for two weeks after Christmas ended on Twelfth Night.

Frances's ex-husband, Lord Essex, had understandably skipped Christmas at court that year. Frances's decision to marry Robert at Whitehall on Saint Stephen's Day added insult to injury, as it was the ninth anniversary of her marriage to Essex in the same venue. Essex henceforth regarded James as coauthor of his humiliation, and he became even closer to the Parliamentarians in his loyalties. His defection to the Parliamentarian cause came at a delicate time. Puritanism's wider adherents had felt alienated since their lack of substantial gains at the Hampton Court Conference nine years earlier. In 1614, their cause found voice when James had to summon a new parliament. As shown by his desperate fundraising for Robert's wedding, the King had exhausted other possible sources of revenue. He needed Parliament to vote him money.

After three years in abeyance, they had absolutely no intention of doing so until James listened to their complaints, including Puritan concerns over the Church of England and collective resentment against Robert, who James insisted should be at his side in the procession for Parliament's opening ceremony on April 5, 1614. Robert held the reins to James's horse, even though the task should have been carried out by the jovial Earl of Worcester in his capacity as the King's Master of the Horse.

First in Parliament's metaphorical crosshairs was the combination of James's extravagance with his continued generosity to Scottish courtiers in England. As earl of Somerset, Robert sat in the Lords, along with his new father-in-law, Lord Suffolk, and the latter's uncle Lord Northampton. Essex was also in the House of Lords, where he maintained momentum against the court. He was supported by several allies, including James's former favorite Philip—even he seemed to think that things at court had gone too far with the scandal of Frances's affair with Robert, her divorce, their swift marriage, and the extrajudicial pressure the King had exerted to get Robert what he wanted.

The Lords' murmurings of discontent were nothing compared to the Commons' cries of outrage. The Howards were accused of ordering MPs whose constituencies lay in their estates to block every attempt to reach a compromise. Even without their machinations, the Parliament of 1614 would likely have proved contentious to the point of failure. Feelings against the King and the court ran high. There had already been innuendo-laden criticism of James's money and private life, when an MP for Norfolk launched into a very odd speech in which he tried to compare the court under Robert as akin to a cistern. Nobody seemed to grasp the metaphor until it lumbered toward its pun-heavy final point: Why should the people be taxed once more to fill the royal cistern, "if it shall daily run out thanks to private cocks?"[35] "Cock" had the same double meaning in Jacobean England as it does in modern English. Another MP had stated the King had wants because of his wantons.[36]

The Parliament of 1614 maintained criticism of the court by stressing a symbiosis between the King's favorites and his extravagance. Why should they respect James's household when, from the court, "we have received nothing but ill examples of all riot and dissoluteness'?[37] An MP stunned his colleagues when he revealed in a speech that, in the last four years, James had granted tens of thousands of pounds in English cash to his Scottish favorites, with Robert the chief beneficiary. Parliament then heard that, as one of his wedding gifts to Robert, James assumed responsibility for his outstanding debts to a further tune of £34,000. Carr and James's Scottish gentlemen were referred to by an MP as "their master's spaniels but this country's wolves."[38]

An impasse was reached between what James regarded as the

mendacity and anti-Scottish xenophobia of the Commons and what they regarded as the financial incontinence of an erratic megalomaniac. After only two months, James disbanded a parliament that had been so contentious, and which had achieved so little, that it acquired the moniker "the Addled Parliament."

17

ALL THE VIOLENCE OF MY LOVE

Love is a fiend, a fire, a heaven, a hell
Where pleasure, pain, and sad repentance dwell
—Richard Barnfield, *The Affectionate Shepherd* (1594)

After the failure of the Addled Parliament, Robert and the Howards dominated every aspect of court life. Robert appeared unassailable. He turned thirty in 1614–15, his blond hair had started to recede, he grew a goatee beard and mustache, he was always dressed in the height of fashion, and James still adored him. The Howards' patriarch, Lord Northampton, died eight days after the Addled Parliament was dissolved. Seventy-four years of age, he had been battling with cancer for some time when he contracted fatal gangrene from an attempt to remove a tumor in his leg. The King transferred many of Northampton's offices to Robert, including that of Lord Privy Seal, a position on the Privy Council. At the same time, Robert's father-in-law, Lord Suffolk, was appointed Lord High Treasurer, possibly due to his promise to find new ways to fund the monarchy that did not require consulting Parliament. James welcomed Suffolk's promises, especially since he had already resorted to the short-term benefit and long-term disaster of selling off Crown lands piece by piece.

Suffolk had previously served as Lord High Chamberlain, a position he yielded for Treasurer and which was also transferred by James to Robert; this made the King's favorite the senior official in the running of the royal household. James silenced the murmurings in council against Robert's appointment by lecturing the councillors that "no man should marvel that he bestowed a place so near himself as his friend, whom he loved above all men living."[1] Any discomfort that Robert's critics felt was likely to extend from the moral to the literal, because the Lord High Chamberlain's many responsibilities included assigning accommodation to courtiers as they moved from house to house, as well as allocating "bouche of the court." From the French word for mouth, "bouche" was food, fuel, and furniture provided at the royal household's expense when an individual was at court. If he felt like it, Robert could lodge his critics in the draughtiest or most odorous room possible. Between them, Robert and his father-in-law had established a duumvirate that held court and government in their grasp.

Throughout 1614 and 1615, the Howards repeatedly proved their usefulness to James. To meet some of the running costs of the royal households, the family leaned on their friends in London to raise a loan of £100,000 from the guilds for the King. They also harnessed the King's financial woes to steer him in their preferred direction of a pro-Habsburg foreign policy. If Prince Charles married Philip III's daughter the Infanta* Maria-Anna, there would be a generous dowry from Spain, which was believed to have vast wealth thanks to its empire in the Americas.

Beyond the palace walls, mockery of Robert and his wife Frances flourished unabated. In London, Frances's claims of virginity after her first marriage were still disbelieved, and the medical inspection that she had undergone, with her face so heavily veiled that no one present could be sure of her identity, had become the city's favorite joke. Smut joined with skepticism to produce ditties about Frances like:

She was a lady fine of late,
She could not be entered, she was so straight;†
But now, with use, she is so wide,
A Carr may enter on every side.[2]

---

* The traditional title for Spanish princesses.

† Tight.

At court, nobody dared be so open. However, while the King's opponents could not complain, they could plan.

Robert had an enemy of the Archbishop of Canterbury, George Abbot. A serious, pious man of fifty, Abbot was a former vice chancellor of the University of Oxford, where he had been educated, and a member of one of the six committees that had helped translate King James's Authorized Bible, which was placed in every Anglican church after its completion in 1611. Abbot was the same archbishop who had wept in moral discomfort when the King ordered him to annul Frances's first marriage. Since then, he had regarded Robert and Frances as a pernicious influence at the heart of the monarchy, and he was also concerned about the ramifications of closer ties with Catholic Spain. Abbot made common cause with many in the Puritan faction, including Lord Pembroke, Philip's brother, who knew better than most the King's tastes. Like Jacob with God in the wilderness, the Archbishop had to wrestle with his conscience. If getting rid of Robert meant finding another handsome man to catch the King's eye, then so be it. As Abbot put it, it was a case of "one nail (as the proverb is) being to be driven out by another."[3]

Even for an archbishop of Canterbury, unseating Robert and the Howards in 1614 was a daunting prospect. In pursuit of an ally formidable enough to help them, Archbishop Abbot approached the Queen about the possibility of enticing the King away from Robert with a candidate of their own. At first, Anna hesitated. Even if they were successful in ousting Robert, she doubted that the dividend would be worth the investment. She explained, "My Lord, you and the rest of your friends know not what you do. I know your master better than you all, for if this young man be once brought in, the first persons that he will plague must be you that labour for him. Yea, I shall have my part* also. The King will teach him to despise† and hardly entreat us all, that he might seem to be beholden to none but himself."[4]

* I shall endure the same treatment.

† Reject.

Which past favorite she was alluding to—whom she had helped but received no thanks from—is unclear. The obvious candidate is Sir James Hay, whose promotion to the Bedchamber in 1603 she had secured in conjunction with Cecil. Whoever it was, Anna evidently felt she had exerted herself to no gain and some loss in the past, and she initially saw no reason to repeat the experience in 1614. She was bounced from her noninvolvement after her dislike of Robert was augmented by how insufferable she found the Howards. The Queen and the family could have been allies—they were both social conservatives, sympathetic to Catholicism, and supportive of an alliance with the Habsburgs. Several of the Howards had, however, succeeded in turning Anna into an enemy by showing her insufficient respect at court and, on several occasions, by insulting her. One of them had described Anna as no different in James's eyes than a Howard; as a queen consort, she was "only the best subject, yet no less a subject than I."[5]

Anna's brother King Christian IV returned for another visit in July, and by then she seemed to have made up her mind to support the Archbishop. At some point during the hunting, fencing, firework displays, and bear baiting—one event they attended was the public "execution" of a captive bear who had mauled a child—held in celebration of Christian's visit, the Queen and the Archbishop found their man. After he and Prince Charles escorted Christian to his waiting warship at Woolwich and said farewell, James went back to Apethorpe Hall to hunt as a guest of the farouche Sir Anthony Mildmay, one of his hosts during his first journey into England in 1603. At Apethorpe, Sir James Graham, a Scottish courtier and a Gentleman of the Privy Chamber, asked the King's permission to present a family friend, who was new to court. The young man had recently returned from a gentlemen's finishing school in France, where he had been sent by his mother, Lady Mary Compton.[6] Graham tactfully left out the detail that Lady Compton, who had a modest income and grand ambitions, had sunk much of her limited resources into her son's education, gambling that he had the looks and charm necessary to win their family a fortune at court.

The King agreed to grant a brief audience to Graham's friend,

Lady Compton's twenty-one-year-old son George Villiers.* His mother's confidence in George's looks was justified. They were almost invariably the first thing noticed by others, many of whom commented on them in detail. He was tall, with unblemished skin, straight white teeth, dark hair, and blue eyes. A courtier and friend of the Herbert family wrote that he had just seen "one of the handsomest men in the whole world."[7] William Laud, a future archbishop noted for his liturgical traditionalism, confided to his diary that he had wet dreams about George, "who came into bed with me; where he behaved himself with great kindness towards me, after that rest, wherewith wearied persons are wont to solace themselves."[8] James's chaplain, the Reverend John Hacket, said of George that "from the nails of his fingers, nay, from the sole of his foot to the top of his head, there was no blemish in him. His looks, his every motion, every bending of his body, was admirable. And yet his Carriage and every stoop of his deportment, more than his excellent form, were the beauty of his beauty."[9] A lawyer, who thought George's personality left much to be desired, conceded that "everything in him [is] full of delicacy and handsome features."[10] The future Bishop of Gloucester, then serving at court as Queen Anna's chaplain, was one of the more restrained when he wrote of George, "He has a very lovely complexion, he is one of the handsomest-bodied men in England. His conversation is pleasant, and his disposition is sweet."[11]

James greeted George politely and welcomed him to court. Robert immediately perceived the potential threat posed by "one of the handsomest-bodied men in England."[12] The Queen and the Archbishop had the same thought, albeit, in their case, it produced hope rather than fear. They discreetly encouraged Graham to continue promoting George, and money was found to improve his wardrobe. Robert demanded that James turn his face away the next time Graham approached him, a sign of intense royal displeasure and corresponding social disgrace. James refused and pointed out that Graham had done nothing wrong, but Robert would not relent until James did what he asked.

* Pronounced *Villars.*

Robert's victory, expressed through the King's reluctant humiliation of Graham, stalled the Queen and the Archbishop's plans. The captain of James's guard, Sir Thomas Erskine, passed on court news to his cousin the Earl of Mar, who was in Scotland: "I think your Lordship has heard before this time of a youth," he wrote, "his name is Villiers, a Northamptonshire man; he begins to find favour with his Majesty"—but it was a lukewarm favor that had been cooled by Robert's reassertion of his dominance over King and court, where he was "more absolute than he ever was."[13] George's comparative irrelevance at this stage is indicated by the mistakes Erskine made about him—he was from Leicestershire, not Northamptonshire—and the normally observant Erskine did not feel the need to pass on, or discover, many other particulars about him, which suggests that he did not expect George to figure as either a prominent or long-term presence.

Throughout autumn, the situation evolved. James repented his rudeness to Graham, to whom he made a point of talking at a public event to show the rest of court that he was no longer out of favor. Anna and the Archbishop maintained close but discreet contact with Graham and, when a position opened in the Bedchamber, Graham, at their urging, suggested George Villiers for the post. Again, however, Robert handed his opponents a defeat when he secured the vacant position for one of his relatives.

Nonetheless, James's pointed politeness to Graham had been noted; by the latter weeks of 1614, some observers of the royal household felt that, while George Villiers was not advancing as fast as his friends might like, the first cracks might be appearing in the King's relationship with Robert. Court gossip had it that while George's career seemed "to be at a stand, or at least not to go very far forward; for when it was expected he should be made one of the Bedchamber, one Carr, a bastard kinsman of the Lord Chamberlain is stepped in, and admitted to the place . . . yet most men do not believe that the world goes altogether so well on that side as it was wont."[*14]

Robert had not been quick enough to prevent the Queen's fac-

* Things are not going as well for Robert Carr as they used to.

tion securing a lesser position for George Villiers. They managed to persuade the King to appoint George as one of his cupbearers, and the appointment went through before Robert could prevent it.[15] The role of cupbearer was of small importance in comparison to a position in the Bedchamber. There were several cupbearers, who took turns on alternate months waiting on the King at his meals. It was nonetheless a foot in the proverbial door for George, helped by James's loquaciousness at dinner and supper. Whereas Elizabeth I had preferred to eat her meals in relative silence, the pleasure that James took in conversation over his meals had been noted by visitors to his court for years.[16] George was charming, a quick study, and relatively well-informed about politics and diplomacy. Where he was less knowledgeable, he was intelligent enough not to hide it, instead freely admitting what he did not know. It was a trait of which James approved, partly because it gave him an opportunity to extol at length his own views.

Usefully if surprisingly for the Queen and the Archbishop, Robert then proceeded to set fire to his own future, as his hubris became their greatest asset. He started to reject James's requests that he spend the night, even when the King begged him. The couple fought so loudly that it could be heard on the other side of James's bedroom door, which meant that the entire court soon knew about it. Their arguments grew in frequency and vitriol. James accused Robert of needlessly antagonizing the Queen, and Robert responded with accusations of his own. "Ye have daily told me so many lies of myself," James reproved him, urging him to stop listening to court gossip about risks to his position. At one point, Robert said something so hurtful that James told him he had just managed to "rebuke me more sharply and bitterly" than had George Buchanan. James could not sleep from distress after their quarrels, when Robert fell into what James called "a frenzy" of anger, followed by "continual dogged sullen behaviour towards me." Eventually, James felt it would be better if he expressed his thoughts in writing, thereby providing us with a letter that chronicles their relationship as it unraveled. We know that there was more than one letter on the topic; James acknowledges a previous missive that had upset Robert, who felt its tone was cold. James apologized for that—"As God shall save me, I meant not in the letter I wrote unto you to be sparing in the least jot of uttering my affection towards you."

In the letter that survives, James asked Robert why he was now ruled by "strange streams of unquietness, passion, fury, and insolent pride" and despaired at his "new art of railing upon me, nay, to borrow the tongue of the devil." Was he deliberately waiting until nighttime to start a fight, knowing that it would end up "bereaving me of my rest . . . it seemed ye did it out of purpose to grieve and vex me"? There were mutual recriminations, one of which James piously announced he would not bring up, only to then hurtle into a full discussion of it: "I leave out of this reckoning your long creeping back and withdrawing yourself from lying in my chamber, notwithstanding my many hundred times earnestly soliciting you to the contrary." He insisted, however, that their recriminations did not carry equal weight, because Robert's were founded on court gossip—"Consider likewise of the difference of the things that ye lay to my charge and that I lay to yours. Here is not 'he said' or 'she said'; no conjectural presumptions, nor things gathered out of outward appearance. I charge you with nothing but things directly acted or spoken to myself."

What further proof did Robert need of James's love for him? He had done everything

> as ye could have wished, having written this letter, having quite turned my countenance from Graham (the like whereof I never did to any man without a known offence), I having received your nephew into my bedchamber, the fashion thereof being done in needless bravery* of the Queen . . . Do not all court graces and place come through your office as Chamberlain, and rewards through your father-in-law's that is Treasurer? Do not ye two, as it were, hedge in all the court with a manner of necessity to depend upon you?

He appealed to memories of their former happiness—"Ye have deserved more trust and confidence of me than ever man did; in secrecy

---

* Contempt, defiance.

above all flesh." He made no secret of his heartbreak "as never grief since my birth seized so heavily upon me," which he felt was so severe that it might kill him. He could not sleep, he was drinking too much again, and he could not hide from anyone how miserable he was. Everyone in his household noticed Robert's "long being with me at unseasonable hours, loud speaking on both [our] parts, and their observation of my sadness after your parting."

He pleaded with Robert not to let it "appear that any part of your former affection is cooled towards me" and "to hold grip of me but out of mere love." For it was by love, not by plots or anger, that Robert could control him, which James admitted when he wrote, "I told you twice or thrice that ye might lead me by the heart and not by the nose." He conceded that he had shouted at Robert during their arguments, threatening him that "all the violence of my love will in that instant be changed [to] as violent a hatred." He vowed that as "God is my judge my love hath been infinite towards you; and only the strength of my affection towards you hath made be bear these things in you and bridle my passions to the uttermost of my ability. Let me be met with your entire heart."[17]

His pleas had little obvious effect. Courtiers noticed how Robert "now rejects the caresses of the King."[18] Lost in a fugue of his own importance, Robert's metamorphosis from his earlier modest affability had produced an extreme confidence that had degenerated into arrogance. However, his tensions with the King were also due in no small part to the fact that he had fallen in love with his wife. Some later writers, noting the devotion Robert felt to Frances, concluded that any intimacy he had previously shared with James was done cynically to advance his status. Yet, as his position at court became precarious, Robert could have saved himself by resuming his sexual and romantic relationship with James. He did not do so, which suggests that his earlier relationship with the King, from Robert's fall from his horse in 1607 until his marriage to Frances Howard in 1613, was sincere. James's letter and the observations of courtiers indicate that James and Robert shared a love, which endured longer in James than it did in Robert.

With blood in the water, the Queen, the Archbishop, and their supporters revived their efforts. At Christmas, the Queen staged a masque, *Mercury Vindicated from the Alchemists,* in which she gave George Villiers the most prominent role. A male masquer's costume would flatter George's appearance—his long and muscular legs in particular—and George's mother, Mary, was brought to court to advise him, as was his stepfather, Sir Thomas Compton.[19] George danced so well at the masque that the King, despite his usual boredom on such occasions, asked if *Mercury Vindicated from the Alchemists* could be repeated two days later.

The Queen and her faction maintained their momentum in the months that followed. George seemed to feel some discomfort at his newfound role as pawn, and he even attempted to win Robert's friendship, an offer to which Robert replied, "you shall [have] none of my favour. I will, if I can, break your neck, and of that be confident."[20] That rather settled hopes of rapprochement. George henceforth became far more enthusiastic in the plots against Robert, who became so jealous that he hurled himself at George with the intention of punching him in the face before they were pulled apart by their respective friends.

On April 23—the feast of England's patron saint George—the King was visiting the Queen and their son, the new heir Prince Charles. Robert was absent for two reasons. The first was that, as the King's Lord High Chamberlain, etiquette did not require him to attend events in the Queen's Apartments. The second was the dynamic created by the fact that Anna detested him. Among the courtiers milling around the Queen's Apartments was George Villiers. What serendipity. Archbishop Abbot watched on in awe at the Queen, who, apparently on impulse, asked her husband "to do her that special favour and to knight this noble gentleman," as it was his patron saint's day, too. James did not have a sword for the ceremony, but—according to Abbot—the Queen, "striking while the iron was hot," spotted that Prince Charles was carrying a sword that day. Yet another fortuitous coincidence.

Robert was furious when he heard that George Villiers had been knighted. He set off for the Queen's Apartments, where, as he told a friend, he intended to make James promise that he would never appoint George as a Gentleman of the Bedchamber. Another vacancy had opened up, after a former Gentleman and favorite, James Hay, was sent on a diplomatic mission to France. Somebody overheard Robert's boast and raced to tip off the Archbishop, who warned the Queen. Before James had even left her rooms, Anna convinced her husband to announce to the assembled courtiers that George would be the new Gentleman of the Bedchamber. Having done so, he could not renege on his word.

In her private letters to George, through which she delivered instructions on how he was to behave, Anna referred to him as her pet dog, lest he be in any doubt as to who held the leash or the keys to his future prosperity. She liked George, whose manners were exquisite, a trait that was bound to win the Queen's approval. She enlisted him in her decades-long quest to improve James's own manners, which, she admitted ruefully, was a frustrating crusade. She wanted George to help look after him, which included remaining loyal to him and protecting him from those who might try to exploit him. One of her notes to George, in which she gives her blessing to his closeness with James, reads:

> My kind dog,
>
> I have received your letter which is very welcome to me. You do very well in lugging the sow's ear* and I thank you for it and would have you do so still upon condition that you continue [to be] a watchful dog to him and be always true to him.
>
> So, wishing you all happiness,
> Anna R.[21]

As he got to know him better through his service as a Gentleman of the Bedchamber, James began referring to George as "Steenie," a contemporary diminutive of Stephen and, in Villiers' case, a reference to the first Christian martyr, Saint Stephen the Protomartyr, who is described in the Bible as having "the face of an angel."[22]

Watching George's rise, Robert panicked. As he had proven when he faced blackmail by Thomas Overbury and sent servants

* Comparing the task of improving James's manners to turning a sow's ear into a silk purse.

to ransack the homes of mutual acquaintances who might have received Overbury's letter, Robert tended to react explosively when he felt threatened. In his worry over George Villiers, he asked James to grant him a pardon that would guarantee him immunity against prosecution, not only for crimes that he had previously committed but any that he might commit in the future. The Venetian ambassador speculated that this indicated Robert had been guilty of embezzlement and feared its imminent discovery; there were wild rumors that he had requested the pardon because he planned to abscond with the Crown Jewels.[23]

When the issue was raised at council, the Lord Chancellor, Lord Ellesmere, knelt before the King to remind him that there was no precedent in the length and breadth of English history for a blanket pardon, much less for a preemptive one. Robert, who was present, countered that it was "the malice of his enemies that had forced him to ask for a pardon."[24] Ellesmere sarcastically replied that, as Lord High Chamberlain, Robert oversaw the royal household, so why not "give him the jewels, the hangings, and the tapestry, and everything that was in the palace, since it was in the pardon that no account was to be taken of him for anything."[25]

The Queen, Lord Ellesmere, and other councillors mounted such effective counterarguments that the requested pardon was still unresolved when James set off hunting a few weeks later in August. George joined him and, as a Gentleman of the Bedchamber, slept in a trestle bed at the foot of James's. Among the places they visited was Goadby Marwood, George's childhood home in Leicestershire.[26] On their journey back to London, the King's retinue spent a few nights at Farnham Castle, where, at some point in the night, George left his bed and climbed into the King's. A few years later, George teasingly asked the King if he loved him more "than at the time I shall never forget at Farnham, where the bed's head could not be found between the master and his dog."[27]

With the benefit of hindsight, some of George's modern biographers have suspected that he initiated a sexual relationship with James in order to secure his victory over Robert.[28] The timing lends credence to this interpretation—the King's relationship with Robert was strained and the latter's political credibility had been undermined by his suspicious request for a pardon. Everywhere one looked at court, one could see evidence of Robert's declining clout, be it through the opposition he faced in council or in day-to-day etiquette, the bellwether of a courtier's standing. When the favorite entered the Privy Chamber, courtiers who had once fawned over Robert now refused even to doff their hats as a basic courtesy to him. Just before he set off for the hunting expedition on which he and George slept together, James had been irritated by Robert's attempts to secure a promotion for his ally the Bishop of Winchester; he had vetoed the advancement with an accompanying reproof to Robert to stop pushing so hard. James told him that he had been "needlessly troubled this day with your desperate letters."[29] It is plausible that George decided this was the time to strike. Equally, we can never know if George made the decision, or James issued an invitation, in the nocturnal privacy at Farnham.

Whether it was premeditated or improvised, George's timing was perfect. However, even he did not appreciate by how much until their return to London, when, two years after his lonely death in the Tower, the revenant of Thomas Overbury appeared.

In those two years, the circumstances preceding Overbury's death had bothered Sir Ralph Winwood. One of Overbury's few remaining friends, Winwood was troubled when he discovered that, shortly before he died, Overbury had voided his bowels "sixty or more" times.[30] Was it possible that, in a century obsessed with the specter of poison, Overbury had been both a genuine victim of the crime and an overlooked one? Winwood spoke to men who worked at the Tower of London; they confirmed that there had been suspicions among the staff when Overbury died in 1613. Winwood took his concerns to the Privy Council, who summoned Sir Gervase Elwes,* the Lieutenant of the Tower, for questioning. He admitted that there had not only been concerns after Overbury died, but while he lived. Somebody planning his murder had got to Richard Weston, the Tower employee assigned to wait on Overbury during his imprisonment, who was so frightened by those who had contacted him that he confessed to Elwes, concocting

* Sometimes given as Helwys or Yelwys.

with him a plan "to deceive those who sent the poisons, by pretending to administer them, but not doing so."[31]

Frustrated by Weston's lack of progress, those wishing Overbury dead had taken advantage of the fact that he was using enemas to recover his health and bribed one of the apothecarist's assistants.[32] Poison was then applied through the enemas, which, to Winwood's mind, explained the "sixty or more stools" that Overbury passed just before his death. When the Privy Council asked Elwes why he had never said anything at the time, he replied that he was afraid of enraging "great persons."[33]

James thought that Elwes's and Winwood's claims were precisely the kind of "foul conspiracy" that had prompted Robert to request his pardon.[34] The King's discussions with the council reveal that he wanted a thorough enquiry into Overbury's death because, "When innocency is not clearly tried, the scar of calumny can never be clearly cured."[35] Questioned again about the identity of the "great persons," Elwes revealed that the person who had brought instructions to Weston at the Tower was Anne Turner, a doctor's widow from Cambridgeshire. Turner was a great friend of Robert's wife, Frances; they were close enough for Frances to address her as "dearest Turner" in their letters. She was erroneously described as Frances's servant; Turner lived in her household but was wealthy in her own right. She had invented a way to dye ruffs golden yellow, which was the latest fashionable craze among the upper classes at court and in London.

She had long been on the periphery of court life. Before her husband's death, Turner had been romantically involved with Sir Arthur Mainwaring, a gentleman in Prince Henry's household. After her arrest, scandal fed on what was left of Anne Turner's reputation. Whether it is true that she had forced her husband to accept her affair with Mainwaring or that she opened an expensive high-class brothel in which she served as madam, we do not know. It is unlikely that all, or even most, of the rumors that attached themselves to her in 1615 held much truth.

Turner was brought in for questioning, during which she confirmed that Elwes had told the truth—when Overbury had been out of favor and nobody at court had shown him any kindness, except Frances, it had been a lethal charade on her part. The tarts and pies that she had baked to send to Overbury at the Tower were laced with a poison that Turner had procured at Frances's request from a London apothecarist. When that had failed, they recruited Weston and then the apothecarist's assistant.

James was confronted with these revelations after returning from his hunting trip with George. He ordered the Privy Council to conduct further questioning to see if there were grounds for a full investigation, telling them that they were to be intimidated by no one, even a member of the royal family or somebody close to them, from discerning the truth.

Robert had gone with the King to Royston, where he discovered that questions were being asked back in London about the circumstances of Overbury's death. He received James's permission to return from the rural hunting lodge to the capital. En route, Robert encountered the Lord Chief Justice, Sir Edward Coke,* who was making the same journey in the opposite direction. Correctly guessing that Coke was carrying more news about the investigation, Robert halted and asked Coke to come back to London with him. Coke refused, even when Robert became emotional.

The Lord Chief Justice had an impeccable reputation as a servant of the law. Even if he had allowed personal animus to color his actions, it would not have gone in Robert's favor. Coke admired the Queen and had recently become friendly with the Villiers family after George's mother, Mary, approached him about the possibility of a marriage between his daughter and George's brother John.

Robert hurried on to London while Coke went to Royston, where he discussed Anne Turner's claims with the King. The next day, having conferred with his in-laws, Robert rushed back to Royston, once again passing Coke in the opposite direction. This time, they passed one another with nothing more than a mutual salute. At Royston, James told Robert that he needed to go back to London and prepare for the now-inevitable investigation. This

* Pronounced *Cook*.

was not an easy decision for James to make, nor an easy order to give. He wept as he kissed Robert's cheek and said, "For God's sake, when shall I see thee again?" He buried his face in the crook of Robert's neck—"lolled about his neck," sniffed a disgusted courtier—and whispered prayers that God would allow him to see Robert again. The same courtier reported that James threw himself into Robert's arms "at the stair's head, at the middle of the stairs, and at the stair's foot" as he escorted Robert to his carriage. As Robert trundled away from Royston, James was overheard whispering, "I shall never see his face more."[36]

His sorrow was soon tempered by surprise when Robert sent back another set of demands, including a list of those who should be allowed to sit on the investigation against him and his wife. Apparently not above emotional blackmail, Robert's now-lost letter invoked the execution of James's mother after she was tried by her enemies. Guessing that Robert's Howard father-in-law, Lord Suffolk, had helped author the letter, James fired back a response in which he pointedly ordered Robert "to show this letter to your father-in-law and that both of you read it twice at least." James bluntly informed them that, even if it meant losing the Howards' help in government, justice would be done: "In a business of this nature, I have nothing to look unto but first my conscience before God, and next my reputation in the eyes of the whole world." In deciding whether it had been a grotesque manipulation "to rake up from the bottomless pit the tragedy of my poor mother, I appeal to your own judgement." Robert should also cease his attacks on his critics in the council, including his requests for the dismissal of Lord Ellesmere since he had "served me more than thirteen years with all honour and faithfulness."

James continued that neither Robert nor the Howards would have had anything to fear had they behaved as if they were innocent and welcomed the discovery of the truth of what had happened to Overbury, but that he must "to my great regret confess and avow that, from the beginning of this business, both your father-in-law and ye have ever and at all times behaved yourselves quite contrary." He referred to the Howards as "that family," swore that "I will never care to lose the hearts of any for justice sake," and vowed that "God so favour me as I have no respect in this turn* but to please Him in whose throne I sit."[37]

Instead of heeding James's warnings, Robert sent his men to the home of Overbury's former attendant, where they found, confiscated, and destroyed letters between him and Anne Turner.[38] When the commission investigating him heard about this, they ordered that Robert and Frances be detained in separate chambers. James's second cousin Ludovic, Duke of Lennox, was on the committee and lent his voice to those urging James not to let the couple escape justice. Thus far, there was no evidence tying Robert to the murder. Everything suggested that Frances had acted of her own volition. However, Robert was doing so much to protect her, and his position, that the public was increasingly unlikely to believe that he was innocent, even if it was proved in a court of law. James reluctantly ordered the couple's arrest, and they were conveyed under guard to the Tower of London, where, two months later, on December 9, Frances gave birth to their daughter, Lady Anne Carr.

Frances's custody passed in comfortable accommodation but separate from her husband's. Three weeks after her daughter's birth, she was visited by James's former favorite Philip Herbert, Earl of Montgomery, and the King's Captain of the Guard, Sir Thomas Erskine. They confronted Frances with the evidence acquired from Anne Turner and the others. Turner had been publicly hanged ten days before Christmas. On the scaffold, she had delivered an incendiary speech to the enormous crowd, in which she repented her actions and left a devastating portrait of James's court as a sinkhole of moral corruption: "God bless the King and send him better servants about him, for there is no religion in the most of them, but malice, pride, whoredom, swearing, and rejoicing in the fall of others. It is so wicked a place as I wonder the earth did not open and swallow it up."[39] Her speech became a sensation, disseminated in thousands of pamphlets.[40] Overbury's former attendant, Richard Weston, was also executed, as were the apothecarist who had provided the poisons, James Franklin, and Sir Gervase Elwes, who despite his testimony was condemned as an accessory

* Case/sequence of events.

to the murder in having failed to report his suspicions at the time. Elwes's conviction gave an idea of the opprobrium the case had attracted among prosecutors and the people of London, in whom it had inspired revulsion and fascination in equal measure. Until Anna had pulled back its window hangings to show herself, the Queen's carriage had been chased through the streets by an angry mob who believed an incorrect rumor that such a splendid carriage was carrying Frances from her prison at the Tower back to freedom at the palace.

With four executions and a mountain of evidence against her, the council wanted Frances to confess, but the decision would have to be hers. As a noblewoman, Frances was protected from the specter of torture on two fronts. Even in the reign of Henry VIII, when torture had once been illegally applied to a female preacher suspected of heresy, there had been uproar at its use on a woman—and torture of an aristocrat was unheard of. Frances knew, however, that she had lost the game. She confessed to Philip and Erskine that she had secured Overbury's death by poison. She admitted that she had done so because she worried that Overbury would somehow find a way to rekindle his closeness to Robert and prevent their marriage, and also because she hated him for "the most unworthy things which he had said about her person."[41] She insisted that her husband "neither knew anything about it, nor took any part in it."[42]

Since Robert had not confessed and Frances's testimony was not believed in its entirety, trials for the pair would have to proceed. This was partly a consequence of Robert's manic attempts before his imprisonment to frustrate the investigation.

A date in May was set for the couple's trials. Regardless of their outcome, Robert would be unable to return to the royal court, at the very least not for some time, possibly forever, and certainly never to his former prominence. James discreetly presented Anna with a beautiful set of diamonds that he had once gifted to Robert, who loved them. Anna, with characteristic flair and a breathtaking lack of magnanimity in victory, handed the diamonds over to George with the instruction that he was to be seen wearing them, often, about the court. He was.

In the four months that elapsed after Frances's confession, James feared what might come out at Robert's trial. He sent a messenger to him in the Tower of London with strict instructions that the messenger was to arrive "in such secrecy none living may know of it and that, after his speaking with him in private, he may be returned back again as secretly."[43] Robert replied that he would be vindicated at trial. James wrote to the Tower's new Lord Lieutenant, Sir George More, with the request that he speak to Robert and make him see that avoiding a trial was in everybody's best interests. Public scrutiny of the King, and disgust at the Somersets, intensified. Robert asked to write privately to James, who rebuffed the request, accepting that "I cannot hear a private message from him without laying an aspersion upon myself of being an accessory to his crime."[44]

Robert continued in his insistence that he had been party to no crime, and in his refusal to confess to something he had not done. James despaired that Robert was not intelligent enough to understand that there were plenty of other matters that he might be asked about on the stand, which neither he nor James wanted aired to the public. Of Robert's refusal to seek a plea bargain, he said, "God knows it is only a trick of his idle brain."[45]

Frances was tried at Westminster Hall on May 24. Crowds had been camping out since six o'clock in the morning to get a ticket to the spectators' gallery—an off-duty lawyer paid ten shillings for "a reasonable place."[46] She did not retract her admission of guilt and, after receiving the expected death sentence, begged her judges that they would petition the King to show her mercy. She was then escorted to the river, where she was rowed back to her quarters at the Tower.

James spent the night at his wife's house at Greenwich Palace. She kept him company there throughout the twenty-fifth, while Robert stood trial at Westminster Hall. James took nothing to eat and, according to a courtier, was in "restless motion" all day.[47] Every time he saw a boat arrive at the palace wharf, he sent down a messenger to see if it brought news of what was happening at the trial, "cursing all that came without tidings."[48] A courtier at Greenwich wrote, "It seemed something was feared should in passion have broken from him [Robert], but when his Majesty had heard that nothing had escaped him more than what he was forced to answer to the business then in hand, his Majesty's countenance soon changed, and he hath ever since continued in a good disposition."[49]

It does not seem overly difficult to guess the question James feared that had nothing to do with "the business then in hand." The fact that everybody at court knew was one thing, but the damage to the Crown was likely to prove incalculable if, on the stand, Robert was asked outright in a packed courtroom if he had committed buggery with the King and answered honestly. There have been suggestions that the dreaded question was something to do with foreign or ecclesiastical policy—either that James had signed a secret alliance with Spain or that he was considering converting to Catholicism. The latter can be dismissed quickly as James never showed, previously or subsequently, any serious inclination to leave the Protestant faith. Nor does the Spanish theory convince, when one considers that James had publicly signed a treaty with Spain fourteen years earlier, the Spanish ambassador was in favor at court, and the King was openly discussing the possibility of marrying his heir to a Spanish princess. When there were discussions of deepening England's friendship with Spain, James was open about it.[50] It seems a stretch to conclude that the question that left James so frightened that he could not sit still, eat, or concentrate, pertained to foreign policy.

The prosecution came close to asking the question James feared, perhaps deliberately so. At the trial, they stated that the reason Robert's intimacy with his former "bedfellow and minion" Overbury had turned to "a mortal malice or hatred, mixed with deep and bottomless fears" was because Overbury had threatened to reveal two different kinds of secrets. They asserted that some of these secrets were of "a high and dangerous nature"; since "high" meant noble, important, political, or significant, the adjective covered some of the political matters that Overbury might have read in the state papers Robert had habitually passed to him. They then specified that, excluding this, Overbury had also frightened Robert with his capacity to reveal "secrets of all natures."[51] These insinuations came from the mouth of Sir Robert Cecil's cousin Sir Francis Bacon, who knew Robert and Overbury well.

There is other tantalizing fragmentary evidence suggestive of the fact that the prosecution had encountered firm evidence about Robert's intimacy with the King, which they chose not to include but were not above hinting at in the courtroom. During his investigations, Sir Edward Coke had found a letter in Robert's rooms, written to him in James's hand, which Coke loyally threw into the fire. We know about its existence only because Coke mentioned it years later to a friend, apparently as a non sequitur after they had been discussing the anti-sodomy laws.[52]

Bereft of the King, the minion, and the father-in-law who had always covered up his intellectual failings, Robert at trial was suddenly once again the teenager fresh to court who embarrassed himself with a fumbled Latin monologue. He did not seem to understand most of the legal points, he fixated on trivialities, and his speech was so lacking in substance that even the lords invited to judge him "shook their heads and blushed to hear such slender excuses come away from him, of whom much better was expected."[53] Robert's defense of himself was so intellectually feeble that the prosecution felt there was no need to rebut. He was found guilty, a verdict he received by vowing on damnation of his soul that he was innocent.

James could not bring himself to sign Robert's or Frances's death warrants. Instead, he commuted the couple's sentence to life imprisonment, whereby they would be kept in comfortable confinement at the Tower of London. All eyes were henceforth on the new favorite. The Queen hosted more masques with George Villiers as the main dancer. Gazing on from the audience, the Venetian ambassador praised George's "exquisite manner [which] rendered himself the admiration and delight of everybody."[54]

18

GEORGE

Good caution never comes better than
when a man is climbing.
—Sir John Harington
(1560–1612)

George's rooms at Hampton Court were on the ground floor, overlooking the palace gardens and facing east toward the Chase. In the redistribution of patronage that followed the Overbury scandal, James took some posts from the Howards but permitted them to keep others. All of imprisoned Robert's positions had to be reallocated. His former post on the council as Lord Privy Seal was assigned to the Earl of Worcester, who in turn relinquished the position in the household as Master of the Horse, which he had held since 1601. In his mid- to late sixties, Lord Worcester was perhaps a little old for the post, which was one of the more physically demanding senior roles in the royal household. Rancor had fueled his longevity—his dislike for Robert Carr, who had hoped to become Master of the Horse himself, had inspired him to resist retirement on at least two occasions when Robert was in favor. With omertà blanketing Robert's name, Worcester stepped aside for George to succeed him as Master of the Horse in January 1616.

It was an important and prestigious role, with control of the royal stables, alongside responsibility for organizing the monarch's hunting as well as the royal household's travel when they moved between their residences. On the occasions when James was in residence with his wife or son, this would require liaison with their Masters of the Horse. As the King's Master of the Horse, George headed a staff of two hundred. He was entitled to generous bouche of court and had his own assigned quarters in each major royal residence, which left the holder of the post free from the potential tyranny of the Lord Chamberlain. The latter was one of several reasons why Lord Worcester had been comfortable in displaying his distaste for Robert, even at the zenith of Robert's influence.

Proximity to the monarch or their consort ensured the Master of the Horse was a trusted courtier. Those who occupied the position had either proved their mettle with the organizational logistics that the post entailed—Queen Anna kept the same Master of the Horse for sixteen years—or they were emotionally significant to the monarch—for the first thirty years of Elizabeth's reign, the office was held by her favorite Robert Dudley, Earl of Leicester.

Sentiment and competence were not mutually exclusive. George was ideally suited to serve as Master of the Horse. He was a superb equestrian with a deep knowledge of breeding and breeds, which he put to good use during his first year as Master by purchasing a purebred Arab stallion for the royal studs.[1] Even allowing for the myopia caused by love, James was not exaggerating when he told another courtier, who commented on the improved pedigree of the stables, that they should "thank the Master of the Horse for providing me with such a number of fair, useful horses, fit for my hand. In a word, I protest I never was master of such horses."[2]

George's appointment as Master of the Horse gave him a reason to be with James throughout most of the day. At night, now that George was no longer a Gentleman of the Bedchamber, they were more inventive. Between 2004 and 2008, a specially constructed passageway linking George's bedroom at Apethorpe Hall* to James's was discovered during restoration work.

His beautiful Hampton Court apartments were doubly significant to George since, five months after he was sworn in as Master of the Horse, James appointed him Keeper of the Honour of Hampton Court.[3] A post previously held by a Howard, the Keeper was typically tasked with overseeing the maintenance of the palace's estates by a large staff. In the months between gaining the two posts, George had also been inducted to the Most Noble Order of the Garter, England's highest chivalric honor. His prominence and lavish accommo-

* Renamed Apethorpe Palace in 2015.

dation were a far cry from the straitened financial circumstances in which he had first come to court, when he attended "the horse-race in Cambridgeshire in an old black suit, broken out in divers places" and could not afford "a room in the inn to lodge in, and was therefore glad to lie in a trundle-bed in a gentleman's chamber."[4]

George came from an old gentry family. His father and namesake had died when he was an adolescent, after which his widowed mother, Mary, had moved with her four children into a dower house, while the family's manor went to George's eldest half brother from his father's first marriage. Money in Mary's household had been neither entirely absent nor plentiful, even after her remarriage to a local landowner.

As he rose at court, George confounded Queen Anna's fears that any new favorite would soon reject his backers—he continued to make his regular, respectful reports to her, and he told Archbishop Abbot that, in light of everything Abbot had done for him, "he was so infinitely bound unto me that all his life long he must honour me."[5] Sir James Graham, who had first introduced George to the King but who died in early 1616, did not live long enough to reap the benefits of George's gratitude. George also took genuine pleasure in helping those who had been kind to him during his obscurity. He invited his childhood teacher, the Reverend Anthony Cade, to visit him at court and presented him to the King. George had been sent by his parents to the local village school, where Cade was a kind schoolmaster who, unlike many of his contemporaries, did not beat or harangue his students if they struggled academically. George offered to find Cade a position at court; Cade thanked him for the opportunity to visit but told him that life at court was not something to which he aspired. George instead found him a comfortable post in the countryside in old age.[6]

George brought his full siblings to court. His sister, Lady Susan Feilding, attracted attention on account of her beauty; she was also a talented hunter, as was her husband, Sir William Feilding, who was appointed a Gentleman of the Privy Chamber. George's brother John Villiers was one year George's senior, and they had studied in France together; John took George's former post as a Gentleman of the Bedchamber, where he was soon joined by their brother Christopher.

Nicknamed Kit in the family, and a year younger than George, who was very protective of him, he was mocked by courtiers behind his back for lacking the good looks of his brother and sister.

Excluding George, the greatest beneficiary in the Villiers family was its matriarch, his remarkable mother. Born Mary Beaumont in about 1570 into a junior branch of an old Leicestershire landowning family, she had no dowry but a few connections. Court snobs would later take vicious delight in exaggerating Mary's "lowly" origins, which makes it difficult to discern how much is true in the stories they told about her. We know that, in her late teens, she went to live in the household of her distant and wealthier relatives, the Villiers family. This renders unlikely a version of events in which it was said that Mary worked as a kitchen maid until she was noticed by the master of the house. Even the family's critics could not deny that George had inherited much of his good looks from his mother, although they cloaked an insult with a compliment in their claim that, when she was a kitchen maid, even "her ragged habit could not shade her beautiful and excellent frame."[7] The same rumor insisted that she had been promoted from the kitchen when the master of the house, entranced by Mary's appearance, pressured his reluctant, sickly wife to accept her as a companion. When the lady of the house died in 1587, Mary allegedly lost little time in replacing her.

It is unlikely that someone from Mary's background, even with little family money, would ever have been put to work in the kitchens. More credibly, she came to the Villiers' household as a companion to the lady of the house, rather than attaining the post solely because the lady's husband bullied her into accepting Mary's presence. Mary's marriage to George's father did not take place in 1587 but in 1590, which further undermines their detractors' account of a social-climbing marriage before the first wife's body was cold.

Mary was ambitious for herself and for her children. George retained fond memories of how loving she had been to him when he was apparently quite a rambunctious child; and he was grateful to her for the French education she had paid for, when it was a financial struggle for her to do so. It had given him his fluency in French, his manners, his deportment, and his skills in dancing, fencing, and hunting. When he returned from school to England, his family had tried to arrange a marriage for him with a courtier's daughter, whose relatives rejected him as too poor.[8]

In 1616, with his rooms in every palace and a staff of hundreds, George therefore appeared understandably content with his good fortune. Despite the factional games that had been played to promote his rise as Robert fell, he tried to avoid further entanglement with court politics. He refused the gift of Robert's seized estate at Sherborne, telling James that he hoped that "the building of his fortunes may not be founded on the ruins of another."[9] He nonetheless accepted in July 1616 the substantial estates of the late Thomas Grey, 15th Lord Grey de Wilton, who had died in 1614 after years in disgrace following his support for some of the early anti-Scottish plots against James. Since Grey de Wilton had died childless, George was not taking the estates from living relatives or their heirs. It did, however, somewhat undercut his virtuous claim that he did not want his prosperity to come at any disadvantage to the King since, had they not been granted to George, Lord Grey de Wilton's lands would have reverted to the Crown.

George's apparent ambivalence about politics was overruled by James himself. Very early in their relationship, James indicated that he expected George to serve as his political confidant by bringing him to meetings of the Privy Council, to which George was sworn in as a councillor in 1617. Despite the terrible end of his relationship with Robert, James had grown accustomed to having his favorite as someone to whom he could dictate his correspondence and discuss policy. George was aware that he was a neophyte when it came to government, and he listened carefully to James's private conversations on the matter, as well as the council's discussions.

He learned a great deal about foreign affairs, which was later to become one of his passions, through the letters that flowed to the King and the council from ambassadors and informants, and the official correspondence that returned in the opposite direction. There were plentiful opportunities for the exercise of diplomacy: English diplomats in the Netherlands secured the freedom of eighty-two Irish, English, and Scottish sailors who had been captured by the Dutch navy and unfairly imprisoned as pirates. The crew of two small merchant ships that had sailed from the restored port of Londonderry in Ireland, they had been in the North Sea when they were taken. Anti-pirate sentiment in the Netherlands was such that "the poor men could scarce be brought alive betwixt their ships and their prisons" thanks to a crowd attempting to lynch them.[10] Widespread persecution of Christians had commenced in China and Japan; James previously had limited, formal communication with Emperor Kotohito of Japan, but there was nothing he could do in practice to ameliorate the persecutions. Armand du Plessis, Bishop of Luçon, was appointed France's new Secretary of State for Foreign Affairs. Better known to posterity as Cardinal Richelieu, the title he acquired from the Pope in 1622, du Plessis swiftly made an impression on foreign governments, who discerned his industriousness and acumen.

Reports arrived from India, where James's new ambassador, Sir Thomas Roe, had presented his credentials to Emperor Jahangir. Less than a century earlier, much of India had been conquered by Jahangir's family, the Mughal dynasty, who had, from their homeland in what is now Uzbekistan, forged an empire that eventually covered most of what later became India, Bangladesh, Afghanistan, and Pakistan. Their empire's wealth was staggering, and the English government was embarrassed to discover that their earlier gift of a gilt carriage for the Emperor had been damaged during the long voyage and arrived at the imperial capital of Agra looking distinctly the worse for wear.[11] Roe, a member of the anti-Carr, anti-Howard faction whose appointment as ambassador had been championed by Archbishop Abbot, won the friendship of the Emperor, who gave him a ruby-decorated goblet as a sign of his favor.[12]

The most strained negotiations preoccupying the Privy Council during George's first year as a member were those between England and the Barbary States, an English term for a confederation of Muslim monarchies and viceroyships on the northwest coast of Africa. In the seven years preceding 1616–17, 466 British ships had been seized by north African pirates; their captured crew were handed over to slave traders, who were not permitted to enslave fellow Muslims and who traded most profitably with the slave markets of the Ottoman Empire, where higher prices were typically paid for slaves with red hair and green or blue eyes.[13] There had also been infrequent raids in southwest England and Ireland in pursuit of captives who possessed those physical characteristics. The Barbary States were nominally under the suzerainty of the Ottoman Sultan Ahmed I, to whom James wrote personally in the thwarted hope that he might be able to intervene.[14] Ahmed I's influence in north Africa was ceremonial rather than functional and so he could do nothing, despite James's promise of renewed economic ties and "beneficial trade unto your dominions" if the slaves were freed and the raids ceased.[15] No satisfactory terms were reached between the British states and those of north Africa, with the consequence that the raids continued for several decades.

Domestic matters in 1616 included reports from George's home county, Leicestershire, of demonic possession. A thirteen-year-old boy called John Smith claimed that fifteen local women were members of a coven who had cast spells facilitating his possession. Nine of these women were hanged due to the boy's testimony; the remaining six were spared only because somebody told James, who was hunting nearby. James still believed deeply in the existence of witchcraft and collected books on sorcery, locking them away to prevent them infecting men with weaker minds. However, an insight into how much his attitudes to witch hunts had changed can be gained from his actions in 1616, when he summoned John Smith to question him about the alleged possession. Quickly discerning that the child had lied, James ordered the immediate release of the five remaining suspects—tragically, the sixth had died in custody—and summoned the two presiding judges to his presence, where he lambasted them for their actions. James's poet laureate, Ben Jonson, requested and received the King's permission to satirize this witch hunt, known as the Leicester Boy case, in a new play called *The Devil Is an Ass.* Writing in the next generation, the author and clergyman Thomas Fuller, whose godfather served as one of James's courtiers, said of the Leicester Boy case that "the frequency of such forged possessions wrought such an alteration upon the judgement of king James, that he, receding from what he had written in his *Daemonologie,* grew first diffident of, and then flatly to deny the workings of witches and devils as but falsehoods and delusions."[16]

This may have been overstating the matter on Fuller's part, but there is no doubt that James was far more skeptical than he had been in his twenties and that he was now more inclined to suspect fraud than possession.

Another item of domestic politics played out from February until July 1616. In February, the Lord Deputy of Ireland retired on health grounds and, in July, was replaced by George's kinsman Sir Oliver St. John.[17] The appointment has been cited as proof that George had become powerful enough to start advancing his family politically, as opposed to merely socially.[18] The details of St. John's career do not necessarily support the conclusion that he owed his appointment to George—he had fought for Elizabeth I against Lord Tyrone in the 1590s, he was a commissioner for the Plantations of Ulster, he owned a large estate in the Irish county of Armagh, he had served in the Irish House of Commons as Member of Parliament for Roscommon since 1613, and he was already vice admiral for the western province of Connacht. While the seventeenth century had a broader definition of kinship than many modern Western societies, St. John's ties to George were not, even in context, close enough for him to be the first relative George would exert himself to promote, certainly at such an early stage in his career. St. John was an uncle of the wife of George's elder half brother. They became allies several years later, probably in 1620, when George secured the viscounty of Grandison for him. In 1621, St. John flatteringly referred to George as "the only author of my fortunes," a piece of panegyric that may account for the subsequent conclusion that George had secured the lord deputyship for him in 1616.[19] While it is unlikely that his relationship with the new favorite did St. John's cause any harm, he was already by the standards of the Jacobean regime in 1616 a logical choice for Lord Deputy.

James turned fifty in June 1616, and the year was overshadowed by four months of ill-health. The royal physicians noticed with concern that his balance was faltering. Whether this was a consequence of his drinking or something else is unclear. There were "frequent falls from horseback," and an old riding wound in his ankle flared up, which gave his right foot "an odd twist when walking." His feet swelled with fluid and he bruised easily.[20]

After James's death, this period in his life would give birth to a caricature in which every physical difficulty was exaggerated both in extent and in endurance. He is frequently described, even today, as bowlegged and chronically weak from infancy, which matches with none of the multiple eyewitness testimonies as to his appearance prior to 1616. During his son's reign, anti-royalist writers would present James as a Neoplatonic nightmare who slobbered on his male favorites, draped himself over them because he could neither walk nor function without them, and refused to wash. Others added the lecherous detail that he constantly fiddled with his codpiece, adding deliberately yet inaccurately to the perception of a king who was morally and literally dirty. Some legends about James, such as the claim that he had a tongue too large for his mouth and filthy fingers because he was afraid of washing, seem to have been outright invented.

James's four months of poor health were not the only difficulty George had to deal with in his first year as favorite. Unlike the Queen, Prince Charles loathed George and, during a visit to Greenwich Palace, Charles put his hand over the fountain to redirect it at him. When he heard about this, James boxed his son's ears. Such an uncharacteristically rough response surprised everybody, perhaps even George, who set out to win the teenage prince's friendship. He only partly succeeded. Prince Charles had thawed from outright hatred to icy politesse by the time he was invested as prince of Wales in November 1616, the month of his sixteenth birthday. The Queen declined to attend, stressing that this was not to be interpreted as an insult to Charles but was simply a consequence of the painful memories it would evoke of a similar ceremony for Prince Henry, six years earlier. It was perhaps just as well that she did so: during the investiture itself, one of the presiding bishops accidentally called Charles by his late brother's name.

George had titles of his own by then. After the King's health and spirits returned, he granted George a barony and a viscounty on August 27, in the week George turned twenty-four. He was thus Lord Villiers when he celebrated Christmas at Whitehall alongside the visiting Princess Pocahontas. Originally named Matoaka, she was a princess from the Algonquian nation in the Americas and famous in England for saving the life of colonist John Smith, who had allegedly been sentenced to death by her father. She had arrived in London with her English husband, John Rolfe, and their son, Thomas, earlier in the year and shortly after her conversion to Christianity. Queen Anna had already thrown a banquet in her honor, as had the Bishop of London, and she had been the Queen's guest for the Christmas masque, *The Vision of Delight,* in which Anna had been relegated from dancer to spectator by her gout. It was to be Pocahontas's only Christmas in England. Tragically, in spring, she contracted either pneumonia or, less probably, smallpox, which ended her life at the age of about twenty-one.

On the Twelfth Day of Christmas, George was made earl of Buckingham. The title had royal associations—previous incumbents had included royal cousins and in-laws. Of more immediate concern were the attached lands and the accompanying income, which made George one of the wealthiest members of the English aristocracy. When some in the council questioned James's generosity, the King left them in very little doubt about where George stood in relation to the rest of them: "I, James, am neither a god nor an angel, but a man like any other. Therefore I act like a man, and confess to loving those dear to me more than other men. You may be sure that I love the Earl of Buckingham more than anyone else, and more than you who are here assembled."[21]

It was not the King's only declaration. The lawyer Simonds d'Ewes, who was visiting his cousin at court, recorded in his diary that, during an audience, the King was staring across the room to where George was standing with other officers of the household. James then suddenly said, "By God, George, I love thee."[22] During another visit to court, d'Ewes observed that when the two men were "hugging one time very seriously" the King "burst forth, 'By God man, never one loved another more than I do thee.'"[23] After a difficult day in council, James asked if George would come to his rooms. When he did, James threw himself into his arms; as a courtier who was present put it, "as soon as he came, he fell upon his neck without any more words."[24] Observing how tactile James and George were with each other, courtier Sir Edward Peyton described George as someone whom the King "would tumble and kiss as a mistress."[25] Francis Osborne, later more famous as an author but then serving at court in the household of Philip Herbert's family, wrote that with George, as with Robert before him, "the love the king shewed was as amorously conveyed, as if he had mistaken their sex, and thought them ladies . . . Nor was his love, or what else posterity will please to call it (who must be the judges of all that history shall inform), carried on with a discretion."[26]

George wrote to James during their infrequent absences from one another, often expressing his gratitude for James's generosity. He also played with the courtly language of gratitude to make obvious allusions to acts of intimacy between him and James, such as when he thanked the King for how he had proved what was in his heart by using his "large bountiful hand" to help George achieve "surfeit," meaning excess or complete satisfaction of a need, "sooner by yours than his own," and he asked if he could soon reciprocate "with mine, that hand which hath been but too ready to execute the motions and affections of that kind obliging heart."[27]

In March 1617, George accompanied James on his first visit to Scotland since the Union of the Crowns. There had been sustained, but until 1617, ineffective, pressure from the Scottish nobility for James to return to "this your first and oldest empire of Scotland."[28] The reasons for his return in 1617 seem to have been his illness and a recurrence of tensions with the Kirk, which James wanted to adjudicate in person. Citing her health, Queen Anna stayed in England, where she had a role on the council that would lead England and Wales's government during James's absence.

During the six weeks it took them to travel from London to Edinburgh, George was amazed by the change in James's spirits. Writing to one of his new allies, Sir Francis Bacon, he observed that "his Majesty, God be thanked, is in very good health, and so well pleased with his journey, that I never saw him better, nor merrier."[29] There were civic and ceremonial visits in England along the route, which explains the month and a half it took to reach Scotland. Some of these were places that James had visited in 1603, such as Durham, where he kept Easter in 1617. Others, such as Lincoln, were firsts for James, who stayed in its Bishop's Palace, watched a cockfight, and attended Sunday service at the cathedral, the spire of which made it the tallest building in the world at the time.

He entered Scotland on May 13 and reached Edinburgh three days later. Unlike his unpopular refusal to engage with the crowds in England, James rode through Edinburgh on horseback, where large numbers had gathered to cheer his return. A Scottish aristocrat called him "the bright star of our northern firmament, the ornament of our age."[30] James likewise used hyperbole and rhetoric in his official proclamation to explain to the people why he had chosen 1617 to return, avoiding any acknowledgment of his broken promise in 1603 to do so at least once every three years. One phrase in the proclamation departed from grandiloquence and rings as heartfelt, or at the very least personal, with its admission that over the past few months James had dreamed of Scotland. He said he had been compelled by "this salmonlike instinct of our mind restlessly, both when we are awake, and many times in our sleep, so stirred up in our thoughts and bended our desires to make a journey thither that we can never rest satisfied till it shall please God we may accomplish it."[31]

James's attitudes to his homeland were contradictory. He seemed to prefer England to Scotland but the Scots to the English. However, he trusted the English aristocracy more than the Scottish and he liked his homes in England more than his residences in Scotland. He maintained a meticulous interest in Scottish government and was rigorous in ensuring his Scottish councillors did their duty. He had installed a new postal system, with more frequent stops for riders, between London and Edinburgh to ensure swift delivery of his orders and reports from the Scottish council. He had spoken out firmly against anti-Scottish speeches in the English parliament and had endured a great deal of criticism rather than part with his Scottish attendants. He had acknowledged that he worried about going physically soft while in England and that his daily routine in Scotland had been better for his health. George was not the only one who noticed the perceptible lift in James's spirits when he reached Scotland. Yet it had taken him fourteen years to return.

In preparation for the King's visit, the Scottish government had ensured that the streets and palaces were cleaned, the accommodation comfortable, the food excellent, and the wine plentiful. They did this partly from respect for James, but also from patriotic paranoia that some of the Englishmen accompanying him would be predisposed to find fault. It was a justified concern. Sir Anthony Weldon, an English courtier who never let irritants like truth or decency get in the way of a malicious anecdote, received Scottish hospitality in public and mocked it in private. Not coincidentally, it is to Weldon's memoirs that we owe the most enduring contemporary caricature of James as an unkempt, unhygienic, slobbering embarrassment who was constantly fiddling with his codpiece. Among Weldon's many hatreds were Scotland and the Scottish. As a member of the visiting English court in 1617, he wrote,

> First, for the country, I must confess it is too good for those who possess it, and too bad for others to be at the charge to conquer it. The air might be wholesome but for the stinking people who inhabit it, the ground might be fruitful had they the will to manure it. Their beasts be generally small, women only excepted, of which sort there are none greater* in all the world.[32]

When one of their Scottish hosts explained to Weldon that the council had made sure there was plenty of healthy poultry, or fowl, set aside for the visitors' tables, Weldon sneered to his friends there was a great deal of fowl in Scotland—"foul houses, foul sheets . . . foul linen, foul dishes."[33]

As with Weldon's later assassination of James by pen, his spite in 1617 was memorably expressed but disputed by others. A fellow courtier wrote home that in Scotland, the royal household was treated to "entertainment very honourable, very general, and very full; every day [there were] feasts and invitations." Of Scotland itself, the courtier concluded, "it is worth the cherishing," and James was "never more cheerful in both body and mind, never so well pleased."[34] James lodged at Holyroodhouse, stayed at his childhood home at Stirling, and visited his former hunting palace at Falkland. As his Master of the Horse, George rode at his side through Edinburgh for the ceremonial opening of Parliament.

---

* Larger.

The Kirk, which had held a General Assembly at Aberdeen a few months before James's arrival, rejected his proposal to introduce certain Anglican features to their church services. They were likewise concerned by the King's intention to reintroduce religious holidays to Scotland. The matter was still unresolved when James left at the end of July. A few months later, once he was back in England, James sent an edict to his Scottish council ordering them to permit festivities for Christmas and Easter, and in May 1618 he relaxed the Scottish Sabbath laws by permitting, to the Kirk's consternation, recreational sports on Sundays. As part of what were later called the Five Articles of Perth, James successfully introduced several Anglican features to Presbyterianism, such as kneeling during Communion and the right to private Communion for the sick. However, he shrewdly pulled back from pushing any further. It was a victory for him with regard to Presbyterianism, but not one that had driven his opponents too far.

James's journey to England was marred by grim weather. It rained almost constantly, and he came off his horse again, badly hurting himself. George applied ointments to the King's back, which remained tender until they reached London. On their arrival, the Queen was shocked by how much weight James had gained. He then caught a chill that he could not shake, and he was suffering from exhaustion. Struggling with gout, the Queen had developed problems with her breathing and her heartbeat, both of which were irregular. After conducting official business from Hampton Court in September, James and Anna decided to nurse their health together by retreating for weeks to Theobalds, where they invited their son Prince Charles to join them. Having always been close to his mother, it was during their time at Theobalds in the autumn of 1617 that Charles developed a rapport with his father, who urged him to consider George as his friend.

Years later, when opprobrium had tainted his name, it was hard to understand how anybody could ever have liked George, much less to account for the friends and admiration he accrued early in his career. Extreme good looks can discombobulate judgment, but not everyone's, nor is it credible that George duped so many. He had real charm and was intensely loyal to his family. Queen Anna's fondness for him is telling, for she had neither a history of, nor reputation for, being easily fooled. Nor was Prince Charles someone who liked easily. Somewhere between shy and cold, he made friendships slowly but deeply, which is what happened in late 1617 when, after his time with his parents at Theobalds, he developed a genuine camaraderie with George. If George wanted to avoid the fate of so many former royal favorites who found themselves cast out into the wilderness when their patron died, he needed to keep the heir on side. How much Charles knew about George's intimacy with the King has never been clear.

George's prominence during James's return to Scotland and then the royal family's retreat to Theobalds were triumphs troubled by tensions. In his first eighteen months as favorite, he had not only witnessed at close quarters James's two relatively serious spells of illness, he had seen how deep James's fearful anguishes could now run. In those moments, the King's calm shattered with alarming speed. While they were in the Lowlands, James had a public meltdown during his visit to the coal mine at Culross, the events of which are related in the prologue.

Navigating James's darker moods required quick thinking on George's part. Masques usually began with a spoken portion, then culminated in dancing; on a night James was tired, when a Christmas masque's spoken section continued far longer than usual, he shouted, "By God, why don't they dance yet?" Polite paralysis from the masquers and musicians ensued, until George leaped in from the sidelines to dance with "exquisite manner," according to the Venetian ambassador.[35] James's spirits lifted. When George and the other masquers had finished dancing, James "embraced and kissed him tenderly."[36]

During the Scottish visit, a cousin of Robert Carr had drunkenly threatened to kill George in revenge for Robert's disgrace. He was pulled away by friends and the King banished him from court.[37] Despite their enmity, in the early days of his ascent George found himself frequently compared to Robert, and seldom to his credit. It was a common view in court and capital that "no other reason appeared in favour of their choice [as favorite] but handsomeness."[38]

Years later, Francis Osborne wrote down his memories of life in James's court. He recalled that, given how obvious James's affection was in public, nobody at court doubted what was happening in private.[39] George's contemporary Sir Henry Rich allegedly turned down an advantageous post in the King's Household because he did not want anybody to assume he owed his position to his looks or an intimate relationship with the King.[40]

When they were back in England, the down-but-not-out Howards attempted to displace George with William Monson—whose sister Bridget was widely suspected to be the veiled virgin who had taken Frances Howard's place during her medical inspection—a handsome young man whose family were the Howards' clients. Having decided not to collectively eviscerate the entire Howard faction after the Overbury convictions, James had left Robert's father-in-law, Lord Suffolk, with one of his former political positions as Lord High Treasurer. Discontented with these remnants of his former glory, Suffolk, his wife, and their allies encouraged Monson, who was in his early twenties, to seduce the King.

The Countess of Suffolk suggested the tried-and-tested method of perfuming his breath and the less conventional beauty treatment of maintaining Monson's complexion with regular facials of milk curd. A lawyer at court wrote in a private letter how the Howards were attempting to "raise and recover their fortunes by setting up this new idol, and take great pains in tricking and pranking him up, besides washing his face with posset-curd."[41] The scheme backfired. James was embarrassed by Monson's oleaginous efforts, which were so painfully obvious that James sent a message to inform Monson that "the King did not like his forwardness, and presenting himself continually about him."[42]

George secured Monson's dismissal from court a few weeks before Suffolk was replaced as Lord High Treasurer by Archbishop Abbot. Further misfortune visited the Howards during a smallpox epidemic. The Countess of Suffolk survived, but with severe scarring. Heartbroken by the loss of her once-famous beauty—what a fellow lady-in-waiting had memorably called "that face of hers that has brought to others such misery and to herself greatness"—she retreated permanently from court.[43]

The King's displeasure at Monson confirmed for courtiers that

George was unlikely to lose his place as favorite in the foreseeable future, a fact further emphasized by James's decision to elevate George's earldom to the marquessate of Buckingham on Twelfth Night 1618. His mother Mary, who was George's closest confidante, was made Countess of Buckingham in her own right, a move without precedent in the English aristocracy. Women had very rarely been granted titles in her own right before. There had been only two examples in the previous century, with the recipients related either by blood or impending marriage to the royal family. It was unheard of to make the mother of a recently ennobled man, who was not herself a member of the nobility, a participant in his title. It is testament to Mary's importance to George, and to the friendship she established with the King, that James granted her the privilege. Predictably, it angered other courtiers, who proved envy's ability to parent spite through some of the early gossip that exaggerated Mary's lowly origins.

Most of the criticism of Mary was unfair, but not all. There were incidents that proved her propensity to be as ruthless as any career courtier. In September 1617, she negotiated the marriage of George's recently knighted elder brother John to Sir Edward Coke's daughter Frances. A fellow courtier thought that John had more kindness and genuine intelligence than the rest of his family, but even his friends could see that his mental health was a concern. John's full mental breakdown did not take place until 1620, yet the warning signs were apparent in 1617, when Frances Coke and her mother were so aghast at the proposed marriage that Lady Coke helped Frances run away. She was hidden in the country homes of various maternal relatives, until her father tracked her down. He too had come to have his doubts about John Villiers's suitability as a bridegroom; however, he could not demur once James ordered the marriage to go ahead. The ceremony was held in the chapel at Hampton Court with the King, the Prince of Wales, George, Mary, and most of their family in attendance. The congregation saw tears streaming down Frances Coke's face when the ring was slipped onto her finger.

19

THE SUN SETS, ONLY FOR TO RISE

> [You] have hung up your Arms to rust, glued up those swords in their scabbards that would shake all Christendom with the brandish, and entertained into your minds such softness, dullness, and effeminate niceness that it would make Heraclitus himself laugh.
>
> —Anonymous, *Haec Vir: Or, The Womanish-Man* (1620)

Throughout 1618, speculation at court focused on the imminent likelihood of Prince Charles's accession to the throne. If James fell off his horse again, either at greater speed or at a fatal angle, or if the illnesses that had left him so weak early in 1616 and again late in 1617 returned, the Prince of Wales might be Charles I before the year was out.

For future generations, Charles's reputation lives in the shadow of a civil war that he was blamed by many for starting. The dignity and the bravery that would, years later, inspire such intense devotion to Charles's cause were already present in him as a young man, as was the obdurate myopia that provoked frustration, rage, and hatred from those who eventually rebelled against him. In 1618, however, the prospect of Charles becoming king provoked neither controversy nor anxiety. The Prince of Wales, who turned eighteen that November, was old enough to rule without the complications of a regency. He was well-educated, less charismatic than his late brother but more intellectual, elegant, and nobody could fairly accuse him of lacking in self-discipline. When he was fourteen, Charles had started running daily races in St. James's Park with his servants and gentlemen.[1] This was a self-set exercise to combat the weak legs that had given him difficulty in his childhood. His competitors were under strict instructions from Charles not to let him win. Charles ran until exhaustion, maintained the routine daily until he could complete the course, then kept going until he could win it on his own merits. For the same reason, he insisted on extra horse-riding lessons until he became an excellent equestrian. He worked hard to overcome his childhood stammer, which returned only in moments of great stress—at which point his accent also rapidly shifted as witnesses heard the Lowland Scottish accent of his infancy mix with the southern English of his later childhood.

At about seventeen or eighteen, Charles became sexually active with a lady of the court. We know of the affair only because of a note from Charles to George, in which he asked George to cover for him if his father asked where he was. To protect the woman's identity, Charles referred to her as she "that must not be named" in their correspondence. Even the note itself is a rare survivor; Charles requested that George deliver all such correspondence into "the custody of Mr. Vulcan," a pun on the name of the Roman god of fire.[2] Knowing of James's abhorrence of the prospect of royal bastards, Charles could make a good guess at what kind of rant he would receive from his father if he discovered Charles was having premarital sex. Presumably, George incinerated the rest but accidentally overlooked this note.

The friendship between Charles and George reassured the Villiers family that their newfound fortune would survive James. Meanwhile, George's prominence at court was further secured through a mixture of his charm and circumspection. He still knew when to draw himself back. In 1618, he tentatively suggested a relative for a vacancy on the Privy Council after a member was dismissed for embezzlement. James had his own candidate in mind, Sir George Calvert. He discussed the matter with the Queen, who agreed that Calvert was a sensible choice. Calvert mistakenly thought he owed his promotion to George and in thanks sent George a jewel, which George returned with the explanation that Calvert's gratitude belonged to the Queen.

Keeping Anna on side was a sensible move, both for George's

present and future. In the anticipated Carolean regime, Anna would almost certainly remain a powerful influence. The Prince of Wales was close to his mother, whom he visited regularly. Mother and son shared common interests, such as the arts and music, and Anna had instilled in Charles a respect for etiquette.

Anna's own health, however, had not been strong for some time. A comet streaked across the sky in September, which was held to presage the death of a great person—possibly Anna, probably James. When both the King and the Queen missed the capital's service of thanksgiving for the Gunpowder Plot's anniversary in November, the coldhearted at court and city started secretly betting over whose funeral would come first, James's or Anna's. Conjecture intensified when the usual Christmas festivities were dramatically scaled back after the Queen's autumn sojourn at Hampton Court was extended on her doctors' orders; she was told that the journey back to London during winter would be ill-advised, as would a busy social schedule. Anna stayed put with her household at Hampton Court, although, keen to silence the whispers that she was at death's door, she made a point of promenading through one of the palace's public galleries with plenty of witnesses. Prince Charles came to visit her often, and was sufficiently stung by unkind gossip that he was doing so only to secure a hefty bequest in her will that he wrote to his father denying it.[3]

James took the opportunity to pass the quieter winter at Theobalds, where he was joined by his household. George tended to him when he was sick and accompanied him on infrequent visits to Hampton Court to see the Queen. Anna's fears about the long-term consequences of her husband's drinking appeared justified. However, so too did her faith in George as somebody who would provide James with companionship when he was healthy and care when he was not. Anna took her duties as a hostess seriously, and meals in the Queen's Household were considered some of the best in England. Her son certainly thought so, writing notes of thanks to his mother every time he enjoyed a "good dinner" as her guest. James too enjoyed a few of those meals, until his physicians advised him that his health was far too fragile to ride in the winter air to Hampton Court. Both he and Anna decided to stay put in their respective countryside palaces until they felt well enough to return to London. Charles moved into Hampton Court to be with his mother in the middle of a miserably cold February.

On the morning of March 2, a messenger arrived at Theobalds from Hampton Court. The Queen had died shortly before dawn, with Prince Charles at her bedside. She had lost the power of speech in her final hours, so she kept running her hands through Charles's hair until the end. James collapsed and had to be carried to his bed.

George was at James's side throughout the complete physical and nervous breakdown that followed. He could barely speak for five days. It was not until the start of April that he was able to sit up properly in bed or feed himself. A curtain of silence descended over the royal household. While the public mourned the late Queen, the King disappeared from view. He managed to sign the letters informing Anna's brothers, mother, and sisters that she had died, but then he relapsed into stupefied grief. In the anxious privacy of Theobalds, it took weeks before he could walk more than a few steps, and it was not until June, three months after Anna's death, that he was seen in public again when he finally returned to the capital on horseback.

Anna of Denmark had been one of the most remarkable queens in British history, which has produced many. Ruthless when she felt it necessary, glamorous, clever, loyal, a consummate dynast, a loving mother, a great patron of the arts, an unrepentant snob, wildly extravagant, vindictive, and popular, she had helped make the Union of the Crowns possible. She had certainly helped make the new dynasty palatable in England. Her capacity to endure and thrive was extraordinary. A career that had commenced with men crushed to death in front of her by a broken-free cannon careering over the decks of a ship tossed in the worst storm in living memory had played out alongside witch hunts, attempted coups, heartbreak, triumph, the scent of gunpowder, and the sound of Shakespeare. She had faced down the Kirk for adhering to Lutheranism. She had confused, outwitted, and intrigued political heavyweights like Queen Elizabeth I and Pope Paul V, both of whom wondered if she had secretly converted to Catholicism.

Considering how James reacted to her death, it is questionable if he was ever told the more distressing details of Anna's final weeks when her tubercular lungs failed her, as did her erratic heart and gout-plagued legs. There had been nights when she woke up panicking because she felt she was drowning in her own blood and others when she was tormented by insomnia. She provided generously for Charles in her will, as expected. Confounding the cynics, Charles refused the inheritance and passed everything over to his father. However, he assumed responsibility for the wages owed to Anna's staff, which he had promised her on the day before she died that he would settle.[4]

Finances reared their head in the weeks after the Queen's death. When he had half recovered from his breakdown, James insisted that Anna deserved a funeral at least as grand as Elizabeth I's.[5] Anna's body was embalmed while the royal household worked to make the order a reality. It was not until the middle of May that the funeral went ahead, thanks to the fundraising initiatives of George's latest ally, Lionel Cranfield. He liquidated certain Crown estates, called in various loans, and diverted some of the rents from Anna's former properties. It was impressive, as well as legal. For his efforts, Cranfield was subsequently appointed Lord Treasurer and, in 1621, James made him earl of Middlesex.

As was customary, James did not attend Anna's magnificent funeral at Westminster Abbey, where she was interred near his mother on May 13. Returning to his poetry, James wrote:

> So did my Queen from hence her court remove
> And left off earth to be enthroned above.
> She's changed, not dead, for sure no good prince dies,
> But, as the sun, sets, only for to rise.

Three weeks after Anna's death, word had arrived from Europe that the sixty-two-year-old Emperor Matthias had died in Vienna. Matthias had no legitimate children, and his death brought to political center stage his cousin Emperor Ferdinand II, who swiftly and decisively abandoned Matthias's conciliatory religious policies in favor of a more aggressive promotion of the Counter-Reformation.[6] The consequences that flowed from those two royal deaths in the spring of 1619—Queen Anna's and that of Emperor Matthias—were to shape the remainder of James's life.

Initially, Ferdinand II's accession was of no immediate interest to James, or at least of no immediate concern. Ferdinand had been a force even while the previous emperor was alive, when he had been Matthias's deputy in several parts of the empire—most significantly in Inner Austria, a collection of duchies covering land that is now part of southern Austria and northern Slovenia. Due to his activities during Matthias's reign, there was no uncertainty about Ferdinand's sympathies. Some English Protestants feared for their coreligionists if, as emperor, Ferdinand chose to expand his successful re-Catholicization of Inner Austria, which he had achieved by investing in Catholic missions into the Austrian provinces, exiling Protestant clergy, prohibiting their employment by the nobility, and banning, then destroying, Protestant books.[7] Despite previously having relatively high numbers of Protestants in her rural communities, Inner Austria had proved a success for the Counter-Reformation through the speed with which it reembraced the old religion.[8] Irrespective of the differences in their denominations, there was a vigorous pan-Protestant populism active within western European Protestantism, and it held that an attack on one community of Protestants was an attack on them all. In James's kingdoms, this belief was particularly lively in the Puritan communities, whose politics and views on foreign affairs were fundamentally shaped by it.

When, as predicted, Ferdinand II extended his anti-Protestant policy to his northeastern kingdom of Bohemia, negating the late emperor's promise of religious toleration, it provoked a rebellion by the Bohemian aristocracy. Converging on the kingdom's capital in Prague, they revoked en masse their oaths of fealty to Ferdinand as king of Bohemia.[9] They found an ally in the Prince of Transylvania, a Protestant who invaded the Emperor's territories from the east in the hope of seizing the Hungarian throne. The Bohemian nobility looked around Europe for a Protestant prince of their own to whom they could offer the Bohemian crown. To James's horror, they chose his German son-in-law, Frederick, who sent an embassy to London to ask for James's advice but did not wait for his reply.

James complained to a councillor, "He wrote to me to know my mind if he should take that crown, but within three days after; and before I could return answer, he put it on."[10] Personally, James felt that the Habsburgs had every right to be furious at what he called "the unjust and needless quarrel" in which Elizabeth and Frederick were involving themselves.[11] Frederick, likely buoyed up by the Prince of Transylvania's victories against the Emperor and certainly encouraged by Elizabeth's faith in it, accepted the Bohemian offer and—joined by a pregnant Elizabeth and their eldest son—went to Prague for his coronation at St. Vitus Cathedral on November 4, 1619.

Having picked a husband for his daughter primarily on the criterion of the groom's diplomatic irrelevance, James was suddenly confronted by the nightmarish probability of the marriage dragging him into a war against the Habsburg empire. More accurately, it would be a war against the Habsburg empires, because the King of Spain was all but certain to support his Austrian cousin.* Ironically, in having married Frederick to a British princess, James had raised Frederick's status sufficiently high for the Bohemian nobility to think of him—and his children—as a worthy royal family for their country.

As queen of Bohemia, James's daughter gained the haunting sobriquet of "the Winter Queen," since it took only until the spring thaw for the full force of Ferdinand II's armies to come crashing down on Bohemia. The Habsburgs ruled their empire—particularly its archduchies in Austria and its kingdoms of Bohemia, Croatia, and Hungary—with much the same dynastic federalism as James ruled the politically separate kingdoms of Scotland, England, and Ireland. Of the three, Bohemia was perhaps the Habsburgs' closest equivalent to Ireland, in that it was the one in which the majority of

* The House of Habsburg had split into two lines in the previous century, when the abdicating Emperor Charles V divided his empires between his brother, Ferdinand I, and son Philip II. The central European side of the family was the Austrian Habsburgs, and Philip's side was known as the Spanish Habsburgs. Sometimes, they had separate ambassadors to the English court, but more often in the late sixteenth and early seventeenth century they used one ambassador to represent the interests of both sides of the dynasty.

the population professed a different religion from their monarch's. Like James in Ireland after 1607, Ferdinand had no intention of allowing Bohemia's aristocracy to challenge him. He was also intent on punishing Frederick for accepting a crown to which, Ferdinand believed, he had no right. The Emperor's forces pushed Frederick and Elizabeth out of Bohemia, and he then swung his army west to conquer Frederick's patrimony of the Palatinate in the Rhineland. Elizabeth and her family accepted an offer of asylum from the Netherlands. When James protested to the Habsburgs' ambassador in London that occupying the Palatinate seemed a disproportionate response to events in Prague, the ambassador replied, "What would you do if anyone had taken London from you?"[12]

London was firmly and vocally on Elizabeth and Frederick's side, as shown by the avalanches of sermons preached and pamphlets printed on the subject. Nearly all urged the King to save his grandchildren's inheritance by declaring war on the Habsburgs. Aristocrats at court donated to volunteer brigades, who were permitted by James to go to Germany to help in the defense of the Palatinate; they and Frederick's other forces were defeated by an army under the command of the Emperor's best general, the Duke of Sesto.

A victorious Ferdinand II dialed up the Counter-Reformation in his empire, claiming that Protestantism had proved its propensity to incubate treason. By 1620, a flood of Protestant refugees flowed westward from Bohemia, Austria, Bavaria, southern Poland, and Hungary. James's daughter remained in the Netherlands, with a depressed husband, four children, and a fifth on the way.

The Bohemian uprising and the Habsburg reprisal were a match in the kindling in Europe, as it helped start a sectarian conflict known later as the Thirty Years' War. Nobody could have foreseen in 1620 just how staggering the war's impact would be. It would claim an estimated six million casualties and, by the time it ended in 1648, it had helped cause two famines that, when combined with its violence, saw the population of the German states, where most of its battles were fought, collapse by about half. For both Protestants and Catholics, the Thirty Years' War was a Manichean struggle for the soul of Europe.[13] Some even saw it as so bloody that it must be the war prophesied as part of the End Times in the book of Revelation.[14] It mutated outward to encompass the continent, with only a few prominent exceptions—the Islamic Ottoman Empire to the south, Orthodox Russia to the east, and the British Isles to the west; France, torn between its Catholicism and its traditional resentment of the Habsburgs, played both sides off against each other as and when it suited them.

Broadly, however, the Thirty Years' War was split along confessional lines. Ferdinand II was joined by the armies of Philip III, King of Spain and Portugal, by Bavaria, and by the Catholic League, an alliance of German Catholic princes and grand dukes. The King of Sweden assumed de facto leadership of the Protestant response, sending a navy and army to land in Europe, where it met up with their allies from the Dutch republic, the kingdoms of Denmark-Norway, the principality of Transylvania, the German states of Prussia, Hesse, and Saxony, and the German Protestant alliance of cities called the Heilbronn League.

James found himself swimming against the tide of both public and court opinion. Even George sympathized with the pro-war lobby, a development cultivated by Princess Elizabeth, who wrote frequently to George from her exile in the Netherlands and recruited him as an ally who she was convinced could persuade her father to go to war. George's support for the Winter Queen's cause was expressed by the substantial sum of £5,000 that he had donated to equip the English volunteer brigade when it left for its doomed defense of the Palatinate. More was needed, and Elizabeth urged George to speak on her behalf to James. Her father's verbal attempts to justify of their cause to the Spanish ambassador was useless, she told George: "I pray tell the King that the enemy will more regard his blows than his words."[15] She liaised with her mother's former ladies-in-waiting, including the Countess of Bedford, who in turn promoted Elizabeth's cause at court and to their relatives on the council. Elizabeth found another important ally in her only surviving sibling, and Charles's support for military intervention strengthened his friendship with George.

James sent money to Elizabeth so that she, her husband, their children, and staff could live comfortably. He hesitated at raising an army for her. He knew the country could not afford it, to say nothing of his own lifelong promotion of peace. Despite George's support for Elizabeth, he was widely identified by public opinion as either cause or symptom of the moral rot that prevented the King from going to war. Anti-court literature like the anonymously authored book *Haec Vir: Or, The Womanish-Man,* which was published in London in 1620, addressed James as the failed king of an enfeebled, effeminate nation that, thanks to the lugubrious example set by his court, "have hung up your Arms to rust, glued up those swords in their scabbards that would shake all Christendom with the brandish, and entertained into your minds such softness, dullness, and effeminate niceness."[16]

In November 1620, as the war in Europe dominated public discourse, James summoned a new parliament, the only body capable of voting sufficient funds to sustain a war. He hoped that, once they saw the cost of a conflict in Europe, Parliament would quail at authorizing the necessary taxes. That would shift or shoulder the blame for nonintervention. He also hoped that news of his convening of Parliament, which had the capacity to fund a war, might make the Habsburgs more cautious in how they treated Elizabeth, Frederick, and the Palatinate in the future. However, remembering the Addled Parliament's excoriation of Robert six years earlier, James feared that the House of Commons would also seize this opportunity to attack George.

20

DARLING SIN

And then says, *Age:* "My friend, come near,
And be not aloof, I thee require.
Come brother, by the hand me take."
—William Dunbar, "Meditation in Winter"
(c. 1504)

In the weeks between the summoning of Parliament on November 13, 1620, and its opening on January 16, 1621, England was hit by a winter so cold that the River Thames froze.[1] From his windows at Whitehall, James could see a vast expanse of ice. Snow howled through the streets, ending the lives of many of the city's homeless people. When the snow stopped, ice holes were drilled for fishing on the river. Torches were lit on the ice, where merchants erected stalls to sell their wares to the hundreds of Londoners skating on the frozen river.

In his apartments, James prepared himself for the anticipated contretemps with Parliament. Since George was English, they might have been expected to go more easily on him than they had on a Scottish favorite such as Robert. However, distaste at what the Overbury trials had revealed about the court's morality meant that anti-favorite sentiment was once again high, as was the perception that every courtier behaved similarly to Frances Howard and Robert Carr.

During the final weeks of Queen Anna's life and in the year and a half since her death, George had acquired palpable political influence, which would make him even more of a target for parliamentary criticism. Anna's decline and death had removed for George both an ally and a brake. In January 1619, he became a senior officer of state as Lord High Admiral, upon the retirement of the previous incumbent, Lord Nottingham, who was in his eighties. As he had when Master of the Horse, George worked hard as admiral and his interest in both foreign affairs and military reform increased. The navy was in a parlous state, and George introduced several reforms, which cut the navy's running cost while increasing its size, its salaries, and the safety of its craft. Socially, in the spring of 1620, he cemented his place at the apex of English high society with his marriage to Lady Katherine Manners, the Earl of Rutland's only surviving child.* Courtiers whispered about the circumstances of the marriage, pointing out maliciously and unnecessarily that seventeen-year-old Lady Katherine's looks were not conventionally beautiful. They also discussed the murky circumstances of Lady Katherine's visit to the home of her future mother-in-law Mary, Countess of Buckingham, where Katherine had allegedly fallen ill and had to spend the night unchaperoned. Her outraged father considered this an insult to his daughter's virtue and insisted that George, who had also been visiting his mother that night, propose to Katherine. Discussions about a marriage between the two families had been ongoing for a few months and, allegedly frustrated at the Manners' foot-dragging on certain points, gossips claimed Mary had deliberately made Katherine sick to "trap" her. While Mary was probably capable of such a Machiavellian move, that does not mean it is true. George seems to have hesitated too about marrying Katherine. However, James thought such a marriage was of great social advantage to George, and his support proved decisive. They were married in a small ceremony at the London home of Katherine's father on May 16.

The King grew to like the new Marchioness of Buckingham very much. Katherine was intelligent, a bibliophile, tactful, firm, and ac-

---

* Katherine Manners's family had recently been visited by tragedy and scandal. Both of her brothers, Henry and Francis, had died in infancy. Three former servants of the family—a mother and her two adult daughters—were accused of witchcraft, resulting in two executions. (The mother, Joan Flower, died before trial.) Katherine's stepmother and father were both convinced that their sons had been killed by malicious spells, so much so that Lord Rutland had it inscribed on his tomb that "he had two sons, both of which died in their infancy by wicked practices and sorcery." The affair was known as that of the "Witches of Belvoir," after the Rutlands' castle in Leicestershire.

customed to life in the English elite. With no queen, she became de facto first lady of the court by helping organize many of the diplomatic receptions and cultural events that had previously been Anna's responsibility. Fortunately for both of them, the Buckinghams' marriage became a happy one in which surviving letters between the couple eloquently display Katherine's affection for her husband and his care for her well-being and reputation.

It did not correlate with any dilution of George's relationship with the King. They spent many evenings and nights alone together. Around the time he recalled Parliament, James had written a new book with George as his amanuensis. The physical act of writing for prolonged periods had become uncomfortable for James, which was why he dictated *Meditation on the Lord's Prayer* to George. To modern eyes, most Jacobean works may seem turgid or long-winded. In context, *Meditation on the Lord's Prayer* is both. It is far less coherent than James's other works and often failed to make clear its point, unlike his previous books on monarchy, religion, or witchcraft. The decline in intellectual standards between his earlier works and *Meditation on the Lord's Prayer* supports the assessment of the new French ambassador, the Comte de Tillières, that "the intelligence of this king is much diminished." He thought James was "as good for nothing as possible . . . and buried for the greater part of his time in wine." After watching James fall over onto the table after drinking heavily at supper one evening, Tillières characterized him as "a King devoted to his own nothingness."[2]

For the opening of Parliament on January 16, James was not only too ill to ride to Westminster, he could not even manage to walk into Parliament itself. His joints gave him pain, his old hunting injuries had flared up, and the swelling had returned. He was carried in on a litter, with George walking at its side.

As James had feared, Parliament lost little time in criticizing the court for its financial corruption, which they insisted should be reformed before there was discussion of any further taxes. The revulsion caused by the Overbury scandal lingered, sustaining suspicion and disgust against any royal favorite.

Investigations were proposed with the clear objective that they would culminate in George's impeachment or disgrace. To prevent this, George displayed a ruthlessness previously either absent or hidden and threw his ally Sir Francis Bacon to the wolves, a move that James supported. Bacon, who had become Lord Chancellor in 1618, was indicted for taking bribes, dismissed from office, fined, and banished from court. To further satisfy and distract Parliament, two more of George's supporters—his elder half brother Sir Edward Villiers and Edward's brother-in-law Sir Giles Mompesson—were banished from court and barred from ever standing for election to Parliament. A London playwright satirized Mompesson as the archetype of a corrupt courtier called Sir Giles Over-Reach in the popular comedy *A New Way to Settle Old Debts*, which depicted the court as a festering sinkhole of financial inequity.

Bacon, Villiers, and Mompesson were offered as sacrifices to save George, but that does not mean they were innocent. In Mompesson's case, he was unquestionably guilty of using his court position to sell fraudulent business licences, squeeze business owners to buy new ones that they did not need but that he mendaciously claimed were a recent legal requirement, and license businesses that sold faulty timber or goods but paid him the cash he asked for. George may have known absolutely nothing about what Mompesson was up to. However, he knew that Bacon had done nothing egregious enough to warrant such a disgrace. He still abandoned him with alacrity to save himself.*

Parliament was not deterred and pressed on with their intention of investigating George. James threatened to dissolve Parliament if they did so but, sensing how unpopular that would be in London, he dismissed it early for summer in June and recalled it in November, by which point both temperature and tempers would have cooled.

Parliament was also focused on sustaining an emerging colonial policy. To the chagrin of some in England and the delight of its investors, including many in Parliament and James's former favorite Philip Herbert, the prominence and rapacity of the East India

---

* There may have been an additional, vindictive element to George's betrayal of Bacon, with whom he was apparently angry after Bacon failed to enthusiastically support John Villiers's controversial marriage to Frances Coke.

Company* led it to act like a quasi-independent state. James's ambassador wrote from India to inform him of the new political status of Emperor Jahangir's twentieth and latest wife, Nur Jahan.[3] Intellectually brilliant, the Empress had been proclaimed her husband's coruler, rather than just his consort. Born on an Afghan roadside to Persian aristocrats who were refugees from a coup in Tehran, she had survived her first husband's execution for treason to become the Emperor's love, wife, and partner in government, making her arguably the most powerful woman in the world. The ambassador informed council and Parliament that the Empress was henceforth the center of Mughal government and must be treated with the same respect as the Emperor.

The first African victims of the Atlantic slave trade to be kidnapped and brought to the English colony in Virginia were disembarked by their captors in 1619 and the process continued in 1620–21. Hundreds of thousands would make the same journey over the next two centuries, as part of the estimated eleven million who were enslaved from Africa and forced across the Atlantic between the mid-sixteenth century and the early nineteenth.[4] It was one of the largest forced displacements of people in human history: in two and a half centuries one million died on the journey, amid conditions so horrific that more than one witness compared them to the gates of Hell opening on Earth. About five million people were enslaved in the Portuguese and Spanish colonies in South America, an estimated half a million were kidnapped to mainland North America, and a further four million to colonies in the Caribbean.[5] Due to a clause in the Magna Carta that, in attempting to limit serfdom in the thirteenth century, had outlawed slavery on English soil, enslavers feared that their victims might be regarded as legally emancipated if they were trafficked to England.[6] Colonies, however, were free to impose or disregard laws from Britain as they saw fit. British slave traders therefore avoided bringing their vic-

* The East India Company (1600–1874), a private English joint-stocks company. Over the course of the seventeenth century, its wealth and influence grew until, by the eighteenth century, it accounted for approximately half the world's registered trade. Its independent wealth enabled it to fund mercenary armies and administrators of its own.

tims to Britain itself—an insidious loophole brilliantly and harrowingly described by some of its victims—while working assiduously to expand and defend slavery in the colonies.[7] Slave traders soon found allies in Parliament, who ensured that enslavement in the colonies was allowed to expand in size, scope, profit, and suffering.

The war in Europe continued. In February, Cardinal Alessandro Ludovisi was elected Pope Gregory XV, and his pontifical reign was defined by his support for the Counter-Reformation. In March, King Philip III died in Madrid, provoking the question of whether his son and successor, sixteen-year-old Philip IV, would be as supportive of the Austrian cause in the Thirty Years' War. James received encouraging signs that he might not be when the Spanish ambassador to London, the Count of Gondomar, refloated the possibility of a marriage between Prince Charles and Philip IV's sister Maria-Anna. In fact, it was a tactical move by Gondomar after explicit secret instructions from his government to dangle the prospect of marriage to the Infanta in order to discourage James from entering the European war against Maria-Anna's relatives. So long as the negotiations continued, James would be even less inclined to abandon peace, especially since Maria-Anna would come with a dowry large enough to help right the monarchy's finances.

The Austrian Habsburgs' cause showed no perceptible sign of flagging, either in its moral certainty or its military action. In the autumn of 1621, the Emperor briefly broke off diplomatic relations with England when James sent another sizeable sum to Elizabeth for her household expenses. The money had been earmarked for domestic use only, a condition to which Elizabeth adhered, but it was enough to provoke Ferdinand II's ire. In February 1622, the widowed Emperor married the Italian noblewoman Eleonora Gonzaga, who shared fully her husband's commitment to the Counter-Reformation, and in May, peace talks, held in Brussels, collapsed as neither side showed any serious willingness to compromise.

In March of the same year, George became a father with the birth of a daughter whom he named in honor of his mother, Mary. James accepted the invitation to stand as the child's godfather, whom he nicknamed "Mall" and treated like a grandchild. A contemporary nickname for a godfather was a "gossop" or "gossip," which was how George sometimes addressed James in his letters. Again, however, there was no diminution of intimacy between the King and George, who in 1623 was awarded the highest title in the English nobility when James made him a duke.

Sometime before the summer of 1622, James intervened to spare a young servant from the death penalty after he was arrested for "buggering" a knight's son. The young men were of a similar age, but the passive partner, the knight's son, was from a much wealthier class. His family was insisting upon the death penalty and exploiting the legal ambiguity in the term "buggery," which drew no distinction between consensual acts and sexual assault. Hearing of the trial's details, James intervened through the Lord Chief Justice to have the young man pardoned, which was legally again an overreach of his royal prerogative.

By the end of 1622, George's property portfolio had swelled considerably. The Boleyns' former palace of Beaulieu in Essex was given to him and, among his four mansions in London, he later acquired the former home of the Catholic martyr Thomas More. George lavished a fortune on his love of beauty by recruiting the art expert Endymion Porter to scour auctions in Europe for him. He hired the famous horticulturalist John Tradescant to design the gardens at his new homes. George's art collection was impressive enough by 1622 to elicit praise from the architect Sir Balthasar Gerbier, who thought that "out of all the amateurs and princes and kings, there is not one who has collected in forty years as many pictures as Your Excellency has collected in five!"[8]

Away from his burgeoning collection of old masters and new commissions, George addressed the King as "dear dad," "daddy," and, latterly and most frequently, "my dear husband." James addressed him as "sweetheart" and "my only sweet wife." At some point after the Queen's death, they may have gone through a sort of ceremony, even if only in front of one another, as there are references in the letters from James to George about "our new marriage ever to be kept hereafter." In the face of parliamentary criticism of George, James told him that he would "rather live banished in any part of the earth with you than live a sorrowful widow's life without you."[9]

It seems unlikely that they had gone through something as formal as the sailors who, four decades earlier, had broken into the Roman church of San Giovanni a Porta Latina to marry eleven couples. For several hundred years in post-legalization Christianity, various communities had preserved a tradition called the *adelphopoiesis,* a "brother-making" ceremony whereby two men could be united by a priest in a lifelong bond.[10] Technically, of course, this was not intended to be a form of homosexual marriage. Equally, it would be obtuse to assume that there were not some couples who attempted to use it for that purpose. The nature of the *adelphopoiesis* remains extremely controversial, and much of its evidence was destroyed or obscured. Even if someone as prodigiously well-read on Church history as James knew about it, we have no certainty as to what the "new marriage" between him and George was. All we can be certain of is that marital language becomes a dominant motif in James and George's private correspondence after 1619.

With James's blessing, George had made his family into the wealthiest in the kingdom. George developed a forensic eye for detail when it came to the mechanics of patronage at the Jacobean court and the ways in which he could keep himself and his family powerful and wealthy. "There has never been a mightier subject in our land's history," concluded an irate nobleman. With no more rungs of the aristocracy for George to climb, James scattered titles to his family. George's brother-in-law was made earl of Denbigh, while his sister, the new Countess, assumed leadership of court festivities in conjunction with her sister-in-law Katherine, Duchess of Buckingham. George's brother John became a viscount and the youngest, Christopher, was made earl of Anglesey. Barred from Parliament, their disgraced half brother Sir Edward was eventually found a lucrative career in Ireland as President of Munster, the most southerly of Ireland's four provinces. The president of each of the provinces acted as the Lord Deputy's regional seconds-in-command. Villiers's relatives and friends were appointed to prominent positions in the Irish government, where their distant kinsman Sir Oliver St. John still served as Lord Deputy, and it was at this point that George bound him closer to the family's cause by asking James to raise him to the title of viscount.

With the family's influence growing in Ireland, George hit on a scheme of selling Irish aristocratic titles to the highest bidder. He and his mother negotiated the fees from wealthy social climbers in England. Over the course of his career, George was responsible for creating, at a price, forty-five new aristocratic titles in the Irish peerage.

Other members of the aristocracy watched the proceedings with eyebrows arched and stomach acid churning. George's former ally, the Lord Treasurer, Lord Middlesex, turned against him. He and his allies tried the Howards' old technique of finding a rival. Theirs was Middlesex's unmarried brother-in-law Sir Arthur Brett, a member of the English volunteer brigade that had gone to the Palatinate. Brett was good-looking, clever, and well-liked, and there were rumors about James's fondness for him late in 1622. However, George remained favorite and, at his urging, Brett was sent home, ostensibly to visit his family at Christmas. He did not return to court until 1626.

The Villiers' reputation was further damaged by the breakdown of John Villiers's marriage to Frances Coke. Unable to live anymore with a husband who suffered at least one severe mental health episode in 1620, Frances ran away. We do not know what afflicted John, although a credible modern suggestion is of bipolar disorder, for which there was not even a name, much less a treatment, at the time. To George's fury, Frances started an affair with one of the Howards—Lord Suffolk's younger son, Sir Robert Howard—and the two of them ran away from court together, where Frances conceived an illegitimate child. George was incensed on his brother's behalf, and his pursuit of vengeance against Frances was vicious. He persuaded James to sign an order that would imprison Sir Robert for adultery in London's Fleet prison. Sentenced to perform public penance as a "fallen woman," Frances Villiers disguised herself as a man and, with her baby son, fled to France, where she started a new life and converted to Catholicism. After James's death, she returned to England, where she reunited with Robert, who had refused to reveal where she had escaped to. They almost certainly married, since the Catholic faith they both adhered to did not acknowledge Protestant weddings, and they had several more children together.

George's commitment to Princess Elizabeth's cause faltered as he came to see the advantage of a Spanish marriage for Prince Charles. Both men were frustrated by the ambassador's foot-dragging over the issue, which gave them the idea of going to Madrid in disguise to propose in person. James was, at best, dubious about the plan but did not overrule them. Posing as merchants, George and Charles left London on February 17, 1623. They stopped in Paris, where, passing themselves off as friends of the ambassador, they went to a ball at the Louvre, where they saw Maria-Anna's sister Queen Anne* dancing. Charles was impressed by Anne's elegance and beauty, which made him even more keen to reach Madrid. They arrived in the Spanish capital on March 7, where they shed their disguises and were treated to a spectacular civic entry.

The ceremony, like the entire "Spanish Match" trip, was a farce. The only people who believed in the mission were George and Charles. The former tried to charm the young Spanish king and, as usual, he was successful. However, although Philip IV liked George, he was not sufficiently swayed to offend the Pope or overturn Spanish foreign policy. When Charles was finally introduced to Maria-Anna, the Infanta responded no more warmly than the bare minimum required of her by politeness. She was disgusted at the prospect of marriage to a heretic, she visibly flinched when Charles kissed her hand at their first meeting, and her reluctance was backed by most of the Spanish royal family. When Pope Gregory XV issued his conditions for permitting a Catholic princess to marry the Prince of Wales, they were so outrageous from the British perspective—they included the overturn of all anti-Catholic laws and a condition that any children born to the couple, including an heir to the throne, must be raised as Catholics—that James, after reading them, realized the Pope had set impossible conditions. He suspected, rightly, that the Pope had done so with the covert support of the Spanish government, who had never intended things to proceed so far. They wanted to push responsibility for the foun-

* Anne of Austria (1601–66). Despite her Spanish birth, she was referred to as "of Austria" because that was the Habsburg dynasty's ancestral home.

dering of negotiations onto James by presenting him with conditions to which they knew he could never agree.

During George's absence, he and the King exchanged letters. Not long after George left for France, James wrote to him, "Sweetheart, I rode this afternoon a great way in the park without speaking to anybody and the tears trickling down my cheeks, as now they do too so much that I scarcely can see to write. I care for nothing save that I may have you in my arms again." George sent him a miniature of himself, which James told him he had hung on a blue ribbon to wear around his heart.[11] James was suffering such "extreme longing that it might kill me." Their tone was sometimes erotic, such as when George added a postscript promising that once he "got hold of your bedpost again, I never again will quit it."[12] He told James that he missed him so much "that none longed more to be in the arms of his mistress."[13] He asked if James remembered the night when they shared a bed for the first time, and in another letter, he told James that he could not wait to have his "legs soon in my arms."[14]

James was afraid that the Spanish might detain Charles and George in Madrid, keeping them hostage. To ensure they were allowed to leave, he lied and said he was considering the Pope's prerequisites. The Prince and the Duke made it back to England in October, where they were greeted with crowds screaming their love for them as they rode toward the palace. The prospect of a Habsburg queen consort was so unpopular with English Protestants that it had managed to turn George, briefly, into a hero. Ignoring the fact that he had gone to Spain with the intention of making Maria-Anna the next queen of England, London was enraptured at his "patriotic" decision to return without her.

James and George wept when they were reunited. In the conversations that followed, George revealed to James that the tales of Spain's great wealth were all show with little substance. Their empire was too large, its military overextended by a bloated foreign policy, the internal government needed drastic reform, and, even if Maria-Anna had said yes, Spain would never have been able to provide the kind of dowry alluded to by their ambassador. Spain rolled out the pomp and ceremony to trick her European adversaries into believing that her wealth was still as substantial as it had been in the previous century.

George returned from Spain humiliated and angry. His resentment at how he had been treated seriously damaged James's happiness at their reunion, as George humiliated him by recommitting himself to the pro-war faction when Parliament reconvened in February 1624. Pro-war MPs praised the victories and bravery of Sweden's king, Gustav II.* They used Gustav as a comparison to shame James for refusing to get involved in the war, even when his daughter's honor was at stake. That Gustav II proved one of the most effective generals of the seventeenth century made James appear even more feeble or, as critics in Parliament called his foreign policy, "effeminate." The English government's response, or lack thereof, was a shameful dereliction of duty to both faith and family. To remain the only major Protestant power that was neutral would, as the MP for Leicester stated in his speech to the House, "diminish our ancient fame of being a valiant nation."[15] Was this pathetic foreign policy any wonder, a pamphleteer rhetorically asked, when the court was dominated—in an echo of other criticisms—by "effeminate persons, sodomites, and other such like monsters," who were more interested in learning how to "curl their hair, pluck their brows and so metamorphise themselves as well in their attire as their demeanour that they appear more like harlots than men"?[16]

George's appearance changed as he presented himself as a warrior rather than the smooth-faced courtier mocked by James's critics. He grew a beard. James hated it and asked him to shave it off, which he refused to do. Arguments between him and James over the war in Europe became more common.

In his interactions with Parliament, James chose combativeness over conciliation. He reminded them that, unlike his Tudor predecessors, he had never come to Parliament to insist that they fund a war. Considering how much money he had saved by peace, it was outrageous for Parliament to query his extravagance when it came to his household. James was correct, in that, when compared

---

* Sometimes referred to in English as Gustavus Adolphus.

to the cost of war, his debts were negligible. He did not seem to realize that even this counted against him. Presumably forgetting Elizabeth I's wars against Spain and Mary I's against France, many MPs characterized the government's pacifist policy as dishonorable, feeble, and "womanish." James continued in his speech by admitting that

> it is true that I, who have been all the days of my life a peaceful King, and have had the honour to be called *Rex Pacificus,** will not without necessity embroil myself in war, it being so far from my nature and from the honour which I have had at home and abroad in endeavouring to avoid the spilling of Christian blood . . . Unless war be upon such necessity that I may judge it to be—as some say merrily about women—*malum necessarium,*† I should be loath to enter it.[17]

In a few sentences, the King had confirmed many of his critics' suspicions against him.

The lawyer Simonds d'Ewes, who referred to sodomy as the "darling sin" of courtiers and had been at court when James and George's relationship first began, lamented the state of public morality while chatting with a friend in London—"I discussed with him the sin of sodomy, how frequent it is in this wicked city, and if God did not provide some wonderful blessing against it, we could not but expect some horrible punishment for it. Especially it being, as we have probable cause to fear, a sin in our prince."[18]

George was still distrusted by those who were inherently hostile to the court, but his firm defection to the pro-war movement after his failure in Spain had sustained at least some of the goodwill he accrued following the Madrid trip. A libel, rhetorically addressed to James, congratulated him on finding a favorite who might finally do some good:

---

* King of peace or peaceful king.

† Unfortunate necessity or unhappily unavoidable.

[He is] the very first
Of all thy favourites e'er undertook
His Country's Cause and thus did overlook
Spanish Deceivings. For he hath done more
Than twenty of thy favourites before.[19]

George and the heir remained close friends, even when, in April 1624, Prince Charles told George that he had forgotten himself during his arguments with James. Regardless of his politics, he needed to remember who was the king and who the subject. No amount of intimacy could change the fact that James was God's anointed, set to rule over them. While Charles shared George's frustration about the war, he also could see how much the political disagreements were distressing his father. George fell ill, possibly with a virus that was active that spring, and he was left bedridden for two weeks. James came to his bedside and, when George recovered, they had reconciled. As he had many times before, George in his turn cared for James when he began to suffer from arthritis, and it seems possible that, in 1624, their sexual relationship ceased. James's comforts were now more often by the fireside, where he liked to read with George's wife, Katherine, or join her in the afternoon to play with her daughter, his goddaughter Lady Mary.

Like Elizabeth I thirty years earlier, James found himself increasingly isolated by the passage of time, despaired of by a younger generation who found his pacifism dishonorable and his hesitancy nothing more than a consequence of aging. In January 1622, George urged James to show Robert Carr mercy. It had been seven years since the Overbury trials. Surely he and Frances could be released from the Tower and go to one of their estates in the country? They did not need to be pardoned; they could be barred from court but free from prison. James agreed and Robert and Frances set off for one of their homes. They had one less to choose from; George had agreed to speak on their behalf only when they sold him, at an outrageously discounted rate, a property that he had long desired.

Portraits from this time in James's life show his physical decline. The sharpness of his features has blurred. The sumptuousness of his clothes throws unintended attention upon his exhausted face and his heavy eyes. In a picture by Daniel Mytens, the angle of James's feet shows the old riding wound to his ankle. Sleep was again difficult for him; he suffered occasionally from hemorrhoids; his fingers hurt more and more, as did his teeth. On February 16, 1624, James awoke to the news that his cousin Ludovic, Duke of Lennox—friend, kinsman, adviser, and, at one point, heir—had died in his sleep in his London residence.[20] James was devastated and paid for Ludovic's funeral at Westminster Abbey. Five months later, Ludovic's brother and heir, the younger Esmé, who had served in James's household for twenty-one years, died of typhoid. His cousins' deaths led to another depressive episode.

As 1624 drew to its end, James struggled to hold to the policy of peace. Those in favor of action had reason to hope that, at some point in 1625, the ailing King would at last declare war. Reflecting on the new powers at court, James's contemporary, former classmate, and Captain of the Guard wrote to another of the Stirling alumni, "It may come that young folks shall have this world. I know not if that will be fit for your Lordship and me."[21]

21

THESE FIFTY YEARS

'Tis true I am a cradle king,
Yet do remember everything.

—James VI and I's last known poem
(c. 1623)

After another Christmas at Whitehall, an exhausted James, "ill troubled with a universal pain in his shoulders, elbows, knees and feet," retreated as usual to his hunting lodges at Newmarket and then Royston. He intended to go to Theobalds for spring, where George would join him.[1] Until then, George sent "merry letters" that made James laugh.[2]

George was in London finalizing details in the Prince of Wales's marriage treaty with Princess Henrietta Maria of France. At the last moment, the French ambassador had thrown a spanner in the works by asking for further concessions for British Catholics, including the Princess's right to hear Mass in public rather than in a private chapel. That would require the construction of a Catholic church in London for the first time in decades, which James and George knew would enrage many Protestants. George wrote acidly to James that the French had proven themselves to speak with "shitten mouths" by trying to add in an eleventh-hour change to the treaty.[3]

George considered delaying his plans to join James at Theobalds and stay on in London to resolve the issue, until Prince Charles reminded him that James's happiness was contingent on George's presence—"if you shall not be ready to go with him to Theobalds . . . he can take no pleasure to be there."[4] On March 2, the King and George reunited at Theobalds. James developed a fever on the fourth but was well enough to focus on the foreign policy issues raised by the French demands.[5] He told George that they needed to call France's bluff—either the French abandoned their latest conditions about Catholicism or the English would call the betrothal off. George went back to London to deliver their ultimatum to the French ambassador.

As James rested at Theobalds, a friend from Scotland sent him a book that he thought he might like, but James's eyes had started to hurt and he could no longer take the pleasure he once had in reading. The Master of the Spicery, keymaster of the kitchens, where the most expensive foods were kept, brought the King "strawberries, cherries, and other fruits" to eat, and James's "hand was in the basket" as soon as he saw them.[6] Over the past few months, James's teeth had caused him more pain. Several had rotted and fallen out, and chewing was difficult.

His Captain of the Guard, Sir Thomas Erskine, noticed that James's temperature was rising. James hated the hot stage of the fever, expressing his fury in several foulmouthed rants against the doctors who bothered him. On March 11, his household canceled a scheduled audience with the Venetian ambassador and another with the Bishop of London, who was waiting for the King's signature on several documents pertaining to the Church. Instead, James passed most of that day playing cards with George, who had returned from London. On the fourteenth, the French ambassador sent word that his government would not press their newest conditions. The marriage treaty arrived at Theobalds, in its previously agreed form. James read through it and signed it. George left again and took it back into London.

The next two days were uncomfortable for the King, who became so hot with illness that he ripped off his clothes and dunked his arms into basins of cold water. A courtier wrote to a friend that in the last twenty-four hours James had suffered seven fits of severe fever. On March 18, a London newsletter broke the story to its readers that the King was seriously unwell at Theobalds. James heard about this and joked that it was hardly a glorious death for a king of England to die of a temperature.

His fever broke on the nineteenth, but the respite lasted for only a day. In the small hours of the twentieth, his temperature soared.

Sir Thomas Erskine spent that night at the King's bedside. Nephew of the by then long-dead "Lady Minny" Mar, Erskine had known James since their childhood at Stirling. His brother Archibald had been the teenager killed in the brawl that left an eleven-year-old James ripping out his hair in distress. Erskine had remained in James's service ever since, never wavering in his loyalty to him.[7] He had been present at the Gowrie House raid, when Alexander Ruthven had allegedly tried to kill James, and was one of the men who had helped kick down the door to rescue him. He had captained James's guard for a quarter of a century.

Erskine was one of the few contemporaries still close to James. Others who had known James in his prime were dwindling into the grave or were, like Erskine's cousin Lord Mar, far away in Scotland. Sandy had been dead for almost twenty years. In 1607, he had been killed trying to break up a fight between his brother and a mutual cousin. The latter tried to push past Sandy, who was accidentally struck by his knife and bled to death. He was survived by his wife and three of their four children. His barony of Spynie passed to his son Alexander.

Patrick, by then 6th Lord Gray, had died five years after Sandy, also in Scotland, to where he had returned from his travels, less to reunite with his wife than to care for his father in old age. Patrick and his wife, Mary, also had four children, the eldest of whom inherited the lordship when Patrick died at home in 1612. His two daughters became prominent figures in the Scottish nobility through their respective marriages to the earls of Monteith and Wemyss.

Anne Murray, possibly James's only mistress, had died in 1618. She had a long and happy marriage with Patrick Lyon, with whom she had six children. She had died a countess, after James made her husband the 1st Earl of Kinghorne in 1606, in recognition of his diligence in supporting law and order in Scotland following the Union of the Crowns.

On the morning of March 20, the sun returned to Theobalds and so did George, who moved into the bedchamber next to James's. He brought with him his mother and his family's doctor, Remington, who provided a syrup to ease James's distress. It had the opposite result. James's urine became severely discolored and he suffered repeated dehydrating bouts of diarrhea. This would later nurture the rumor that, via Dr. Remington, George had poisoned James. Keen to preemptively quash any suggestion of foul play, two of George's servants made a point of taking the syrup themselves from the same container and on the same spoon, as did a few of the royal doctors. None suffered any adverse side effects.

However, George had already offended the King's physicians by refusing to let them treat James until he brought in one of his own experts. It was either needless arrogance or callous one-upmanship and, witnessing the impact of Remington's medicine, James's Dr. Craig flew into a rage and accused George or his mother, Mary, of poisoning the King. George was furious and had Craig thrown out of the palace. Erskine, who had come to dislike George, nonetheless defended him in another letter to Lord Mar, explaining that George's reaction was entirely justified—"If I was in his place, I would do so myself, considering what the world says, and I protest I think he gets [done a] great wrong in saying such tales as goes here about him."[8]

Many rumors would subsequently arise from the altercation between George and Dr. Craig, along with attempts to imagine why George of all people would have wanted to see James dead. He had cared for James throughout his illnesses and the suggestion that he poisoned him so he could go to war against Spain strains credulity. However, George did medically contribute to James's suffering.[9] It is likely that James suffered from several maladies at once, most of them linked to his long-term health problems. George had tried his best to ameliorate them over the past few years but, in March 1625, the attempted cure he and Remington had given James instead inflamed the symptoms of his illness. It remains doubtful if James's doctors could have cured him, even without Remington's interference, especially given what passed for a cure at seventeenth-century sickbeds. It may have been that, along with resenting George for bringing in a rival physician, Craig and his colleagues tried to preemptively exculpate themselves by blaming George for malice or for a mistake.

In reality, nearly everyone at Theobalds had realized the situation was serious since sometime around the second week in March and suspected from about the nineteenth that it might prove fatal. The Prince of Wales was sent for.

James had fathered seven children and buried five—Margaret, Robert, Sophia, and Mary as infants, and Henry at the age of eighteen. Dead for six years was their mother, Anna, who despite the tensions in their marriage was in many ways James's greatest ally. In her absence, he had slowly pickled himself with alcohol, while the court became a byword for corruption. Detested for his pacifism and mocked for his private life, James had spent the final years of his life increasingly politically isolated. As his health ebbed away, he made one final gesture of love by pardoning Robert Carr so that nobody could reprosecute the Overbury case once he was gone.

While they waited for Charles to arrive, George stayed at James's bedside, talking to him and trying to distract him from his fever. He was the last of the men James had loved, beginning with Patrick in the late 1580s. Those romances had, like so much of James's life, been haunted by possibilities, chief among them the peace he had always pursued, politically as well as personally. What George VI would later jokingly call "the business of king-ing" had intruded on nearly all James's romances. Nonetheless, he had experienced moments not just of heartbreak and frustration, but also of real happiness. There had been his first love with Sandy and the languid happiness of six years with Robert Carr, before hubris, avarice, mutual recriminations, Thomas Overbury, and Frances Howard caused one of the scandals of the century. There had been a great love with George Villiers, "my own dear sweet wife," although George's ambition will always render difficult a conclusion about how sincere that was for him. James had also experienced the charm of the transient with Philip and possibly with Hay, as well as the rush of intoxication with Patrick and Huntly.

Of them all, Huntly continued as the great survivor, older than James in 1625 and in better health. He was still the principal nobleman in the Highlands, alongside his wife and Esmé's daughter Henrietta. They had four daughters and two sons. James still occasionally sent pardons north when, as he so often had, Huntly crossed the line from controversial to confrontational.

The Prince of Wales arrived at Theobalds on March 21. As he had with his mother six years earlier, Charles sat by his parent's bedside. It was distressing for those with him to witness James gasping for a drink. Nothing seemed to satiate his thirst. James grabbed Charles's hand as his mouth fell open and squeezed the air in a painful, failed attempt to say something to his son. The King had lost the power of speech, and he had likely endured the first in a series of ministrokes.

Two of James's favorites were still alive, but far away. James Hay, Earl of Carlisle, was in Paris, where he served as the English ambassador. Religion and colonialism had come for Philip Herbert, who had not been to court for some time. In his forties, he was no longer the fresh-faced, dimwitted, and cheerful hunter of 1603. He was bearded, sober, serious, still not especially intelligent but certainly a sincerely conscientious Puritan. He was a husband, a father of four, whose sympathies lay with Parliament, and he was a major shareholder in some of the private companies that would soon help pave the British Empire into existence—the Virginia Company, the East India Company, and the Northwest Passage Company.

Letters were sent to the rest of the Privy Council in London and, in the Great Hall, Theobalds's moon voyaged across the artificial night sky that covered the ceiling. James's breathing slowed but endured through March 24, the twenty-second anniversary of his accession to the English and Irish thrones. He suffered a massive stroke that evening, at which point the physicians decided that their duty must yield to that of the clergy. The royal household's clerics filed into the bedchamber, where Archbishop Abbot led them in prayers for the sick from the Church of England's Book of Common Prayer.

"O Lord, look down from Heaven," they intoned, "behold, visit and relieve this Thy servant: Look upon him with the eyes of Thy mercy, give him comfort, and sure confidence in Thee: Defend him from the danger of the Enemy,* and keep him in perpetual peace, and safety: through Jesus Christ Our Lord. Amen. Hear us, Almighty and Most Merciful God and Saviour. Extend

* Temptation by the Devil.

Thy accustomed Goodness to this Thy servant, which is grieved with sickness . . ."

The prayers shifted from those for the sick to those for the dying. One of James's favorite preachers, the Bishop of Lincoln, joined in readings that reminded the fading James that soon he must, like all Christians, stand before God, by "Whom all must be judged without respect of persons:* I require you to examine yourself and your state, both toward God and man . . ." As James ended in bed a life that had begun in violence, different clerics took turns with the prayers: "Through Thee have I been holden up ever since I was born; thou art He that took me out of my mother's womb; my praise shall be of Thee . . ."

Servants rekindled the fires in the bedchamber's marble grate. The artificial moon yielded one final time to the sun in the Great Hall and the prayers in James's bedchamber continued with the dawn: ". . . he passeth from death unto life."

Shortly after sunrise on March 27, 1625, with his son at his side and the sounds of George's sobs nearby, fifty-nine years of life and fifty-eight of kingship ended as James gasped one last time and died. Thomas Erskine wrote to Mar, "He is gone that I have waited on† these fifty years."[10]

---

* Rank.

† Attended, served.

EPILOGUE

James was buried next to Anna at Westminster Abbey on May 7, 1625. The funeral sermon—preached by the Bishop of Lincoln—drew parallels between James and King Solomon, the biblical exemplar of wisdom with whom James had so often been compared by his supporters. His enemies had done so, too, when they wanted to cast aspersions on his paternity with jokes that both kings had been sons of Davids.

Nine months after James's funeral, his son was crowned King Charles I at the abbey. As a Catholic, his new wife, Henrietta Maria of France, absented herself from the Protestant ceremony, thereby unintentionally earning the first of what would become many notches against her in the English public's mind. George remained as powerful under the new reign as he had been in the old. Despite the closeness of their friendship, there were never any suggestions of a sexual connection between him and Charles I.

George's political dominance lasted for three more years until he was killed at an inn in Portsmouth by a knife-wielding soldier who was, like so many of his comrades, aggrieved at his unpaid wages. James had been right—the European war sought by Charles, George, and their allies was an expense that the British states could not afford. He had been likewise correct in guessing that Parliament preferred talking about war to funding it.

George's widow, Katherine, remarried to an Irish aristocrat, died as Marchioness of Antrim during an outbreak of the plague in Ireland in 1649. She was survived by her second husband and by two of her four children from her marriage to George.

After the disaster of his first wars, Charles I pivoted to a less militarist foreign policy. Since he had fallen completely in love with his wife, peace reigned too in his household with no royal mistresses, favorites, bastards, lovers, or rivals. The couple's first child—a short-lived son—was born and died in 1629. Seven siblings arrived over the next fifteen years, five of whom lived past childhood.[1]

In the same year as his first child's birth, King Charles disbanded Parliament and managed to avoid recalling it for eleven years. During that time, court life was ruled with a reverence for etiquette that mirrored how Queen Anna had transmitted the concept of monarchy, as opposed to James's more relaxed, informal—many said, undignified—style of kingship. While Charles had loved his father, he was determined not to behave like him.

In 1635, Charles ordered the Marquess of Huntly's imprisonment at Edinburgh Castle. In his seventies, Huntly had led a raid that torched the estates of a nearby family whom he blamed for the death in a house fire of his son Lord Melgum. Charles kept the elderly marquess as a comfortably confined prisoner for seven months, before permitting his release as his health failed. While still on his journey home to the Highlands, Huntly received the Last Rites from a Catholic priest in the town of Dundee, where he died on June 13, 1636.

Another of James's favorites—James Hay, Earl of Carlisle—died the same year. He suffered a stroke at his home on the Strand in London, several years after retiring from public life. His title passed to his son. His widow, Lucy Hay, Dowager Countess of Carlisle, served as a lady-in-waiting to Queen Henrietta Maria and would become a political figure in the early dramas of the civil war that began in 1642.

Seduced into complacency by a certainty untroubled by fear, Charles I shared James's belief in the Divine Right of Kings, but he had never experienced the dangers that had forced his father to temper his principles with a determination to survive. Despite his intelligence, Charles did not understand Scotland, much less Presbyterianism, in the way James had and his disastrous attempts to make it even more like Anglicanism helped provoke a rebellion in 1638. Not long after, civil war erupted in Ireland, where Charles was far less culpable for the crisis. As King of Ireland, he had inherited a festering situation from his father, as James had from Elizabeth I and Mary I, both of whom had failed to cut the Gordian knot created by Henry VIII's policies.

Civil war* followed in Wales and England, where populist opposition to Catholicism aimed against the Queen mixed explosively with dissatisfaction at the King and support for Parliament. On the other side of the barricades, admiration for the King marched hand in hand with frustration at the perceived obstinacy of the Puritan faction in Parliament. The civil wars split the nation so brutally that they killed a higher percentage of the English and Welsh population than the First World War.

In the chaos, the royal family fled London in 1642 and made Oxford their rival capital city. Taking no part in the war, Robert Carr, Earl of Somerset, died in London in 1645. About sixty years old at the time, Robert had been saved from legal harassment by James's pardon and had faded into the safety of irrelevance, still possessing enough of his former properties to do so comfortably. His wife Frances had predeceased him by thirteen years, likely because of cancer, which killed her in her early forties.[2] They had no more children following their release from the Tower.†

After the Royalists lost the civil wars, Charles I was placed on trial for treason by the victors, who also, for good measure, accused him of poisoning his father in 1625 and his brother Henry in 1612 (when Charles was eleven). Charles behaved with dignity at his trial, as his grandmother Queen Mary had at hers six decades earlier. In a further similarity, Charles's verdict had been decided upon before he set foot in the courtroom. Philip Herbert, who had, in the years since James's death, succeeded his childless brother as earl of Pembroke, sided with Parliament during the civil wars. He had never ceased to hope for a compromise with the monarchy but, like many Parliamentar-

* The era's conflicts have various names in the different parts of the British Isles. Collectively referred to as the Wars of the Three Kingdoms, they are commonly known as the civil wars in England and Wales; the 1641 rebellion, the Eleven Years' War, or the Irish Confederate Wars in Ireland, and the Bishops' War or the civil wars in Scotland.

† Their daughter, Anne (1615–84), married the Earl of Bedford, a match opposed by her future father-in-law, who, having been at court during the Overbury scandal, warned his son against "the dangerous beauty of Anne Carr." Charles I, who did not believe Anne should be punished because of her parents' notoriety, spoke out on her behalf and the marriage, which was a happy one, went ahead in 1637.

ians in 1647–50, he was outmaneuvered by the radicals on his own side. They excused him from the burden of sitting on the panel that condemned James's son to death; however, they required him not to speak out against the sentence, a promise that he both made and kept. He died in his rooms at the Palace of Whitehall on January 23, 1650, almost a year to the day since Charles I's beheading at Whitehall in front of a large crowd outside his father's Banqueting House.

Whitehall and Hampton Court became homes to prominent members of the various republican regimes that ruled between the abolition of the monarchy in 1649 and its restoration in 1660. Most of the royal family had managed to make it out of England alive during the civil wars and they returned in 1660 with Charles I's son Charles II. Among them was the new king's aunt Elizabeth, James's only surviving child, who had last seen London on the day she left as Frederick's bride. She had been a widow for twenty-eight years and, although Charles I had invited her to come home to live as his guest, she had refused; instead she chose to remain in the Netherlands to better pursue her family's attempts to retake their home in the Rhineland, which they achieved in 1649 after the end of the Thirty Years' War. Two of Elizabeth's sons, Rupert and Maurice, had gone to Britain in the 1640s to fight for their uncle during the civil wars. Maurice had been lost at sea in 1652, but Rupert became a prominent figure at the Restoration court.

While Elizabeth had lived long enough to see her dynasties restored in both the Rhineland and the British Isles, she did not survive for very long after the latter. At her new London home of Leicester House, she died of pneumonia on February 13, 1662. The body of the sixty-five-year-old "Winter Queen" was taken to rest near her parents and brother Henry at Westminster Abbey.

Charles II ruled for twenty-three more years. With his olive skin and dark hair, he resembled his mother's family, the House of Bourbon; his personality was more like his paternal grandfather's. Even more so than had James, Charles II had seen what could happen when monarchy failed. He had endured threats to his life and over a decade in exile. He would have preferred to rule as an absolute monarch, but, as with James, it was a preference, not a prerequisite, and Charles II proved a mendacious pragmatist when it came to politics.

How much this was an inherited trait is unknowable. However, it is interesting that the energetically heterosexual Charles II further echoed his grandfather in his refusal to hide his carousel of lovers at court, his generosity to them, and his lack of vindictive spite once a relationship had cooled. As James had with his male favorites, Charles II typically left his female former favorites with titles, estates, good marriages, and incomes. He fathered over a dozen children with his lovers but none with his Portuguese queen, Catherine of Braganza, who stoically endured public criticism of her religion, household, and marriage.

When Charles II died in 1685, he was thus succeeded by his younger brother, who was James II in England and Ireland, and James VII in Scotland. The first Catholic monarch in the family since Mary, Queen of Scots, he lasted three years on the throne until his religion was used as justification for his overthrow. Driven into exile by his Protestant daughter Mary II and her Dutch husband, William of Orange, James VII and II died in exile as a guest of the French royal family. Parliament introduced a law banning non-Anglicans from the throne, which did not prevent two serious attempts to reclaim the crown, led by James VII and II's Catholic son in 1715 and grandson in 1745. The greatest bastion of support for them was in Scotland, which paid a horrific price, especially in the Highlands, for supporting the 1745 rebellion.

Mary II and her husband had no children. Their heir, Queen Anne, had outlived all her children by the time of her death in 1714. The new laws that had mandated a Protestant monarch saw the succession shift from the descendants of James's son Charles I to that of his daughter. Elizabeth and Frederick's grandson, George, Elector of Hanover, was proclaimed King George I.* It is through

---

* Since the eighteenth century, the numbering of British monarchs has changed. The protocol is now that if a monarch's name has historically been used before in any part of the British Isles, the highest numbering will be used as their only regnal number. Hence why the late Queen Elizabeth (d. 2022) was Elizabeth II throughout the United Kingdom, despite the fact that Scotland had never had a reigning queen Elizabeth before. Likewise, if there is another King James in the future, he will reign as King James VIII, because, although most parts of the UK have only had two kings James, Scotland has had seven and the highest number henceforth takes priority.

him, and Elizabeth "the Winter Queen," that the current British royal family directly descends from James and Anna.

James's remains still rest with his wife's at Westminster Abbey, as do those of four of their seven children—Henry, Elizabeth, Mary, and Sophia. In the centuries since his death, James's reign has been appreciated as one of the most important in British history. Without James, Britain as a nation might not have come into being, even though he failed to achieve a political, as opposed to a dynastic, union during his lifetime. The Jacobean era was culturally rich, politically fraught, diplomatically difficult, and socially explosive. As such, it continues to provoke debate, as does the king whose name was given to the era.

For his role in the King James or Authorized Version of the Bible, James has been admired by many Protestant historians, for whom the details of his private life can sometimes prove vexatious. The legacies of his American policy or lack thereof, his unionism, and his Irish policy, particularly in the northern province of Ulster, remain controversial. Among scholars, there has been great debate over how much culpability James shares for encouraging or, at the very least, facilitating, the increase in witch hunts in late sixteenth-century Scotland and early seventeenth-century England. In political and constitutional history, disagreement continues over whether he should be viewed as either prologue or rebuttal to Charles I. Did James fatally inculcate his son with ideological beliefs that made compromise with the English Parliament impossible and thus sowed the seeds of the civil war? Or does James's ability to avoid civil war, despite his antagonistic relations with Parliament, prove that it was possible for a king of England to disagree with Parliament without it degenerating into civil strife, and that the blame for what happened in the 1640s thus rests squarely on Charles I's shoulders? A few historians have posited a third view, in which James—through his extravagance, political belligerence, lack of dignity, and failure to control the scandals at his English court—bequeathed to Charles I a monarchy on the precipice of catastrophe and that Charles should not so much be indicted for the war but instead commended for staving it off for as long as he did.

In attempting to understand James VI and I as "a particular man," as he once described himself in a letter to Lord Huntly, the portrait that emerges is of a fascinating, complicated, and often difficult man. He was a precocious and sensitive child—it is hard not to flinch when reading of how he was treated by George Buchanan—who became a terrified teenager, desperate for affection and guidance, yet was instead surrounded by the constant threat of kidnapping, which often materialized into reality. He grew into a strong, intelligent, healthy, and determined adult who crushed the threats against him. He toured his soldiers' firesides on the eve of battle, crossed the sea and snow to rescue his wife, and held the government of his kingdom together in the face of significant challenges.

He was deeply flawed—a hypocrite, a genius, a liar, a loyal friend, a pedant, a loving father, a spendthrift, and a man who was capable of great vindictiveness and great kindness. In the last two decades of his life, alcohol and fear wrapped themselves around him, sapping his energies and blunting his intelligence. While there were flashes of wit and intellect almost until the end, James became too dependent on his favorites, and too indifferent to public opinion. Yet unlike either of his parents or his successor, James died in power and in his bed, with his son at his side and a man he loved in the same room.

Of all the many threads to James's personality, perhaps the one that ran through his adult life was the trait first noticed when he was eighteen by the diplomat Albert Fontenay, who wrote that James VI "loves indiscreetly and obstinately, despite the disapprobation of his subjects."[3]

APPENDIX

Terminology and deciphering evidence of intimacy

This appendix will clarify the terminology that is currently preferred in academic discourse on same-sex intimacy in early modern Europe and that which I have used in this book. It will also clarify how witchcraft was discussed, designations like British, Scottish, English, Irish, and Welsh, and what criteria for intimacy were established for ascertaining which of James VI's fifteen alleged lovers can credibly be identified as his sexual or romantic partners.

Bisexuality, heterosexuality, and homosexuality as terms for human sexual-romantic attraction did not originate until the 1860s. They were initially utilized as psychological or psychosexual terms. Their applicability as three broad categories of sexual attraction were expanded upon later, most notably by the Kinsey Scale in the mid-twentieth century, which posited that sexuality could better be understood as a spectrum that also incorporated asexuality. Over the course of the latter half of the twentieth century and the first two decades of the twenty-first, these labels came to be associated with a sociopolitical civil rights movement, especially and initially homosexuality, then latterly bisexuality and asexuality. Some elements of that movement subsequently campaigned in conjunction with issues pertaining to transgenderism, intersex individuals, and those without exclusively heterosexual impulses, desires, and romantic feelings. Over the course of their existence, various names have been attached to these movements. Most relevant in the study of historical cases of homosexual intimacy is the nomenclature associated with gay rights, particularly two English language terms—"homosexual" and "gay"—as the most popular to describe same-sex love and acts of same-sex sexual intimacy.

At the same time as the gay rights movement gained momentum in Western society, an academic subculture emerged in some universities that sought to engage with the experiences of the historically marginalized, silenced, ignored, or oppressed. This subculture yielded important studies, which in their turn helped move the subject into the mainstream of academia and, from there, far more slowly, into popular history. Today, this remains a rich field of academic research, which takes seriously the lexicon of its subject.

Among academic researchers of the history of male same-sex intimacy, the preferred term to use today is "sodomy." This is partly in deference to the fact that sodomy was the term used most frequently in the early modern period. Its use is also justified on the grounds that it separates the discipline from any cultural associations accrued by "homosexual" and "gay" in the late twentieth century and early twenty-first century. "Sodomy," like "buggery," pertains to a biological-erotic act. "Homosexual" and "gay" potentially carry with them unhelpful modern cultural expectations or stereotypes of a certain kind of personality or life experience, mannerisms or romantic aspirations, which an early modern practitioner of homosexual sex could not possibly have understood, nor be expected to have shared.

I understand why such a conclusion has been reached. However, I have demurred from it in this book. The multiplicity of moral implications sodomy had in early modern western Europe means that, for a book focused on the private life of one man, it seemed better to use "sodomy" only when describing specific contemporary reactions to it. While I appreciate that there are concerns regarding cultural expectations associated with words like "gay," the term "sodomy" is one that also carries with it many connotations for most modern readers.

I felt comfortable using "homosexual" as my preferred term to describe instances in which I believe James had sex with another man. If pushed, I think I would describe James as bisexual with a strong preference for his own gender. While I appreciate the point that the vocabulary of homosexuality, heterosexuality, bisexuality, and asexuality emerged in the nineteenth and twentieth centuries, and that they therefore do not belong in any description of a seventeenth-century man, they do however describe an eternal reality and history is, inevitably, the story of the past written with the words of the present. Otherwise, the entirety of this book would be in early modern Scots and early modern English, with a sprinkling of sixteenth-century Danish, Gaelic, Irish, Norn, and Norwegian.

On the subject of using modern vocabulary to describe the past, my instinct is that James VI probably had attention deficit hyperactivity disorder (ADHD). In the main body of this book, I have quoted from contemporary accounts describing his behavior to allow the reader to make up their own mind. At the distance of four centuries, it is impossible to know. Similarly, I think much of James's later behavior bears many of the hallmarks associated with post-traumatic stress disorder (PTSD) from what he endured, not only in his youth but also in adulthood through the Raid of Ruthven, the Gowrie House conspiracy, and the Gunpowder Plot. There, too, however, I decided to leave that as a conclusion for readers to reach or reject themselves, based on the words of James and his contemporaries—as I have with the problems caused by his later relationship with alcohol.

The history of witchcraft and folklore constitutes another rich field of study. I have explained the cultural and socioeconomic milieu in which the North Berwick witch trials incubated. However, I have avoided trying to explain why the testimonies contained the claims that they did. As various fascinating attempts have shown in trying to explain France's Affair of the Poisons (1679–82), the Salem witch trials in Massachusetts (1692–93), or the central European vampire hunts (1730–35), it is not always possible to define with precision what was happening in moments of mass hysteria or paranoia. Broadly speaking, it seems that a lie is taken for truth and many more conclusions are then built on top of it. The specifics of what happens in each case of mass panic or mass speculation differ. Rather than ask an answerless question, I have attempted to portray it as its phenomena appeared to its perpetrators and, where possible, to its victims. I think we can make educated guesses about what kind of man David Seton was to have done what he and his son did to Geillis Duncan, why phenomena like the tempests of 1590 frightened even experienced navigators like Peder Munk, and why Geillis Duncan, Agnes Sampson, and so many others gave their testimonies. My instinct is that the psychology of false confessions, particularly as they pertain to the victims of torture, would likely offer the best explanation as to why Sampson in particular said what she did, when she said it, and the depth of detail she continued to provide, even after physical torture was no longer inflicted upon her. Even that, however, is, and must remain, speculative. We do not know what precisely Agnes Sampson told James VI that convinced him that she was a witch. We do not know what people saw in the dark, the storm, the prison cells, or by candlelight that convinced them, too, that the Devil was walking among them. James VI evidently believed in witchcraft, specifically as a malignant force, as did many of his contemporaries.

Outside quotations, I have used the word "coven" when describing a collective of alleged witches, which, like "homosexuality," is a later term. In the case of coven, it seems to have entered popular use in the mid-seventeenth century.

Unless specified to the contrary, the term "British" is used here geographically, rather than politically. Although James hoped for a political rather than dynastic union between his kingdoms, that did not occur until the two acts of Union, respectively in 1707 (England and Wales, with Scotland, into Great Britain) and in 1800 (Great Britain with Ireland, into the United Kingdom).

The term "north Irish" is used here when referring to the Earl of Tyrone, the Earl of Tyrconnell, the Flight of the Earls in 1607, and the Jacobean plantations of Ulster. I have avoided "Northern Irish" or "northern Irish" in that context, since those terms, especially the former with both initial letters capitalized, have political connotations following the creation of Northern Ireland in 1921. It also functions in current political language as a preferred nationality for some citizens of Northern Ireland, following the Good Friday Peace Agreement in 1998.*

All other national terms—chiefly Scottish, Welsh, English, and Irish—are used in either a geographical or political/national way throughout.

Establishing the criteria of homosexual intimacy in history is complicated by two factors, one modern and one contemporary. The former is a suspicion that any such history is inextricably

* Also known as the Belfast Agreement.

tied to a political agenda, which may lead the author to ignore or inflate evidence to fit their point. I sincerely hope I have not done so here.

The second difficulty is that, of necessity, many same-sex love affairs in history set out to obfuscate themselves. Perhaps the most remarkable fact about studying James VI and I's private life is that there is, comparatively, such an abundance of evidence. This, of course, is because of the position James occupied, which rendered his loves important, as well as more difficult to hide. As both he and his predecessor in England, Elizabeth I, noted, monarchs were set on a stage for the world to watch as their audience.

The consequences of these two difficulties are simultaneously contradictory and interwoven with one another. An excess of caution, or suspicion, has meant that at times an impossible standard of proof seems to be required before historians are permitted to describe a historical relationship as homosexual. Yet Mary Boleyn, for instance, is described as one of Henry VIII of England's mistresses based on little more than a few sentences—one being a comment made by a Catholic prior who had never come to court and the other being a Member of Parliament. There are no letters between Henry and Mary, we do not have a firm date bracket for the liaison, there are no surviving specific mentions of their affair that we know of by any member of their families, nor even an acknowledgment by a mutual acquaintance, except one—Thomas Cromwell, 1st Earl of Essex—who stated that the affair had not happened. Many believe Cromwell was lying, but the fact stands that far less specific evidence remains for that, and for dozens of other alleged royal affairs, than we have for James VI's feelings toward the 1st Lord Spynie or the 6th Earl, later the 1st Marquess, of Huntly. Equally, when it comes to queens or empresses taking male lovers, we do not require firm evidence of sexual contact. Instead, we use things like terms of endearment in letters, time spent together, and common sense. In writing about James's private life, I have highlighted where the language used was tellingly atypical and often with an erotic subtext, in the cases of James's romances in the mid-1580s and early 1600s, and I have done the same for his relationships in the late 1580s, 1610s, and 1620s, in conjunction with the comparatively more substantial documentary paper trail that fortunately survives from those relationships.

It is equally important, however, not to fall into the trap of assuming that every friendship was a camouflaged romance. There are publications that justify the modern skepticism about individuals' romantic lives or friendships being written about with an indifference to context—among the most memorable of which is the example referenced in the endnotes of Richard the Lionheart's alleged love affair with King Philippe II of France.

While most of James's modern biographers believe that he had homosexual relationships, there is less consensus as to the identities of his lovers. Of James VI and I's fifteen named alleged sexual partners, there are three of whom, I believe, we can be all but certain—Anna of Denmark, Robert Carr, 1st Earl of Somerset, and George Villiers, 1st Duke of Buckingham. The caveat exists here only because of the philosophical difficulties posed by obtaining absolute certainty, rather than because of any logically justifiable doubt. Queen Anna did not likely find alternative fathers for her seven children and the intimate letters from James's relationships with Somerset and Buckingham make sense only when read as romantic or erotic.

There are three partners—Patrick Gray, 6th Lord Gray; Alexander Lindsay, 1st Lord Spynie; and Anne Murray, Countess of Kinghorne—for whom, to my mind, the evidence is less specific, but which, in its cumulative if circumstantial form, makes a romantic and/or sexual relationship overwhelmingly the most persuasive conclusion and the alternatives implausible.

I do not think there are reasonable grounds for doubting that James had strong feelings for George Gordon, 6th Earl, and later 1st Marquess, of Huntly, and that those feelings, which often led him to behave unwisely with Huntly, were romantic or sexual, particularly in 1587–88. How Huntly felt and how far he went in his response is less clear, but the surviving evidence strongly suggests that he encouraged, and possibly reciprocated, James's interest. Whatever the truth of their dynamic, it was one with significant political consequences and one that evolved over the years.

I think James was sleeping with somebody in the early years of his English reign (1603–7), possibly more than one person. James Hay was deliberately recruited by the Cecil faction, who hoped to use his good looks to their advantage. Beyond that, all that we can be certain of is that James was attracted to, and close with, two men in his entourage—Philip Herbert, 4th Earl of Pembroke and 1st Earl of Montgomery, and James Hay, 1st Earl of Carlisle. I think the evidence for both candidates being the King's lovers is more substantial than I first gave credence to when I started working on this book.

The mystery surrounding the death of Alexander Ruthven, Master of Ruthven, extends to his relationship with James. I think Ruthven's actions on the day he died, principally in taking James off on his own and locking the doors as they went, and James's acceptance of that, indicate either that they had established, or James thought they were about to establish, a physically intimate relationship. However, a conclusion as to their relationship rests on a conclusion about what happened in the tower just before Ruthven was killed, and that remains one of the great mysteries of Scottish history.

The evidence we have for a relationship between James and Richard Preston, 1st Earl of Desmond, seems to me to weigh on the unlikely side of possible. The four whom I would argue have been misidentified as having sexual contact with King James are Esmé Stuart, 1st Duke of Lennox, Euphemia Douglas, Mistress of Glamis, John Ramsay, 1st Earl of Holderness, and Sir Arthur Brett.

The lexicon I have employed for this telling of James's story will not please every reader. In a topic such as this, it seems unlikely that anything ever will. However, if we were to stand on the edge waiting for the perfect vocabulary that offended no one, I doubt stories like this would ever be told. I might be biased having spent so much time studying James and his world, but it seems to me that would be a great shame.

DRAMATIS PERSONAE

This list includes some of the prominent figures in James's life, including those with multiple titles, with their names CAPITALIZED showing how they were most often referred to in the text.

JAMES VI, King of Scots and later James I, King of England and Ireland

JAMES'S FAMILY

ANNA of Denmark, his wife, Queen of Scots and later Queen of England and Ireland

MARY, Queen of Scots, his mother

DARNLEY—James's father Henry Stuart, Duke of Albany, Earl of Ross, Lord Darnley

James Hepburn, 4th Earl of BOTHWELL, James's stepfather

ESMÉ Stuart, 1st Duke of Lennox, Lord Darnley's cousin

THE DOWAGER COUNTESS OF LENNOX—James's paternal grandmother, Margaret Douglas

MARCH—James's great-uncle Robert Stewart, former Bishop of Caithness, then Earl of Lennox and finally 1st Earl of March

LADY ARBELLA STUART, James's English cousin on his father's side

CHRISTIAN IV, King of Denmark and Norway, James's brother-in-law

JAMES'S CHILDREN—*Henry, Elizabeth, Margaret, Charles, Robert, Mary, Sophia*

HENRIETTA, COUNTESS OF HUNTLY—Henrietta Stuart, later Marchioness of Huntly. James's second cousin, daughter of Esmé Stuart, 1st Duke of Lennox, married to Huntly.

LUDOVIC Stuart, 2nd Duke of Lennox, James's second cousin and eldest son of Esmé Stuart, 1st Duke of Lennox, served in various roles as a prominent adviser to James. From 1583 to 1594, heir presumptive to the Scottish throne.

JAMES'S FAVORITES

PATRICK Gray, Master of Gray, later 6th Lord Gray

HUNTLY—George Gordon, 6th Earl, and later 1st Marquess, of Huntly

SANDY—Alexander Lindsay, 1st Lord Spynie

ALEXANDER Ruthven, Master of Ruthven

PHILIP—Lord Philip Herbert, later 4th Earl of Pembroke and 1st Earl of Montgomery

HAY—Sir James Hay, later 1st Earl of Carlisle

ROBERT Carr, later 1st Earl of Somerset

GEORGE Villiers, later 1st Duke of Buckingham

JAMES'S REGENTS

MORAY—James Stewart, 1st Earl of Moray, James's uncle and first regent

LENNOX—Matthew Stuart, 4th Earl of Lennox, James's grandfather and second regent

MAR—John Erskine, 17th Earl of Mar, James's childhood guardian and third regent

MORTON—James Douglas, 4th Earl of Morton, James's kinsman and fourth regent

AT STIRLING

The DOWAGER COUNTESS OF MAR, James's governess—nicknamed "Lady Minny," Annabella Murray, Lady Mar

SIR ALEXANDER ERSKINE, James's childhood governor—Annabella's brother-in-law and the 18th Earl of Mar's uncle

DRUMQUHASSLE, Master of the Household—John Cunningham, Laird of Drumquhassle

MAR—John Erskine, 18th Earl of Mar, James's schoolroom companion, later Governor of Prince Henry and a Privy Councillor

TULLIBARDINE, Comptroller of the Household—Sir William Murray of Tullibardine, Annabella's brother

LORD GLAMIS, Treasurer of the Household—John Lyon, 8th Lord Glamis (d. 1578)

JAMES'S TUTORS—*George Buchanan, Peter Young, Adam Erskine, David Erskine*

AT THE SCOTTISH COURT

ANNE MURRAY of Tullibardine—James's alleged mistress, a lady-in-waiting to Queen Anna, later Lady Glamis and Countess of Kinghorne

ARRAN, *previously* CAPTAIN STEWART—James Stewart, Earl of Arran, Captain of James's Guard, later a councillor and Lord Chancellor of Scotland (1584–86)

BOTHWELL—Francis Stewart, 5th Earl of Bothwell, James's cousin, and Lord High Admiral of Scotland

CAPTAIN STEWART *see* Arran

EUPHEMIA DOUGLAS—another alleged mistress of James, a lady-in-waiting to Queen Anna, subsequently Mistress of Glamis

GOWRIE—before 1584, William Ruthven, 1st Earl of Gowrie, leader of the Raid of Ruthven coup

GOWRIE—after 1588, John Ruthven, 3rd Earl of Gowrie, son of the 1st Earl of Gowrie, brother of the 2nd Earl of Gowrie and of James's favorite Alexander Ruthven, Master of Ruthven

MAITLAND—John Maitland, 1st Lord Maitland of Thirlestane, Lord Chancellor of Scotland (1586–95)

MELVILL—Andrew Melvill, theologian and Moderator of the Presbyterian General Assembly (sometimes spelled *Melville)*

SIR JAMES MELVILLE, courtier, diplomat, and memoirist

MONTROSE—John Graham, 3rd Earl of Montrose, Treasurer and later Lord Chancellor of Scotland (1599–1604)

SIR THOMAS LYON, Master of Glamis, later Captain of James's Guard, and Treasurer

THE "BONNY" EARL OF MORAY—James Stewart, 2nd Earl of Moray, Queen Anna's alleged lover

THOMAS FOWLER, English lawyer and spy

AT THE COURT OF ELIZABETH I

ELIZABETH I, Queen of England and Ireland

BURGHLEY—William Cecil, 1st Baron Burghley, Elizabeth's chief minister

SIR FRANCIS WALSINGHAM, diplomat, councillor, and Elizabeth's spymaster

LEICESTER—Robert Dudley, 1st Earl of Leicester, Elizabeth's favorite

SIR ROBERT CAREY, courtier, grandson of Elizabeth's maternal aunt

EDWARD SEYMOUR, Lord Beauchamp, son of Elizabeth's kinswoman Lady Katherine Grey

AT JAMES'S COURT IN ENGLAND

ARCHBISHOP ABBOT—George Abbot, Archbishop of Canterbury (1611–33)

ESSEX—Robert Devereux, 3rd Earl of Essex, Puritan-supporting nobleman and Frances Howard's first husband. Son of the previous earl, who was executed for treason against Elizabeth I

FRANCES HOWARD—countess, first of Essex and then of Somerset. Prominent courtier and Robert Carr's wife

THE COUNTESS OF SUFFOLK—Catherine Howard (née Knyvett), Countess of Suffolk, lady-in-waiting to Queen Anna, mother of Frances Howard

TYRONE—Hugh O'Neill, 1st Earl of Tyrone, most prominent nobleman in the north of Ireland. Also known as The O'Neill, Ó Néill Mór, or Chief of the Name. From 1593 to 1603, leader of the Irish uprising against Elizabeth I

TYRCONNELL—Rory O'Donnell, 1st Earl of Tyrconnell. Irish nobleman and Tyrone's ally

MARY Compton (prev. Rayner, prev. Villiers, née Beaumont)—mother of George Villiers, 1st Duke of Buckingham. From 1618 to 1632, Countess of Buckingham in her own right

OVERBURY—Sir Thomas Overbury, diplomat, confidant, friend, and possible lover of Robert Carr

RAMSAY—Sir John Ramsay, Gentleman of the Bedchamber, later 1st Earl of Holderness, killer of Alexander Ruthven

RICHARD Preston, Gentleman of the Privy Chamber, later 1st Earl of Desmond

SIR EDWARD COKE, Attorney General for England and Wales (1594–1606) and Lord Chief Justice (1613–16)

SIR FRANCIS BACON, writer, philosopher, courtier, Attorney General for England and Wales (1613–17), Lord Chancellor of England (1617–21), later 1st Viscount St. Albans

SIR ROBERT CECIL, son of Elizabeth I's Lord Burghley, James's chief adviser, later 1st Earl of Salisbury

SIR ROGER WILBRAHAM, prominent English lawyer, courtier, and memoirist, Solicitor-General for Ireland (1586–1603)

LORD SUFFOLK—Thomas Howard, 1st Earl of Suffolk, prominent member of the Howard faction, held various court offices, including Lord High Treasurer (1614–18). Robert Carr's father-in-law.

ACKNOWLEDGMENTS

My first thanks are to Elizabeth Fremantle, who, during a weekend at mutual friends', suggested that I write a book about King James and the men he loved.

Since that encouragement, I have received much more, especially from my editors, Arabella Pike and Peter Borland. Their advice and support were invaluable. I remain very grateful for it, as well as to those in London and New York who worked on publishing this book.

My thanks to the staff at the Bodleian Library in Oxford, British History Tours, the Church of the Holy Rude in Stirling, Harvington Hall, Historic Environment Scotland, particularly at Stirling Castle, Historic Royal Palaces, the National Archives, the National Library of Scotland, the Royal Collection Trust, Saint Giles's Cathedral in Edinburgh, Stirling District Tourism, Worcester Cathedral Library and Archives, and the Yale Center for British Art.

The friends, colleagues, and loved ones to whom I owe thanks are Tracy Borman, Alastair Bruce, Georgina Capel, James Davis, Allan Davison, Karey Draper, Iain Dupont, Lynsey and Ryan Egan, Owen Emmerson, David Fletcher, Steve Gove, Steve Gunn, Alfred Hawkins, Laura and Tom Hunniwood, DJ Kim, Philippa Lacey, Leanda and Peter de Lisle, Micheál Ó Siochrú, Joanne Sayers, Antonia and Archie Sebag-Montefiore, Sarah Slater, Alexa Reid Smith, Lesley and Gareth Smith, Mari Sveistrup, and Emma Taylor.

This book is dedicated to Brettne Bloom, ten years after we first met through a mutual acquaintance at a Greek restaurant in Manhattan. I hope it conveys some small measure of how much I have cherished those past ten years of working together and the friendship that has grown from them.

Gareth Russell
Portballintrae, Northern Ireland
Christmas 2024

NOTES

Abbreviations

Cal. S.P., Dom.—Mary Anne Everett Green (ed.), *Calendar of State Papers Domestic: James I* (London: Her Majesty's Stationery Office, 1857–59)

Cal. S.P., Scot.—Joseph Bain et al (eds.), *Calendar of State Papers, Scotland* (London and Edinburgh: Her and His Majesty's Stationery Offices, 1898–1936)

Cal. S.P., Simancas—Martin A. S. Hume (ed.), *Calendar of State Papers, Spain (Simancas)* (London: Her Majesty's Stationery Office, 1892–99)

Cal. S.P., Span.—G. A. Bergenroth et al (eds.), *Calendar of State Papers, Spain* (London: Her and His Majesty's Stationery Offices, 1862–1954)

Cal. S.P., Ven.—Rawdon Brown et al (eds.), *Calendar of State Papers Relating to English Affairs in the Archives of Venice* (London: Her and His Majesty's Stationery Offices, 1864–1947)

Cal. S.P., Foreign—William B. Turnball et al. (eds.), *Calendar of State Papers Foreign* (London: Her and His Majesty's Stationery Offices, 1861–1950)

GD—Private Papers in the National Records of Scotland

HMC Bath—Historical Manuscripts Commission, with Marjorie Blatcher (ed. and intro.), *Calendar of the manuscripts of the Marquis of Bath, preserved at Longleat, Wiltshire, 1532–1686* (London: Her Majesty's Stationery Office, 1968)

HMC Buccleuch—Historical Manuscripts Commission, *Report on the manuscripts of the Duke of Buccleuch and Queensberry, K.G., K.T., preserved at Montagu House, Whitehall* (London: Her and His Majesty's Stationery Offices, 1899–1926)

HMC Mar and Kellie—Historical Manuscripts Commission, with Henry Paton (ed.), *Report on the Manuscripts of the Earls of Mar and Kellie* (London: His Majesty's Stationery Office, 1904–1930)

HMC Salisbury—Historical Manuscripts Commission, with R. A. Roberts et al. (eds.), *Calendar of the manuscripts of the Most Honourable the Marquess of Salisbury preserved at Hatfield House, Hertfordshire* (London: Her and His Majesty's Stationery Offices, 1883–1976)

LP—J. S. Brewer et al. (eds.), *Letters and Papers, Foreign and Domestic, of the Reign of Henry VIII: preserved in the Public Record Office, the*

British Museum, and elsewhere in England (London: Her and His Majesty's Stationery Offices, 1862–1932)

ODNB—Lawrence Goldman et al. (eds.), *Oxford Dictionary of National Biography* (Oxford: Oxford University Press, 2004)

OED—John A. Simpson and Edmund S. C. Weinger (eds.), *The Oxford English Dictionary*, second edition (Oxford: Oxford University Press, 1989)

RCIN—Royal Collection Identification Number

SP—State Papers in the National Archives

AUTHOR'S NOTE

1. SP 52/43/15.
2. Robert Ashton (ed. and intro.), *James I by his Contemporaries* (London: Hutchinson & Co., 1969), p. 122.
3. The primary exception is the man who served as Lord Chancellor of Scotland from 1584 to 1586. He is referred to in Chapter 3 by his military title of Captain Stewart and, in later chapters, as the Earl of Arran, the title he acquired from James VI in 1581.
4. See Antonia Fraser, *King James VI of Scotland and I of England* (London: Morrison and Gibb, 1974); Neil Cuddy, "The Revival of the Entourage: The Bedchamber of James I, 1603–1625" in David Starkey (ed.), *The English Court from the Wars of the Roses to the Civil War* (London: Longman, 1987), pp. 214–15; Roger Lockyer, *James VI and I* (London and New York: Longman, 1998); Pauline Croft, *King James* (Houndmills and New York: Palgrave Macmillan, 2003); Alan Stewart, *The Cradle King: A Life of James VI and I* (London: Chatto & Windus, 2003); John Matusiak, *James I: Scotland's King of England* (Stroud: The History Press, 2018); Andrea Zuvich, *Sex and Sexuality in Stuart Britain* (Stroud: Pen & Sword, 2020), and Steven Veerapen, *The Wisest Fool: The Lavish Life of James VI and I* (Edinburgh: Birlinn, 2023). The latter, pp. 108–9, offers an excellent discussion of the king's homosocial, homoerotic, and bisexual behaviors. For a thorough exploration of James's Scottish relationships through their political and dynastic consequences, see Steven J. Reid, *The Early Life of James VI: A Long Apprenticeship, 1566–1585* (Edinburgh: John Donald, 2023) and Alexander Courtney, *James VI, Britannic Prince: King of Scots and Elizabeth's Heir, 1566–1603* (London and New York: Routledge, 2024).
5. See David H. Wilson, *King James VI and I* (Oxford: Oxford University Press, 1967) and Maurice Lee Jr., *Great Britain's Solomon: King James VI and I in his Three Kingdoms* (Champaign: University of Illinois Press, 1990).

PROLOGUE

1. David M. Bergeron, *King James and Letters of Homoerotic Desire* (Iowa City: University of Iowa Press, 1991), p. 175.
2. He was George Villiers, 1st Baron Villiers (1616–17).
3. John Hacket, *Scrinia Reserata: A Memorial Offer'd to the Great Deservings of John Williams* (London: Edw. Jones, 1693), p. 123.
4. Godfrey Goodman, Bishop of Gloucester, *The Court of King James the First* (London: Richard Bentley, 1839), I, pp. 225–26.
5. HMC Bath, ii, p. 71.
6. Patrick Fraser Tytler, *A History of Scotland* (Edinburgh: William Tait, 1843), VIII, p. 197.
7. Ashton, *James I by his Contemporaries,* p. 2.
8. Thomas Barlow, Bishop of Lincoln, and Sir Everard Digby, *The Gunpowder-treason with a discourse of the manner of its discovery, and a perfect relation of the proceedings against those horrid conspirators, wherein is contained their examinations, tryals, and condemnations* (London: Tho. Newcomb and H. Hills, 1679), p. 3.

1: A BONNY SON

1. David Tweedie, *David Rizzio and Mary Queen of Scots: Murder at Holyrood* (Stroud: Sutton, 2006), p. 140.
2. Jayne Elizabeth Lewis, *Mary Queen of Scots: Romance and Nation* (London and New York: Routledge, 1998), p. 27.
3. Sir James Melville, with Gordon Donaldson (ed. and intro.), *The Memoirs of Sir James Melville of Halhill* (London: The Folio Society, 1969), pp. 43–44.
4. Melville, *Memoirs,* p. 44.
5. Tweedie, *David Rizzio and Mary Queen of Scots,* p. 143.
6. James Melville of Halhill (1535–1617), an invaluable eyewitness through his memoirs of the Stewart court under Mary and James VI. He was knighted at Anna of Denmark's coronation (1590), but as he appears in this text often, on either side of his knighthood, and is most frequently referred to in history as Sir James, I have referred to him as Sir James Melville throughout.
7. Melville, *Memoirs,* p. 44.
8. Melville, *Memoirs,* p. 51.
9. John Guy, *My Heart Is My Own: The Life of Mary Queen of Scots* (London: Harper Perennial, 2004), p. 249.
10. Melville, *Memoirs,* p. 52.
11. Tweedie, *David Rizzio and Mary Queen of Scots,* p. 142.
12. Tweedie, *David Rizzio and Mary Queen of Scots,* p. 143.

13. Guy, *My Heart Is My Own,* p. 252.
14. Melville, *Memoirs,* p. 52.
15. Melville, *Memoirs,* p. 52.
16. Claude Nau, and J. Stevenson (ed.), *Memorials of Mary Stewart* (Edinburgh: W. Paterson, 1883), p. 31.
17. Nau, *Memorials of Mary Stewart,* p. 31.
18. Matusiak, *James I,* p. 7.
19. John Maxwell, 4th Lord Herries, and Robert Pitcairn (ed.), *Historical Memoirs of the Reign of Mary, Queen of Scots, and a portion of the reign of King James the Sixth* (Edinburgh: Abbotsford Club, 1836), p. 79.
20. James Mackay, *In the End Is My Beginning: A Life of Mary Queen of Scots* (Edinburgh and London: Mainstream, 1998), p. 162.
21. Herries, *Historical Memoirs,* p. 79.
22. Stewart, *Cradle King,* pp. 15–16.
23. Caroline Bingham, *The Making of a King: The Early Years of James VI and I* (London: Collins, 1968), p. 28.
24. Mackay, *In the End Is My Beginning,* p. 186.
25. Mackay, *In the End Is My Beginning,* p. 187.
26. Cal. S.P., Span., I, 620.
27. Cal. S.P., Foreign, VIII, 185.
28. Jamie Cameron (post.), with Norman Macdougall (ed.), *James V: The Personal Rule, 1528–42* (East Linton: Tuckwell Press, 1998), p. 325.
29. Jane Dunn, *Elizabeth and Mary* (London: HarperCollins, 2003), p. 14.
30. Leonie Frieda, *Catherine de Medici* (London: Weidenfeld & Nicolson, 2003), pp. 127–28, 153–54.
31. Samuel Haynes (ed.), *A Collection of State Papers, Relating to Affairs in the Reigns of King Henry VIII, King Edward VI, Queen Mary and Queen Elizabeth: From the year 1542 to 1570* (London: Bowyer, 1740), p. 511.
32. Herries, *Historical Memoirs,* p. 74; Caroline Bingham, *James VI of Scotland* (London: Weidenfeld & Nicolson, 1979), pp. 7–8.
33. Cal. S.P., Span., I, 638.
34. Cal. S.P., Span., I, 638.
35. Cal. S.P., Foreign, VIII, 215.
36. Antonia Fraser, *Mary Queen of Scots* (London: Ebenezer Baylis and Son, 1969), p. 316.
37. Nau, *Memorials of Mary Stewart,* p. 163.
38. Melville, *Memoirs,* p. 149.
39. Cal. S.P., Scot., II, 322.
40. Dunn, *Elizabeth and Mary,* p. 363.

41. Fraser, *Mary Queen of Scots,* p. 315.
42. Fraser, *Mary Queen of Scots,* p. 316.
43. This is the interpretation favored in Guy, *My Heart Is My Own,* pp. 328–30.
44. The difficulty in navigating the evidence that remains from 1567 is shown by the division among modern historians who have written at length about Mary's career. James Mackay, Julian Goodare, Alison Weir, Retha Warnicke, Linda Porter, and Kate Williams broadly or entirely conclude that Mary was the victim of abduction and coercion. See Mackay, *In the End Is My Beginning,* pp. 201–3; Julian Goodare, "Mary [Mary Stewart], ODNB, XXXVII, pp. 84–85; Alison Weir, *Mary Queen of Scots and the Murder of Lord Darnley* (London: Jonathan Cape, 2003), pp. 351–57; Retha M. Warnicke, *Mary Queen of Scots* (London and New York: Routledge, 2006), pp. 153–54; Linda Porter, *Crown of Thistles: The Fatal Inheritance of Mary Queen of Scots* (London: Macmillan, 2013), pp. 449–51; Kate Williams, *Rival Queens: The Betrayal of Mary, Queen of Scots* (London: Cornerstone, 2018), pp. 202–7. In contrast, Antonia Fraser, Jenny Wormald, John Guy, and Jane Dunn query some, or all, of the official version of events in which Mary was coerced, abducted, or assaulted. See Fraser, *Mary Queen of Scots,* pp. 315–16; Jenny Wormald, *Mary Queen of Scots: A Study in Failure* (London: George Philip, 1988), pp. 163–64; Guy, *My Heart Is My Own,* pp. 328–30; Dunn, *Elizabeth and Mary,* pp. 362–66. Reaching a conclusion is further complicated by the 2008 research paper of early modern obstetrics expert Lesley Smith, who argued that the twins miscarried by Mary in 1567 were considerably further along in gestation than the seven weeks claimed at the time, strongly suggesting that Mary's sexual relationship with Bothwell predated her alleged abduction by several months. See Lesley Smith, "Mary Queen of Scots: the 'daughter of debate,'" *Journal of Family Planning and Reproductive Health* (2008), 34(2), pp. 125–27.
45. SP 59/13, fos. 174v-175r.
46. II Kings 11:2–3, 20; II Chronicles, 22:9; 24:7.
47. John Graham Dalyell, *Fragments of Scottish History* (Edinburgh: Archibald Constantine, 1798), Appendix XIII.
48. Bingham, *The Making of a King,* p. 35.

2: CAIN BAIRN

1. Fraser, *Mary Queen of Scots,* p. 341. She applied for an annulment from Rome eight years later in 1576.
2. Dunn, *Elizabeth and Mary,* p. 370.

3. Melville, *Memoirs*, p. 108.
4. Fraser, *Mary Queen of Scots*, pp. 375–78 and Appendix, "The English and Scottish Versions of the Long Casket Letter," pp. 556–68; Warnicke, *Mary Queen of Scots*, pp. 174–80; cf. Wormald, *Mary Queen of Scots*, pp. 174–78.
5. Gordon Donaldson, *All the Queen's Men: Power and Politics in Mary Stewart's Scotland* (London: Batsford Academic and Educational, 1983), pp. 93–95.
6. The Hamiltons renounced their support for Mary in February 1573 under an amnesty, the Pacification of Perth.
7. Bingham, *The Making of a King*, pp. 42–43, 46–48.
8. Bingham, *James VI of Scotland*, p. 37.
9. Bingham, *The Making of a King*, p. 61.
10. Bingham, *James VI of Scotland*, p. 37; Melville, *Memoirs*, p. 96n.
11. David Calderwood with David Laing (ed.), *Calderwood's History of the Kirk of Scotland* (Edinburgh: The Woodrow Society, 1849), III, pp. 242–43.
12. Melville, *Memoirs*, pp. 100–1.
13. George Buchanan, *The History of Scotland Written in Latin by George Buchanan* (London: Edward Jones, 1690), p. 215.
14. W. Mackay Mackenzie, *The Medieval Castle in Scotland* (London: Methuen & Co., 1927), pp. 39, 175–76; Norman MacDougall, *James IV* (East Linton: Tuckwell Press, 1989), pp. 113–14, 146–49, 155–57; Aonghus MacKechnie, "Court and Court Architecture, 1424–1660," in Richard D. Oram and Geoffrey P. Stell (eds.), *Lordship and Architecture in Medieval and Renaissance Scotland* (Edinburgh: John Donald, 2005), pp. 296–97, 306.
15. Bingham, *The Making of a King*, pp. 80, 94.
16. David Irving (ed.), *Memoirs of the Life and Writings of George Buchanan* (Edinburgh: Bell and Bradfute, 1807), pp. 160–61.
17. Bingham, *The Making of a King*, p. 82.
18. Cal. S.P., Scot., V, 9.
19. Bingham, *James VI of Scotland*, pp. 33–34.
20. G. F. Warner and J. P. Gilson (eds.), *Catalogue of Western Manuscripts in the Old Royal and King's Collections* (London: The British Museum, 1921), p. xxviii.
21. Melville, *Memoirs*, p. 174.
22. Francis Osborne, *Advice to a Son: or Directions for your better conduct through the various and most important encounters of this life* (Oxford: Henry Hall, 1656), p. 2.
23. Fraser, *Mary Queen of Scots*, p. 181.

24. Buchanan, *Memoirs,* pp. 3, 13.
25. Buchanan, *Memoirs,* p. 27.
26. Buchanan, *Memoirs,* pp. 3, 8, 42.
27. Roger A. Mason, "From Buchanan to Blaeu: The Politics of Scottish Chorography, 1582–1654," in Caroline Erskine and Roger A. Mason (eds.), *George Buchanan: Political Thought in Early Modern Britain and Europe* (Farnham and Burlington, VT: Ashgate, 2012), pp. 14, 16–18.
28. Peter Hume Brown, *George Buchanan and his times* (Edinburgh: Oliphant, Anderson and Ferrier, 1906), p. 377.
29. Even James's title as *Rex Scotorum,* "king of Scots" or "king of the Scottish" rather than "king of Scotland," was used to prove Buchanan's point that Scotland's kings did not rule over the land, as did a king of England, France, or Portugal. Rather, he was the Scottish people's king, ruling for them, rather than above them. The nuances of this were often lost, even at the time, when many contemporaries referred to James and his mother as king or queen of Scotland.
30. R. Chambers, *A Biographical Dictionary of Eminent Scotsmen* (Glasgow: Blackie & Son, 1835), I, p. 407.
31. R. J. Knecht, *The Rise and Fall of Renaissance France, 1483–1610* (London: Fontana, 1996), p. 431.
32. Knecht, *The Rise and Fall of Renaissance France,* pp. 424–25.
33. The consensus among scholars rejects the belief that the massacre was premeditated, but the debate continues as to how far the Guise faction should be blamed—see Knecht, *The Rise and Fall of Renaissance France,* pp. 425, 427; Henri Nouguères, *Le Saint Barthélemy* (Paris: Robert Laffont, 1959), pp. 119–21.
34. Brown, *George Buchanan,* p. 254.
35. For the debate over, and reality of, James III's death at the Battle of Sauchieburn, see Norman MacDougall, *James III* (Edinburgh: John Donald, 1982), pp. 255–58, 262–63.
36. Veerapen, *Wisest Fool,* p. 29.
37. Courtney, *Britannic Prince,* p. 49.
38. Courtney, *Britannic Prince,* p. 26.
39. Nau, *History,* pp. 29–30.
40. Melville, *Memoirs,* p. 103.
41. Bingham, *The Making of a King,* p. 36.
42. G. P. V. Akrigg (ed.), *Letters of James VI and I* (Berkeley and Los Angeles: University of California Press, 1984), p. 41; Courtney, *Britannic Prince,* p. 31.
43. Melville, *Memoirs,* p. 103.

44. Reid, *The Early Life of James VI*, p. 36.
45. Melville, *Memoirs*, p. 103. Drumquhassle's money issues motivated many of his later disastrous forays into politics—he was subsequently and accurately accused of embezzlement. It is unclear when it impacted his role as Master of James's Household, as documentation for that office is lacking for 1573–79; see Reid, *The Early Life of James VI*, p. 94.
46. Michael Wasser, "Scotland's First Witch-Hunt: The Eastern Witch-Hunt of 1568–1569," in Julian Goodare (ed.), *Scottish Witches and Witch-Hunters* (London and New York: Palgrave Macmillan, 2013), pp. 17–33.

3: COUSINS

1. Morton was the King's cousin, twice removed, as a first cousin of James's grandmother Margaret Stuart, Countess of Lennox (d. 1578).
2. Bingham, *The Making of a King*, pp. 99–100.
3. Melville, *Memoirs*, p. 109; Reid, *The Early Life of James VI*, p. 155. He had also seen military service farther afield in the Holy Roman Empire and Sweden as well as, possibly, in Russia. Both he and James VI were descendants in the male line of King Robert II (r. 1371–90).
4. Melville, *Memoirs*, p. 104.
5. The ongoing project by George Lasry, Norbert Biermann, and Satoshi Tomokiyo of translating correspondence to and from Mary, Queen of Scots during her imprisonment in England has raised the strong possibility that Atholl only pretended to relinquish his loyalty to her and hoped to influence James into supporting his mother's return. See Courtney, *Britannic Prince*, p. 34n.
6. They were second cousins, once removed, as descendants of Joan Beaufort, Queen of Scots (d. 1445) via her son John Stewart, 1st Earl of Atholl (d. 1512).
7. Wormald, *Mary Queen of Scots*, p. 171; Melville, *Memoirs*, p. 70.
8. William Forbes Leith (ed.), *Narratives of the Scottish Catholics Under Mary Stuart and James VI* (Edinburgh: William Paterson, 1885), p. 133.
9. The closest comparison today for an age that was regarded as not quite a minor but not yet an adult might be the ages of sixteen and seventeen, at which certain activities, such as learning to drive or the age of consent, are permitted by law, depending on jurisdiction, but there remains an understanding that the individual has not yet reached full maturity. Full, adult legal rights, including the right to vote, drink alcohol, apply for a credit card, or get a tattoo, are not typically granted

until eighteen. In James's era, fourteen was typically regarded as the point of maturity for a male, but this varied when it came to monarchs. In James's family, his mother had been declared old enough, at twelve, to nominate her own regent, which remained a necessity given her continued residence in France. It was at that point that Marie of Guise officially became regent. James V had also been declared legally of age when he was twelve.

10. Melville, *Memoirs*, p. 105.
11. Dalyell, *Fragments of Scottish History*, p. 21.
12. Thomas Thomson (ed.), *The Historie and Life of King James the Sext: Being an Account of the Affairs of the Scotland, from the Year 1566, to the Year 1596* (Edinburgh: publishing house unspecified, 1825), p. 165; James Maitland, *Early Records of the University of St Andrews: The Graduation Roll, 1413–1579, and the Matriculation Roll, 1473–1579* (Edinburgh: Scottish Historic Society, 1926), p. 288.
13. Cal. S.P., Scot., V, 336.
14. Cal. S.P., Scot., V, 336; David Laing (ed.), *Original Letters relating to the Ecclesiastical Affairs of Scotland* (Edinburgh: Bannatyne Club, 1851), II, p. 263. His name is sometimes given as Alexander.
15. Cal. S.P., Scot., V, 336.
16. Erskine was granted the governorship of Edinburgh Castle in lieu.
17. Cal. S.P., Scot., V, 336.
18. Reid, *The Early Life of James VI*, p. 89.
19. Bingham, *The Making of a King*, p. 116.
20. Laing, *Original Letters relating to the Ecclesiastical Affairs of Scotland*, II, p. 263.
21. Melville, *Memoirs*, p. 104.
22. Calderwood, *History of the Kirk*, III, pp. 442–43.
23. Richard Fawcett, *Stirling Castle: The restoration of the Great Hall* (York: Council for British Archaeology, 2001), p. 19.
24. Cal. S.P., Scot, V, 408.
25. Bingham, *The Making of a King*, p. 107.
26. Bingham, *James VI of Scotland*, p. 52.
27. Simon Thurley, *Palaces of Revolution: Life, Death and Art at the Stuart Court* (London: William Collins, 2021), p. 9.
28. Cal. S.P., Scot, V, 623.
29. Victor von Klarwill (ed.), *Queen Elizabeth and Some Foreigners: Being a series of hitherto unpublished letters from the archives of the Hapsburg family* (London: John Lane, 1928), p. 81.
30. Melville, *Memoirs*, p. 105.
31. Bingham, *The Early Life of James VI*, p. 56.

32. Cal. S.P., Scot, V, 512.
33. Calderwood, *History of the Kirk*, III, p. 468.
34. Cal. S.P., Scot., V, 536.
35. Cal. S.P., Scot., V, 548.
36. Cal. S.P., Scot., V, 550.
37. Cal. S.P., Scot., V, 554.
38. Cal. S.P., Scot., V, 536.
39. Cal. S.P., Scot., V, 536, 542.
40. Cal. S.P., Scot., V, 536.
41. Cal. S.P., Scot., V, 646.
42. Cal. S.P., Scot., V, 547, 554, 673, 684.
43. Cal. S.P., Scot., V, 673.
44. Cal. S.P., Scot., V, 660.
45. RPS 1584/5/29.
46. Calderwood, *History of the Kirk*, III, p. 562.
47. Calderwood, *History of the Kirk*, III, p. 569.
48. Melville, *Memoirs*, p. 106.
49. Calderwood, *History of the Kirk*, III, p. 574.
50. Calderwood, *History of the Kirk*, III, p. 559.

4: HATE AND WAIT

1. Christopher Hunter et al. (eds.), *The Correspondence of Robert Bowes, of Aske, Esquire* (London and Edinburgh: The Surtees Society, 1834), p. 143.
2. Reid, *The Early Life of James VI*, p. 281.
3. Earlier in the century, a queen of England, Katherine Parr (d. 1548), had pipped him to the post as the first to be published, in her case by producing two books on theology. For contrasting contemporary responses to James's poetry, see Richard McCabe, "The Poetics of Succession 1587–1605: The Stuart Claim" in Susan Doran and Paulina Kewes (eds.), *Doubtful and Dangerous: The Question of Succession in Late Elizabethan England* (Manchester: Manchester University Press, 2014), pp. 192–211, and Steven W. May, "The Circulation in Manuscript of Poems by King James VI and I" in James M. Dutcher and Anne Lake Prescott (eds.), *Renaissance Historicisms: Essays in Honor of Arthur F. Kinney* (Newark, 2008), pp. 206–24.
4. The House of Hamilton would have outranked Lennox, on the grounds that they descended from one of James II's grandsons. However, the family's influence and wealth had been destroyed during Morton's regency.
5. Melville, *Memoirs*, pp. 107–8. Arran's side of the family was descended

from a younger son of the first Stewart king, Robert II (r. 1371–90). Quarrels over the comparative superiority of descent from a more recent king or through a more antique one, but through the male line, had occurred before in Scottish history.

6. Cal. S.P., Scot., VI,142.
7. For further arguments that the relationship did not contain a sexual component, see Lee, *Great Britain's Solomon,* pp. 45–46; Rosalind K. Marshall, "Stuart [Stewart], Esmé, first duke of Lennox," in ODNB, LV; John Miller, *The Stuarts* (London and New York: Hambledon and London, 2004), pp. 38–39; Reid, *The Early Life of James VI,* pp. 130–33; Noel Malcolm, *Forbidden Desire in Early Modern Europe: Male-Male Sexual Relations, 1400–1750* (Oxford: Oxford University Press, 2024), pp. 273–74; Courtney, *Britannic Prince,* pp. 48–49; Susan Doran, *From Tudor to Stuart: The Regime Change from Elizabeth I to James I* (Oxford: Oxford University Press, 2024), pp. 38–39. Cf. Wilson, *King James,* pp. 32–36; David Mathew, *James I* (London: Eyre & Spottiswoode, 1967), pp. 35–37; Michael Young, *James VI and I and the History of Homosexuality* (London: Macmillan Press, 2000), pp. 11–12, 39–42; Croft, *King James,* pp. 15–16, and Veerapen, *Wisest Fool,* pp. 48–50, 60–61.
8. Genesis 18:16–33 and 19:1–29.
9. Fraser, *Mary Queen of Scots,* p. 318n.
10. Mark D. Jordan, *The Invention of Sodomy in Christian Theology* (Chicago: University of Chicago Press, 1997), p. 29.
11. Joseph Cady, "The 'Masculine Love' of the 'Princes of Sodom' 'Practising the Art of Ganymede' at Henri III's Court: The Homosexuality of Henri III and His *Mignons* in Pierre L'Estoile *Mémoires-Journaux*" in Konrad Eisenbichler and Jacqueline Murray (eds.), *Desire and Discipline: Sex and Sexuality in the Premodern West* (Toronto: University of Toronto Press, 1996), pp. 128–31.
12. For the argument that Henri III had male lovers, see Gary Ferguson, *Queer (Re)Readings in the French Renaissance* (London: Routledge, 2008), pp. 182–84; Laurence Senelick, "King Henri III and His Mignons," *The Gay and Lesbian Review* (July–August 2020); Louis Crompton, *Homosexuality and Civilization* (Cambridge, MA: Harvard University Press, 2003), pp. 328–31; cf. Pierre Chevallier, *Henri III: Roi shakespearien* (Paris: Fayard, 1985); Jean-François Solnon, *La Cour de France* (Paris: Tempus/Perrin, 2014); Nicolas Le Roux, *Un régicide au nom de Dieu* (Paris: Gallimard, 2006); Knecht, *The Rise and Fall of Renaissance France,* pp. 491–92, and Estelle Paranque, "Devotion, Influence, and Loyalty: Reevaluating Queen Louise de Lorraine-

Vaudémont's Political and Diplomatic Role in Early Modern France" in *Early Modern Women: An Interdisciplinary Journal* (2022).

13. Katherine B. Crawford, "Love, Sodomy, and Scandal: Controlling the Sexual Reputation of Henry III," in *Journal of the History of Sexuality* (October 2003), p. 524.
14. Crawford, "Love, Sodomy, and Scandal," p. 532.
15. Veerapen, *Wisest Fool,* p.50.
16. After the Turkish conquest of 1453, Constantinople retained its Byzantine name, which was given in Ottoman Turkish as *Ḳosṭanṭīnīye.* In 1930, the 1,600th anniversary of the city's founding, it was officially renamed as Istanbul, which it had been referred to as by many of its residents for some time.
17. Malcolm, *Forbidden Desire in Early Modern Europe,* p. 4.
18. Crawford, "Love, Sodomy and Scandal," p. 521.
19. Calderwood, *History of the Kirk,* III, pp. 486–87.
20. SP 53/12/12.
21. Prince Alexandre Labanoff (ed.), *Lettres, instructions et mémoires de Marie Stuart, reine d'Écosse* (London: Charles Dolman, 1845), V, pp. 185–87.
22. Reid, *The Early Life of James VI,* pp. 16, 65–71.
23. Gordon Donaldson (ed.), *Scottish Historic Documents* (Edinburgh and London: Scottish Academic Press, 1970), pp. 150–53.
24. It remains possible that the ongoing translation of the exiled Mary's correspondence by Lasry, Biermann, and Tomokiyo will one day confirm that Esmé and Mary played an impressive double bluff.
25. Veerapen, *Wisest Fool,* p. 64.
26. Already ill at the time of Riccio's murder, Patrick Ruthven, 3rd Lord Ruthven, had fled to England, where he died three months later.
27. S. J. Reid, "Of bairns and bearded men: James VI and the Ruthven Raid" in S. J. Reid and M. Kerr-Peterson (eds.), *James VI and Noble Power in Scotland 1578–1603* (London: Routledge, 2017), p. 32.
28. Melville, *Memoirs,* p. 108.
29. Calderwood, *History of the Kirk,* III, p. 678.
30. Bingham, *The Making of a King,* pp. 175–76.
31. Gowrie had several reasons for the raid, one of which may have been genuine concern over the amount of money Esmé was spending in his improvements to the royal household. For the financial and fiscal concerns that motivated Gowrie, see Reid, *The Early Life of James VI,* pp. 142, 190, 207–9, and Julian Goodare, "The Debts of James VI of Scotland" in *Economic History Review* (2009), pp. 935–37.
32. Cal. S.P., Scot., VI, 231.

33. Cal. S.P., Simancas, III, 311.
34. Bingham, *The Making of a King*, p. 183; Lady Elizabeth Cust, *Some Account of the Stuarts of Aubigny in France, 1422–1672* (London: privately printed, 1891), pp. 95–96.
35. This included permitting him access to the hunt again and building a new kennel for his hunting hounds. See Reid, *The Early Life of James VI*, p. 204.
36. Veerapen, *Wisest Fool*, p. 72. As the separate burial of a heart at a dynasty's ancestral home was not uncommon, the Duchess of Lennox may also have sent her late husband's heart to create a sense of dynastic continuity between him and his son Ludovic as the dukedom's heir in Scotland.
37. Bingham, *The Making of a King*, p. 184.
38. James VI, King of Scots, *The Essayes of a Prentise, in the Divine Art of Poesie* (Edinburgh, 1585), Hvr.
39. Melville, *Memoirs*, pp. 107–8.
40. Melville, *Memoirs*, p. 111.
41. Melville, *Memoirs*, p. 111.
42. Melville, *Memoirs*, p. 111.
43. Alexander Hay, *The Scottish Nobilitie in An. Dom.1577* (London: printed for the Grampian Club, 1873), pp. 11–12.
44. Lee, *Great Britain's Solomon*, pp. 98, 241; Lockyer, *James VI and I*, pp. 20–21; Harry Potter, *Blood Feud: The Stewarts and the Gordons at War in the Age of Mary, Queen of Scots* (Stroud: Tempus, 2002), pp. 124–27.
45. Melville, *Memoirs*, p. 111.
46. *The History of the Life of King James*, p. 198.
47. Akrigg, *Letters of James VI and I*, p. 97.
48. Calderwood, *History of the Kirk*, IV, pp. 197–98.
49. Cal. S.P., Scot., VI, 603; Hunter et al., *The Correspondence of Robert Bowes, of Aske, Esquire*, pp. 525–28.

5: THE MASTER OF GRAY

1. Cal. S.P., Scot., VI, 694.
2. Margaret H. B. Sanderson, *Scottish Rural Society in the Sixteenth Century* (Edinburgh: John Donald Publishers, 1982), p. 72.
3. The Scottish Guard had been created for King Charles VII of France (d. 1461), and Scottish monarchs, such as James II, had sent young noblemen to serve in its ranks. It remained predominantly a Scottish unit until the reign of James VI. From the early seventeenth century, it retained its name but consisted mostly of French officers. It lasted

until the overthrow of King Charles X in 1830, when it was disbanded for the last time.

4. Tytler, *A History of Scotland*, VIII, p. 197.
5. Tytler, *A History of Scotland*, VIII, p. 197.
6. Melville, *Memoirs*, p. 127.
7. Child weddings in the Scottish elite were very rare in the sixteenth century. Elizabeth Lyon would also have been extremely young, as her most likely year of birth is c. 1563.
8. John Philip Wood (ed.), *The Peerage of Scotland* (Edinburgh: George Ramsay & Co, 1813), I, pp. 670–71; H. A. Doubleday, Duncan Warrand, and Lord Howard de Walden (eds.), *The Complete Peerage, or a History of the House of Lords and All its Members from the Earliest Times* (London: The St Catherine Press, 1926), pp. 100–1.
9. Melville, *Memoirs*, pp. 127–28.
10. Wood, *The Peerage of Scotland*, I, p. 671.
11. Cal. S.P., Scot., VII, 247.
12. SP 53/13/37.
13. M. Greengrass, "Mary, Dowager Queen of France" in Michael Lynch (ed.), *Mary Stewart: Queen in Three Kingdoms* (Oxford: Basil Blackwell, 1988), Table 1 and pp. 175–76, 179–80, 186–88.
14. Letter from Albert Fontenay to Claude Nau, August 15, 1584, Ashton, *James I by his Contemporaries*, pp. 1–3. The quotations following by Fontenay are taken from the same source.
15. Leanda de Lisle, *After Elizabeth: The Death of Elizabeth and the Coming of King James* (London: Harper Perennial, 2006), pp. 49, 57.
16. Bingham, *James VI of Scotland*, p. 76.
17. Veerapen, *Wisest Fool*, p. 88; Cal. S.P. Scot., IX, 701.
18. Wood, *The Peerage of Scotland*, I, pp. 670–71; Doubleday, Warrand, and Howard de Walden, *The Complete Peerage*, pp. 100–1.
19. Cal. S. P., Scot., X, 156.
20. Ruth Grant, "George Gordon, sixth Earl of Huntly and the Politics of the Counter-Reformation in Scotland, 1581–1595" (D. Phil. thesis submitted to the University of Edinburgh, 2010), pp. 74–76.
21. Melville, *Memoirs*, p. 208.
22. Calderwood, *History of the Kirk*, IV, p. 487.
23. Bingham, *James VI of Scotland*, p. 43.
24. Veerapen, *Wisest Fool*, p. 109.
25. Akrigg, *Letters of James VI and I*, p. 63.
26. SP 52/36/85.
27. Labanoff, *Lettres*, VI, p. 82.
28. Cal. S.P., Scot., VIII, 2, 8.

29. Bingham, *James VI of Scotland,* p. 92.
30. Russell had allegedly behaved aggressively at the meeting, to which he turned up uninvited, but the details of what led to his murder remain contested. See W. C. Dickinson, "The Death of Lord Russell," 1585 in *Scottish Historical Review* (April 1923), pp. 181–86.
31. Akrigg, *Letters of James VI and I,* p. 64.
32. Cal. S.P., Scot., VIII, 41.
33. Melville, *Memoirs,* p. 132.
34. Melville, *Memoirs,* p. 132; for Patrick specifically encouraging the English government to "seize the opportunity" created by Francis Russell's murder and to refuse to conclude the negotiations for the treaty until Arran was disgraced, see Cal. S.P., Scot., VIII, 94.
35. Cal. S.P., Scot., VIII, 94.
36. Melville, *Memoirs,* p. 136; Reid, *The Early Life of James VI,* p. 271.
37. Akrigg, *Letters of James VI and I,* pp. 66–68.
38. Melville, *Memoirs,* p. 161.
39. Bingham, *James VI of Scotland,* p. 93; Maurice Lee Jr., *John Maitland of Thirlestane and the Foundation of the Stewart Despotism in Scotland* (Princeton, NJ: Princeton University Press, 1959), p. 86. For the argument that James harnessed the post-Arran aftermath to subdue the Kirk to the monarchy's benefit, by the way in which he repealed part of the "Black Acts," see Courtney, *Britannic Prince,* pp. 86–88. Cf. Alan MacDonald, *The Jacobean Kirk, 1567–1625: Sovereignty, Polity and Liturgy* (New York and London: Routledge, 1998), pp. 29–31.
40. Cal. S.P., Scot., VIII, 536.
41. Julian Goodare, "James VI's English Subsidy," in Julian Goodare and Michael Lynch (eds.), *The Reign of James VI* (East Linton: Tuckwell, 2000), pp. 120–21.
42. Similar entrapment tactics with Catholic plots had been tried before by Walsingham and Burghley as far back as 1567, when Mary was still Queen of Scots. See Guy, *My Heart Is My Own,* pp. 265–66.
43. Cal. S.P., Foreign: Elizabeth I, XXI, i, Appendix "December 1587."
44. F. A. MacCunn, *Mary Stuart* (London: Methuen & Co., 1905), p. 301.
45. Tytler, *A History of Scotland,* VII, p. 95.
46. Veerapen, *Wisest Fool,* pp. 97–98.
47. Rait and Cameron, *King James's Secret,* p. 5.
48. Bingham, *James VI,* p. 88.
49. Akrigg, *Letters of James VI and I,* pp. 76–77.
50. GD 1/371/3, f. 337.
51. Cal. S.P., Scot. X., 249.
52. SP 52/41/74.

53. GD 1/371/3, f. 336.
54. Akrigg, *Letters of James VI and I*, pp. 80–81. The penultimate sentence, referencing Patrick's "great credit there," is interesting. It suggests the possibility that James had always known of Patrick's work as an informant. Knowing of James's talent for dissimulation, he may even have encouraged his favorite to do so. It would have made it easier for James to pass on to London messages that he wanted conveyed but for which he did not want to take public responsibility. This cannot be proved, as the nature of early modern espionage required a subterfuge that disguised its realities from contemporaries and from historians alike. Equally plausible is the scenario in which James had learned of Patrick's duplicity after the fact, or simply suspected it, and in January 1587 ordered that he put his "great credit" to Scotland's use.
55. Melville, *Memoirs*, pp. 140–41.
56. Melville, *Memoirs*, pp. 140–41.
57. Fraser, *Mary Queen of Scots*, pp. 546–48.
58. Calderwood, *History of the Kirk*, VI, p. 17.
59. Rait and Cameron, *King James's Secret*, p. 191; HMC, Sixth Report, Part I, p. 639; Akrigg, *Letters of James VI and I*, p. 86.
60. Akrigg, *Letters of James VI and I*, p. 87.
61. Marcus, *Collected Works*, p. 197.
62. Bingham, *James VI of Scotland*, p. 88.
63. Bell, *Despatches of Courcelles*, pp. 40–41.
64. Neale, *Parliaments*, II, p. 104.
65. Paul Johnson, *Elizabeth I: A Study in Power and Intellect* (London: Weidenfeld & Nicolson, 1974), p. 291.
66. *Warrender Papers*, II, p. 11.
67. Akrigg, *Letters of James VI and I*, pp. 84–85.
68. Cal. S.P., Scot., IX, 280.
69. Cal. S.P., Scot., IX, 556.
70. Calderwood, *History of the Kirk*, IV, pp. 612–13.
71. Cal. S.P., Scot., IX, 427, 530, 556.
72. HMC Salisbury, X, p. 388; Cal. S.P., Scot., X, 23, 26, 65. See the latter, doc. 26 in particular, for James's damning private assessment of Patrick in April 1589 as a man of "worse conscience, no honesty or credit, extreme[ly] proud and ambitious . . ."

6: NIGHTLY BEDFELLOWS

1. Veerapen, *Wisest Fool*, pp. 114–15; Potter, *Blood Feud*, p. 128, suggests that romantic jealousy motivated James's strong opposition in 1583 to

Huntly's proposed marriage with a daughter of Sir Thomas Kerr of Ferniehurst.

2. Cal. S.P., Scot., X, 3.
3. Cal. S.P., Scot., X, 3.
4. Potter, *Blood Feud,* p. 139.
5. Cal. S.P., Scot., IX, 404.
6. Cal. S.P., Scot., X, 3; Potter, *Blood Feud,* pp. 113–14, 125–27, 138–39.
7. C. Rodgers (ed.), *Estimate of the Scottish Nobility During the Minority of James VI* (London: Grampian Club, 1873), p. 31.
8. Potter, *Blood Feud,* p. 126.
9. Croft, *King James,* p. 33.
10. Cal. S.P., Scot., IX, 384.
11. Cal. S.P., Scot., IX, 404.
12. Cal. S.P., Scot., IX, 404.
13. Alexander is first mentioned by name as an infant in an entail dated to March 1564. Sandyford is now part of Glasgow. It may simultaneously have been an affectionate shortening of "Alexander," coupled with a nod to his being known as Alexander Lindsay of Sandyford.
14. Akrigg, *Letters of James VI and I,* pp. 102–3.
15. Cal. S.P., Scot., IX, 549.
16. Cal. S.P., Scot., IX, 593.
17. Cal. S.P., Scot., IX, 455.
18. Cal. S.P., Scot., IX, 542, 554.
19. Cal. S.P., Scot., X, 19.
20. Cal. S.P., Scot., X, 27.
21. Cal. S.P., Scot., X, 19.
22. Russ McDonald, *Shakespeare and the Arts of Languages* (Oxford: Oxford University Press, 2013), p. 6; OED, III, 7.b, d.
23. William Shakespeare, *Othello,* Act I, scene iii.
24. OED, III, 7.b.
25. OED, III, 8.
26. My thanks to Dr. James Davis of Queen's University, Belfast, for discussing the use of "proper man" in this context.
27. Most famously, by interpreting an incident in the twelfth century when England's King Richard I (d. 1199) shared a bed with France's King Philippe II (d. 1223) as proof that they were lovers. See John Harvey, *The Plantagenets* (London: B. T. Batsford, 1948), pp. 33–35. The bed-sharing between the two kings was an unusual but public act, intended in their case to highlight political amity between them, as was their serving of one another at meals. See Jean Flori, *Richard Coeur de Lion: le roi-chevalier* (Paris: Payot, 1999), pp. 453–56.

28. R. W. Hoyle, "Henry Percy, sixth earl of Northumberland, and the fall of the House of Percy, 1527–1537" in G. W. Bernard (ed.), *The Tudor Nobility* (Manchester: Manchester University Press, 1992), pp. 182–84, 205 and Gareth Russell, "His Dear Bedfellow: The debate over Harry Percy," *Tudor Life* (February 2016), pp. 2–5.
29. Mary Anne Everett Wood, *Letters of Royal and Illustrious Ladies of Great Britain* (London: Henry Colburn, 1846), II, pp. 357–58.
30. Akrigg, *Letters of James VI and I,* p. 98.
31. Cal. S.P., Scot., IX, 435, 455, 457.
32. Cal. S.P., Scot., IX, 448, 456, 457, 459.
33. James VI, King of Scots, *An Fruitful Meditation* (1588) and *An Meditation* (1589). Around this time, he wrote a third theological work, also on the Apocalypse, *A Paraphrase upon the Revelation to the Apostle John,* which remained unpublished until the 1610s.
34. Melville, *Memoirs,* p. 159.
35. Cal. S.P., Scot., IX, 589.
36. He subsequently reverted to his surname after Beatrix's death and his subsequent marriage to Helen Chisholm.
37. Cal. S.P., Scot., IX, 142.
38. Cal. S.P., Scot., IX, 116, 165.
39. Stewart, *The Cradle King,* p. 106.
40. *Warrender Papers,* II, pp. 80–81.
41. Cal. S.P., Scot., IX, 368.
42. Ashton, *James I by his Contemporaries,* pp. 98, 100.
43. Cal. S.P., Scot., X, 2, 3, 21.
44. Cal. S.P., Scot., IX, 403, 404; David Moysie, *Memoirs of the Affairs of Scotland* (Edinburgh, 1830), p. 72.
45. 25 Hen. 8. c. 6.
46. Leviticus 20:13.
47. *Historie and Life of King James the Sext,* p. 64.
48. Hannay had sasine of land in Herriggs and was admitted to the guild on April 26, 1569. See Col. William van der Poel Hannay (printed privately: Clan Hannay Society, 1969), p. 238.
49. Compton, *Homosexuality and Civilization,* p. 384.
50. Most British executions for homosexuality occurred in the eighteenth and nineteenth centuries. After Parliament passed the Offences against the Person Act (1862), homosexual sex ceased to be a capital offense, but remained punishable by imprisonment until the decriminalization of homosexuality by the Sexual Offences Act (1967). Heterosexual buggery—anal sex between a man and a woman—remained technically illegal in the United Kingdom until the Criminal Justice

and Public Order Act (1994). Homosexuality was decriminalized in Canada in 1969, in New Zealand in 1986, and in Australia between 1994 and 1997. Having adopted the English buggery laws prior to independence, homosexuality ceased to be a capital crime in any of the states of the United States in 1873, and the last laws criminalizing homosexual sex were invalidated by *Lawrence vs. Texas* (2003). Homosexuality was decriminalized in the Republic of Ireland with the Criminal Law (Sexual Offences) Act (1993).

51. Colin L. Talley, "Gender and Male Same-Sex Erotic Behaviour in British North America in the Seventeenth Century" in *Journal of the History of Sexuality,* VI, iii (January 1996), pp. 385–86; Robert F. Oaks, "'Things Fearful to Name': Sodomy and Buggery in Seventeenth-Century New England," *Journal of Social History* (Winter 1978), pp. 268–70.
52. Leviticus 20:10, 17.
53. Croft, *King James,* p. 28.
54. Jordan, *The Invention of Sodomy in Christian Theology,* p. 29.
55. Young, *James VI and I and the History of Homosexuality,* pp. 49–50.
56. Young, *James VI and I and the History of Homosexuality,* pp. 49–50.
57. Malcolm, *Forbidden Desire in Early Modern Europe,* p. 75.
58. Cynthia B. Herrup, *A House in Gross Disorder: Sex, Law, and the 2nd Earl of Castlehaven* (Oxford: Oxford University Press, 1999), p. 33.
59. Gary Ferguson, *Same-Sex Marriage in Renaissance Rome: Sexuality, Identity, and Community in Early Modern Europe* (Ithaca, NY: Cornell University Press, 2016), pp. 26–27.
60. James VI, King of Scots, *Basilikon Doron* (Edinburgh: Robert Walde, 1603), p. 31.
61. Young, *James VI and I and the History of Homosexuality,* p. 77.
62. Ferguson, *Same-Sex Marriage in Renaissance Rome,* pp. 13–19, 25. This précis comes from compiling Montaigne's account with that of another contemporary observer, the Venetian ambassador, Antonio Tiepolo.
63. Ferguson, *Same-Sex Marriage in Renaissance Rome,* p. 13.
64. Ferguson, *Same-Sex Marriage in Renaissance Rome,* p. 13.
65. James VI, *Basilikon Doron,* p. 20.
66. Cal. S.P., Scot., IX, 430.
67. Bingham, *James VI of Scotland,* p. 100.
68. Stewart, *Cradle King,* p. 93.
69. Cal. S.P., Simancas, IV, 17.
70. Cal. S.P., Scot., IX, 460.
71. Cal. S.P., Scot., IX, 485.

72. Bingham, *James VI of Scotland,* p. 101.
73. Cal. S.P., Scot., IX, 494.
74. Cal. S.P., Scot., IX, 532.
75. Bingham, *James VI of Scotland,* p. 110. James also took the opportunity to successfully petition the Spanish government to show similar mercy and release any Scotsmen, most of them Protestant merchants, then being detained by the Spanish Inquisition. See Colin Martin and Geoffrey Parker, *Armada: The Spanish Enterprise and England's Deliverance in 1588* (New Haven and London: Yale University Press, 2022), pp. 368–69.
76. Cal. S.P., Scot., IX, 554, 588.

7: TO BE YOUR FELLOW, YOU MAY DENY ME

1. Cal. S.P., Scot., IX, 554.
2. Cal. S.P., Scot., IX, 542.
3. Melville, *Memoirs,* p. 159; Cal. S.P., Scot., IX, 545.
4. Cal. S.P., Scot., IX, 554.
5. Cal. S.P., Scot., X, 2.
6. SP 52/43/15.
7. SP 52/43/15.
8. SP 52/43/15.
9. Grant, "George Gordon, Sixth Earl of Huntly and the Politics of the Counter-Reformation in Scotland," pp. 310–13.
10. Cal. S.P., Scot., IX, 593.
11. Cal. S.P., Scot., X, 2.
12. Cal. S.P., Scot., IX, 593.
13. Cal. S.P., Scot., X, 28, 29, 69, 71.
14. Lee, *John Maitland,* p. 182.
15. Colville, *Letters,* p. 91.
16. Cal. S.P., Scot., X, 19.
17. Cal. S.P., Scot., X, 19.
18. Young, *James VI and I and the History of Homosexuality,* p. 17.
19. Cal. S.P., Scot., X, 249.
20. Veerapen, *Wisest Fool,* p. 129.
21. Edward IV, Richard III, Henry VII, Henry VIII, and Queen Jane had married English subjects albeit, in Richard III's and Henry VII's cases, subjects who were regarded as princesses by many of the population. Henry VIII and Mary I married foreign royalty.
22. The Kalmar Union (1397) was the personal union of a single monarch for Norway, Denmark, Sweden, Iceland, Greenland, and the Faroe, Orkney, and Shetland Islands. The latter two became part of Scotland

in 1469, and Sweden seceded from the union in 1523 by electing a different monarch. The union between the others continued under various constitutional arrangements until 1814, when Norway was placed in personal union with Sweden following the Norwegian-Swedish War. Norway declared independence in 1905 by a plebiscite, which also voted to reestablish their monarchy. A younger brother of the King of Denmark accepted the invitation to become the first king of a postindependence Norway. Iceland left the union with Denmark by plebiscite in 1944.

23. B.M. Cotton MSS Caligula D.I., f. 385.
24. Knecht, *The Rise and Fall of Renaissance France,* p. 574.
25. Knecht, *The Rise and Fall of Renaissance France,* p. 571.
26. Akrigg, *Letters of James VI and I,* pp. 92–93.
27. Akrigg, *Letters of James VI and I,* pp. 93–94.
28. Akrigg, *Letters of James VI and I,* p. 93.
29. Akrigg, *Letters of James VI and I,* pp. 102–3.
30. See Veerapen, *Wisest Fool,* p. 124, for the suggestion that James VI's delays may have been part of the reason for Frederik II pressing ahead with a different marriage for Elisabeth.
31. There had also briefly been discussion of a possible marriage between Anna and Prince Maurice of Nassau.
32. Akrigg, *Letters of James VI and I,* p. 95.
33. Ethel Carleton Williams, *Anne of Denmark: Wife of James VI of Scotland, James I of England* (London: Longman, 1970), p. 14.
34. Cal. S.P., Scot., X, 236.
35. Cal. S.P., Scot., X, 236.
36. Murdin, *State Papers,* p. 637.
37. Carleton Williams, *Anne of Denmark,* p. 16.
38. Salisbury MSS, III, 438.
39. Akrigg, *Letters of James VI and I,* p. 98.
40. Cal. S.P., Scot., X, 249.
41. Cal. S.P., Scot., X, 249.
42. Cal. S.P., Scot., X, 249.
43. Carleton Williams, *Anne of Denmark,* p. 19.
44. G. Stephens, "James VI. In Tonsberg, 1589. With Photograph of an old Oaken Tablet erected in the Church of St Mary, in Commemoration of his Visit," *Proceedings of the Society of Antiquaries of Scotland* (November 1875), pp. 462–64.
45. Stephens, "James VI. In Tonsberg," p. 464.
46. Stephens, "James VI. In Tonsberg," p. 462.
47. Moysie, *Memoirs of the Affairs of Scotland,* p. 80.

48. Moysie, *Memoirs of the Affairs of Scotland,* p. 80.
49. Moysie, *Memoirs of the Affairs of Scotland,* p. 80.
50. Retha M. Warnicke, "Henry VIII's Greeting of Anne of Cleves and Early Modern Court Protocol," in *Albion* (1996), pp. 580–82.
51. Akrigg, *Letters of James VI and I,* p. 95.
52. Akrigg, *Letters of James VI and I,* pp. 102–3.
53. Michael Roberts, *The Early Vasas: A History of Sweden, 1523–1611* (Cambridge: Cambridge University Press, 1968), pp. 319–20.
54. Cal. S.P., Scot., IX, 568.
55. Their brother, the future King Christian IV, also briefly joined the princesses at Güstrow.
56. Ellis, *Original Letters,* III, 149.
57. Knud J. V. Jespersen, trans. Ivan Hill, *A History of Denmark* (London: Palgrave, 2004), pp. 116–17; Karen Larsen, *A History of Norway* (Princeton: Princeton University Press, 1948), pp. 251–52.
58. Carleton Williams, *Anne of Denmark,* p. 6.
59. Stewart, *The Cradle King,* p. 113.
60. Carleton Williams, *Anne of Denmark,* p. 24.
61. Roger B. Manning, *Hunters and Poachers: A Social and Cultural History of Unlawful Hunting in England, 1485–1640* (Oxford: Oxford University Press, 2003), p. 25.
62. GD 1/240/2.
63. GD 1/240/2.
64. Akrigg, *Letters of James VI and I,* pp. 102–3.
65. SP 52/45/11.

8: THE DAMNABLE LIFE AND DEATH OF A NOTABLE SORCERER

1. At the time of writing, the King's Wark restaurant. In 1590, the same building functioned as a customs house.
2. Stewart, *The Cradle King,* p. 117.
3. Helen Douglas-Irvine, *The Royal Palaces of Scotland* (London: Constable & Co., 1911), p. 100.
4. Carleton Williams, *Anne of Denmark,* p. 14.
5. Veerapen, *Wisest Fool,* p. 152; 1 Samuel 10:1, 16:13; 1 Kings 1:30; 2 Kings 9:6. The four kings described as being anointed are Saul, David, and Solomon (kings of Israel) and King Jehu, ruler of a kingdom that is variably referred to as the kingdom of Samaria or the northern kingdom of Israel.
6. Veerapen, *Wisest Fool,* p. 155.
7. Stewart, *The Cradle King,* p. 120.
8. Balfour, *The Scots Peerage,* VIII, p. 291.

9. Douglas, *Peerage of Scotland,* II, p. 517.
10. David Masson (ed.), *The Register of the Privy Council of Scotland: Vol. IV: A.D. 1585–1592* (Edinburgh: Her Majesty's General Register House, 1881), IV, p. 542; Balfour, *The Scots Peerage,* VIII, p. 97.
11. Akrigg, *Letters of James VI and I,* p. 93.
12. Cal. S.P., Scot., X, 742. The source's wording makes it unclear if the affair took place before or during Jean's marriage to Sandy Lindsay—she is described on August 20, 1592, as "now wife of Spynie, and late lady and mistress of Airdrie."
13. Carleton Williams, *Anne of Denmark,* p. 33.
14. Marion Gibson, *Witchcraft: A History in Thirteen Trials* (London: Simon & Schuster, 2023), p. 30.
15. Brian P. Levack, *The Witch-Hunt in Early Modern Europe* (London and New York: Longman, 1995), p. 200.
16. Levack, *The Witch-Hunt in Early Modern Europe,* pp. 21–23, Table 1.
17. Julian Goodare, "Witch-hunting and the Scottish state," in *The Scottish Witch-hunt in Context* (Manchester and New York: Manchester University Press, 2002), pp. 124–25.
18. James Sharpe, "Witch-hunting and witch historiography: some Anglo-Scottish comparison" in Goodare, *The Scottish Witch-hunt in Context,* p. 182.
19. Orna Alyagon Darr, *Marks of an Absolute Witch: Evidentiary Dilemmas in Early Modern England* (Farnham and Burlington, VT: Ashgate, 2011), pp. 120–21.
20. Ronald Hutton, "The global context of the Scottish witch-hunt" in Goodare, *The Scottish Witch-hunt in Context,* p. 31.
21. Diane Purkiss, *The Witch in History: Early Modern and Twentieth-century Representations* (London and New York: Routledge, 1996), p. 76.
22. Gibson, *Witchcraft,* pp. 31–33.
23. Gibson, *Witchcraft,* pp. 36–37.
24. Yeoman, "Hunting the rich witch in Scotland," in Goodare, *The Scottish Witch-hunt in Context,* p. 107.
25. Yeoman, "Hunting the rich witch in Scotland," p. 108.
26. Anonymous, *Newes from Scotland* (London: William Wright, 1591).
27. Stewart, *The Cradle King,* p. 125.
28. Anonymous, *Newes from Scotland.*
29. Melville, *Memoirs,* p. 156.
30. Ian B. Cowan, "The Darker Vision of the Scottish Renaissance: The Devil and Francis Stewart" in Ian Cowan and Duncan Shaw (eds.), *The Renaissance and Reformation in Scotland: Essays in Honour of*

Gordon Donaldson (Edinburgh: Scottish Academic Press, 1983), p. 130.

31. His name is sometimes given as Rinian—other times as Archibald—Chirnside. See Cal. S.P., Scot., X, 554, 559.
32. Anonymous, *Newes from Scotland.*
33. Stewart, *The Cradle King,* p. 126.
34. Gibson, *Witchcraft,* p. 42.
35. Further potential evidence that Napier was not executed comes from the way her case was used by James's critics within the Kirk, several of whom preached sermons citing her acquittal as proof that God was angry at James for his sins; see Calderwood, *History of the Kirk,* IV, pp. 129–30. While this was in reference to the acquittal that James sought to overturn, the subsequent silence in the contemporary records about Napier lends credence to the theory that she died of natural causes. Whether in prison or after release remains unclear.
36. Stewart, *The Cradle King,* p. 127.
37. Akrigg, *Letters of James VI and I,* p. 114.
38. Akrigg, *Letters of James VI and I,* p. 118.
39. Carleton Williams, *Anne of Denmark,* p. 40.
40. Carleton Williams, *Anne of Denmark,* p. 43.
41. Stewart, *The Cradle King,* p. 129.
42. Carleton Williams, *Anne of Denmark,* p. 41.
43. James Craigie (ed.), *The Poems of James VI of Scotland* (Edinburgh: W. Blackwood and Sons, 1955–8), p. 106.
44. GD 1/240/5.
45. This was not strictly accurate in legal terms, although it was in practical terms. Bothwell agreed to undergo a trial for form's sake, but with the verdict arranged beforehand.
46. Akrigg, *Letters of James VI and I,* p. 122.
47. Cowan, "The Darker Vision of the Scottish Renaissance," p. 139.

9: THESE RUMORS SET DANGEROUS FIRES

1. Cal. S.P., Scot., XI, 300.
2. Carleton Williams, *Anne of Denmark,* pp. 36–37.
3. Carleton Williams, *Anne of Denmark,* p. 109.
4. Melville, *Memoirs,* pp. 153–54.
5. Melville, *Memoirs,* p. 160.
6. Carleton Williams, *Anne of Denmark,* pp. 35–36.
7. Carleton Williams, *Anne of Denmark,* p. 41; Moysie, *Memoirs of the Affairs of Scotland,* p. 184; Potter, *Blood Feud,* p. 118.
8. Carleton Williams, *Anne of Denmark,* p. 41.

9. *The Register of the Privy Council of Scotland: A.D. 1585–1592.*
10. Keith Brown, *Bloodfeud in Scotland: Violence, Justice and Politics in Early Modern Scotland* (Edinburgh: John Donald, 1986), p. 160; Ian A. Olson, "The Dreadful Death of the Bonny Earl of Murray," in *Folk Music Journal* (1993), pp. 281–310; Potter, *Blood Feud*, p. 179.
11. James had never forgiven Moray for sheltering Bothwell after his escape during the North Berwick witch trials, which convinced even some of those who knew there was no truth in the claims of an affair between Moray and the Queen that James had a motive for supporting Moray's murder. See Calderwood, *History of the Kirk*, V, pp. 146–47.
12. GD 1/371/3 f. 353.
13. Veerapen, *Wisest Fool*, p. 186.
14. Sarah Fraser, *The Prince Who Would Be King: The Life and Death of Henry Stuart* (London: William Collins, 2017), p. 3.
15. Fraser, *The Prince Who Would Be King*, p. 7.
16. Ezekiel, 41:2; Ian Campbell and Aonghus MacKechnie, "The 'Great Temple of Solomon' at Stirling Castle" in *Architectural History* (2011), pp. 91–118.
17. Melville, *Memoirs*, p. 166.
18. Fraser, *The Prince Who Would Be King*, p. 14.
19. Melville, *Memoirs*, pp. 166–67.
20. Cal. S.P., Scot., XI, 593.
21. Cal. S.P., Scot., XI, 638.
22. Bingham, *James VI of Scotland*, p. 125.
23. Cal. S.P., Scot., XI, 533, 534, 545, 549.

10: EXPECTATIONS

1. Calderwood, *History of the Kirk*, V, p. 382.
2. GD 124/10/65; Akrigg, *Letters of James VI and I*, p. 114.
3. Melville, *Memoirs*, p. 177.
4. David Masson (ed.), *The Register of the Privy Council of Scotland: Vol. V: A. D. 1592–1599* (Edinburgh: Her Majesty's General Register House, 1882), p. 409.
5. *The Register of the Privy Council of Scotland: A. D. 1592–1599*, V, pp. 409–10.
6. John Spottiswoode, with Rev. Michael Russell and M. Napier (eds.), *History of the Church of Scotland* (Edinburgh: J. G. & F. Rivington, 1847–51), III, p. 21.
7. Calderwood, *History of the Kirk*, V, p. 440.
8. Stewart, *The Cradle King*, pp. 143–45.
9. Thomas Boleyn was heir presumptive to his Irish grandfather's earl-

dom of Ormond, the inheritance of which was delayed for fourteen years (1515–29) by the counterclaim of his kinsman Sir Piaras Butler. The matter was resolved in Boleyn's favor in 1529, several years before his daughter's marriage into the royal family, but after her betrothal to the King. He was also earl of Wiltshire in the English nobility, as previous earls of Ormond had been until an Act of Attainder (1461–62) and a partial restoration (1475). The entailment between the two earldoms was not restored until 1529.

10. Lacey Baldwin Smith, *Henry VIII: The Mask of Royalty* (London: Jonathan Cape, 1971), pp. 268–70.
11. Terence Hartley (ed.), *Proceedings in the Parliaments of Elizabeth I, 1593–1601* (London: Leicester University Press, 1995), pp. 158–60.
12. By 1600, those six kings were Sweyn Forkbeard (r. 1013–14), Canute the Great (r. 1016–35), William the Conqueror (r. 1066–87), William II (r. 1087–1100), Stephen (r. 1135–54), and Henry II (r. 1154–89). There have been five more at the time of writing—James I (r. 1603–25), Charles I (r. 1625–49), William III (r. 1689–1702), George I (r. 1714–27), and George II (r. 1727–60).
13. For discussions of Edward VI's cause of death, see Jennifer Loach, with G. W. Bernard and Penry Williams (eds.), *Edward VI* (New Haven: Yale University Press, 1999), pp. 160–62; Frederick Holmes, Grace Holmes, and Julia McMorrough, "The Death of Young King Edward VI," *New England Journal of Medicine* (5 July 2001), pp. 60–62, and Linda Porter, *Mary Tudor: The First Queen* (London: Piatkus, 2009), pp. 184–86.
14. Leanda de Lisle, *The Sisters Who Would Be Queen: The Tragedy of Mary, Katherine and Lady Jane Grey* (London: HarperPress, 2008), pp. 288–89.
15. De Lisle, *After Elizabeth*, pp. 29–30.
16. Francis Edwards, *Plots and Plotters in the Reign of Elizabeth I* (Dublin: Four Courts, 2002), p. 186.
17. De Lisle, *After Elizabeth*, p. 30n.
18. He continued to keep an eye on them, however. See Akrigg, *Letters of James VI and I*, pp. 200–2.
19. Robert Persons, *A Conference about the Next Succession to the Crown of Inglande, divided into two partes* (Doleman: Antwerp, 1594–5); RCIN1046003.
20. Akrigg, *Letters of James VI and I*, p. 184.
21. Akrigg, *Letters of James VI and I*, pp. 178–80.
22. HMC Salisbury, VI, 31.
23. Jenny Wormald, "James VI and I, *Basilikon Doron* and *The Trew Law of Free Monarchies:* The Scottish Context and the English Translation"

in Linda Levy Peck (ed.), *The Mental World of the Jacobean Court* (Cambridge: Cambridge University Press, 1991), p. 51.

24. James VI, *Basilikon Doron*, p. 46.
25. James VI, *Basilikon Doron*, p. 41.
26. That the monarch himself was above the law had not been so recently tested. Some argued that it could be justified historically by the deposition of King Edward II in 1326–27.
27. Latymer, "Treatyse," Bodleian Library, C. Don., f. 24.
28. Cal. S.P., Span., I, 177, 178.
29. Mary Anne Everett Green, *The Lives of the Princesses of England* (London: Henry Colburn, 1855), p. 88.

11: CROCK OF GOLD

1. For Anna's awareness of the favorites in 1603–4, see Chapter 13. The most compelling evidence that she knew before 1603 comes from one of her future allies in England, who, when recollecting his friendship with her years later in 1627, wrote that Anna had "been bitten with Favourites both in England and Scotland." See Ashton, *James I by his Contemporaries*, p. 127 and F. H. Mares (ed.), *Studies in Tudor and Stuart Literature: The Memoirs of Robert Carey* (Oxford: Oxford University Press, 1972), p. 66.
2. Melville, *Memoirs*, p. 160.
3. Adrian Goldsworthy, *Caesar* (London: Weidenfeld & Nicolson, 2007), p. 81.
4. Douglas, *The Peerage of Scotland*, p. 306.
5. The cause of Sophia Ruthven's sudden death is not clear. The consequences of a miscarriage have been suggested, as has cancer.
6. James Maidment (ed.), *The Chronicles of Perth* (Edinburgh: Maitland Club, 1831), p. 7.
7. Carleton Williams, *Anne of Denmark*, p. 61.
8. Calderwood, *History of the Kirk*, VI, p. 68.
9. Calderwood, *History of the Kirk*, VI, p. 68.
10. Calderwood, *History of the Kirk*, VI, pp. 49–50.
11. Cal. S.P., Scot., XIII, ii, 535.
12. Calderwood, *History of the Kirk*, VI, p. 85.
13. Cal. S.P., Scot., XIII, ii, 537.
14. Records of the Parliament of Scotland, November 1, 1600, "Act regarding the disinheriting and inability of the brother and posterity of [John Ruthven], earl of Gowrie."
15. Calderwood, *History of the Kirk*, VI, pp. 68–70; Cal. S.P., Scot., XIII, ii, 545.

16. Cal. S.P., Scot., XIII, ii, 574.
17. Cal. S.P., Scot., XIII, ii, 537.
18. J. D. Davies, *Blood of Kings: The Stuarts, the Ruthvens, and the Gowrie Conspiracy* (Shepperton: Ian Allan, 2010), pp. 31–32.
19. For the debate over the Gowrie House incident, see W. F. Arbuckle, "The Gowrie Conspiracy," in *Scottish Historical Review* (1957), pp. 1–24, 89–100; Ashton, *James I by his Contemporaries*, for a reprint of the official account of the incident, "Gowrie's Conspiracy: A Discourse of the unnatural and vile Conspiracy, attempted against the King's Majesty's Person," pp. 44–54; Maurice Lee Jr. (ed.), *The "Inevitable" Union and Other Essays in Early Modern Scotland* (East Linton: Tuckwell, 2003), pp. 99–115; Maureen M. Meikle, "A Meddlesome Princess: Anna of Denmark and Scottish Court Politics, 1589–1603" in Goodare and Lynch, pp. 138–40; Amy L. Juhala, "Ruthven, John, third earl of Gowrie," ODNB, XLVIII, pp. 407–8; Davies, *Blood of Kings;* Jenny Wormald, "The Gowrie Conspiracy: Do We Need to Wait Until Judgement Day?" in Kerr-Peterson and Reid, pp. 194–206; Jemma Field, *Anna of Denmark: The Material and Visual Culture of the Stuart Courts, 1589–1619* (Manchester: Manchester University Press, 2020), pp. 135–36; Veerapen, *Wisest Fool*, pp. 207–11; and Courtney, *Britannic Prince*, pp. 217–19.
20. Arbuckle, "The Gowrie Conspiracy: Part II," p. 89.
21. Stewart, *The Cradle King*, p. 159.
22. Francis Osborne, *The Works of Francis Osborne* (London: A Bancks, 1673), seventh edition, p. 536.
23. Calderwood, *History of the Kirk*, VI, p. 68.
24. LP, XVI, 573; Cameron, *James V*, p. 265.
25. Charles Carton, *Charles I: The Personal Monarch* (London: Routledge & Kegan Paul, 1983), pp. 1–2.
26. Veerapen, *Wisest Fool*, p. 213.
27. Logan Pearsall Smith (ed.), *The Life and Letters of Sir Henry Wotton* (Oxford: Clarendon Press, 1907), I, pp. 314–15.
28. For a summary of the evidence on Anna of Denmark's relationship with Catholicism, see Leeds Barroll, *Anna of Denmark, Queen of England: A Cultural Biography* (Philadelphia: University of Pennsylvania Press, 2001), "Appendix: Anna of Denmark and Catholicism," pp. 162–72.
29. Carleton Williams, *Anne of Denmark*, p. 60.
30. Carleton Williams, *Anne of Denmark*, p. 60.
31. De Lisle, *After Elizabeth*, pp. 136–37.
32. De Lisle, *After Elizabeth*, pp. 136–37.

12: UNION JACK

1. Goodman, *Court of King James*, II, p. 70.
2. Margarette Lincoln, *London and the Seventeenth Century: The Making of the World's Greatest City* (New Haven and London: Yale University Press, 2021), p. 2.
3. De Lisle, *After Elizabeth*, p. 144.
4. Sarah Gristwood, *Arbella: England's Lost Queen* (London: Bantam, 2003), pp. 200–1.
5. De Lisle, *After Elizabeth*, p. 139.
6. Stewart, *The Cradle King*, p. 167.
7. De Lisle, *After Elizabeth*, p. 149. He was correct. No member of the royal family was born in Scotland until Elizabeth II's younger sister, Princess Margaret, at Glamis Castle, the childhood home of their Scottish mother, in 1930. It was not until the 1850s that monarchs again spent months of the year living in Scotland.
8. Calderwood, *History of the Kirk*, VI, pp. 215–16.
9. Akrigg, *Letters of James VI and I*, p. 201.
10. The Duke of Northumberland's plot to place his daughter-in-law on the throne and the subsequent involvement of certain prominent noble supporters in the Wyatt Rebellion (1553–54), the Revolt of the Northern Earls (1569), and the Essex rebellion (1601). The legitimacy of the threat posed by other prominent aristocratic plots—for instance, by the Duke of Buckingham (1521), the White Rose intrigue (1538), the Earl of Surrey's disgrace (1546), and the Duke of Norfolk against Elizabeth I (1572)—is contested, because the participants lacked either the malice attributed to them by the government or the intelligence to turn their malice into a viable threat. The major rebellions against the Tudors in England in the 1500s—the Pilgrimage of Grace (1536–37), the Western Rising (1549), and Kett's Rebellion (1549), or intrigues like the Babington Plot (1586)—lacked substantial aristocratic involvement and did not originate within the nobility.
11. John Nichols, *The Progresses, Processions and Magnificent Festivities of James the First* (London: The Society of Antiquaries, 1828), I, p. 70.
12. De Lisle, *After Elizabeth*, p. 161.
13. James Spedding, *An Account of the Life and Times of Francis Bacon* (London: Trübner & Co., 1878), III, p. 413.
14. Sir Roger Wilbraham, ed. Harold Spencer Scott, *The Journal of Sir Roger Wilbraham for the years 1593–1616* (London: The Camden Miscellany, 1902), p. 55.
15. Wilbraham, *Journal*, p. 56.
16. Wilson, *King James*, p. 165.

17. HMC Salisbury, XV, p. 30.
18. D. M. Palliser, *Tudor York* (Oxford: Oxford University Press, 1979), p. 1.
19. HMC Salisbury, XV, p. 52.
20. Pauline Croft, "Can a Bureaucrat Be a Favourite? Robert Cecil and the Strategies of Power" in J. H. Elliott and L. W. B. Brockliss (eds.), *The World of the Favourite* (New Haven and London: Yale University Press, 1999), p. 85.
21. E. A. Wrigley and R. S. Schofield, *The Population History of England, 1541–1871* (Cambridge: Cambridge University Press, 2010), pp. 207–15; Barry Coward, *The Stuart Age* (London: Longman, 2003), table, p. 7.
22. Coward, *The Stuart Age*, p. 8.
23. Penry Williams, *The Later Tudors: England, 1547–1603* (Oxford: Oxford University Press, 1995), p. 4.
24. Williams, *The Later Tudors*, pp. 10–11.
25. A. L. Beier and Roger Finlay (eds.), *London, 1500–1700: The Making of the Metropolis* (London and New York: Longman, 1986), p. 23.
26. There were four legislatures within the Channel Islands—individual parliamentary bodies for Alderney, Jersey, and Sark, and another for the islands of Guernsey, Hern, Jethou, and Lihou.
27. UK Parliament, *Union of the Crowns*, February 10, 2023.
28. Fynes Moryson, *An Itinerary written by Fynes Moryson, Gent.* (London: John Beale, 1617), III, p. 480.
29. Nichols, *The Progresses, Processions and Magnificent Festivities*, I, p. 87.
30. HMC Hatfield, XV, p. 65.
31. De Lisle, *After Elizabeth*, p. 185.
32. Paul E. J. Hammer, "Elizabeth's Unsettling Succession," *Huntingdon Library Quarterly* (2015), pp. 553–61.
33. Sir James Balfour (ed.), *The Scots Peerage: Founded on Wood's Edition of Sir Robert Douglas's Peerage of Scotland* (Edinburgh: David Douglas, 1910), V, pp. 357–58.
34. Cal. S.P., Ven., X, 39.
35. Ashton, *James I by his Contemporaries*, pp. 62–63.
36. Thomas Dekker, with Rev. Alexander Grosart (ed.), "The Wonderful Year, 1603" in *The Non-Dramatic Works of Thomas Dekker* (London: Printed Privately, 1885) II, p. 258.
37. Cal. S.P., Ven., X, 55.
38. De Lisle, *After Elizabeth*, p. 235.
39. Fraser, *The Prince Who Would Be King*, p. 7.
40. Calderwood, *History of the Kirk*, VI, p. 231.

41. William Fraser, *Memorials of the Earls of Haddington* (Edinburgh: T. & A. Constable, 1889), II, p. 211.
42. Spottiswoode, *History of the Church of Scotland*, III, p. 140.
43. John Hill Burton, *The History of Scotland from Agricola's Invasion to the Revolution of 1688* (Edinburgh: William Blackwood and Sons, 1870), VI, p. 170.
44. Veerapen, *Wisest Fool*, p. 227.
45. HMC Salisbury, XV, p. 143.
46. Fraser, *James VI*, p. 94.
47. Edmund Lodge (ed.), *Illustrations of British History, Biography, and Manners* (London: G. Nicol, 1791), III, pp. 163–64.
48. Carleton Williams, *Anne of Denmark*, p. 81.
49. Carleton Williams, *Anne of Denmark*, p. 81.

13: PHILIP

1. No portraits of Philip survive from the earlier period in his career. However, a large family study painted by Anthony van Dyck in 1636 shows Philip's adult children, including his eldest son, Charles, allegedly the relative who most closely resembled Philip.
2. Edward Hyde, 1st Earl of Clarendon, *The History of the Rebellion and Civil Wars in England* (Oxford: Oxford University Press, 1843), I, p. 24.
3. Philip Jenkins, *A History of Modern Wales, 1536–1990* (New York: Longman, 1992), p. 17.
4. Jenkins, *A History of Modern Wales*, p. 19.
5. J. Gwynfor Jones, *Wales and the Tudor State: Government, Religious Change and the Social Order, 1534–1603* (Cardiff: University of Wales Press, 1989), pp. 16, 18, 20–21.
6. For Wales, the United Kingdom's census of 1891 recorded 54 percent of the population speaking Welsh.
7. This was repealed by the devolution referendum (2011), which passed with 63.49 percent in favor.
8. LP, XII, ii, 167, 424, 1060.
9. Sir Anthony Weldon, *The court and character of King James whereunto is now added The court of King Charles: continued unto the beginning of these unhappy times: with some observations upon him instead of a character* (London: J. Collins, 1651), p. 59.
10. Weldon, *The court and character of King James*, p. 59.
11. Mares, *Memoirs*, p. 66.
12. Cuddy, "The Revival of the Entourage: The Bedchamber of James I, 1603–1625", p. 197.

13. Thomas Platter the Younger, intro. and ed. Clare Williams, *Thomas Platter's Travels in England, 1599* (Jonathan Cape, 1937), p. 199.
14. De Lisle, *After Elizabeth*, p. 147.
15. Francis Osborne, *The Works of Francis Osborn, Esq: Divine, Historical, Moral, Political* (London: A. and J. Churchill, 1700), tenth edition, p. 399.
16. Clarendon, *History of the Rebellion*, I, p. 24. See the same for the role played by Philip's appearance—"the comeliness of his person."
17. Mares, *Memoirs*, p. 66; CP 104/57, 188/81.
18. Cal. S.P., Dom., 1603–10, p. 151.
19. Ashton, *James I by his Contemporaries*, p. 155.
20. Ashton, *James I by his Contemporaries*, p. 155.
21. George Crawfurd, *The Peerage of Scotland: Containing an Historical and Genealogical Account of the Nobility of that Kingdom* (Edinburgh: George Stewart, 1716), p. 92.
22. Veerapen, *Wisest Fool*, pp. 236–37.
23. Lodge, *Illustrations of British History*, III, p. 38.
24. Anna had use of Greenwich Palace from 1603, but the lease was not formally transferred to her until 1616.
25. HMC Salisbury, XV, p. 345.
26. HMC Salisbury, XV, p. 253.
27. Fynes Moryson, *A History of Ireland, from the Year 1599 to 1603* (Dublin: S. Powell, 1793), p. 17.
28. They had established their primacy after victory at the Battle of Moira (637), though they never conquered the whole province and continued to have rivals, especially in the northeast. See Jonathan Bardon, *A History of Ulster* (Dundonald: The Blackstaff Press, 1992), pp. 20–21.
29. The response to Tyrone's Rebellion accounted for about 41 percent of Elizabeth's entire military expenditure during her forty-five-year reign. See Doran, *From Tudor to Stuart*, p. 75.
30. Bardon, *A History of Ulster*, p. 108.
31. Bardon, *A History of Ulster*, p. 115.
32. De Lisle, *After Elizabeth*, p. 217.
33. Philip S. Robinson, *The Plantation of Ulster: British Settlement in an Irish Landscape, 1600–1670* (Dublin and New York: The Ulster Historical Foundation, 1984), p. 38.
34. Jenny Wormald, "James VI and I," in ODNB, XXIX, p. 650.
35. Later evidence indicates that Queen Anna, too, had accepted Philip Herbert's position as favorite. However, it is unclear whether she had actively promoted Herbert, c. 1603, or accepted his primacy later. See Cuddy, "The Revival of the Entourage: The Bedchamber of James I, 1603–1625", p. 189n.

36. Stewart, *The Cradle King*, p. 195.
37. II Chronicles 15:16, 16a (Geneva Bible translation, 1599 edition).
38. Exodus 1:19.
39. Exodus 1:19a (Geneva Bible translation, 1599 edition).
40. Stewart, *The Cradle King*, p. 191.
41. Ashton, *James I by his Contemporaries*, p. 186.
42. Stewart, *The Cradle King*, pp. 198–99.
43. Stewart, *The Cradle King*, p. 196.
44. Stewart, *The Cradle King*, p. 197.
45. Stewart, *The Cradle King*, p. 198.
46. Akrigg, *Letters of King James VI and I*, 98.
47. Authorized Version, also known as the King James Version, Preface.

14: CHILDREN OF WRATH

1. Carleton Williams, *Anne of Denmark*, p. 105.
2. A daughter of the "bonny Earl of Moray" who had been killed by Lord Huntly in 1592. Lady Margaret Stewart's year of birth is unclear and is complicated by similar confusion about the years in which her sisters, Griselda and Elizabeth Stewart, were born. A date in 1591 has been suggested, the year before her father's murder, but so too has 1588–89. She was between twenty-two and twenty-five when she married Lord Nottingham.
3. Mary Howitt (ed.), *Biographical Sketches of the Queens of England* (London: Virtue & Co., 1883), p. 431.
4. Ephraim Burford, *Bawds and Lodgings: A History of London Bankside Brothels, c. 100–1675* (London: Peter Owen, 1976), p. 175.
5. The population size of London c. 1603 continues to be a source of debate, with estimates ranging from 140,000 to 215,000. In part this is because of migration in, and out, of the adjoining countryside, the number of vagrants or those without homes, and the fluctuations caused by the plague. It was also because of growing imprecision as to what constituted London itself. See Lincoln, *London and the Seventeenth Century*, pp. 7, 55.
6. Gretchen Gerzina, *Black London: Life before Emancipation* (New Brunswick: Rutgers University Press, 1995), pp. 5–6.
7. Cal. S.P., Dom., 1603–10, p. 151.
8. HMC Buccleuch, I (Hist. MSS. Com.), i, 203; Cal. S.P., Dom., 1611–18, pp. 162, 171–2; William Page (ed.), *A History of the County of Hertford* (London: His Majesty's Stationery Office, 1912), pp. 253–65.
9. Talk delivered by Dr Elizabeth Norton, "Tudor Palaces of London," at Southwark Cathedral, September 16, 2023.

10. Simon Thurley, *Palaces of Revolution: Life, Death and Art at the Stuart Court* (London: William Collins, 2021), p. 28.
11. SP 14/216.
12. Stewart, *The Cradle King*, p. 221.
13. This aspect of the plot remains obscure and may have been so to the plotters themselves. Why they would put a princess on the throne over her brother, who was younger and a male, is unclear. Charles's youth would have made him an easier candidate to reeducate as a Catholic and control as a puppet for longer. It may be that they were unsure of whether Charles would accompany his father and brother to Parliament and thus made plans to kidnap Elizabeth. If Charles had not attended Parliament, he might have been proclaimed king once the plotters had assessed the situation after the explosion. The assumption too was that Queen Anna would be assassinated.
14. Even today, mystery endures as to which priest hides were Saint Nicholas Owen's work and if more remain undiscovered. He certainly created a hide at Broad Oaks Manor, and convincing cases can be made for the extraordinary survivals at Harvington Hall, Oxburgh Hall, Huddington Court, and Sawston Hall.
15. Tony Reynolds, *St. Nicholas Owen: Priest-Hole Maker* (Leominster: Gracewing, 2014), pp. 125–9.
16. Fraser, *James VI*, pp. 109–11.
17. Digby and Barlow, "A Speech Made by King James to both Houses of Parliament, upon occasion of the discovery of the Gunpowder Plot; designed to be executed on the 5 Nov. 1605," pp. 2–4.
18. Stewart, *The Cradle King*, p. 223.
19. Cal. S.P., Ven., X, 445.
20. Mark 5:25–34; Cal. S.P., Ven., X, 544.
21. Carleton Williams, *Anne of Denmark*, p. 115.
22. Carleton Williams, *Anne of Denmark*, p. 116.
23. Carleton Williams, *Anne of Denmark*, pp. 116–17.
24. Ashton, *James I by his Contemporaries*, pp. 242–44.
25. Anonymous, *The Kinge of Denmarkes Welcome* (London: Edward Allde, 1606), pp. 8–9.
26. Sara Jayne Steen (ed.), *The Letters of Lady Arbella Stuart* (Oxford: Oxford University Press, 1994), p. 184.
27. Lodge, *Illustrations of British History*, III, p. 34.
28. Goodare, "Subsidy," pp. 120–21.
29. CP 103/46.
30. CP 103/46.
31. Ashton, *James I by his Contemporaries*, pp. 63–4.

32. Cal. S.P., Ven., X, 526.
33. Ashton, *James I by his Contemporaries,* pp. 8–10.
34. James VI, *Basilikon Doron,* p. 21; Doran, *From Tudor to Stuart,* pp. 284–85.
35. Ashton, *James I by his Contemporaries,* pp. 66–67.
36. Stewart, *The Cradle King,* p. 216.
37. E. H. Phelps Brown and Sheila V. Hopkins, "Wage-rates and prices: evidence for population pressure in the sixteenth century," in *Economia* XXIV (1957), p. 306.
38. Coward, *The Stuart Age,* Table, "The rise in prices, 1501–1650," p. 17.
39. Veerapen, *Wisest Fool,* p. 221.
40. Goodman, *Court of James,* II, p. 25.
41. Stewart, *The Cradle King,* p. 215.
42. Stewart, *The Cradle King,* p. 215.
43. Veerapen, *Wisest Fool,* p. 254.
44. *House of Commons Journal,* I, 22 March 1604, "Die Jovis, 22o Martii, 1603 [O.S.], House attends the King."
45. HMC Portland, IX, p. 113.
46. Ashton, *James I by his Contemporaries,* pp. 232–33.
47. HMC Salisbury, XV, p. 167; Philip Gawdy, with Isaac Herbert Jeayes (ed.), *Letters of Philip Gawdy of West Harling, Norfolk, and of London* (London: J. B. Nichols and Sons, 1906), pp. 21, 163.
48. HMC Salisbury, XV, p. 167.
49. Constantia Maxwell (ed.), *Irish History from the Contemporary Sources* (London: George Allen and Unwin, 1923), pp. 203–4.
50. Edgar R. Samuel, "'Sir Thomas Shirley's Project for Jewes'—the Earliest Known Proposal for the Resettlement," *Jewish Historical Society of England* (1970), pp. 195–97.
51. James Stevens Curl, *The Londonderry Plantation, 1609–1914* (Chichester: Phillimore & Co., 1986), pp. 29–31.
52. Brendan Bradshaw, *The Irish Constitutional Revolution of the Sixteenth Century* (Cambridge: Cambridge University Press, 1979), pp. 123–29.
53. Sir John Harington, with Thomas Park (ed.), *Nugae Antiquae* (London: J. Wright, 1804), p. 154.
54. Harington, *Nugae Antiquae,* p. 345.
55. Ashton, *James I by his Contemporaries,* p. 248.
56. Stewart, *The Cradle King,* p. 177.
57. HMC Salisbury, XVII, p. 70.
58. Akrigg, *Letters of James VI and I,* 121.
59. Doran, *From Tudor to Stuart,* pp. 216–17.

60. HMC Salisbury, 134/48.
61. Stewart, *The Cradle King*, p. 177.
62. Stewart, *The Cradle King*, p. 178.
63. Lodge, *Illustrations of British History*, III, p. 245.
64. Cal. S.P., Ven., X, 141.
65. Young, *James VI and I and the History of Homosexuality*, p. 28.
66. Ashton, *James I by his Contemporaries*, pp. 5–8.
67. Cal. S.P., Ven., X, 125.
68. Fraser, *James VI*, p. 97.

15: ROBERT

1. Ashton, *James I by his Contemporaries*, pp. 95–7.
2. Clarendon, *The History of the Rebellion and Civil Wars in England*, I, p. 24.
3. Arthur Wilson, *The History of Great Britain, Being the Life and Reign of King James the First* (London: Richard Lownds, 1653), p. 83.
4. Cuddy, "The Revival of the Entourage: The Bedchamber of James I, 1603–1625," p. 210; Stewart, *The Cradle King*, p. 258. The same courtier had contemptuously referred to Philip as "the Welsh earl."
5. Clarendon, *The History of the Rebellion and Civil Wars in England*, I, p. 24.
6. Clarendon, *The History of the Rebellion and Civil Wars in England*, I, p. 24.
7. Harington, *Nugae Antiquae*, pp. 390–97.
8. David M. Bergeron, "King James and Robert Carr: Letters and Desire" in *Explorations in Renaissance Culture* (Jan. 1996), p. 1.
9. Maurice Lee Jr. (ed.), *Dudley Carleton to John Chamberlain, 1603–1624* (New Brunswick: Rutgers University Press, 1972), letter dated December 30, 1607.
10. Harington, *Nugae Antiquae*, pp. 390–97.
11. Cal. S.P., Dom., 1603–1610, p. 417.
12. The chronology of Thomas Overbury and Robert Carr's earlier acquaintanceship has several possibilities. Overbury's father, Nicholas, recalled that his son had recently turned twenty when he returned from his visit to Edinburgh, which, if correct, would date the pair's meeting to some point in 1601–2. Nicholas Overbury also stated that his son and Robert traveled into England together and it was on that journey that they became close. This would place the start of their friendship to the spring of 1603, when Robert traveled to England in the household of his patron, Sir George Home, when the latter accompanied the King. This date would tally with Thomas Overbury's

description in 1613 of love existing between him and Robert Carr for nine years. A credible explanation is that Thomas Overbury and Robert Carr first met during the former's Edinburgh trip in 1601, but that they became close during their shared participation in the long royal progress from Edinburgh to London in the spring of 1603—see *Winwood Memorials*, III, p. 479, and Alistair Bellany, *The Politics of Court Scandal in Early Modern England: News culture and the Overbury affair, 1603–1660* (Cambridge: Cambridge University Press, 2002), p. 41.

13. Stewart, *The Cradle King*, pp. 259–60; Anne Somerset, *Unnatural Murder: Poison at the Court of James I* (London: Weidenfeld & Nicolson, 1997), pp. 123–24.
14. Somerset, *Unnatural Murder*, p. 63.
15. Stewart, *The Cradle King*, p. 266.
16. Stewart, *The Cradle King*, p. 267.
17. Howard M. Colvin (ed.), *History of the King's Works* (London: Her Majesty's Stationery Office, 1963–82), IV, ii, p. 237.
18. Akrigg, *Letters of James VI and I*, p. 312.
19. Thurley, *Palaces of Revolution*, p. 37.
20. Thurley, *Palaces of Revolution*, p. 37.
21. Barroll, *Anna of Denmark*, pp. 102–3.
22. Strong, *Henry Prince of Wales*, p. 46.
23. Cal. S.P., Ven., X, 513, 514.
24. Goodman, *Court of King James*, I, p. 251.
25. Akrigg, *Letters of James VI and I*, pp. 320–21.
26. Somerset, *Unnatural Murder*, p. 21.
27. Jessica L. Malay (ed.), *Anne Clifford's autobiographical writing, 1590–1676* (Manchester: Manchester University Press, 2018), p. 76.
28. A match between Henry and a German Protestant princess was considered but rejected because it was considered diplomatically redundant after his sister Elizabeth's marriage to a German Protestant prince.
29. Manningham, *Diary*, p. 236.
30. Downshire MSS, III, p. 83.
31. Francis Bacon, 1st Viscount St Albans, *Baconiana, or, Certain genuine remains of Sr. Francis Bacon, Baron of Verulam, and Viscount of St. Albans in arguments civil and moral, natural, medical, theological* (London: Robert Chiswell, 1679), pp. 23–24.
32. St. Albans, *Baconiana*, p. 24.
33. St. Albans, *Baconiana*, p. 23.
34. Stewart, *The Cradle King*, p. 260.

16: PRIVATE COCKS

1. Alford, *All His Spies*, p. 345.
2. Croft, "The Reputation of Robert Cecil," p. 61.
3. Fraser, *The Prince Who Would Be King*, p. 243.
4. Alison Plowden, *The Stuart Princesses* (London: Sutton, 1996), p. 20.
5. Charles Cornwallis, *An Account of the Baptism, Life, Death and Funeral of the Most Incomparable Prince Frederick Henry, Prince of Wales* (London: J. Freeman, 1751), pp. 29–32.
6. Fraser, *The Prince Who Would Be King*, p. 249.
7. Fraser, *The Prince Who Would Be King*, p. 249.
8. Fraser, *The Prince Who Would Be King*, p. 254.
9. Cal. S.P., Ven., XII, 812.
10. Norman McClure (ed.), *The Letters of John Chamberlain* (Philadelphia: The American Philosophical Society, 1939), I, pp. 423–24.
11. Plowden, *The Stuart Princesses*, p. 27.
12. Stewart, *The Cradle King*, p. 251.
13. Cal. S.P., Dom., 1611–18, LXXI, p. 161.
14. BL, MS Cotton Titus B. vii, fol. 483v.
15. Somerset, *Unnatural Murder*, p. 157.
16. McClure, *The Letters of John Chamberlain*, I, pp. 443–44.
17. Somerset, *Unnatural Murder*, p. 63.
18. Lee, *Dudley Carleton to John Chamberlain*, May 6, 1613.
19. Philip Gibbs, *King's Favourite: The Love Story of Robert Carr and Lady Essex* (London: Hutchinson, 1909), p. 160.
20. Even some of Overbury's friends admitted that he had "irritated and provoked almost all men of place and power by his extreme neglect of them, and needless contestation with them, upon every occasion." See HMC Buccleuch, I, pp. 131–32.
21. Somerset, *Unnatural Murder*, p. 123.
22. Gibbs, *King's Favourite*, p. 160.
23. Gibbs, *King's Favourite*, p. 160.
24. Gibbs, *King's Favourite*, p. 161.
25. Gibbs, *King's Favourite*, p. 161.
26. Gibbs, *King's Favourite*, p. 161.
27. Bergeron, "King James and Robert Carr," pp. 7–8.
28. Gibbs, *King's Favourite*, p. 163.
29. Michael Sparke, *The Narrative History of King James, for the First Fourteen Years* (London: Richard Cotes, 1651), p. 66.
30. Gibbs, *King's Favourite*, p. 163.
31. St. Albans, *Baconiana*, p. 32.
32. Devonshire MSS, IV, 125.

33. Bellany, *The Politics of Court Scandal in Early Modern England,* pp. 53–54.
34. Stewart, *The Cradle King,* p. 263.
35. Gardiner, *Parliamentary Debates,* p. 11; Foster, *Proceedings in Parliament, 1610,* II, p. 344.
36. Samuel Rawson (ed.), Parliamentary Debates in 1610: Edited, From the Notes of a Member of the House of Commons (New York: AMS Press, 1968), p. 13.
37. Thomas L. Moir, *The Addled Parliament of 1614* (Oxford: Clarendon Press, 1958), pp. 142–48.
38. Moir, *The Addled Parliament of 1614,* pp. 137–39.

17: ALL THE VIOLENCE OF MY LOVE

1. McClure, *The Letters of John Chamberlain,* I, p. 548.
2. Bodleian MS, Rawl. Poet. 26, fol. 17v.
3. Bellany, *The Politics of Court Scandal in Early Modern England,* p. 66.
4. Stewart, *The Cradle King,* p. 269.
5. Somerset, *Unnatural Murder,* p. 121.
6. The date of Villiers's time in France is unclear. He and his elder brother, John, received legal permission to study abroad in May 1609, they are known to have still been in Angers in 1611, and they returned either in 1612 or in 1613; see Roger Lockyer, *Buckingham: The Life and Political Career of George Villiers, First Duke of Buckingham, 1592–1628* (London and New York: Longman, 1981), pp. 10–11.
7. Francis Bamford (ed.), *A Royalist's Notebook: The Commonplace Book of Sir John Oglander* (New York: Benjamin Blom, 1971), p. 41.
8. James Bliss (ed.), *The Works of the Most Reverend Father in God William Laud DD, Sometime Archbishop of Canterbury* (Oxford: Clarendon Press, 1885), III, p. 170.
9. Hacket, *Scrinia Reserata,* p. 120.
10. James Orchard Halliwell (ed.), *The Autobiography and Correspondence of Sir Simonds D'Ewes* (London: Richard Bentley, 1845), I, p. 166.
11. Goodman, *Court of King James,* pp. 225–26.
12. Goodman, *Court of King James,* pp. 225–26.
13. HMC Mar and Kellie, II, 56.
14. McClure, *The Letters of John Chamberlain,* I, p. 559.
15. Lockyer, *Buckingham,* p. 17.
16. *Life and Letters of Sir Henry Wotton,* I, pp. 314–15.
17. Akrigg, *Letters of James VI and I,* pp. 335–40.
18. M. C. Hippeau (ed.), *Mémoires inédits du Comte Leveneur de*

Tillières, ambassadeur en Angleterre sur la Cour de Charles Ier, et son mariage avec Henriette de France (Paris: Poulet–Malassis, 1862), p. 4.

19. Lockyer, *Buckingham,* p. 17; Barroll, *Anna of Denmark, Queen of England,* p. 211n78.
20. Lockyer, *Buckingham,* p. 22.
21. Carleton Williams, *Anne of Denmark,* p. 173.
22. Acts 6:15.
23. Samuel Rawson Gardiner, "On certain Letters of Diego Sarmiento de Acuña, Count of Gondomar, giving an account of the affair of the Earl of Somerset, with Remarks on the career of Somerset as a public man" in *Archaeologia* (1867), p. 175.
24. Gardiner, "On certain Letters," pp. 175–76.
25. Gardiner, "On certain Letters," pp. 175–76.
26. Lockyer, *Buckingham,* pp. 10–11, 22.
27. Weldon, I, p. 411.
28. Lockyer, *Buckingham,* p. 22.
29. Akrigg, *Letters of James VI and I,* pp. 341–42.
30. Gardiner, "On Certain Letters," p. 170. There had also been skepticism in London about Overbury's cause of death, expressed in contemporary rhymes such as "'Tis painful rowing 'gainst a big swoll'n tide/Nor dare we say why Overbury died." How much this influenced Winwood's doubt is unclear. See Bellany, *The Politics of Court Scandal in Early Modern England,* p. 6.
31. Cal. S.P., Dom., 1611–1618, LXXXI, 86.
32. Cal. S.P., Dom., 1611–1618, LXXXI, 86.
33. Veerapen, *Wisest Fool,* p. 312.
34. Somerset, *Unnatural Murder,* p. 293.
35. Somerset, *Unnatural Murder,* p. 293.
36. Scott, I, p. 411.
37. Akrigg, *Letters of James VI and I,* pp. 343–45.
38. Stewart, *The Cradle King,* pp. 273–74.
39. SP 14/83/21.
40. For an example, see "Mistress Turner's Farewell to all women" in Bellany, *The Politics of Court Scandal in Early Modern England,* fig. 5.
41. Gardiner, "On certain Letters," pp. 177–79.
42. Gardiner, "On certain Letters," pp. 177–79.
43. Akrigg, *Letters of James VI and I,* pp. 350–51.
44. Akrigg, *Letters of James VI and I,* p. 353.
45. Akrigg, *Letters of James VI and I,* pp. 352–53.
46. McClure, *The Letters of John Chamberlain,* II, p. 6.

47. James Spedding, "Review of the evidence respecting the conduct of King James I in the case of Sir Thomas Overbury," in *Archaeologia* (1867), pp. 112–13.
48. Spedding, "Review of the evidence," pp. 112–13.
49. SP 14/87/40.
50. A marginally more credible suggestion is that James may have held out the tantalizing prospect of granting religious toleration to British Catholics as part of Prince Charles's marriage negotiations, which would have been very unpopular, especially in London. The Spanish royal family was unlikely to agree to the marriage without it or, at the bare minimum, without receiving substantial concessions that would permit the celebration of Mass in public for the first time since 1558. It cannot, however, have been a shock to the Puritan lobby that the question of religious toleration for Catholics would at least be discussed during the royal marriage talks; furthermore, James would reject that same condition when it was proposed in similar circumstances by the French government in 1625.
51. St. Albans, *Baconiana,* p. 26.
52. Stewart, *The Cradle King,* p. 278; Bourcier, *The Diary of Sir Simonds d'Ewes,* pp. 92–93.
53. Somerset, *Unnatural Murder,* p. 346.
54. Cal. S.P., Ven., XV, 188.

18: GEORGE

1. Lockyer, *Buckingham,* p. 26.
2. C. M. Prior, *The Royal Studs of the Sixteenth and Seventeenth Centuries* (London: Horse and Hound Publications, 1935), p. 74.
3. Cal. S.P., Dom., 1611–1618, LXXXVII, p. 187.
4. Lockyer, *Buckingham,* p. 17.
5. Lockyer, *Buckingham,* p. 20.
6. Lockyer, *Buckingham,* p. 9.
7. Lockyer, *Buckingham,* p. 8.
8. Lockyer, *Buckingham,* p. 11.
9. Lockyer, *Buckingham,* p. 27. The manor had been Robert's from 1608 to 1610, when James bought it back from him at the price of twenty times its annual rental income, in order that it form part of the lands bestowed upon Prince Henry on his investiture as Prince of Wales. In late 1613, a year after Prince Henry's death, Robert bought the estate back from the Crown, for the price James had paid for it in 1610. It was then seized during his disgrace.
10. Lee, *Dudley Carleton to John Chamberlain,* p. 207.

11. Nandini Das, *Courting India: England, Mughal India and the Origins of Empire* (London: Bloomsbury, 2023), pp. 150–51.
12. Das, *Courting India*, p. 203.
13. Bernard Capp, *British Slaves and Barbary Corsairs, 1580–1750* (Oxford: Oxford Academic, 2022), pp. 22–38.
14. Akrigg, *Letters of James VI and I*, pp. 356–57.
15. Akrigg, *Letters of James VI and I*, p. 357.
16. Thomas Fuller, *The church-history of Britain from the birth of Jesus Christ until the year MDCXLVIII* (London: John William, 1655), V, pp. 451–52.
17. Better known in Irish history as Lord Grandison, after the viscounty he acquired in 1620.
18. Victor Treadwell, *Buckingham and Ireland, 1616–1628: A study in Anglo-Irish Politics* (Dublin: Four Courts Press, 1998), pp. 48–50.
19. Treadwell, *Buckingham and Ireland*, p. 48. Another complicating factor may be that Grandison retrospectively and sycophantically credited George for achievements in his career in which George had played no part. A similar tactic was taken by Henry Yelverton, who, in 1617, had become Attorney General without George's patronage. However, later, when Yelverton had attracted George's patronage, he gave George the credit for the earlier appointment: see Lockyer, *Buckingham*, pp. 40–41.
20. Frederick Holmes, *The Sickly Stuarts: The Medical Downfall of a Dynasty* (Stroud: Sutton, 2005), pp. 46–47.
21. Young, *James VI and I and the History of Homosexuality*, p. 70.
22. Bourcier, *The Diary of Sir Simonds d'Ewes*, p. 57.
23. Bourcier, *The Diary of Sir Simonds d'Ewes*, p. 87.
24. Bourcier, *The Diary of Sir Simonds d'Ewes*, p. 87.
25. Young, *James VI and I and the History of Homosexuality*, p. 175.
26. Osborne, *The Works of Francis Osborn*, pp. 274–76.
27. Bergeron, *King James and Letters of Homoerotic Desire*, p. 192; Alan Bray, *The Friend* (London and Chicago: University of Chicago Press, 2003), pp. 166–72; Michael B. Young, "James VI and I: Time for a Reconsideration?" in *Journal of British Studies*, LI, iii (July 2012), pp. 561–63. See the latter for how the letter is referencing acts of mutual masturbation between the pair and that George must have known there was a chance it could be read by others. The full relevant passage reads, "That is the difference betwixt that noble hand and heart, one may surfeit by the one, but not by the other, and sooner by yours than by his own; therefore give me leave to stop, with mine, that hand which hath been but too ready to execute the motions and affections of that kind obliging heart to me."

28. Wormald, "James VI and I," p. 649.
29. Nichols, *The Progresses, Processions and Magnificent Festivities*, III, pp. 280–81.
30. Calderwood, *History of the Kirk*, VII, p. 245.
31. Stewart, *The Cradle King*, p. 286.
32. Nichols, *The Progresses, Processions and Magnificent Festivities*, III, p. 347.
33. Nichols, *The Progresses, Processions and Magnificent Festivities*, III, p. 347.
34. Nichols, *The Progresses, Processions and Magnificent Festivities*, III, p. 347.
35. Cal. S.P., Ven., XV, 188.
36. Cal. S.P., Ven., XV, 188.
37. Veerapen, *Wisest Fool*, pp. 323–24.
38. Osborne, *The Works of Francis Osborn*, I, pp. 274–76. As early as c. 1611–12, the charge had been popular enough to inspire mocking poetry in London, such as: "Some are made great by birth, some have advance,/I know one made a Lord for his good face/Some climb by wit, some are made great by chance./That had no more wit than would bear the place." See Bellany, *The Politics of Court Scandal in Early Modern England*, p. 6.
39. Osborne, *The Works of Francis Osborn*, pp. 274–76.
40. Osborne, *The Works of Francis Osborn*, p. 276.
41. McClure, *The Letters of John Chamberlain*, II, p. 144.
42. McClure, *The Letters of John Chamberlain*, II, p. 144.
43. Malay, *Clifford*, p. 76.

19: THE SUN SETS, ONLY FOR TO RISE

1. William Benchley Rye, *England as seen by Foreigners in the Days of Elizabeth and James the First* (London: John Russell Smith, 1865), p. 133.
2. Leanda de Lisle, *White King: Traitor, Murderer, Martyr* (London: Chatto & Windus, 2018), p. 14.
3. E. Beresford Chancellor, *The Life of Charles I* (London: George Bell & Sons, 1886), p. 47; Ellis, *Original Letters*, III, pp. 102–4.
4. Carleton Williams, *Anne of Denmark*, p. 201.
5. Field, *Anna of Denmark*, p. 302.
6. Geoffrey Parker, *The Thirty Years' War* (London and New York: Routledge, 1987), pp. 96–98.
7. Robert Bireley, *Ferdinand II: Counter-Reformation Emperor* (Cambridge: Cambridge University Press, 2014), p. 38.

8. Bireley, *Ferdinand II*, p. 33.
9. Bireley, *Ferdinand II*, p. 100.
10. Stewart, *The Cradle King*, p. 302.
11. Michael Questier, *Dynastic Politics and the British Reformations, 1558–1630* (Oxford: Oxford University Press, 2019), p. 289.
12. Stewart, *The Cradle King*, p. 305.
13. Quentin Outram, "The demographic impact of early modern warfare," *Social Science History*, XXV, pp. 270–72.
14. Revelation 6:1–11.
15. Nadine Akkerman, *Elizabeth Stuart, Queen of Hearts* (Oxford: Oxford University Press, 2021), p. 143.
16. Young, *James VI and I and the History of Homosexuality*, p. 128.

20: DARLING SIN

1. Alexander Harris, with Augustus Jessop (ed.), *The Œconomy of the Fleete: Or an Apologeticall Answeare of Alexander Harris (Late Warden There)* (London: The Camden Society, 1879), p. 191.
2. Young, *James VI and I and the History of Homosexuality*, pp. 94–96.
3. The previous ambassador had occasionally underestimated the expansion of Nur Jahan's influence and acumen from 1616–20. See Das, *Courting India*, pp. 299–302, and Ruby Lal, *Empress: The Astonishing Reign of Nur Jahan* (New York: W. W. Norton, 2018), pp. 138–39.
4. James Walvin, *A World Transformed: Slavery in the Americas and the Origins of Global Power* (London: Robinson, 2022), p. xvi.
5. Walvin, *A World Transformed*, Map 1, p. 102; David Eltis and David Richardson, *Atlas of the Transatlantic Slave Trade* (New Haven and London: Yale University Press, 2015), p. 257.
6. Walvin, *A World Transformed*, pp. 239–40; Hamid Ghany, "Emancipation and Magna Carta," *Trinidad and Tobago Guardian*, July 31, 2016. This had seemingly been corroborated by a legal ruling early in the reign of Elizabeth I, the Cartwright Case (1569), which had ruled that a man who had enslaved and trafficked a Russian had behaved illegally because slavery was illegal in England. However, advertisements to capture "runaway slaves" in Britain and Ireland conversely show that the practical application of slavery's horrors continued after the Cartwright Case. The debate on the legality of slavery's status on English, and later British, soil, endured until several court cases, including *Harvey v. Chamberlain* (1696), which explicitly stated, "no man can have property in the person of another while in England," and more famously the cases of *Shanley v. Harvey* (1729) and *Somerset v. Stewart* (1772).

7. Olaudah Equiano, ed. Vincent Carretta, *The Interesting Narrative and Other Writings* (London: Penguin, 2003), pp. 91–94, 219.
8. Goodman, *Court of King James, II*, pp. 375–76.
9. Bergeron, *King James and Letters of Homoerotic Desire*, p. 175.
10. For the fraught debate on the *adelphopoiesis* controversy and its wider context, see John Boswell, *Christianity, Social Tolerance, and Homosexuality: Gay People in Western Europe from the Beginning of the Christian Era to the Fourteenth Century* (Chicago and London: University of Chicago Press, 1980) and the same author's *The Marriage of Likeness: Same-Sex Unions in Pre-Modern Europe* (London: HarperCollins, 1994); William L. Countryman, *Dirt, greed, and sex: sexual ethics in the New Testament and their implications for today* (Philadelphia: Fortress Press, 1988); Robin Scroggs, *The New Testament and Homosexuality: Contextual background for contemporary debate* (Philadelphia: Fortress Press, 1993); Peter Linehan, "In Isherwood country—*The Marriage of Likeness: Same-sex union in pre-modern Europe* by John Boswell" in *Times Literary Supplement* (February 24, 1995); Bernadette Brooten, *Love Between Women: Early Christian Responses to Female Homoeroticism* (Chicago and London: University of Chicago Press, 1996); Stefano Parenti, "Same-Sex Unions in Premodern Europe, New York 1994" in *Byzantinische Zeitschrift*, LXXXIX (1996); Paul Halsall, "Lesbian and Gay Marriage through History and Culture," (Fordham University, June 1, 1996, now available online via Fordham University's website); Claudia Rapp, "Ritual Brotherhood in Byzantium" in *Traditio*, LII (1997) and the same author's *Brother-Making in Late Antiquity and Byzantium: Monks, Laymen, and Christian Ritual* (Oxford: Oxford University Press, 2016).
11. Akrigg, *Letters of James VI and I*, p. 392.
12. Bergeron, *King James and Letters of Homoerotic Desire*, p. 176.
13. Bergeron, *King James and Letters of Homoerotic Desire*, p. 176.
14. Bergeron, *King James and Letters of Homoerotic Desire*, p. 199.
15. Young, *James VI and I and the History of Homosexuality*, p. 143.
16. Young, *James VI and I and the History of Homosexuality*, p. 114.
17. *Journal of the House of Lords*, III, pp. 250–51.
18. Bourcier, *The Diary of Sir Simonds d'Ewes*, pp. 92–93.
19. Alastair Bellany and Thomas Cogswell, *The Murder of King James I* (New Haven and London: Yale University Press, 2015), pp. 135–36.
20. David M. Bergeron, *The Duke of Lennox, 1574–1624: A Jacobean Courtier's Life* (Edinburgh: Edinburgh University Press, 2023), p. 208.
21. Maurice Lee Jr., *Government by Pen: Scotland under James VI and I* (Urbana: University of Illinois Press, 1992), p. 52.

21: THESE FIFTY YEARS

1. Bellany and Cogswell, *The Murder of King James I*, p. xxiii.
2. Bellany and Cogswell, *The Murder of King James I*, p. 77.
3. Hardwicke SP I, p. 464.
4. Bellany and Cogswell, *The Murder of King James I*, p. 77.
5. Bellany and Cogswell, *The Murder of King James I*, p. 77.
6. Veerapen, *Wisest Fool*, p. 372.
7. From 1619, the 1st Earl of Kellie.
8. Bellany and Cogswell, *The Murder of King James I*, p. xxv.
9. Norman Chevers, *Did James the First of England Die from the Effects of Poison, or from Natural Causes?* (London and Calcutta: R. C. Lepage & Co., 1862), p. 66; Bellany and Cogswell, *The Murder of King James I*, pp. 528–29.
10. HMC Mar and Kellie, II, p. 227.

EPILOGUE

1. The princesses Anne (1637–40) and Catherine (1639) died in infancy. Princess Elizabeth (1635–50) died as a teenager.
2. Alastair Bellany, "Howard, Frances," ODNB, XXVIII, 2004.
3. Ashton, *James I by his Contemporaries*, pp. 1–3.

BIBLIOGRAPHY

Ackroyd, Peter, *Shakespeare: The Biography* (London: Chatto & Windus, 2005).

Akkerman, Nadine, *Elizabeth Stuart, Queen of Hearts* (Oxford: Oxford University Press, 2021).

Akkerman, Nadine, and Birgit Houben (eds), *The Politics of Female Households: Ladies-in-Waiting across Early Modern Europe* (Leiden: Brill, 2014).

Akrigg, G. P. V. (ed.), *Letters of James VI and I* (Berkeley and Los Angeles: University of California Press, 1984).

Alford, Stephen, *Burghley: William Cecil at the Court of Elizabeth I* (New Haven: Yale University Press, 2008).

Alford, Stephen, *Kingship and Politics in the Reign of Edward VI* (Cambridge: Cambridge University Press, 2002).

Alford, Stephen, *All His Spies: The Secret World of Robert Cecil* (London: Allen Lane, 2024).

Allen, Paul C., *Philip III and the Pax Hispanica, 1598–1621: The Failure of Grand Strategy* (New Haven and London: Yale University Press, 2000).

Amussen, Susan Dwyer, *An Ordered Society: Gender and Class in Early Modern England* (Oxford: Basil Blackwell, 1988).

Anonymous, *The Kinge of Denmarkes Welcome* (London: Edward Allde, 1606).

Ansdell, Ian, *Gordon: The Origins of the Clan Gordon and their Place in History* (Newtowngrange: LangSyne, 2024).

Arbuckle, W. F., "The Gowrie Conspiracy," *Scottish Historical Review* (1957).

Archer, Ian W., *The Pursuit of Stability: Social Relations in Elizabethan London* (Cambridge: Cambridge University Press, 1991).

Armitage, David, *The Ideological Origins of the British Empire* (Cambridge: Cambridge University Press, 2000).

Armitage, David, *The Complete Soldier: Military Books and Military Culture in Early Stuart England, 1603–1645* (Leiden: Brill, 2009).

Ashton, Robert (ed. and intro.), *James I by his Contemporaries* (London: Hutchinson & Co., 1969).

Aveling, Hugh, *Northern Catholics: The Catholic Recusants of the North Riding of Yorkshire, 1558–1790* (New York: Hillary House, 1966).

Baker, Anastasia Christine, "Anna of Denmark: Expressions of Autonomy and Agency as a Royal Wife and Mother" (MA thesis submitted to Portland State University, 2012).

Balfour, James (ed.), *The Scots Peerage: Founded on Wood's Edition of Sir Robert Douglas's Peerage of Scotland* (Edinburgh: David Douglas, 1910).

Bamford, Francis (ed.), *A Royalist's Notebook: The Commonplace Book of Sir John Oglander* (New York: Benjamin Blom, 1971).

Bardon, Jonathan, *A History of Ulster* (Dundonald: The Blackstaff Press, 1992).

Barlow, Thomas, and Everard Digby, *The Gunpowder-treason with a discourse of the manner of its discovery, and a perfect relation of the proceedings against those horrid conspirators, wherein is contained their examinations, tryals, and condemnations* (London: Tho. Newcomb and H. Hills, 1679).

Barroll, Leeds, *Anna of Denmark, Queen of England: A Cultural Biography* (Philadelphia: University of Pennsylvania Press, 2001).

Beier, A. L., and Roger Finlay (eds), *London, 1500–1700: The Making of the Metropolis* (London and New York: Longman, 1986).

Bell, Robert (ed.), *Poetical Works of Henry Howard, Earl of Surrey and Minor Contemporaneous of Thomas Sackville, Lord Buckhurst* (London: John W. Parker and Sons, 1854).

Bell, Robert (ed.), *Extract from the despatches of M. Courcelles, French ambassador at the court of Scotland* (Charleston, SC: Bibliolife, 2009).

Bellany, Alastair, *The Politics of Court Scandal in Early Modern England: News culture and the Overbury affair, 1603–1660* (Cambridge: Cambridge University Press, 2002).

Bellany, Alastair, "Howard, Frances," ODNB, XXVIII.

Bellany, Alastair and Thomas Cogswell, *The Murder of King James I* (New Haven and London: Yale University Press, 2015).

Bergeron, David M., *King James and Letters of Homoerotic Desire* (Iowa City: University of Iowa Press, 1991).

Bergeron, David M., "King James and Robert Carr: Letters and Desire," *Explorations in Renaissance Culture* (Jan. 1996).

Bergeron, David M., *Royal Family, Royal Lovers* (Columbia, MO: University of Missouri Press, 1991).

Bergeron, David M., *The Duke of Lennox, 1574–1624: A Jacobean Courtier's Life* (Edinburgh: Edinburgh University Press, 2023).

Bernard, George W. (ed.), *The Tudor Nobility* (Manchester: Manchester University Press, 1992).

Bingham, Caroline, *The Making of a King: The Early Years of James VI and I* (London: Collins, 1968).

Bingham, Caroline, *James VI of Scotland* (London: Weidenfeld & Nicolson, 1979).

Bingham, Caroline, *James V, King of Scots: 1512–1542* (London: Collins, 1971).

Bireley, Robert, *Ferdinand II: Counter-Reformation Emperor* (Cambridge: Cambridge University Press, 2014).

Blakeway, Amy, *Regency in Sixteenth-Century Scotland* (Woodbridge: Boydell Press, 2015).

Bliss, James (ed.), *The Works of the Most Reverend Father in God William Laud DD, Sometime Archbishop of Canterbury* (Oxford: Clarendon Press, 1885).

Boardman, Stephen, *The Early Stewart Kings: Robert II and III, 1371–1406* (East Linton: Tuckwell, 1996).

Bohstedt, John, *The Politics of Provisions: Food Riots, Moral Economy, and Market Transition, c. 1550–1850* (Farnham: Ashgate, 2010).

Borman, Tracy, *Thomas Cromwell: The Untold Story of Henry VIII's Most Faithful Servant* (London: Hodder and Stoughton, 2014).

Borman, Tracy, *Witches: A Tale of Sorcery, Scandal and Seduction* (London: Jonathan Cape, 2013).

Bowie, Karin, *Public Opinion in Early Modern Scotland, c. 1560–1707* (Cambridge: Cambridge University Press, 2020).

Bradshaw, Brendan, *The Irish Constitutional Revolution of the Sixteenth Century* (Cambridge: Cambridge University Press, 1979).

Brady, Ciarán, *The Chief Governors: The Rise and Fall of Reform Government in Tudor Ireland, 1536–1558* (Cambridge: Cambridge University Press, 1994).

Bray, Alan, *Homosexuality in Renaissance England* (New York: Columbia University Press, 1995).

Bray, Alan, *The Friend* (London and Chicago: University of Chicago Press, 2003).

Bray, Alan, "Homosexuality and the Signs of Male Friendship in Elizabethan England," *History Workshop*, XXIX (1990).

Brown, E. H. Phelps, and Sheila V. Hopkins, "Wage-rates and prices: evidence for population pressure in the sixteenth century," *Economia*, XXIV (1957).

Brown, Keith M., *Bloodfeud in Scotland, 1578–1625: Violence, Justice and Politics in an Early Modern Society* (Edinburgh: John Donald, 2003).

Brown, Keith M., *Noble Power in Scotland from the Reformation to the Revolution* (Edinburgh: Edinburgh University Press, 2011).

Brown, Peter Hume, *George Buchanan and his times* (Edinburgh: Oliphant, Anderson and Ferrier, 1906).

Buchanan, George, *The History of Scotland written in Latin by George Buchanan* (London: Edward Jones, 1690).

Buchanan, Patricia Hill, *Margaret Tudor, Queen of Scots* (Edinburgh: Scottish Academic Press, 1985).

Buffey, Emily, "The Early Modern Dream Vision (1558–1625): Genre, Authorship and Tradition" (D. Phil. thesis submitted to the University of Birmingham, 2016).

Burford, Ephraim J., *Bawds and Lodgings: A History of London Bankside Brothels, c. 100–1675* (London: Peter Owen, 1976).

Burgess, Glenn, Rowland Wymer, and Jason Lawrence (eds), *The Accession of James I: Historical and Cultural Consequences* (New York: Palgrave Macmillan, 2006).

Burns, J. H., *The True Law of Kingship: Concepts of Monarchy in Early Modern Scotland* (Oxford: Oxford University Press, 1996).

Burton, John Hill, *The History of Scotland from Agricola's Invasion to the Revolution of 1688* (Edinburgh: William Blackwood and Sons, 1870).

Byrne, Conor, *Lady Katherine Grey: A Dynastic Tragedy* (Stroud: The History Press, 2023).

Calderwood, David, with David Laing (ed.), *Calderwood's History of the Kirk of Scotland* (Edinburgh: The Woodrow Society, 1849).

Cameron, Annie I., and Robert S. Rait (eds), *The Warrender Papers: Volume II* (Edinburgh: T. & A. Constable and The Scottish History Society, 1932).

Cameron, Jamie (post.), with Norman Macdougall (ed.), *James V: The Personal Rule, 1528–42* (East Linton: Tuckwell Press, 1998).

Canny, Nicholas, *Making Ireland British, 1580–1650* (Oxford: Oxford University Press, 2001).

Capp, Bernard, *British Slaves and Barbary Corsairs, 1580–1750* (Oxford: Oxford Academic, 2022).

Carroll, Stuart, *Martyrs and Murderers: The Guise Family and the Making of Europe* (Oxford: Oxford University Press, 2011).

Carton, Charles, *Charles I: The Personal Monarch* (London: Routledge & Kegan Paul, 1983).

Chambers, R., *A Biographical Dictionary of Eminent Scotsmen* (Glasgow: Blackie & Son, 1835).

Chancellor, E. Beresford, *The Life of Charles I* (London: George Bell & Sons, 1886).

Chevallier, Pierre, *Henri III: Roi shakespearien* (Paris: Fayard, 1985).

Chevers, Norman, *Did James the First of England Die from the Effects of Poison, or from Natural Causes?* (London and Calcutta: R. C. Lepage & Co., 1862).

Clarendon, Edward Hyde, 1st Earl of, *The History of the Rebellion and Civil Wars in England* (Oxford: Oxford University Press, 1843).

Connolly, Steven J., *Contested Island: Ireland, 1460–1630* (Oxford: Oxford University Press, 2007).

Cornwallis, Charles, *An Account of the Baptism, Life, Death and Funeral of the Most Incomparable Prince Frederick Henry, Prince of Wales* (London: J. Freeman, 1751).

Courtney, Alexander, *James VI, Britannic Prince: King of Scots and Elizabeth's Heir, 1566–1603* (London and New York: Routledge, 2024).

Cowan, Ian, and Duncan Shaw (eds), *The Renaissance and Reformation in Scotland: Essays in Honour of Gordon Donaldson* (Edinburgh: Scottish Academic Press, 1983).

Coward, Barry, *The Stuart Age, 1603–1714*, third edition (Harlow: Edinburgh Gate, 2003).

Coward, Barry, *The Stuart Age* (London: Longman, 2003).

Craigie, James (ed.), *The Poems of James VI of Scotland* (Edinburgh: W. Blackwood and Sons, 1955–58).

Cramsie, John, *Kingship and Crown Finance under James VI and I, 1603–1625* (Suffolk and Rochester: Boydell & Brewer, 2002).

Cranstoun, James (ed.), *Satirical Poems of the Time of the Reformation* (Edinburgh and London: William Blackwood and Sons, 1843).

Crawford, Alexander Lindsay, 8th Earl of Balcarres and 25th Earl of, *Lives of the Lindsays: Or, a Memoir of the Houses of Crawford and Balcarres* (London: John Murray, 1849).

Crawford, Katherine B., "Love, Sodomy, and Scandal: Controlling the Sexual Reputation of Henry III," in *Journal of the History of Sexuality* (October 2003).

Crawfurd, George, *The Peerage of Scotland: Containing an Historical and Genealogical Account of the Nobility of that Kingdom* (Edinburgh: George Stewart, 1716).

Croft, Pauline, *King James* (Houndmills and New York: Palgrave Macmillan, 2003).

Crompton, Louis, *Homosexuality and Civilization* (Cambridge, MA: Harvard University Press, 2003).

Cuddy, Neil, "Anglo-Scottish Union and the Court of James I, 1603–1625," *Transactions of the Royal Historical Society*, V, xxxix (1989).

Curl, James Stevens, *The Londonderry Plantation, 1609–1914* (Chichester: Phillimore, 1986).

Cust, Elizabeth, *Some Account of the Stuarts of Aubigny in France, 1422–1672* (London: privately printed, 1891).

Dalyell, John Graham, *Fragments of Scottish History* (Edinburgh: Archibald Constantine, 1798).

Daniel-Rops, H., *The Church in the Seventeenth Century*, trans. J. J. Buckingham (London: J. M. Dent & Sons, 1963).

Darr, Orna Alyagon, *Marks of an Absolute Witch: Evidentiary Dilemmas in Early Modern England* (Farnham and Burlington, VT: Ashgate, 2011).

Das, Nandini, *Courting India: England, Mughal India and the Origins of Empire* (London: Bloomsbury, 2023).

Davies, J. D., *Blood of Kings: The Stuarts, the Ruthvens, and the Gowrie Conspiracy* (Shepperton: Ian Allan, 2010).

Dawson, Jane E. A., *The Politics of Religion in the Age of Mary, Queen of Scots: The Earl of Argyll and the Struggle for Britain and Ireland* (Cambridge: Cambridge University Press, 2002).

Dawson, Jane E. A., *Scotland Re-Formed, 1488–1587* (Edinburgh: Edinburgh University Press, 2007).

Dawson, Jane E. A., *John Knox* (New Haven and London: Yale University Press, 2016).

Dekker, Thomas, with Alexander Grosart (ed.), *The Non-Dramatic Works of Thomas Dekker* (London: Printed Privately, 1885).

Dekker, Thomas, with G. B. Harrison (ed.), *The Wonderfull Yeare, 1603* (London: Bodley Head, 1924).

Dickinson, W. C., "The Death of Lord Russell, 1585," *The Scottish Historical Review* (April 1923).

Donaldson, Gordon, *All the Queen's Men: Power and politics in Mary Stewart's Scotland* (London: Batsford Academic and Educational, 1983).

Donaldson, Gordon (ed.), *Scottish Historic Documents* (Edinburgh and London: Scottish Academic Press, 1970).

Donaldson, Gordon (ed.), *Registrum Secreti Sigilli Regum Scotorum: The Register of the Privy Seal of Scotland* (Edinburgh: Her Majesty's Stationery Office, 1982).

Doran, Susan, *From Tudor to Stuart: The Regime Change from Elizabeth I to James I* (Oxford: Oxford University Press, 2024).

Doran, Susan, "Revenge her Foul and Most Unnatural Murder? The Impact of Mary Stewart's Execution on Anglo-Scottish Relations," *History*, LXXXV (2000).

Doran, Susan, and Paulina Kewes (eds), *Doubtful and Dangerous: The Question of Succession in Late Elizabethan England* (Manchester: Manchester University Press, 2014).

Doubleday, H. A., Duncan Warrand, and Thomas Scott-Ellis, 8th Baron Howard de Walden (eds), *The Complete Peerage, or a History of the House of Lords and All its Members from the Earliest Times* (London: The St Catherine Press, 1926).

Douglas-Irvine, Helen, *The Royal Palaces of Scotland* (London: Constable & Co., 1911).

Duerloo, Luc, *Dynasty and Piety: Archduke Albert and Habsburg Political Culture in an Age of Religious Wars* (London and New York: Routledge, 2016).

Dunn, Jane, *Elizabeth and Mary* (London: HarperCollins, 2003).

Dures, Alan and Francis Young, *English Catholicism, 1558–1642: Continuity and Change* (London: Routledge, 2021).

Dutcher, James M., and Anne Lake Prescott (eds), *Renaissance Historicisms: Essays in Honor of Arthur F. Kinney* (Newark: University of Delaware Press, 2008).

Edwards, Francis, *Plots and Plotters in the Reign of Elizabeth I* (Dublin: Four Courts, 2002).

Eisenbichler, Konrad, and Jacqueline Murray (eds.), *Desire and Discipline: Sex and Sexuality in the Premodern West* (Toronto: University of Toronto Press, 1996).

Elliott, J. H., and L. W. B. Brockliss (eds.), *The World of the Favourite* (New Haven and London: Yale University Press, 1999).

Ellis, Steven G., *Ireland in the Age of the Tudors, 1447–1603: English Expansion and the End of Gaelic Rule* (London: Longman, 1998).

Eltis, David, and David Richardson, *Atlas of the Transatlantic Slave Trade* (New Haven and London: Yale University Press, 2015).

Equiano, Olaudah, with Vincent Carretta (ed.), *The Interesting Narrative and Other Writings* (London: Penguin, 2003).

Erskine, Caroline, and Roger A. Mason (eds.), *George Buchanan: Political Thought in Early Modern Britain and Europe* (Farnham and Burlington, VT: Ashgate, 2012).

Falls, Cyril, *Elizabeth's Irish Wars* (London: Methuen, 1950).

Fawcett, Richard, *Stirling Castle: The restoration of the Great Hall* (York: Council for British Archaeology, 2001).

Fenwick, Hubert, *Scotland's Castles* (London: Robert Hale, 1976).

Ferguson, Gary, *Queer (Re)Readings in the French Renaissance* (London: Routledge, 2008).

Ferguson, Gary, *Same-Sex Marriage in Renaissance Rome: Sexuality, Identity, and Community in Early Modern Europe* (Ithaca, NY: Cornell University Press, 2016).

Ferrell, Lori Anne, *Government by Polemic: James I, the King's Preachers, and the Rhetorics of Conformity, 1603–1625* (Stanford, CA: Stanford University Press, 1998).

Field, Jemma, "Anna of Denmark and the Politics of Religious Identity in Jacobean Scotland and England, c. 1592–1619" in *Scottish Society for Northern Studies* (2018).

Field, Jemma, *Anna of Denmark: The Material and Visual Culture of the Stuart Courts, 1589–1619* (Manchester: Manchester University Press, 2020).

Fincham, Kenneth, and Peter Lake, "The Ecclesiastical Policy of James I," *Journal of British Studies,* XXIV, ii (1985).

Fischlin, Daniel, and Mark Fortier (eds), *Royal Subjects: Essays on the Writings of James VI and I* (Detroit: Wayne State University Press, 2001).

Flori, Jean, *Richard Coeur de Lion: le roi-chevalier* (Paris: Payot, 1999).

Forge, J. W. Lindus, *Oatlands Palace* (Walton-on-Thames: Walton and Weybridge Local History Society, 1982).

Foster, Elizabeth Read (ed.), *Proceedings in Parliament, 1610* (New Haven and London: Yale University Press, 1966).

Fraser, Antonia, *King James VI of Scotland and I of England* (London: Weidenfeld & Nicolson, 1974).

Fraser, Antonia, *Mary Queen of Scots* (London: Ebenezer Baylis and Son, 1969).

Fraser, Antonia, *The Gunpowder Plot: Terror and Faith in 1605* (London: Weidenfeld & Nicolson, 1996).

Fraser, Sarah A., *The Prince Who Would Be King: The Life and Death of Henry Stuart* (London: William Collins, 2017).

Fraser, William, *Memorials of the Earls of Haddington* (Edinburgh: T. & A. Constable, 1889).

Frieda, Leonie, *Catherine de Medici* (London: Weidenfeld & Nicolson, 2003).

Gajda, Alexandra, *The Earl of Essex and Late Elizabethan Political Culture* (Oxford: Oxford University Press, 2012).

Gardiner, Samuel Rawson, "On certain Letters of Diego Sarmiento de Acuña, Count of Gondomar, giving an account of the affair of the Earl of Somerset, with Remarks on the career of Somerset as a public man," *Archaeologia,* XLI, (i) (1867).

Gardiner, Samuel Rawson (ed.), *Parliamentary Debates in 1610: Edited, From the Notes of a Member of the House of Commons* (New York: AMS Press, 1968).

Gawdy, Philip, with Isaac Herbert Jeayes (ed.), *Letters of Philip Gawdy of West Harling, Norfolk, and of London* (London: J. B. Nichols and Sons, 1906).

Gerzina, Gretchen, *Black London: Life before Emancipation* (New Brunswick: Rutgers University Press, 1995).

Ghany, Hamid, "Emancipation and Magna Carta," *Trinidad and Tobago Guardian,* 31 July 2016.

Gibbs, Philip, *King's Favourite: The Love Story of Robert Carr and Lady Essex* (London: Hutchinson, 1909).

Gibson, Marion, *Witchcraft: A History in Thirteen Trials* (London: Simon & Schuster, 2023).

Goldsworthy, Adrian, *Caesar* (London: Weidenfeld & Nicolson, 2007).

Goodall, John, "Murder on the palace floor: The Palace of Holyroodhouse, the official residence in Scotland of His Majesty the King," *Country Life* (October 16, 2024), pp. 61–69.

Goodare, Julian, "Mary [Mary Stewart]," ODNB, XXXVII.

Goodare, Julian, "The Scottish Presbyterian Movement in 1596," *Canadian Journal of History* (Spring–Summer 2010).

Goodare, Julian (ed.), *The Scottish witch-hunt in context* (Manchester and New York: Manchester University Press, 2002).

Goodare, Julian (ed.), *Scottish Witches and Witch-Hunters* (London and New York: Palgrave MacMillan, 2013).

Goodare, Julian, and Alisdair M. MacDonald (eds.), *Sixteenth-Century Scotland: Essays in Honour of Michael Lynch* (Leiden: Brill, 2008).

Goodare, Julian, and Michael Lynch (eds.), *The Reign of James VI* (East Linton: Tuckwell, 2000).

Goodare, Julian, and Stephen I. Boardman (eds.), *Lords and Men in Scotland and Britain, 1300–1625: Essays in Honour of Jenny Wormald* (Edinburgh: Edinburgh University Press, 2014).

Goodman, Godfrey, *The Court of King James the First* (London: Richard Bentley, 1839).

Grant, Ruth, "George Gordon, sixth Earl of Huntly and the Politics of the Counter-Reformation in Scotland, 1581–1595" (D. Phil. thesis submitted to the University of Edinburgh, 2010).

Gray, Iain, *Lindsay: The Origins of the Clan Lindsay and their Place in History* (Newtowngrange: LangSyne, 2024).

Green, Mary Anne Everett, *The Lives of the Princesses of England* (London: Henry Colburn, 1855).

Gristwood, Sarah, *Arbella: England's Lost Queen* (London: Bantam, 2003).

Guy, John, *My Heart Is My Own: The Life of Mary Queen of Scots* (London: Harper Perennial, 2004).

Guy, John, *Elizabeth I: The Forgotten Years* (London: Viking, 2016).

Hacket, John, *Scrinia Reserata: A Memorial Offer'd to the Great Deservings of John Williams, DD* (London: Edw. Jones, 1693).

Halliwell, James Orchard (ed.), *The Autobiography and Correspondence of Sir Simonds D'Ewes* (London: Richard Bentley, 1845).

Hammer, Paul E. J., *The Polarisation of Elizabethan Politics: The Political Career of Robert Devereux, 2nd Earl of Essex, 1585–1597* (Cambridge: Cambridge University Press, 1999).

Hammer, Paul E. J., "Elizabeth's Unsettling Succession," *Huntingdon Library Quarterly* (2015).

Hannay, William van der Poel, *The Hannay Family* (printed privately: Clan Hannay Society, 1969).

Harington, John, with Thomas Park (ed.), *Nugae Antiquae* (London: J. Wright, 1804).

Harris, Alexander, with Augustus Jessop (ed.), *The Œconomy of the Fleete: Or an Apologeticall Answeare of Alexander Harris (Late Warden There)* (London: The Camden Society, 1879).

Hartley, Terence (ed.), *Proceedings in the Parliaments of Elizabeth I, 1593–1601* (London: Leicester University Press, 1995).

Harvey, John, *The Plantagenets* (London: B. T. Batsford, 1948).

Hay, Alexander, *The Scottish Nobilitie in An.Dom.1577* (London, printed for the Grampian Club, 1873).

Haynes, Samuel (ed.), *A Collection of State Papers, Relating to Affairs In the Reigns of King Henry VIII, King Edward VI, Queen Mary and Queen Elizabeth: From the year 1542 to 1570* (London: Bowyer, 1740).

Hayward, Maria, *Stuart Style: Monarchy, Dress and the Scottish Male Elite* (New Haven and London: Yale University Press, 2020).

Hernán, Enrique García, with Liam Liddy (trans.), *Ireland and Spain in the Reign of Philip II* (Dublin: Four Courts Press, 2009).

Herries, John Maxwell, 4th Lord, and Robert Pitcairn (ed.), *Historical Memoirs of the Reign of Mary, Queen of Scots, and a portion of the reign of King James the Sixth* (Edinburgh: Abbotsford Club, 1836).

Herrup, Cynthia B., *A House in Gross Disorder: Sex, Law, and the 2nd Earl of Castlehaven* (Oxford: Oxford University Press, 1999).

Hewitt, George R., *Scotland under Morton, 1572–80* (Edinburgh: John Donald, 1982).

Hill, J. W. F., *Tudor and Stuart Lincoln* (Cambridge: Cambridge University Press, 1956).

Hippeau, M. C. (ed.), *Mémoires inédits du Comte Leveneur de Tillières, ambassadeur en Angleterre sur la Cour de Charles Ier, et son mariage avec Henriette de France* (Paris: Poulet–Malassis, 1862).

Holmes, Frederick, *The Sickly Stuarts: The Medical Downfall of a Dynasty* (Stroud: Sutton, 2005).

Holmes, Frederick, Grace Holmes, and Julia McMorrough, "The Death of Young King Edward VI," *New England Journal of Medicine* (July 5, 2001).

Howitt, Mary (ed.), *Biographical Sketches of the Queens of England* (London: Virtue & Co., 1883).

Hunter, Christopher, et al. (eds.), *The Correspondence of Robert Bowes, of Aske, Esquire* (London and Edinburgh: The Surtees Society, 1834).

Irving, David (ed.), *Memoirs of the Life and Writings of George Buchanan* (Edinburgh: Bell and Bradfute, 1807).

James VI, King of Scots, *The Essayes of a Prentise, in the Divine Art of Poesie* (Edinburgh: printing house unspecified, 1585).

James VI, King of Scots, *An Meditation* (Edinburgh: publisher unspecified, 1589).

James VI, King of Scots, *An Fruitful Meditation* (Edinburgh: publisher unspecified, 1588).

James VI, King of Scots, *Basilikon Doron* (Edinburgh: publisher unspecified, 1599).

James VI, King of Scots, *Daemonologie, in a Forme of a Dialogue* (Edinburgh: publisher unspecified, 1597).

James VI, King of Scots, *The Trew Lawe of Free Monarchies* (Edinburgh: publisher unspecified, 1598).

Jenkins, Philip, *A History of Modern Wales, 1536–1990* (New York: Longman, 1992).

Jespersen, Knud J. V., with Ivan Hill (trans.), *A History of Norway* (Princeton: Princeton University Press, 1948).

Johnson, Paul, *Elizabeth I: A Study in Power and Intellect* (London: Weidenfeld & Nicolson, 1974).

Johnstone, Nathan, *The Devil and Demonism in Early Modern England* (Cambridge: Cambridge University Press, 2006).

Jones, J. Gwynfor, *Wales and the Tudor State: Government, Religious Change and the Social Order, 1534–1603* (Cardiff: University of Wales Press, 1989).

Jordan, Mark D., *The Invention of Sodomy in Christian Theology* (Chicago: University of Chicago Press, 1997).

Juhala, Amy L., "Ruthven, John, third earl of Gowrie," ODNB, XLVIII.

Jung, Leo, "Samuel's Conscience," *Hebrew Studies*, Vol. 26 (1985).

Kamen, Henry, *Philip of Spain* (New Haven and London: Yale University Press, 1997).

Kanemura, Kei, "Kingship by Descent or Kingship by Election?: The Contested Title of James VI and I," *Journal of British Studies*, LII, ii (April 2013).

Kann, Robert A., *A History of the Habsburg Empire, 1526–1918* (London: University of California Press, 1974).

Kerr-Peterson, Miles, *A Protestant Lord in James VI's Scotland: George Keith, Fifth Earl Marischal* (Woodbridge: Boydell, 2019).

Kerr-Peterson, Miles, and Steven J. Reid (eds.), *James VI and Noble Power in Scotland, 1578–1603* (London: Routledge, 2019).

Klarwill, Victor von (ed.), *Queen Elizabeth and Some Foreigners: Being a series of hitherto unpublished letters from the archives of the Hapsburg family* (London: John Lane, 1928).

Knecht, R. J., *The Rise and Fall of Renaissance France, 1483–1610* (London: Fontana, 1996).

Labanoff, Alexandre (ed.), *Lettres, instructions et mémoires de Marie Stuart, reine d'Écosse* (London: Charles Dolman, 1845).

Laing, David (ed.), *Original Letters relating to the Ecclesiastical Affairs of Scotland* (Edinburgh: Bannatyne Club, 1851).

Lake, Peter, *Bad Queen Bess?: Libels, Secret Histories, and the Politics of Publicity in the Reign of Queen Elizabeth I* (Oxford: Oxford University Press, 2016).

Lake, Peter, *Moderate Puritans and the Elizabethan Church* (Cambridge: Cambridge University Press, 1982).

Lake, Peter, with Michael Questier (eds.), *The Antichrist's Lewd Hat: Protestants, Papists, and Players in Post-Reformation England* (New Haven and London: Yale University Press, 2002).

Lal, Ruby, *Empress: The Astonishing Reign of Nur Jahan* (New York: W. W. Norton, 2018).

Larsen, Karen, *A History of Norway* (Princeton: Princeton University Press, 1948).

Le Roux, Nicholas, *Un régicide au nom de Dieu* (Paris: Gallimard, 2006).

Lee Jr., Maurice, *Great Britain's Solomon: James VI and I in His Three Kingdoms* (Urbana and Chicago: University of Illinois Press, 1990).

Lee Jr., Maurice, *John Maitland of Thirlestane and the Foundation of Stewart Despotism in Scotland* (Princeton: Princeton University Press, 2020).

Lee Jr., Maurice, *The "Inevitable" Union and Other Essays in Early Modern Scotland* (East Linton: Tuckwell, 2003).

Lee Jr., Maurice, *Dudley Carleton to John Chamberlain, 1603–1624* (New Brunswick: Rutgers University Press, 1972).

Lee Jr., Maurice, *Government by Pen: Scotland under James VI and I* (Urbana: University of Illinois Press, 1992).

Leith, William Forbes (ed.), *Narratives of the Scottish Catholics Under Mary Stuart and James VI* (Edinburgh: William Paterson, 1885).

Levack, Brian P., *The Witch-hunt in Early Modern Europe* (London and New York: Longman, 1995).

Levy Peck, Linda, *Court Patronage and Corruption in Early Stuart England* (London: HarperCollins, 1990).

Levy Peck, Linda (ed.), *The Mental World of the Jacobean Court* (Cambridge: Cambridge University Press, 1991).

Lewis, Jayne Elizabeth, *Mary Queen of Scots: Romance and nation* (London and New York: Routledge, 1998).

Lincoln, Margarette, *London and the Seventeenth Century: The Making of the World's Greatest City* (New Haven and London: Yale University Press, 2021).

Lindley, David, *The Trials of Frances Howard: Fact and Fiction at the Court of King James* (London and New York: Routledge, 1993).

Lindquist, Eric, "The Failure of the Great Contract Proposal," *Journal of Modern History,* LVII, iv (1985).

Lisle, Leanda de, *The Sisters Who Would Be Queen: The Tragedy of Mary, Katherine and Lady Jane Grey* (London: HarperPress, 2008).

Lisle, Leanda de, *After Elizabeth: The Death of Elizabeth and the Coming of King James* (London: Harper Perennial, 2006).

Lisle, Leanda de, *White King: Traitor, Murderer, Martyr* (London: Chatto & Windus, 2018).

Loach, Jennifer, with George W. Bernard and Penry Williams (eds), *Edward VI* (New Haven: Yale University Press, 1999).

Lockyer, Roger, *James VI and I* (London and New York: Longman, 1998).

Lockyer, Roger, *Buckingham: The Life and Political Career of George Villiers, First Duke of Buckingham, 1592–1628* (London and New York: Longman, 1981).

Lodge, Edmund (ed.), *Illustrations of British History, Biography, and Manners* (London: G. Nicol, 1791).

Love, Ronald S., *Blood and Religion: The Conscience of Henry IV, 1553–1593* (Montreal and London: McGill-Queen's University Press, 2001).

Lynch, Michael, *Scotland: A New History* (London: Pimlico, 2002).

Lynch, Michael (ed.), *Mary Stewart: Queen in Three Kingdoms* (Oxford: Basil Blackwell, 1988).

MacCunn, F. A., *Mary Stuart* (London: Methuen & Co., 1905).

MacDougall, Norman, *James IV* (East Linton: Tuckwell Press, 1989).

MacDougall, Norman, *James III: A Political Study* (Edinburgh: John Donald, 1982).

Machielsen, Jan (ed.), *The Science of Demons: Early Modern Authors Facing Witchcraft and the Devil* (London: Routledge, 2020).

Mackay Mackenzie, W., *The Medieval Castle in Scotland* (London: Methuen & Co., 1927).

Mackay, James, *In the End Is My Beginning: A Life of Mary Queen of Scots* (Edinburgh and London: Mainstream, 1998).

Maidment, Julian (ed.), *The Chronicles of Perth* (Edinburgh: Maitland Club, 1831).

Malay, Jessica L. (ed.), *Anne Clifford's autobiographical writing, 1590–1676* (Manchester: Manchester University Press, 2018).

Malcolm, Noel, *Forbidden Desire in Early Modern Europe: Male-Male Sexual Relations, 1400–1750* (Oxford: Oxford University Press, 2024).

Manning, Roger B., *Hunters and Poachers: A Social and Cultural History of Unlawful Hunting in England, 1485–1640* (Oxford: Oxford University Press, 2003).

Mares, F. H. (ed.), *Studies in Tudor and Stuart Literature: The Memoirs of Robert Carey* (Oxford: Oxford University Press, 1972).

Marshall, Peter, *Storm's Edge: Life, Death and Magic in the Islands of Orkney* (London: William Collins, 2024).

Marshall, Rosalind K., "Stuart [Stewart], Esmé, first duke of Lennox," ODNB, LV.

Marshall, Rosalind K., *Scottish Queens, 1031–1714* (Edinburgh: Birlinn, 2019).

Martin, Colin, and Geoffrey Parker, *Armada: The Spanish Enterprise and England's Deliverance in 1588* (New Haven and London: Yale University Press, 2022).

Masson, David (ed.), *The Register of the Privy Council of Scotland: Vol. IV: A.D. 1585–1592* (Edinburgh: Her Majesty's General Register House, 1881).

Masson, David (ed.), *The Register of the Privy Council of Scotland: Vol. V: A.D. 1592–1599* (Edinburgh: Her Majesty's General Register House, 1882).

Mathew, David, *James I* (London: Eyre & Spottiswoode, 1967).

Mathieson, William Law, *Politics and Religion in Scotland, 1560–1695: A Study in Scottish History from the Reformation to the Revolution* (Glasgow: James MacLehose and Sons, 1902).

Matusiak, John, *James I: Scotland's King of England* (Stroud: The History Press, 2018).

McClure, Norman (ed.), *The Letters of John Chamberlain* (Philadelphia: The American Philosophical Society, 1939).

McCoog, Thomas M., *The Society of Jesus in Ireland, Scotland, and England, 1589–1597* (London: Routledge, 2012).

McCullough, Peter, *Sermons at Court: Politics and Religion in Elizabethan and Jacobean Preaching* (Cambridge: Cambridge University Press, 1998).

McDonald, Alan, *The Jacobean Kirk, 1567–1625: Sovereignty, Polity and Liturgy* (New York and London: Routledge, 1998).

McDonald, Russ, *Shakespeare and the Arts of Languages* (Oxford: Oxford University Press, 2013).

McGinley, Kevin J., and Nicola Royan (eds.), *The Apparelling of Truth: Literature and Literary Culture in the Reign of James VI* (Newcastle-upon-Tyne: Cambridge Scholar Publishing, 2010).

McGrath, Alistair, *In the Beginning: The Story of the King James Bible and How It Changed a Nation, a Language, and a Culture* (New York: Doubleday, 2001).

McManus, Clare, *Women on the Renaissance Stage: Anna of Denmark and Female Masquing in the Stuart Court, 1590–1619* (New York: Manchester University Press, 2022).

Melville, James, with Gordon Donaldson (ed. and intro.), *The Memoirs of Sir James Melville of Halhill* (London: The Folio Society, 1969).

Milligan, Iain, *Sovereign of the Isles: How the Crown Won the British Isles* (London: Unicorn, 2020).

Moir, Thomas L., *The Addled Parliament of 1614* (Oxford: Clarendon Press, 1958).

Morgan, Hiram, "Extradition and a Treason-Trial of a Gaelic Lord: The Case of Brian O'Rourke," *Irish Jurist*, XXII, ii (January 1987).

Morgan, Hiram, *Tyrone's Rebellion: The Outbreak of the Nine Years War in Tudor Ireland* (Woodbridge: Royal Historical Society, 1993).

Morgan, John, "Popularity and Monarchy: The Hampton Court Conference and the Early Jacobean Church," *Canadian Journal of History*, LII, ii (2018).

Moryson, Fynes, *An Itinerary written by Fynes Moryson, Gent.* (London: John Beale, 1617).

Moryson, Fynes, *A History of Ireland, from the Year 1599 to 1603* (Dublin: S. Powell, 1793).

Moysie, David, *Memoirs of the Affairs of Scotland* (Edinburgh: The Bannatyne Club, 1830).

Mullan, David G., *Episcopacy in Scotland: The History of an Idea, 1560–1638* (Edinburgh: John Donald, 1986).

Murdin, William (ed.), *A collection of state papers relating to affairs in the reign of Queen Elizabeth: Transcribed from original papers and other authentic memorials never before published, left by William Cecill, Lord Burghley, and reposited in the library at Hatfield House* (London: William Bowyer, 1759).

Nau, Claude, with J. Stevenson (ed.), *Memorials of Mary Stewart* (Edinburgh: W. Paterson, 1883).

Neale, John E., *Elizabeth I and her Parliaments* (London: Jonathan Cape, 1953–57).

Nicholls, Mark, *A History of the Modern British Isles, 1529–1603: The Two Kingdoms* (Oxford: Blackwell, 1999).

Nichols, John, *The Progresses, Processions and Magnificent Festivities of James the First* (London: The Society of Antiquaries, 1828).

Nicolson, Adam, *When God Spoke English: The Making of the King James Bible* (London: HarperCollins, 2011).

Nouguères, Henri, *Le Saint Barthélemy* (Paris: Robert Laffont, 1959).

Ó Ciardha, Éamonn, and Micheál Ó Siochrú (eds.), *The Plantation of Ulster: Ideology and Practice* (Manchester: Manchester University Press, 2012).

Ó Muraíle, Nollaig (ed.), *Turas na dTaoiseach nUltach as Éirinn from Ráth Maoláin to Rome* (Dublin: Four Courts Press, 2007).

O'Neill, James, *The Nine Years War, 1593–1603: O'Neill, Mountjoy and the Military Revolution* (Dublin: Four Courts Press, 2018).

Oaks, Robert F., "'Things Fearful to Name': Sodomy and Buggery in Seventeenth-Century New England," *Journal of Social History* (Winter 1978).

Olson, Ian A., "The Dreadful Death of the Bonny Earl of Murray," *Folk Music Journal* (1993).

Oram, Richard D., and Geoffrey P. Stell (eds.), *Lordship and Architecture in Medieval and Renaissance Scotland* (Edinburgh: John Donald, 2005).

Orr, D. Alan, "God's Hangman: James VI, the Divine Right of Kings, and the Devil," *Reformation and Renaissance Review*, XVIII, ii (2016).

Osborne, Francis, *Advice to a Son: or Directions for your better conduct through the various and most important encounters of this life* (Oxford: Henry Hall, 1656).

Osborne, Francis, *The Works of Francis Osborn, Esq: Divine, Historical, Moral, Political* (London: A. and J. Churchill, 1700).

Otele, Olivette, *African Europeans: An Untold History* (London: C. Hurst, 2020).

Outram, Quentin, "The demographic impact of early modern warfare," *Social Science History*, XXV.

Page, William (ed.), *A History of the County of Hertford* (London: His Majesty's Stationery Office, 1912).

Palliser, D. M., *Tudor York* (Oxford: Oxford University Press, 1979).

Paranque, Estelle, "Devotion, Influence, and Loyalty: Reevaluating Queen Louise de Lorraine-Vaudémont's Political and Diplomatic Role in Early Modern France," *Early Modern Women: An Interdisciplinary Journal* (2022).

Paranque, Estelle, and Valerie Schutte (eds.), *Forgotten Queens in Medieval and Early Modern Europe: Political Agency, Myth Making, and Patronage* (London: Routledge, 2018).

Parker, Geoffrey, *The Thirty Years' War* (London and New York: Routledge, 1987).

Patterson, Jonathan, "Obscenity and Censorship in the Reign of Henri III," *Renaissance Quarterly*, LXX (2017).

Persons, Robert, *A Conference about the Next Succession to the Crown of Inglande, divided into two partes* (Antwerp: Doleman, 1594–95).

Peters, Timothy, and Peter Garrard, "The nature of King James VI/I's medical conditions: New approaches to the diagnosis," *History of Psychiatry* (2012).

Platter the Younger, Thomas, with Clare Williams (ed.), *Thomas Platter's Travels in England 1599: Rendered from the German and with Introductory Matter* (London: Jonathan Cape, 1937).

Pollnitz, Aysha, *Princely Education in Early Modern England* (Cambridge: Cambridge University Press, 2015).

Porter, James, "Psalms for King James: Jean Servin's Music for George Buchanan's Latin Psalm Paraphrases (1579)," *British Academy Review*, XII (January 2009).

Porter, Linda, *Crown of Thistles: The Fatal Inheritance of Mary Queen of Scots* (London: Macmillan, 2013).

Porter, Linda, *Mary Tudor: The First Queen* (London: Piatkus, 2009).

Potter, Harry, *Blood Feud: The Stewarts and the Gordons at War in the Age of Mary, Queen of Scots* (Stroud: Tempus, 2002).

Prior, C. M., *The Royal Studs of the Sixteenth and Seventeenth Centuries* (London: Horse and Hound Publications, 1935).

Purkiss, Diane, *The Witch in History: Early Modern and Twentieth-century Representations* (London and New York: Routledge, 1996).

Questier, Michael, *Dynastic Politics and the British Reformations, 1558–1630* (Oxford: Oxford University Press, 2019).

Redmond, Joan, "Memories of violence and New English identities in early modern Ireland," *Historical Research* (March 2016).

Reid, Steven J., *The Early Life of James VI: A Long Apprenticeship, 1566–1585* (Edinburgh: John Donald, 2023).

Reynolds, Tony, *St. Nicholas Owen: Priest-Hole Maker* (Leominster: Gracewing, 2014).

Riddell, William Renwick, "The Death of King James I, A Medico-Legal Study," *Journal of Criminal Law and Criminology*, XIX, I (Spring 1928).

Ring, Morgan, *So High a Blood: The Life of Margaret, Countess of Lennox* (London: Bloomsbury, 2017).

Ritchie, Pamela E., *Mary of Guise in Scotland, 1548–1560: A Political Career* (East Linton: Birlinn, 2022).

Roberts, Michael, *The Early Vasas: A History of Sweden, 1523–1611* (Cambridge: Cambridge University Press, 1968).

Robinson, Philip S., *The Plantation of Ulster: British Settlement in an Irish Landscape, 1600–1670* (Dublin and New York: The Ulster Historical Foundation, 1984).

Rodgers, C. (ed.), *Estimate of the Scottish Nobility During the Minority of James VI* (London: Grampian Club, 1873).

Russell, Conrad, *Parliaments and English Politics, 1621–1629* (Oxford: Oxford University Press, 1979).

Russell, Gareth, "His Dear Bedfellow: The debate over Harry Percy," *Tudor Life* (February 2016).

Russell, Gareth, *Young and Damned and Fair: The Life and Tragedy of Catherine Howard at the Court of Henry VIII* (London: William Collins, 2017).

Rye, William Benchley, *England as seen by Foreigners in the Days of Elizabeth and James the First* (London: John Russell Smith, 1865).

Samuel, Edgar R., "'Sir Thomas Shirley's Project for Jewes'—the Earliest Known Proposal for the Resettlement," *Jewish Historical Society of England* (1970).

Sanderson, Margaret H. B., *Scottish Rural Society in the Sixteenth Century* (Edinburgh: John Donald Publishers, 1982).

Senelick, Laurence, "King Henri III and His Mignons," *Gay and Lesbian Review* (July–August 2020).

Sharpe, Kevin, *Image Wars: Promoting Kings and Commonwealths in England, 1603–1660* (New Haven and London: Yale University Press, 2010).

Sharpe, Kevin, and Peter Lake (eds.), *Culture and Politics in Early Stuart England* (Houndsmills: Macmillan, 1994).

Shire, Helena Mennie, *Song, Dance and Poetry of the Court of Scotland under King James VI* (Cambridge: Cambridge University Press, 1969).

Simson, Robert (ed.), *The Annals of Derry and thence of the City of Londonderry to the Present Time* (Londonderry: Hempton, 1847).

Slack, Paul, *Poverty and Policy in Tudor and Stuart England* (London: Longman, 1988).

Smith, Bruce R., *Homosexual Desire in Shakespeare's England: A Cultural Poetics* (Chicago and London: University of Chicago Press, 1991).

Smith, Lacey Baldwin, *Henry VIII: The Mask of Royalty* (London: Jonathan Cape, 1971).

Smith, Lesley, "Mary Queen of Scots: the 'daughter of debate,'" *Journal of Family Planning and Reproductive Health*, XXXIV, ii (2008).

Smith, Logan Pearsall (ed.), *The Life and Letters of Sir Henry Wotton* (Oxford: Clarendon Press, 1907).

Smuts, R. Malcolm, *Political Culture, the State, and the Problem of Religious War in Britain and Ireland, 1578–1625* (Oxford: Oxford University Press, 2023).

Solnon, Jean-François, *La Cour de France* (Paris: Tempus/Perrin, 2014).

Somerset, Anne, *Elizabeth I* (London: Phoenix Giant, 1997).

Somerset, Anne, *Unnatural Murder: Poison at the Court of James I* (London: Weidenfeld & Nicolson, 1997).

Sparke, Michael, *The Narrative History of King James, for the First Fourteen Years* (London: Richard Cotes, 1651).

Spedding, James, *An Account of the Life and Times of Francis Bacon* (London: Trübner & Co., 1878).

Spedding, James, "Review of the evidence respecting the conduct of King James I in the case of Sir Thomas Overbury," *Archaeologia,* XLI (1867).

Spottiswoode, John, with Michael Russell and M. Napier (eds.), *History of the Church of Scotland* (Edinburgh: J. G. & F. Rivington, 1847–51).

St. Albans, Francis Bacon, 1st Viscount, *Baconiana, or, Certain genuine remains of Sr. Francis Bacon, Baron of Verulam, and Viscount of St. Albans in arguments civil and moral, natural, medical, theological* (London: Robert Chiswell, 1679).

Starkey, David (ed.), *The English Court from the Wars of the Roses to the Civil War* (London: Longman, 1987).

Stephens, G., "James VI. In Tonsberg, 1589. With Photograph of an old Oaken Tablet erected in the Church of St Mary, in Commemoration of his Visit," *Proceedings of the Society of Antiquaries of Scotland,* XI (November 1875).

Stevenson, David, *Scotland's Last Royal Wedding: The Marriage of James VI and Anne of Denmark* (Edinburgh: John Donald, 2001).

Stewart, Alan, *The Cradle King: A Life of James VI and I* (London: Chatto & Windus, 2003).

Stewart, Alan, *Close Readers: Humanism and Sodomy in Early Modern England* (Princeton: Princeton University Press, 1997).

Stewart, Laura A. M., "The Political Repercussions of the Five Articles of Perth: A Reassessment of James VI and I's Religious Policies in Scotland," *Sixteenth Century Journal,* XXXVIII, iv (2007).

Stoyle, Mark, *West Britons: Cornish Identities and the Early Modern British State* (Exeter: University of Exeter Press, 2002).

Talley, Colin L., "Gender and Male Same-Sex Erotic Behavior in British North America in the Seventeenth Century," *Journal of the History of Sexuality,* VI, iii (January 1996).

Taylor, Elizabeth Maria, "James I: Monarchial Representation and English Identity," (Doctoral thesis submitted to Louisiana State University, 2020).

Thompson, James Westfall, *The Wars of Religion in France, 1559–1576* (New York: Frederick Ungar Publishing, 1909).

Thomson, Thomas (ed.), *The Historie and Life of King James the Sext: Being an Account of the Affairs of the Scotland, from the Year 1566, to the Year 1596* (Edinburgh: publishing house unspecified, 1825).

Thurley, Simon, *Palaces of Revolution: Life, Death and Art at the Stuart Court* (London: William Collins, 2021).

Todd, Margo, *The Culture of Protestantism in Early Modern Scotland* (New Haven and London: Yale University Press, 2002).

Treadwell, Victor, *Buckingham and Ireland, 1616–1628: A study in Anglo-Irish Politics* (Dublin: Four Courts Press, 1998).

Tweedie, David, *David Rizzio and Mary Queen of Scots: Murder at Holyrood* (Stroud: Sutton, 2006).

Tytler, Patrick Fraser, *A History of Scotland* (Edinburgh: William Tait, 1843).

Veerapen, Steven, *The Wisest Fool: The Lavish Life of James VI and I* (Edinburgh: Birlinn, 2023).

Walker, Anita M., and Edmund H. Dickerman, "The King Who Would Be Man: Henri III, Gender Identity and the Murders at Blois, 1588," *Réflexions Historiques* (Summer 1998).

Walker, Nigel, *Crime and Insanity in England* (Edinburgh: Edinburgh University Press, 1968).

Walvin, James, *A World Transformed: Slavery in the Americas and the Origins of Global Power* (London: Robinson, 2022).

Warner, G. F., and J. P. Gilson (eds.), *Catalogue of Western Manuscripts in the Old Royal and King's Collections* (London, 1921).

Warnicke, Retha M., *Mary Queen of Scots* (London and New York: Routledge, 2006).

Warnicke, Retha M., "Henry VIII's Greeting of Anne of Cleves and Early Modern Court Protocol," *Albion* (1996).

Watson, Constance, "The secrets of Oxburgh Hall," *Catholic Herald* (September 2020).

Weir, Alison, *Mary Queen of Scots and the Murder of Lord Darnley* (London: Jonathan Cape, 2003).

Weldon, Anthony, *The court and character of King James whereunto is now added The court of King Charles: continued unto the beginning of these unhappy times: with some observations upon him instead of a character* (London: J. Collins, 1651).

White, Stephen D., *Sir Edward Coke and the grievances of the commonwealth* (Manchester: Manchester University Press, 1979).

Wilbraham, Roger, with Harold Spencer Scott (ed.), *The Journal of Sir Roger Wilbraham for the years 1593–1616* (London: The Camden Miscellany, 1902).

Williams, Ethel Carleton, *Anne of Denmark: Wife of James VI of Scotland, James I of England* (London: Longman, 1970).

Williams, Kate, *Rival Queens: The Betrayal of Mary, Queen of Scots* (London: Cornerstone, 2018).

Williams, Penry, *The Later Tudors: England, 1547–1603* (Oxford: Oxford University Press, 1995).

Wilson, Arthur, *The History of Great Britain, Being the Life and Reign of King James the First* (London: Richard Lownds, 1653).

Wilson, David H., *King James VI and I* (Oxford: Oxford University Press, 1967).

Wood, John Philip (ed.), *The Peerage of Scotland* (Edinburgh: George Ramsay & Co., 1813).

Wood, Mary Anne Everett (ed.), *Letters of Royal and Illustrious Ladies of Great Britain* (London: Henry Colburn, 1846).

Wormald, Jenny, *Mary Queen of Scots: A Study in Failure* (London: George Philip, 1988).

Wormald, Jenny, "James VI and I," ODNB, XXIX.

Wormald, Jenny, *Court, Kirk and Community: Scotland, 1470–1625* (Edinburgh: Edinburgh University Press, 1991).

Wormald, Jenny, "James VI and I: Two Kings or One?" *History*, LXVIII (1983).

Wrigley, E. A., and R. S. Schofield, *The Population History of England, 1541–1871* (Cambridge: Cambridge University Press, 2010).

Yellowlees, Michael, *"So Strange a Monster as a Jesuit": The Society of Jesus in Sixteenth-Century Scotland* (Isle of Colonsay: House of Lochar, 2003).

Young, Michael, *James VI and I and the History of Homosexuality* (London: Macmillan Press, 2000).

Young, Michael, "James VI and I: Time for a Reconsideration," *Journal of British Studies*, LI, iii (2012).

Zuvich, Andrea, *Sex and Sexuality in Stuart Britain* (Stroud: Pen & Sword, 2020).

IMAGE CREDITS

FIRST INSERT

James, aged eight months *(Public Domain)*
James's mother, Mary, Queen of Scots *(Public Domain)*
Magnificent Stirling Castle *(Empato/Getty Images)*
A man of many words *(Public Domain)*
Grim but clever *(Public Domain)*
James's elegant and unpopular French cousin *(Public Domain)*
James as a teenager *(Public Domain)*
Ruthven Castle *(PaulT (Gunther Tschuch))*
James's godmother *(Bridgeman Images)*
A coven *(Pictorial Press Ltd/Alamy Stock Photo)*
James personally interrogates *(Bridgeman Images)*
James's remarkable wife *(Fitzwilliam Museum/Bridgeman Images)*
Gowrie House *(Penta Springs Limited/Alamy Stock Photo)*
James in his early thirties *(Penta Springs Limited/Alamy Stock Photo)*
A sketch with costume ideas *(Reproduced by permission of Chatsworth Settlement Trustees/Bridgeman Images)*
The Habsburg Archduchess *(Royal Collection Trust/© His Majesty King Charles III, 2024/Bridgeman Images)*
James, painted around 1606 *(Public Domain)*

SECOND INSERT

The before-and-after signatures *(Pictorial Press Ltd/Alamy Stock Photo)*
Influential, glamorous *(Yale Center for British Art)*
The tomb of James and Anna's daughter *(Angelo Hornak/Getty Images)*
Robert Carr *(Yale Center for British Art)*
Bloody Tower *(Yale Center for British Art)*
James's son Henry *(Royal Collection Trust/© His Majesty King Charles III, 2024/Bridgeman Images)*
James, mid-forties *(Yale Center for British Art)*
James's daughter Elizabeth *(Public Domain)*

Queen Anna *(Royal Collection Trust/© His Majesty King Charles III, 2024/Bridgeman Images)*
James's son Prince Charles *(Yale Center for British Art)*
Robert Carr's rival *(© National Portrait Gallery, London)*
An exhausted and unwell James *(Digital Image Library/Alamy Stock Photo)*

INDEX

M